Visualization

Excerpts from 5 STAR reviews on Amazon
VISUALIZATION
CREATING YOUR OWN UNIVERSE

"...if you allow yourself an open mind, he will take you on an enriching journey that will leave you feeling differently in the end. His Perception of Reality is unique and enriching. Mr. Kapuscinski presents his views and opinions, drawing the reader in, but letting the reader reach their own conclusions. (R. Piecuch USA)

The purpose of the book is to inform readers that we can attain freedom in the here and now... by creating our own universe. ...The writing... is top-notch... an inspirational book that will change your life perspective. (*J. Linson* USA)

...As with all of this author's books, it is extremely well written, it is mind-boggling and eye opening, and it will challenge your current ideological beliefs. It could very possibly change the way you look at life and your place in this world. Yes, it is that thought provoking and profound.
I am a student of History and Philosophy... ...As I was reading this book I couldn't help but wish he was one of my professors in college because his books challenge me to think more than my college professors did!
...(the author) has truly achieved in one lifetime what might take others multiple lifetimes. Because of this unique perspective he has based on his vast experiences, his books are a gift to us in that they truly will open your mind and your heart if you let them. (*M. Brown*, USA, TOP 500 REVIEWER)

Stanislaw Kapuscinski (aka Stan I.S. Law)... is not only gifted in writing, but gifted in life itself. He has so much wonderful knowledge to share with the world to make it a better place, and not only that, but he delivers it in a way that just captivates the reader!
I just love his work... ...I really could not put it down...
I can't recommend it enough! (*Mary Leckie* USA)

Author Stanislaw Kapuscinski shows us a whole new world of possibilities. Kapuscinski provides us the catalyst to become ever more aware of the connection between the power of the mind and the world around us.
He generously provides a wealth of insights while leaving you to draw your own conclusions. He provides profound secrets that have been buried in obsolescence, encouraging you to filter the truth for yourself and create your own universe. In the end you know you have been exposed to a life changing body of work that leaves you with the tools to exact that change in your own life.
I highly recommend it! (Amy Taylor, USA)

Brilliant! ...this major work expanded on and complemented the author's three volumes of essays: Beyond Religion I, II, and III. Fantastic read. (Brian, USA)

Other books by Stanislaw Kapuscinski

DICTIONARY OF BIBLICAL SYMBOLISM
KEY TO IMMORTALITY
DELUSIONS—Pragmatic Realism
BEYOND RELIGION Volumes I
BEYOND RELIGION Volumes II
BEYOND RELIGION Volumes III
[Three Collections of Essays on Perception of Reality]

Fiction by Stan I.S. Law
(aka Stanislaw Kapuscinski)
Novels

WALL—Love, Sex, and Immortality
[Aquarius Trilogy Book One]
PLUTO EFFECT
[Aquarius Trilogy Book Two]
OLYMPUS—Of Gods and Men
[Aquarius Trilogy Book Three]
YESHUA—Missing Years of Jesus
PETER AND PAUL—Intuitive Sequel to Yeshûa
MARVIN CLARK—In Search of Freedom
GIFT OF GAMMAN
ENIGMA OF THE SECOND COMING
ONE JUST MAN [Winston Trilogy Book One]
ELOHIM [Winston Trilogy Book Two]
WINSTON'S KINGDOM [Winston Trilogy Book Three]
THE PRINCESS
GATE—Things my Mother told Me
ALEC [Alexander Trilogy Book One]
ALEXANDER [Alexander Trilogy Book Two]
SACHA—THE WAY BACK
[Alexander Trilogy Book Three]
THE AVATAR SYNDROME
[Prequel to the Headless World]
HEADLESS WORLD
[Sequel to the Avatar Syndrome]
NOW—BEING AND BECOMING

Short stories
THE JEWEL AND OTHER SHORT STORIES
Sci-Fi Series 1
Sci-Fi Series 2
Cats & Dogs Series

VISUALIZATION
Creating Your Own Universe

An Overview of Human Potential by
Stanisław Kapuściński
(aka Stan I.S. Law)

PUBLISHED BY INHOUESPRESS

Copyright © Stanislaw Kapuscinski 1999, 2004, 2010
Ebook Edition March 04, 2012
2nd Paperback Edition 2015
http://stanlaw.ca

All rights reserved. No part of this publication may be reproduced, stored in a retrieval system or transmitted in any form, or by any means electronic, mechanical, photocopying, recording or otherwise, without the prior written permission of the publisher.

Published by
INHOUSEPRESS
1470 St–Jacques, suite 7, Montreal, Qc., H3C 4J4

Cover design and layout
Bozena Happach

ISBN 978-1-987864-03-8

Paperback Edition 2015
INHOUSEPRESS

CONTENTS
PREFACE
INTRODUCTION

HISTORICAL BACKGROUND

Chapter 1. Visions	21
Chapter 2. Myth and Reality	41
Chapter 3. Politics and Society	58
Chapter 4. Religions and Science Fiction	78
Chapter 5. Groups and Traditions	97
Chapter 6. Medical View	111
Chapter 7. Scientific Perspective	126
Chapter 8. Visualizing Infinity	143
Chapter 9. Apports and other Phenomena	165

THE PROCESS

Chapter 10. Universal Laws and Chaos	175
Chapter 11. The Problem with Karma and Reincarnation	195
Chapter 12. Aging and Longevity	221
Chapter 13. Art and Creativity	233
Chapter 14. Health and Healing	246
Chapter 15. Visualization in Sports	253

CREATING YOUR OWN UNIVERSE

Chapter 16. Re-defining Self	260
Chapter 17. Reviewing the Elements	277
Chapter 18. Duality and Oneness	293
Chapter 19. Relaxation	306
Chapter 20. Creative Process	316
Chapter 21. Programming	328
Chapter 22. Negative Programming	340
Chapter 23. Reverse Effects of Visualization	357
Chapter 24. The Universal and the Particular	369
Chapter 25. Creating Your Own Universe	382

BIBLIOGRAPHY

Whatever is received is received according to the nature of the recipient

Thomas Aquinas

PREFACE

"I have here made only a nosegay of culled flowers, and have brought nothing of my own but the string that ties them."

As the above words of seigneur de Montaigne imply, there is nothing here that you don't already know. But if you are anything like I am, indeed—like most of my friends, then you seldom find time, or take the trouble, to reach within deep enough to become aware of your knowledge. I hope this book will help you to know yourself better.

What follows is not intended as a scientific dissertation. Nor is it an attempt to impose my views, nor influence your thinking in any way. What I am offering is a compendium of my observations which may motivate you to begin observing the world through your own eyes a little more diligently. You might call it my vision of the world I live in. To protect myself from an egocentric viewpoint, I took great pains to share with you also the visions of many men throughout history, many men and women who are making history today, and some lesser visionaries whose views I find particularly attractive. Your vision, the program that controls your views and therefore your life, will forever remain your own. I wish to stress, however, that you must have a vision or else remain no more than an effect of your subconscious.

I am not concerned with the visible universe.

Once the universe becomes detectable to our senses, it is too late to change it. The book will show that we have our being within a continuous process of creating the reality we live in.

I am fascinated by the process itself. There are excellent popular books on the subject of how to procure results. Here, we shall concentrate on the cause. Although we shall not ignore the results, neither physics nor astrophysics need concern us here other than to broaden our perspective. What we shall discus principally is the "Visual Universe". The universe which we do or can visualize and, in the process of doing so, we shall give it reality. The tangible universe thus becomes the result of our quest, not the quest itself. What we are after is the process. The Creative Process. The methods which empower us to be as gods.

From the hoary days of history in which we, humans, became aware of ourselves, of our distinctiveness, we have been engaged in doing just that. Every single one of us has been creating his or her subjective realities. We made our beds and we must sleep in them. We created our heavens and our hells. We did it all unwittingly. We had no idea that it had been up to us what world we chose to live in. We became adept at blaming the stars, the governments, schools and educational systems, and finally our parents. It may be that all these elements had some peripheral influence on the universes we live in. But the degree to which we permit external conditions, or the environment, to influence us has always been up to us. Up to our free will. Up to our ability to lead a Conscious Life.

It is time to stop being a result. It is time to stop bobbing up and down like a cork cast by some whimsical deity on the vast oceans of life. We are the architects of our destiny. We are gods.

It is time to learn to be the Cause.

In the course of this book, I shall prove that neither you nor I, nor the universe around us really exists. At least, not as we perceive it with our senses. We shall have to learn to probe it with our mind, to visualize it with our inner vision. I shall also show how an individual vision can and did change the course of history.

Perhaps now, it is our turn.

An apology is due to my readers who decide to join me on my meandering through various subjective universes. There will be a lot of repetition when dealing with certain aspects of the creative process. The reason is that for thousands of years we have been conditioned to think in a particular way, which I consider false. I shall show that I am not alone in my opinion. Unfortunately, there are very few who will agree with me. Those who do, however, shall in time become masters of their domain.

To prove my point, I shall draw upon myths, history, politics and science, as well as philosophies and the more esoteric interpretations of some ancient and modern religions. I shall attempt to show that the truth had always been available to us under different guises. I shall also show why it is only now that we are in position to dive headlong into the ocean of infinite possibilities—an ocean which heretofore had been accessible only to the few.

***

Finally, I must stress that this is not yet another self-help book to add to the countless others adorning the bookshelves of your local book-merchant. Rather, it is a book that will enable you to write your own set of rules that will, in turn, govern your own personal universe. It is a book that, I hope, will help you to stand on your own feet with such confidence that nothing will ever upset your balance again.

And you will do so whatever others do.

***

*You shall always find what you created in your mind,
for instance, a benevolent God or an evil Devil.
Between them are countless facets.
Therefore, concentrate on the depth
of your consciousness and on what you consider to be
positive and good.*

Hans Bender
German Psychologist,
(1907 - 1991)

INTRODUCTION

I am convinced all of humanity is born with more gifts than we know. Most are born geniuses and just get de-geniused rapidly.

Buckminster Fuller

My dharma, my purpose, became evident early in my life. However, just as most of us, I remained blind to it. Yet even as all roads lead to Rome, all events in our lives lead to the fulfillment of our dharma. Dharma is our *raison d'être*. If we die accidentally before realizing it, we merely continue where we left off in our future incarnation.

My purpose is to help people fulfill their own dharma.

In order to fulfill our personal purpose we must first discover what it is and then have the means to carry it out. No one can help us with the first part. To discover one's true calling is often a long process of growing up, of keeping one's eyes and ears wide open, and most of all, in keeping an open mind. Each time we shackle our imagination with any restrictions, each time we impose limitations on our innate potential, we delay the discovery of our true purpose.

And discover our purpose we must. As the great Indian mystic Sai Baba once said: "When a cat or a dog dies he leaves the world the same as before he lived in it, but a man should leave the world a better place than when he came into it. For no other reason was he born, for no other reason does he die."[1]

If we fail to discover our specific purpose in life, we shall continue to reincarnate ourselves in an endless cycle of Awagawan, treading water on the eternal mill, hardly advancing, hardly being alive. Two thousand years ago Jesus called such people dead. "Let the dead bury their dead", he admonished when a man wanted to serve tradition rather than fulfill his true calling.[2] Perhaps, as you read this book, you will gradually come to realize that contrary to the mores, customs and traditions of this world, contrary to the tens-of-thousands of laws, rules and regulations designed to limit our freedom—we can be free. We can be free here, on earth; we do not have to die to go to heaven, we can become masters of our kingdoms, our universes—right now.

There are many ancient truths that reverberate throughout the ages guiding mankind towards fulfillment. There are also truisms that gather the quintessence of those truths as they pertain to an individual. The ancient king David had enunciated one such axiom in one of his psalms.[3] This great visionary left us a legacy, which proclaimed that we must shrug off *all* limitations. Few of his contemporaries understood David's words. Today, some 3000 years later, we can no longer plead ignorance. We are no longer ignorant plebes unable to read or write. The ancient knowledge is available to all that yearn for it.

To all who take the trouble to look.

Those who do, soon discover that a great part of that which enables us to claim our heritage is lying dormant in the realm of our imagination. Imagination fosters a vision that constitutes the *first* step.

How many of us realize that practically every effort, every creative act we perform is preceded by an act of visualization? We 'imagine' what it would be like if such-and-such a thing, condition, or dream were to come true. We dream, we hope, we envision, fancy, idealize. All these mental acrobatics form an integral part of the great realm of 'virtual' universes. Universes which, nevertheless, are real to our subjective consciousness, but not yet manifested in the physical realm. They are part of the endless ocean of infinite possibilities. They are part of a realm whence nothing is impossible, nothing too difficult, where the joy of being, of success, takes precedence over all other considerations. This realm is our true kingdom. It is also the kingdom of God, or perhaps, the kingdom of the gods. It is the kingdom of heaven.

A great deal has been written on how to enter this kingdom. We have inherited a magnificent treasury of information on this subject, a veritable road map to its most intricate byways. The incredible storehouse of knowledge offered in the scientific document called the Bible has been perverted by many into a means of controlling people. We have been told that we can only 'go' to heaven after we die. What insidious palter! The Bible teaches us how to live, not how to die. Heaven is a state of consciousness that does not tolerate limitations. It is the realm of all people that identify with such awareness. Until we learn to study the ancient scriptures with this attitude we shall fall prey to many who will exploit those very same inspired writings to subject us to their will, to their need for power, to their desire to wield the carrot and the stick of heaven and hell over our gullible heads.

There are other ancient documents outlining different methods of arriving at the desirable state of awareness. Regrettably the various scriptures of whatever religion are so shrouded in the mists of yore, so protected by stalwart ramparts of symbolism, that few manage to uncover their teaching. Once, such safeguards had been necessary to protect the many from the abuse by the few. Yet for over two millennia those safeguards only partially succeeded in protecting us from the manipulations of fierce religious oligarchies.

Now, as we enter the Age of Aquarius, the heretofore

secret knowledge is laid open to us all. Not because we are so much smarter or manifest a higher moral or ethical level, but because finally the critical mass of people capable of achieving the understanding has been attained. Finally we can all reach out for the watering can and begin tending our own gardens. With the introduction of electricity to the homes of masses, we have entered the new age. This magnificent period shall take us, over the next 2000 years, into unprecedented heights of individualism. We shall no longer impersonate sheep led by our not-so-noble leaders, no longer rely on the security offered by our primitive herd instinct manifested in the allegiance to groups such as nations, political systems or even various religions. We shall rise above all such traditional needs, spread our wings and soar into celestial heights of the kingdom itself.

We shall give credence and substance to the ancient King David's words: "Ye are gods".

***

I often wondered why various events led me to become an architect; to specialize in design above all other professional disciplines, when my primary interest has always been the "inner realm." This primary interest took many forms, but more than anything I have always been preoccupied with uncovering the scope of human potential. It is now apparent that the art of designing was the necessary training ground for the work that I started on completion of my forty-year internship as an architect.

In my professional capacity I had no choice but to visualize every project in its entirety, before putting a single line on paper. No architect can begin the fascinating process of design without envisaging the needs of his client, visualizing the specific characteristics of the site: slopes, aspect, prospect, context water level, bearing capacity of subsoil, the time, space, construction, and costs parameters. To this already complex vision an architect must add the analyses of general climatic conditions: annual snow/rainfall, the temperature ranges and variations, exposure to prevailing winds/sun. Then, before we begin to visualize the internal and external spaces, we must picture the parameters of the program. Since few people are trained in the art of visualization, it behooves an architect to guide his client through the maze of function/uses, spaces, horizontal and vertical circulation, access and egress, masses of controlling bylaws, conditions arising from all the previous items. When finally a preliminary plan, a horizontal projection of the vertical components can be put on paper, an architect must visualize the requirements of the eventual structural integrity, of mechanical and electrical requirements and constraints, before the specialists are called to the conference table.[4] I have often been told by my staff of many 'specialists', that is architects, engineers and draftsmen combining into a team to work on buildings of my design, that I have allowed for all the succeeding functions before they were even converted into detail plans. In other words, I became competent in the art of visualization. It took me another ten years to realize that what is true of the architectural profession is true of all aspects of life.

Of course, the process of visualization is not limited to architects. Before my own ideas could germinate, my prospective client must have gone, at least partially, though the creative process himself. He or she must have had an idea, "slept on it", let it grow into a coherent outline, develop this vision into a plan of action, part of which was selecting an architect. And so it is with all visions. They are precursors of all thoughts, actions, and manifestations in the physical reality.

Nothing in this world happens by chance.

But I was lucky. We all are. A review of my past led me to believe that all events in my life had been arranged by some as yet unknown powers to guide me inexorably towards the fulfillment of my destiny. A broader examination of my environment confirmed that what had been true of myself is also true of other people, perhaps all of us, and even families, nations and races. Einstein's expression: "God does not play dice with the universe," comes to mind. Only whereas Einstein was referring to the workings of the universe, I noticed that the same maxim applied to the human condition.

In my early life fate played in yet another way into the unfolding arms of my dharma. I was a "war child". The Germans invaded Poland when I was merely six years old. For the next five years I was forced to visualize countless toys which today's child picks up in Toy-o-Rama or other emporium bent on destroying a child's innate imagination. In my childhood we all learned imagining that stale bread is tasty, that inner walls covered with hoarfrost made the room acceptably warm, that the Gestapo barging into our meager quarters in the middle of the night did not come merely to shoot us, that eight people living and sleeping in one room gave us plenty of space, that carrying water from the nearest public hand-pump a kilometer away would not freeze solid on the way home, that tomorrow would, ultimately, be a better day.

And it was.

The art of visualization helped us all to survive, remain reasonably healthy in mind and body, without today's inevitable daily doses of vitamin supplements, without meat, butter, and fruit, without most of the victuals. We have all learned that it is indeed true that it is not what we put into our mouth that sustains us, but that which comes out of it.[5] Words of hope, of good cheer, of love, compassion, understanding and tolerance helped to visualize a better world. Those words of hope came "out of our mouths." Our dreams had been so intense that finally, after five years, they came true. As all dreams do.

If you know how to dream.

***

Surely, it is better to visualize one's needs, one's actions, before they occur and be ready for their consequences. The boy-scouts motto "be prepared" is the motto underlying the process of visualization. Though it may sound like an oxymoron, eventually we become fully prepared for the unknown. But more than this. Often without conscious participation, a process of visualization at some level of our consciousness precedes most if not all of our actions. We may have daydreamed, we may have fantasized with half-closed eyes reclining in our favorite armchair, or we might have dreamt in the fullness of the night. One way or another, every action, every deed is the result of previous thoughts and thoughts are the structural elements of the process of visualization. We can learn to build houses, complex structures, we can also learn to build our bodies, our health, and our mental acuity. We can build favorable conditions for our lives, our marriages, our artistic endeavors, our wealth. We can build anything we want—if we have enough faith that we can. The techniques will be outlined below.

The rest will be up to every one of us.

There is a catch.

NO ONE CAN DO IT FOR US.

We cannot hire an expert to make us healthy. We cannot hire a master to make us a concert violinist or a champion golfer. They can offer help, assistance. But the work, the visualization, must be done by us. We must learn how to play our parts ourselves. It is *our* universe we are building. We alone can be sovereign in our own kingdom. We cannot delegate the rod of power. It is always tailor-made for the individual. To walk in someone else's footsteps is to play second fiddle, to be second best. Such a position is unbecoming to gods.

But having said that, we mustn't take objective life too seriously. In the physical universe, all we do is play our part, as well as we possibly can, enjoying it to the utmost—but never forgetting that our true kingdom is not of this world.

***

FOOTNOTES

(1). BABA by Arnold Schulman, [Simon & Shuster, Canada]. Born Sathia, a Brahmin, in Puttaparthi, on November 23, 1926.
(2). Matthew 8:22
(3). Psalm 82:6
(4). I am forced to admit, with considerable regret, that I had colleagues within my profession who did not follow the route I've outlined above. Many design steps are often bypassed for the sake of expediency, at the expense of quality and professional ethics.
(5). compare Matthew 15:11

HISTORICAL BACKGROUND

All the world is a stage and the men players.
The life is a tale told by an idiot
Full of sound and fury, saying nothing.

Shakespeare

Chapter 1
Visions

All visions are subjective. Subjective religious visions are called Revelations. Subjective non-religious visions (unless held by famous people) are often referred to as Hallucinations. Hallucinations can be subdivided into artistic, political, social, idealistic, and a whole array of inspired non-religious fantasies, delusions or insights. Revelations fall essentially into two categories, the pragmatic (aimed at organizing people) and the prophetic (aimed at scaring people). Both deal with influencing others directly. There has never been a prophecy of a carrot that was not accompanied by a stick. The prophetic visions are usually symbolic in nature, i.e. misunderstood by all that attempt to give them a fundamentalist interpretation. There is a very basic characteristic of all visions. They can never really be shared. People who claim allegiance to a vision of another human being become followers, never those who implement the original vision.

They follow what they *think* the vision was, never what it was *de facto*.

The same is true of all visions.

No more can the vision of a mystic be fully shared with another person than an artist's vision with his audience. The artist and the mystic attempt to convey their singular, subjective insights, which we then receive and examine at our own subjective level. Each one of us receives or experiences differently the very same Beethoven's symphony, the same Mendelssohn's violin concerto or Pablo Picasso's Guernica. In spite of copious examples, we each have a different interpretation of Jesus' Kingdom of Heaven. No two people agree precisely on Buddha's vision of the middle path, fewer still will fall in step on Lao Tzu's Tao. Not even 'interpretations' are alike. We can only wonder at what the artist or mystic *really* had in mind. The original visions remain subjective and inimitable. Other peoples' visions can be aspired to, even exceeded, *but never equaled*.

I recall an elderly lady asking Picasso who was attending his first exhibition in London, England, what a particular painting of his represented. The inscrutable master took it off the wall, turned it sideways, upside-down, pondered it for a while and replaced it on the wall. "To you, Madame, this painting can represent anything you want," he said, "to me, it represents £10,000."

To repeat, all visions are by definition subjective.

The prophet and the crank both respond to energies beyond their intellectual or mental understanding. To protect his sanity, the prophet escapes into the realm of the 'divine'. He (or she) blames or praises God for his (or her) visitation. Today, unless the non-religious visionary can channel his vision into an artistic or pragmatic application, they are compelled, and often do, escape to the psychiatrist. Few do justice to their experience. All deal with the unknown. The degree of their sanity is directly proportional to their ability to recognize the process of visualization.

There is a byproduct of the visionary process, which must be recognized but never confused with the vision itself. When an astrophysicist translates his or her vision into a theorem, backs it up with adequate equations for the vision to be 'testable', it is then called a prediction. Yet what we test is not the vision, but an interpretation of a vision; rather like a painting is a two-dimensional representation of artist's holistic or *gestält* vision, or a religion an interpretation of an avatar's vision.[1] Predictions ensue from visions, but they are initiated at the consciousness level.

Visions have their origin in the Ocean of Infinite Possibilities.

In the absolute unknown.

To understand Picasso's painting we must enter his studio, insinuate ourselves into his thoughts, with luck into his heart, soul, examine his stream of consciousness and then perhaps, just perhaps... we might share in his vision. The same is true about the products of all artists, composers, visionaries. Asking an artist what does his or her painting, or sculpture, or a musical composition represent is equivalent to an open admission of total inability to understand the answer. Unless the visionary is a writer or a gifted orator, that which he or she conveys is not meant to be conveyed with words. It must be felt, appreciated or even understood at a higher level.

The greatest offenders in this field are the, so-called, experts or critics. They are like Pharisees who do not enter the Kingdom yet bar others from doing so themselves. They build walls between the visionary and the recipient. They insinuate their own version of the interpretation in lieu of the original experience. Whether a vision is religious or not, it must be experienced, never interpreted—unless the interpretation is made by the experiencer himself for himself. Then, and only then, the interpretation remains subjective and thus true at the personal level. At best, a subjective interpretation may be offered, never imposed. It may be offered as an illustration attesting to the richness of the original vision, never as a substitute of the vision itself.

The same is true of all 'hallucinations' and of all 'revelations'.

There are no exceptions.

Ultimately, those who attempt to share their subjective Revelations become exploited by those who wish to benefit from other people's insights. This has never yet proven successful. The dismal failure of major religions to implement the precepts underlying the visions on which the various religions purport to have been based attest incontrovertibly to this thesis. Those who suffer from Hallucinations (capital H implies great visions) are luckier, as they become known as scientists, artists, poets, leaders or philosophers. The non-religious visionaries do not require followers for their implementation (though there are obvious financial benefits if there are such). There are also those who as a result of their visions lose contact with objective reality. There are dangers in crossing the road—there are dangers inherent in visions.

More often than not, a vision is inspired by desire.

A prophet, a scientist or an artist does not imagine receiving a revelation. They condition their unconscious mind to respond to whatever inputs are available and feed such information to their conscious awareness. The process is often automatic, the condition—sensitivity and willingness to face the unknown. The desire to achieve, when strong enough and directed towards altruistic ends, will result in a surprising response from the Source of all inspiration. The word altruistic is very important. The late mystic and writer Paul Twitchell once said that altruism is not a virtue but an act of self-preservation. Roger Buckminster Fuller, the gentle giant, observed that only when he committed his efforts towards the good of the greatest number, the results exceeded the norm. At the age thirty-two, he noted:

"In 1927 I also committed all my productivity potentials toward dealing only with our whole planet Earth.... This decision was not taken on a recklessly altruistic do-gooder basis, but in response to the fact that my Chronofile clearly demonstrated that in my first thirty-two years of life I had been positively effective in producing life-advantage wealth—which realistically protected, nurtured, and accommodated X numbers of human lives for Y numbers of forward days—only when I was doing so entirely for others and not for myself." [2]

Mr. Fuller further adds that the larger the number for whom he worked, the more positively effective he became. This is the evidence of a man whose vision encompassed the whole "Spaceship Earth." We can safely assume that the prerequisite to a successful vision is the benefit of the largest possible number of people, or the greatest common good. This dictum is no longer a religious rhetoric, but a sound scientific observation.

The question remains: What is the source of visions? While the process of visualization can become a controlled technique, the actual energy which manifests visions is still lost in religious jargon. We hear of God whispering in one's ear, of angels conveying messages, and such other esoteric projections as of ghosts or spirits tapping on *ouija* boards. The problem seems to lie in our inability to combine human resources. The mystics refuse to submit to rigorous scientific examination, while the scientists—usually skeptics—refuse to recognize the evidence of their eyes, just because it does not fit in with their pragmatic experiments. The same Doubting Thomases cannot reproduce a bolt of lightening, but they do not deny its existence. Yet a vision of an unknown origin vastly outperforms the effects of a lightening. In the chapter on *Politics and Society* we shall see how visions of individual men leave indelible imprints on humanity for centuries to come. Both categories of visions are the result of emotional stimulation. The first is the consequence of the mystic's preoccupation with the 'divine' properties or characteristics of their 'messages'. A mystic is so committed to his vision that he'll often choose to lose his life rather than deny his vision. Early Christianity offers ample evidence of this thesis. On the other hand, contrary to popular belief, a scientist would often choose to remain in the dark ages then submit to any new 'revelation' which would undermine his or her established *status quo*. There are exceptions, but the manner in which Socrates, Galileo, Bruno, and more recently Einstein had been treated in Greece, Italy, Germany and France respectively, may well justify other scientists' and even philosophers' reticence to tread on unproven grounds.

Nevertheless, there are quanta of energy which, while as yet non-measurable, leave an ample trace of their influences, rather like the invisible, non-measurable quarks do on the screen of a cyclotron.[3] While the energies stimulated by the process of visualization cannot be measured, they leave a very visible, observable and measurable trace on the health, wealth and general well-being of the participants in the pragmatic experiment.

The fact that a particular energy is regarded as 'non-physical' means that our scientists have not yet learned to identify it with their instrumentation. Our ignorance, however, does not preclude its existence, or its effect on the physical reality. We can neither detect with our senses nor measure the intensity of the energy of love. Yet all who experienced love, are as sure of its existence as they are of their physical environment. There are those who relegate love to their hormonal influxes or to the dictates of our instinct of self preservation, but such would never explain love based on indisputable altruism. And even our most recent history is rich with examples of such impersonal "energy". The late Mother Theresa comes to mind. Conversely, the human eye cannot detect photons outside a very small spectrum.[4] Yet none would dispute the existence of radio, radar, TV, or ultraviolet rays which can burn blindness into the human iris. Since human mind invented the instruments necessary to record that which is invisible, it is safe to assume that, in time, it will increase its scope to experience, scientifically, that which to-date is not as yet understandable. To draw on the Revelation part of visions, I am reminded of a phrase: For *nothing is secret, that shall not be made manifest: neither anything hid, that shall not be known and come abroad.*[5] I cannot think of any scientist who would not gladly subscribe to the above statement. It sounds more like Einstein talking rather than a man recognized by most as a "religious visionary", though, as already mentioned, it was the very same Einstein who affirmed (perhaps wistfully) that God does not play dice with the universe.

In the meantime, under the overwhelming evidence of countless witnesses, we must accept that such energies exist. The visualization of events at a distance, or those taking place in the past or the future, are easier to recognize once we accept the assurances of our physicists that time doesn't really exist. Although both Aristotle and Newton believed in absolute time, later scientists put dents in the previous theories. First Einstein showed time's relativity to movement (velocity) and space, and later, the best known theoretical physicist living today, Stephen Hawking, elaborated on its fluctuations and other disturbing properties.[6] Einstein's own visions are reviewed in the chapter on *Scientific Perspective*.

I would suggest, however, that at the present level of our ability and knowledge, the key to understanding this phenomenon is the acceptance that Soul, or the individualized awareness manifesting through the medium of a human mind and body, has its being *outside* the constrains of time and space. The next step would be to identify with this awareness. To say: "I am aware of myself therefore I am." Self-awareness implies the awareness of Self.

The Self will be discussed at length in the chapter on *Redefining Self*.

If the premise is correct than it follows that we, today,

are everything that we ever have been, or ever shall be. At the very least, we are endowed with an inner awareness of all our experiences. I am reminded of Socrates suggesting a similar premise to Meno:

"The soul, then, as being immortal... and having seen all things that exist... has knowledge of them all; and it is no wonder that she should be able to call to remembrance all that she ever knew about virtue, and about everything; for as all nature is akin, and the soul has learned all things, there is no difficulty in her eliciting or as men say learning, out of a single recollection all the rest, if a man is strenuous and does not faint; for all enquiry and all learning is but... recollection."[7]

What changes is not the reality of the world but our awareness of it. As we grow and mature, we become more and more aware of our true nature, which while residing within the physical envelope of the body, it is not the body as such. In this context, visions would be momentary insights into the totality of knowledge latent in our own timeless selves.

Nevertheless, for the present, most of us shall probably associate the origin of visions with various myths. Yet it is from visions of individual men that we inherited insights which influenced the course of history. Paul of Tarsus promulgated the Christ's vision of Good News (ignored by close to one billion Christians). Muhammad gave us a wonderful vision of submission of our Self to the Highest Being (Allah, the Merciful, the Compassionate), only to lose heart and reinforce it with a stick and carrot philosophy which is responsible to this day for mass-murder and other bloodthirsty perversions. Perhaps the Moslem had been (and still are) inspired by the Christian deviations which came into being during the days of the Crusades or the *un*Holy Inquisition. While the Christians and the Moslem declare periodic mutually beneficial truces, the Moslem continue to extend their struggle against the Hindus who, in turn, enjoy slaughtering the Christians, all in the name of the All Merciful and Compassionate Allah. Not to be left behind, the Christians, presumably in the name of the Prince of Love, excelled in butchering the Moslem in ex-Yugoslavia's Kosovo.

In another and very different example of the distortion of the original visions, it is to the Hindu vision that we owe the most numerous Pantheon, much broader in scope and complexity than the Greek or the Roman aggregations, yet, amazingly, also springing from a monotheistic origin! It is India that gave us the concept of Brahma, "who engineered the entire universe, down to the insignificant ant" yet, in the words of Swami Prabhupada: "Brahma is not the ultimate creator... the supreme intelligence behind all creations is the Absolute Godhead, Sri Krishna."[8]

It is indeed of some considerable disdain that, in all cases I came across, the misinterpretation of the original vision brought about more harm than good to humanity. Since the masses had always been taught that they must be told what is best, the leaders of the various religions must bear the burnt of responsibility for the crimes committed in the name of the various visions. To protect ourselves, we must enter, once again, into the no-man's land where Truth or God *is*, in the words of Jalal ud-Din Rumi, beyond the realm or ideas of doing right and doing wrong. The degree of love advocated by Christ is in direct opposition to the degree of hatred generated by the Crusades, Inquisition, fundamentalism, egoism and particularly indifference. The Krishna vision is in direct opposition to the burning of temples, slaughter of members of opposing sects, or debasing exploitation including the maiming of children so that they might be more successful at procuring alms.

The euphoric love sang of Muhammad, as heard by the Sufis, does not resonate with the willful maiming of beggars who have their hands, arms and feet cut off for theft—all in the name of the Koran. The word Islam means submission, not imposition. Submission to Allah, the source of all good not submission to vengeance devoid of love, compassion or mercy. Since Koran claims that Allah is *all* merciful, how come his henchmen are *all* vengeful? 'God' is suspended somewhere in the middle, where the opposites meet. One can but wonder if the world would not be a better place if neither prophet nor savior nor any avatar attempted to share their vision with us, lest we would have no vision to pervert.

We have been warned: "...neither cast ye your pearls before swine."[9]

Apparently there is a very good reason for this warning. I recall a story told me by another seeker for truth. A man had been sitting at the feet of his Master. He had been told to love his enemies. The man became very sad, but accepted humbly the admonition. Suddenly his face lit up. He got up and went outside. Returning some minutes later, he seemed filled with joy. "Why are you so happy?" asked the Master. The man smiled. "I had no enemies, Master," said the man. "When you told me to love them, I was sad. But now I am joyful." "How come?" asked the Master. "I went out and hit the first man I met in the face. He now hates me. I now have an enemy I can love."

Although I feel that any of the major religions, if understood properly, would raise mankind to a higher level, the sad part is that even the most noble of visions at their very source are confined or diluted by the limitations of the human language. In 1962 Mahatma Gandhi, best known as the father of modern India, wrote:

"While I believe that the principal books [scriptures] are inspired, they suffer from a process of double distillation. Firstly, they come through a human prophet; and then through the commentaries of interpreters. ...as [God's] message is received through the imperfect human medium, it is always liable to suffer distortion in proportion as the medium is pure or otherwise."[10]

To the proud Christians who deign to rise above the "imperfect human medium" by deifying Christ, let me quote the words of their Lord: "Why callest thou me good? there is none good but one, that is, God..."[11] Was their Master wrong?

Alas, distilled of not, we cannot put a genie back into the bottle. A vision once brought into the world, remains part of the human heritage. No matter how misunderstood, how misapplied, mishandled or misused—it is ours to deal with. It may be promulgated publicly, to all nations, but its fulfillment will always be an individual task. Never that of a group or organization. The organizations were *not* created "unto the image and likeness" of God. You and I are. And we must balance prudence with courage. Heaven is not for the cowardly or the weak. It also not for fools.

***

And then we have the 'lesser' visionaries; and the lesser are all too often the blind bent on leading the blind. Today I've read in my local paper that a Rev. Jerry Falwell, a chancellor (sic!) of a university, claims that antichrist is alive and well, walking the earth this moment. The pompous preacher also pushes his presumption that since Christ was Jewish, therefore the antichrist must be Jewish.[12] By this inscrutable logic one can only wonder what nationality were Adam and Eve. Eden[13] is reputed to have been at the environs of Tigris. That would make the First Couple Iraqi or Syrian. But surely, as such a nationality would be highly offensive to the Jews and Falwell, we might be wiser to assume that Adam and Eve were simply displaced Fundamentalist Baptists from the Bible belt of Southern United States.

Each to his vision—*chacun a son goût.*

And then there are those who expect the world to end any minute and/or after the good guys get whisked up into heaven (rapture)[14], while the remaining population, after a perfunctory decimation, will spend the next 1000 years in the goody-goody land, with the reincarnated Jesus on the throne of Jerusalem. In this vision the world will last a millennium longer.[15] *Voilà*, another vision. Hasn't Jesus done enough for those people? He offered us his vision; he gave us his life. What else do they want? I am told that the local psychiatric institution can supply us with volumes of other visions, equally as imaginative and equally devoid of any contact with reality.

Yet visions have always preoccupied the human mind.

The ancient Egyptians, the Greeks and Romans, the Hebrew of the Old Testament, and the later prophets ranging from Nostradamus (1503-66) to Edgar Cayce (1877-1945), all visualized their gods as powerful beings outside and beyond their influence. They created their gods so real that many of them committed whole lives to their service. Throughout history man suffered from a great need to serve some higher Being, if not 'spiritual' then at least of heroic stature. The global myths of all religions are filled with man's search for heroes to worship; filled with men of Herculean proportions. Little has changed to this day. The bourgeoisie of various nations take vicarious pride in their composers, artists, historical notables, dignitaries, eminencies, heavyweights, leaders, luminaries, 'somebodies'... as if they, themselves, actually contributed to the achievements of such allegedly superior people. My own 'hero', the late Joseph Campbell identifies this need for hero worship with a subliminal desire to identify with the hero's individuality.[16] It seems much easier than striving to become a hero oneself—much easier than to aspire to one's own vision.

Leaders of various faiths amply exploit this apparently inherent inner need. The adherents of most major religions, including the Hindu, the Christians, and the Moslem, are as manipulated today as they have been for centuries. All in the name of some 'externalized' heavenly, inaccessible deity, who apparently commissioned the few to rule over the many. The need to externalize one's potential is all the more enigmatic when examining the various scriptures. The Bible offers many examples of attempts by the more advanced minds, the prophets, to explain to their followers that God-within and God-without are One. Even the biblical names such as Eliah or Elijah seem to imply that the *El* and the *Jah* are one and the same. In biblical context, *El* is established as the hero within—the Divine Presence within us, and *Jah*, an abbreviation of *Jehovah* or *YHWH*—the ancient tertragrammaton representing the universal male and female principles, are one and the same.[17] Jesus has reiterated this same thesis in his statement "I and my father are one." The prophets, including Jesus, refuse to identify any power outside their own being as being superior in *quality* to that which governs their own consciousness. They submit to the scope, or the magnitude differential, but not to the attributes *per se*. In other words, they recognize that macrocosm is greater than microcosm, but in size only, not in quality.

A similar principle is voiced by the Hindu teacher Swami Prabhupada, who basing his knowledge on the authority of the Srimad-Bagavatam (the Hindu scripture) explains: "...the transcendentalists affirm that the soul and the Supersoul are two different identities, qualitatively one but quantitatively different."[18] This view might well have been also espoused by Teilhard de Chardin in his vision of the Noosphere.[19] Such visions, however, have been enunciated long before the vast majority of people were ready to receive them. The pearls had been cast before swine. It is apparent that only visions which lend themselves towards the exploitation of people, of keeping the masses in ignorance and thus easier to control, met with success. The opium of the masses had to be carefully handled, lest the proletariat would suspect that the original vision in no way resembled the sociopolitical version fed to them. Only recently the 'masses' appear to raise their ugly heads. Perhaps they are beginning to suspect that they have been lied to for centuries. Perhaps we are just getting ready—today.

Perhaps we are reaching a critical mass.

There are those amongst us who might consider it blasphemous to regard ourselves as "gods in waiting", rather than as incorrigible sinners. This book is not for them. It is not that they are wrong in their view. It simply means that they (still) live in a relative world, best explained in Srimad-Bagavatam quoted below:

"In the relative world the knower is different from the known, but in the Absolute Truth both the knower and the known are one and the same thing. In the relative world the knower is the living spirit or superior energy, whereas the known is inert matter or inferior energy." [20]

To accept this version of reality, this vision, all we must do is to change our point of view. Those who externalize their God shall come, in time, to internalize Him as did Christ, in whose steps his believers claim to be following. The same teacher affirmed that while he and his father are one, he and we are one. By a process of simple mathematics, we appear all to be One. A sentiment to which all the great Myths subscribe fully.

Another mystic offers a different but reinforcing vision from India whom Dr. Chopra quotes in one of his lectures:

"You are where your attention takes you. In fact, you are your attention. If your attention is fragmented, you are fragmented. When your attention is in the past, you are in the past. When your attention is in the present moment, you are in the presence of God. And God is present in you."

If we substitute the word vision for attention, we shall cross oceans of time to arrive at the present moment of great realization. In order to become One, we must not dwell in the past, we must have our attention in the present.

There are assuredly others, who may think it blasphemous to betray their version of the exclusivity of the

Christian creed. For them I quote John's vision in his Apocryphal Acts: *"A lamp am I to you that perceive me, a mirror am I to you that know me"*.

In all these propositions we deal with visions of reality. To some they are mired with good and evil, a dichotomous existence, devoid of freedom, resigned to one's fate written for them in the stars. Yet "It is not in our stars but in ourselves that we are underlings."[21] Their hearts and minds are encumbered and bound with traditions, with interpretations of other mentors, of other scriptures, of other people's visions. To them I quote a Sufi poet, Jalal-ud-Din Rumi: "Beyond the ideas of doing right and doing wrong there is a field. I'll meet you there." There we find a God who embodies that which the opposites have in common. There and only there we find singularity of Life.

To those who share this vision, life is an open-ended opportunity in which we can visualize a reality in which everyone of us can and will create his and her own universe.

One other aspect of visions seems to escape some scholars or commentators on the subject of reality. People who have visions, be they religious or lay prophets, invariably translate the expected fate of their own (i.e. subjective) universe to be that of other people's, or the objective reality. It is a common error not necessarily of the seers as such but certainly of a vast majority of interpreters. One of the best known examples are the prophesies of Jesus Christ, who is reported to have had a number of visions pertaining to his own future. This is perfectly understandable. A man with universal vision is capable of experiencing the totality of his existence or being. By this I mean that since our spiritual awareness has it's being outside the matrix of time and space, we can, theoretically, experience our distant past as well as our distant future at any time of our journey. What we cannot normally do is to assign a chronological factor to such experiences. We can predict what will happen, we cannot say when. No one can. The factor of unpredictability controls our reality. The variables are simply too great. The science of quantum mechanics shed some light on this problem (see chapter on *Scientific Perspective*). The theoretical physicist Stephen Hawking, mentioned before, writes:

"The fourth dimension, time, is also finite in extend, but it is like a line with two ends or boundaries, a beginning and an end. ...when one combines general relativity with the uncertainty principle of quantum mechanics, it is possible for both space and time to be finite without any edges or boundaries."[22]

To me, this sounds very unfortunate. It sounds like a vicious circle. Like walking in a circle. At best a sphere. Round and round in ever repeating patterns, depressing like Nietzsche's Nihilism. I greatly admire Stephen Hawking, but I don't like his vision. Perhaps this is what happens when one tries to contain the universe in a few simple equations. The scientists claim to have evolved past the mechanical view of the universe. I wonder... But there is another problem. The theoretical physicists seem to equate the Big Bang with the Big Cause. No wonder they walk in circles.

Rather like serpents swallowing their own tail.

I can predict, here and now, that most people, perhaps all, will eventually stop walking in circles. That eventually we shall all achieve a greater awareness of our Higher Self, of our true nature. That we shall be in this universe but not of this universe. That we shall gradually come to an understanding that the source of our being lies within our own awareness. What I cannot say, is *when* will this happen. Nor can anyone else.

Returning to Jesus. When he predicted the end of the world, he was asked when would this (event) take place. He replied: "But of that day and hour knoweth no man, no, not the angels of heaven, but my Father only."[23] This admission is preceded by a long and detailed account of what takes place in human consciousness before the spirit is liberated from its earthly embodiment. The whole prophetic monologue is, of course, steeped in symbolic language. In my DICTIONARY OF BIBLICAL SYMBOLISM,[24] I attempted to empower everyone interested in the inner meaning of the Bible to draw his or her own conclusions. (Not my, but *their own*).

The same is true of the Biblical prophets who gained awareness of the progression and evolution of their own psyche, their own *nephesh* or animal soul, which today we can best refer to as the subconscious. The religious fraternities quote the various seers to substantiate their claim and to prop up their speculations regarding the past and/or future events which had or are going to occur in the objective reality. Since in the course of human events *all* things will happen, sooner or later, their speculations regarding the past cannot fail. The same is true of the future. The question is *when*. We are on much safer ground if we interpret *all* the prophecies, of *all* the prophets, as pertaining to their own, particular, individualized psyche. The fact that the various biblical prophets did experience similarities in their visions only proves that, sooner of later, we shall all experience the events described or prophesied in our own realities, in our own subjective universes which we have created over countless millions of years. If we do accept this thesis, then at least we shall go down (or up!) informed, and therefore prepared.

I feel I must stress the futility of attempting to tie in the time factor to one's visions.

In addition to Jesus' example quoted above, throughout history various people predicted successive "ends of the world." Have you notice that we are still here? Even partial destruction of our mother earth did not come about. I am sure it will—though—some day... Some day the sun will burn out its nuclear fuel, it will shrink, collapse, and then expand to become a red giant, many times it's present diameter. The earth, with or without us, shall be cooked to cinder. Some day all prophecies shall come true.

Only, please, don't hold your breath.

Edgar Cayce who succeeded, with his extraordinary powers, in helping thousands of his *contemporaries* with their mental and physical troubles, failed completely as regards the chronology of his 'cataclysmic' predictions. While his projection of *trends* affecting humanity had been fairly accurate, his prophecies regarding global geological upheavals failed to materialize.[25] The same can be said of Jeffrey Goodman Ph.D., who in his book *We Are The Earthquake Generation* researches an impressive list of prophets ranging from Nostradamus, through the abovementioned Cayce to an array of contemporary seers, to give us a pessimistic but completely false image of our future, ahm... present, or perhaps even the past.

According to Goodman's checklist of major events predicted by various psychics, by the year 2000 we shall have experienced major subsidences on East and West coasts of the U.S.A., major section of Western United States shall have fallen into the ocean as coastline moves from its present position to Nebraska and Kansas; large portions of Wisconsin, Michigan and Illinois will have dipped into the expanded Great Lakes, and similar inundations will have taken place in Florida, Louisiana, Texas, China, USSR (which no longer exist but the psychics failed to predict its demise) as will part of the British Isles, Norway, Sweden, Denmark, Finland, as will most of Japan and Hawaii, etc., etc., etc.... While, as of writing the first draft of this book, we still have nine months (out of the 1990-2000 period) for the prophesies to be fulfilled, I am not holding *my* breath. Perhaps I am discouraged by previous predictions in the same book according to which we have already witnessed (*inter alia*) Palm Springs sink under water; San Diego, Los Angeles and San Francisco destroyed; California coastline pushed back to Bakersfield, Fresno and Sacramento; land rising in the Bering Strait creating a land bridge between Siberia and

Alaska, etc., etc., all this by 1980-85. And furthermore, by the year 1990 New York City was to have been completely broken up, land was to have risen between Gibraltar and Morocco closing off the Mediterranean sea from the Atlantic, the earth's axis of rotation was to have tipped a few degrees and all this to the horrendously clamorous accompaniment of unprecedented earthquakes all over the world.

Ooops....

With such dismal record, even with best intentions, the seers could never make a believer out of me.

A projection (as against a prophetic prediction) is an intelligent and knowledgeable person's estimate of future development, based on the data available today. Alvin Toffler's *Future Shock* offers very perceptive analyses of possible social development, Basil Booth's & Frank Fitch's *Earthshock* examine probabilities of future disasters by reviewing the best available scientific data from the past, or John Naisbitt's & Patricia Aburdene's *Megatrends* and *Magatrends 2000*, which extend and implement the work started by Toffler. The books are among the best examples of such projections. They cover as wide a range of our (immediate) future as can be. But none of them have anything to do with prophecy. Their projections have an excellent chance of coming true.

It has been said that prophesying is the second oldest profession in the world. We all know what is the first.

***

FOOTNOTES

(1). The word 'holistic' should perhaps be spelled with a 'w', i.e. wholistic, implying a completeness which is the derivative if the word holy or saintly.

(2). Fuller, R. Buckminster CRITICAL PATH, St. Martins's Press, New York 1981; pg.125

(3). A subatomic particle accelerator, also called atom-smasher.

(4). Visible light (violet, blue, green, yellow, orange and red) is flanked with ultraviolet on one side and infrared on the other. Its wavelength varies from 0.000076 centimeters to 0.000038 centimeters at the violet end. Until 1800 other photons were unknown to man.

(5). Luke 8:17. See also Kapuscinski, S., BEYOND RELIGION, VOL. 2, *Mystery* (Inhousepress 2000)   Hereafter my books of essays are referred to as BEYOND RELIGION, Vol. 1 or 2.

(6). Hawking, Stephen W., A BRIEF HISTORY OF TIME Bantam Books 1988.

(7). DIALOGUES OF PLATO, Random House, New York 1937, pg.360

(8). SRIMAD-BHAGAVATAM interpreted by A.C. Bhaktivendanta Swami Prabhupada; The Bhaktivendanta Book Trust. Los Angeles, California; pg. 48-9.

(9). Matthew 7:6.

(10). Gandhi, Mohandas Karamchand, ALL RELIGIONS ARE TRUE, (Bharatiya Vidya Bhavan, Bombay 1962)

(11). Matthew 19:17

(12). Falwell's opinions have been reported by Associated Press, in the Montreal Gazette, on January 16, 1999, pg. A 17. If anyone wishes to contest my views on the subject, I refer them to BEYOND RELIGION. Vol. 2, essay entitled "*Antichrist*" (Inhousepress, Montreal 2000: Smashwords Edition 2010]

(13). Eden, Hebrew word for "delight" is a state of consciousness; as is heaven and hell, and all states in between. See BEYOND RELIGION Vol 2. *"Heaven"* [Inhousepress 2000]

(14). 1 Corinthians 15:50-53 and 1 Thessalonians 4:15-18

(15). This or a very similar version, putatively based on the Bible, has been presented by Hal Lindsey in his bestseller: THE 1980's COUNTDOWN TO ARMAGEDDON (Bantam Books 1981)

(16). Campbell Joseph THE HERO WITH A THOUSAND FACES, (Princeton University Press, 1973)

(17). refer to Kapuscinski, S., DICTIONARY OF BIBLICAL SYMBOLISM, (Inhousepress 2001; also available as eBook with Part One free download)

(18). SRIMAD-BHAGAVATAM, First Canto, text 21, interpreted by A.C. Bhaktivendanta Swami Prabhupada;   (The Bhaktivendanta Book Trust. Los Angeles, California) pg. 120.

(19). de Chardin, Teilard, THE PHENOMENON OF MAN, (Harper & Row, New York, 1965)

(20). SRIMAD-BAGAVATAM. The quotation is from the First Canto "Creation", Text 11, page 104.

(21). Shakespeare, William, JULIUS CAESAR.

(22). Hawking, Stephen, W., BRIEF HISTORY OF TIME   (Bantam Books1988).

(23). Matthew 24:36. Also see essay on *Mystery* in BEYOND RELIGION vol 2.

(24). Published by Inhousepress 2001

(25). EDGAR CAYCE ON PROPHECY, by Mary Ellen Carter; Warner Books 1968

Chapter 2
Myth and Reality

*It is not in our stars but in ourselves
that we are underlings.*

Shakespeare

"What is the secret of the timeless vision? From what profundity of the mind does it derive? Why is mythology everywhere the same, beneath its varieties of costume? And what does it teach?" asks Campbell. [1]

Joseph Campbell (1904-1987) dedicated his life to unraveling these timeless questions. He wasn't the first. As far back as man's memory can reach, mythology enriched man's mind, his life, his customs. It nourished man's soul which, while never sated, had kept hunger at bay. Campbell postulates that a single archetypal hero inspired all world mythologies. He discovered the same vision permeating all nations, all peoples of the world—throughout the ages. He concludes that all share the same dream the same desire: to become One. He reaches the same conclusion as do all the heroes, that eventually "the essence of oneself and the essence of the world: these two are one."

This mystery rests at the source of every myth. We start our journey, naked, ignorant, cast out from our true home by a loving though stringent Father. We spend many lives building false realities, false hopes of achievements. We run after illusions, after ephemeral gratifications, titles and wealth. And then?

"Vanity of vanities, saith the Preacher, vanity of vanities;

all is vanity." [2]

And then we stand timidly at Narcissus's shoulder and gaze with him into the pool. Perhaps it dawns on us also that what we search for has always been within our reach. Was John gazing into the same mysterious deep when he realized that: "a lamp am I to you that perceive me, a mirror am I to you that know Me"?[3] Had Narcissus reached the very same conclusion?

Solomon with his thousand wives searched for his soul outside his own being. He tried to sate his hunger in the splendor of his temple only to find that his own vineyard has he not kept.[4] How strange that his song's words are so close to the symbol of the Age of Aquarius. We all look outside for what is only discernible within. The grass is always greener... We search for gods in temples, churches, hiding behind marble statues, within beguiling paintings. We substitute symbols for reality. And then again, perhaps curiously, perhaps timidly, we gaze into the pool.

But the waters are roiled. We never keep still long enough for them to settle. To become a true mirror of our soul. We turn away.

The search goes on.

"The myths have been invented by wise men to strengthen the laws and teach moral truths," says Horace in *Ars Poetica*.[5] Perhaps among the Romans. But other myths have been twisted, the truth behind the allegories metamorphosed into half-truth, bent to serve other ends. Bent to control people. "Myths are living organisms that change constantly..." counters Ms. O'Flaherty after an intimate communion with countless Hindu gods, demigods and demons.[6]

Myths personify the qualities to which we all aspire.

They lay at the source of religions, at the gateway to the inner kingdoms beyond the reach of most mortals. The Olympian gods did not create the Greeks; the Greeks created the Olympian gods. The gods, the half-gods, the muses and the satyrs are little more than who we might be or become, or hope to become, or even look down upon. But we all seem to need images, heroes, who embody that which we dare not embody. Zeus, Hera, Ares, Aphrodite, Artemis... are they not even today attributes to which many aspire? Do we not long for power, control, wisdom, beauty, even love, which we hope to find in the Eleusinian fields?

What is Religion to some is Myth to another. In both cases the origin of beliefs has fallen in desuetude. "Dead are all the gods" affirmed Nietzsche.[7] I feel like paraphrasing a proclamation the English reserve for their kings: "The gods are dead, God save the gods!"

"Truth is One, the sages call it by many names" say the Vedas.

There are many excellent books on myths. Most are concerned with the roots which they provide for religions. After all, religion is what is meant to keep us on an even keel. But perhaps in our travels we might cast our glance backwards once in a while. To examine, no matter how briefly, not where we are going, but whence we came. "Before Abraham was, I am," said Jesus.[8] But what *was* before Abraham?

That which *is* does not change. What constitutes a change is the act of becoming. That which changes, does so in cycles. Brahma's breath creates and dissolves the world as expressed thousands of years later in the Big Bang and Big Crunch theory. Even as Brahma sleeps between his respirations, a man too goes through a cycles of sleep, perhaps dreams, and returns to build his own, subjective world once again. *"So God created man in his own image..."*[9] Does therein lie our image and likeness? In our ability, or fate, to build our worlds only to destroy them, and then, on and on, to recreate them again and again...? Is this what defines our immortality? Is this what Hamlet rebelled against when he mused: *"To die, to sleep; No more; ... For in that sleep of death what dreams may come..."*[10] Are our successive reincarnations memories of dreams past? Sai Baba calls the (death) dream *samadhi*; he calls life (physical embodiment) a memory of a dream. Joseph Campbell illustrates a similar cosmogonic cycles derived from the Mandukya Upanishad wherein the dream period is the phase of emanations and dissolutions separating the deep sleep and the waking eons.[11]

Only the Christian Myths, and possibly the Hebrew, are said to limit life to a single accident of birth, but even this interpretation appears to be undergoing a change. More and more Christians tolerate and even espouse the concept of reincarnation. Heretofore, the exclusion of the concept of rebirth was contrary to all knowledge of all sages of all times. One can only wonder who was responsible for imposing such restrictions on our "longevity", not to say immortality. According to the religions built on the Christian myths, once we gain entry into heaven, we are destined to remain there in a perfect stasis forever. Until hell freezes over. They call it for "ever-and-ever", as if just one 'ever' wasn't long enough.

What a dull prospect.

All religions vie for the monopoly on Truth. Those which predate Judeo-Christian myths, (even some resuscitated later such as Theosophy or Eckankar) prefer to claim the honor of being the 'mother' of all religions, that all that followed evolved from 'their' original roots. Such claim enables its adherents not to detract from other religions, only to regard them with a degree of condescension as an elder brother would when discussing philosophy with his preteen sibling.

The most ancient myths, which survived to the present day, differ from latter visions, in as much as they tend to describe our primordial past as much as our projected future. Our 'modern' religions, including Judaism, Christianity and Islam, pale in comparison the Puranas, the Vedas and the records of Jainism. Furthermore, the "modern" religions appear to have been directed at select groups of people. The ancient ones, address humanity as a whole.

The Hindu mythologies are among those that had been much more concerned with cosmology and cosmogony than later religions. For the Hindu avatars, for some reason, the contemplation of millions upon millions of years that would define the duration of our earth/world's life seemed to have been of great importance. The myths are based on Sanskrit texts, an Indo-European language closely related to Greek and Latin. The main sources of myths, ranging from approximately 1200 B.C to 200 B.C., include Rg Veda, Atharva Veda, Brahmanas, Mahabharata (the great epic of India), and the Ramahama. Later sources, the Puranas,[12] are preoccupied in great detail with cosmology and cosmogony, or the creation and the origin of the world. Here we are not concerned with religion which ensued from the various myths, but with the vision of the world held by our eastern forefathers. There is considerable harmony in the basic vision. The Hindu Puranas, the Secret Doctrine of Buddhism as postulated in Theosophy and the mythology of the Jains all confirm the cyclic nature of our universe. Today's theoretical astrophysicists are just beginning to agree.

But wherein the myths share, in principle, some aspects of cosmogony, they differ considerably in its evolution. They all reach back to prehistory. They all postulate eons of existence, predating our present earth and its formation. After that, the visions go their separate ways. To illustrate the point, let us review just a few of them. An in-depth analysis (beyond the scope of this book) would lead us to realize that much of the ancient myth has survived to this day or has been resurrected in the modern day science.

Among the most ancient myths are those upheld in Jainism.

The Jains hold that everything, including matter, is eternal, while the Spirit is the seat of consciousness. Their vision describes the world of spiritual perfection, slowly descending into material depravity, only to rise like phoenix from its decadent ashes and climb, once again, to the glories of spiritual perfection. Unfortunately, we do not remain at the top of the twelve-prong cycle very long, but begin a descent, once more to the nether regions—but this too is temporary. We rise again; we grow in awareness of health and beauty, in stature and reach once again the apex, as the cyclic mythology demands. At least, not to put undue pressure on the reader, the cycles are counted in "ten millions of ten millions of one hundred millions of one hundred millions" of periods of countless years. We have ample time to visualize this mythical offering. Although at the apex of the cycle people had been four-miles tall and one hundred and twenty-eight ribs strong, and enjoyed a life span of "two periods of countless years", the rest of the cycles are not all fun and games, particularly during the lower swing of the circle. Should one wish to free oneself from this endless cycle, one can aspire to Nirvana, which can be achieved following a period of twelve years of self-denial. Alternatively, if one dies at the very top of the cycle, one is so perfect that one enters directly into the realm of the gods. The relatively good news is that we are in the descending series which began in 522 B.C., and will last for another twenty-one thousand years. The bad news is that after this period we have another bout with the descending ages before we can begin our upward climb.

If we attempt to adjust the Mosaic vision of ancient Hebrews of us having been created unto the image of God, some interesting speculations ensue. It would suggest that we have been born pure, we descend to a materialistic nadir, and then rise again to a higher ethical ground. I can see little evidence of such a cycle among most of my friends.

The Hindu vision is truly cosmogonic.

Its ancient brush paints a more disturbing picture. While the Jains offer a cycle in which there is also an upward trend toward self-betterment, the Hindus deny us this relief. They start, as do the Jains, at the very top, in a glorious Golden

Age, Satya Yuga (more accurately—the Age of Truth). This age of bliss and beauty is by far the longest of the four ages of the Maha Yuga, and lasts 1,728,000 years. I would suggest it is equivalent to the period humanity had spent in Eden. It is followed by the Silver Age during which we are still blessed with considerable virtue and beauty for the next 1,296,000 years. Then things begin to deteriorate more rapidly. We lose a lot of our spiritual values and seem to straddle the ethical fence. This Bronze Age lasts for 864,000 years. Mercifully, the last age in which humanity sinks to the lowest level and is steeped in materiality and egotism is shortened to 432,000 years only. It is appropriately called the Iron Age (Kali Yuga)[13], the least noble of the four metals.

But here we part company with the previous vision.

While the Jains start on the upward direction to recover their lost virtues (perhaps as in the Christian purgatory), at the end of Kali Yuga the Hindu world is completely annihilated. It is destroyed by fire and water. This non-world persists in a dormant mode for a long, long time, until finally the Gods decide to give us another chance. Then, and only then we begin anew. The one consolation is that we begin, once more, at the top.

The interesting aspect of the Hindu vision is that it stipulates not evolution but devolution of the human race. It implies that by separating ourselves from the Universal, by taking on an individual identity, soul, we cannot but head the wrong way. Given time, we are bound to fall pray to egoism. So why bother? Why make the effort at all? Here, once again, we can take advantage of enlightenment that will absolve us, as individuals, from the necessity of incarnating ourselves in a human form. This is the good news. The bad news is that we have already entered the present Iron Age, the Kali Yuga, some time ago. And worse still, we have a long, long way to go before the cosmic dissolution.

And now for the most complex vision in which I limit myself to the anthropogenetic vision, to which cosmogony is virtually incidental.

The Theosophists, led by the late Helena Pertrovna Blavatsky who took it upon herself to decipher ancient writings hidden in the upper reaches of Tibet, add a slight twist on the above. In her greatest work, *The Secret Doctrine*, Blavatsky refers to the "very old book" which predates all other known sources, and on which, she claims, future scriptures of various religions have been based. Any attempt to abbreviate Blavatsky's writings would be regarded by any serious theosophist as doomed to failure. Nevertheless, I doubt that many readers are willing to examine, in detail, some 1,400 pages of her *Isis Unveiled*, and to follow with *The Secret Doctrine* which in its very *abbreviated* form adds another two-hundred and fifty.[14] To extrapolate a comparison to the visions of the Jains and Hindus is equally as difficult. Yet the cosmogony of Theosophy is such as to demand at least a cursory scrutiny.

The myths embrace the Atlanteans, the Lemurians, and reach further back as though with a blink of an eye. Time is nothing to Theosophy, as indeed it seems like nothing to all who have read it. In the midst of all this, HPB (as Ms.Blavatsky was known to her colleagues) stresses the reality of the present. No mean achievement.

The Theosophic cosmogony also revolves in cycles. Yet they do not strike me as truly repetitive. From the mists of prehistory, reaching back countless millions of years, the humanity evolves in a series of Root-Races. They are seven in number and now we have reached the middle of the fifth Root-Race, which became established *su generis* approximately a million years ago. Each Root-Race is in turn divided into seven Sub-Races, which, in turn, are composed of seven Family-Races. This last subdivision has a life-span of some 30,000 earth-years, and is made up of innumerable tribes and nations lasting some 4,000 to 5,000 years each.

This very start gives us a perspective on the transiency of political systems. Their ephemeral existence, as in the larger scheme of things, relegates them to transient cauldrons of iniquity, wherein our time might be better spent on matters of other than parochial importance. We might see ourselves as a race of people, rather than pawns in the hands of power-hungry autocrats. It could be the first step towards our liberation.

But to continue.

Each Root-Race goes through repetitive cycles of golden, silver, bronze and iron ages. The subgroups echo this rotation, rather as in the Hindu mythology, but it allows for a greater awareness of present conditions. In Theosophy, after the age of Kali steeped in materiality, we know that a new Satya Yuga is just around the corner. The corner might spell a few thousand years of waiting, but presents a more rewarding prospect than global dissolution. And if we are prepared to settle for latter rewards, then, with a dose of optimism, we can devise a sub-sub-cycle which will place us in a mini-age of silver or gold often enough to combat an ongoing bout with manic depression.

A broader view is more pessimistic. We have only just completed the first 5,000 years of the Iron Age cycle of Kali Yuga, which began with the death of Krishna. In terms of mega-cycles, we have a long wait for the new Golden age. I am grateful that my own thoughts have evolved along the lines that we all create our subjective realities, no matter how illusory, and my own reality seldom strays far from the golden area.

A word about our past.

In Theosophy, we had not been created by God in an Eden, but rather we result from a cooperation between Nature and the Higher Beings. Nature took us as far as she could along the upward path, and then gods granted us the mind which facilitated continued struggle. As for the distant future, we have two more Root-Races to go, before we join our Hindu friends and cease to be. Rather like in a Big Crunch which our astrophysicists are determined to impose on us. As for the timing, don't hold your breath, the present Iron Age, the Kali Yuga still has some 427,000 years to go. That's the bad news or the good news, depending whether you enjoy your life in Kali Yuga. The other good or bad news is that each Family-Race more or less disappears every 30,000 years only, a mere blink of the cosmic eye. Strangely enough the tectonic plate movements, the periodic shifting of the earth's magnetic poles and the unexpected bombardment from our asteroid belt could easily accelerate this schedule. So—maybe we should take a deep breath, after all.

Those who find the Theosophic vision too complex or too mythical to influence their reality, think again. Some Christians and most North American motels display a Bible on their bedside table. Albert Einstein is said to have kept there the *Secret Doctrine*.

To a greater or lesser degree, all the above myths are cyclic. But there is a particular perversion of these myths which left a considerable mark on Western Society. No religions sprang from it but indirectly it was responsible for many deaths. The myth is that of Sisyphus, or the myth of Eternal Return. While the myths of Jainism, Buddhism or Hinduism precede the present Big Bang / Big Crunch theories, they do not predict the imminent exact repetition of previous cycles. This is left to the myth of Sisyphus. In punishment for his disrespect, Zeus condemned king Sisyphus to forever push a heavy rock up a steep hill. Always the same hill, always the same stone, always up to the same elevation and distance—only to slip near the top, and watch the rock roll back down the slope. He came to symbolize all abortive labor, all effort without any hope of reward. What is more, he represents the futility of immortality. After all, what is the point of being immortal if one is only to repeat, *ad nauseam*, the same abortive cycle? It is no more a cycle—it is a *circle*.

There have been exceptions to this interpretation. The Stoics seem to have derived a great peace of mind in knowledge that there is nothing to be gained by emotional involvement. It gave them strength based on indifference.

This, in terms of the Christian myth, is a perversion. The Stoical peace of mind does not spring from assurance of intrinsic goodness of the Absolute, but from the futility of effort.

Yet the futility embodied in Sisyphus has been accepted by later minds. We see the influence of the concept in Friedrich Nietzsche's *Übermensch*, the 'Overman' often translated as the 'Superman' (*Thus Spake Zarathustra* 1883) overriding the masses sentenced to eternal mediocrity. Albert Camus (*The Myth of Sisyphus*) and other existentialists such as Jean Paul Sartre (*Being and Nothingness* 1943 and *Existentialism* 1946) have adopted a parallel disconsolate philosophy.

Ivan Turgenev's (*Fathers and Sons*) Nihilism, from the Latin root *nihil* meaning *nothing*, together with Nietzsche's *Übermensch*, are said to have contributed direct fuel for Hitler's paranoia associated with his desire to breakaway from the "eternal return" by attempting to create an Aryan Superrace. All are in direct opposition to the Christian philosophy which, in the words of St. Augustine (*City of God*) affirm: "...Christ died once for our sins, and rising again, dies no more."

And so to the Christian myths.

In my essay sharing its title with this chapter (*Beyond Religion Vol.1.*), I pointed out that Christian myths are as enigmatic as any we examined above. It seems that Ms. O'Flaherty was right in pointing out that "myths are living organisms that change constantly". The review of the Christian mythology points to the same conclusion. Not only are dogmas added at random, whenever need arises, but the Creed, the very pillar of the Christian mythic structure, undergoes fundamental changes.

From the original concise statement in Nicæa (A.D. 325) which included a declaration of the nature of Christ, the creed had been revised a mere half a century later at the First Council of Constantinople (A.D. 381). The present form was reached only in the seventh century, but not without some succeeding changes. In the ninth century the Vatican decided that the Holy Ghost proceedeth not only from the Father, but also from the Son: *Et in Spiritum Sanctum, Dominum et vivificantem, qui ex Patre **Filioque** procedit.* This predates the Son in relation to the Spirit, equating the Son with the Father. Jesus' many assurances to the contrary fell on deaf sacerdotal ears.[15] This is particularly surprising since in the Apostles' creed offered below, it is stated that the Son was conceived *by* the Holy Ghost. It seems that the church created a mystery in which the Son is conceived by that which issues from himself. Still, all religions thrive on mysteries, which make the priesthood indispensable to act as intermediaries between the divine and us. Yet, would it not be simpler to say that the Son was 'self-born'? This term is not unknown in other mythologies. The God Brahma, Jehovah, Osiris are all second persons of various Trinities and are all self-engendered. Spinoza, and Pythagoras before him, both asserted that Brahma is the universe itself.[16] It is a way of saying that Brahma is the manifested reality, the Logos, the Word made flesh—all attributes assigned to Jesus Christ. But in any case, we are offered no clue why it took the Roman church nine centuries to reach this conclusion.

The Creed itself can be also analyzed in the context of myth and reality. Below I offer the Apostles' creed as adopted by the Roman Catholics. Bold letters are, to my knowledge, facts. The italic script indicates the accumulated myths.

I believe in God the Father Almighty, Maker of heaven and earth; and in **Jesus** *Christ his only Son, our Lord,* who was *conceived by the Holy Ghost,* **born of** *the* **Virgin Mary, suffered under Pontius Pilate, was crucified, died and buried**; *he descended into hell; the third day he rose from the dead; he ascended into Heaven, and sitteth at the right hand of God, the Father Almighty; from thence he shall come to judge the quick* *and the dead. I believe in the Holy Ghost; the holy Catholic Church; the communion of saints; the forgiveness of sins; the resurrection of the body; and the life everlasting.*

To recap, the historical reality consists of thirteen words. "Jesus, born of Mary, suffered under Pontius Pilate, was crucified, died and buried." The rest (ninety-five words) is myth: "a living organism that changes constantly..."

It should be stressed, that the Christian (or the Judaic) myths should never be confused with the document called the Bible, an assembly of books written over many centuries. The Bible is neither a historic nor religious dissertation. From the days it had been written we inherited no other compendium of knowledge recorded for posterity; certainly not of such a scale. Essentially the Bible equates the universe with the anthropomorphic man, and defines it (the man/universe) in human terms. It could be called a historical record of scientific thought development, but never as record of history or religious myths.

We started this discussion by attempting to define the purpose of myths. Various distinguished scholars offer divergent views. Marx, equating them with religions, considered them the opium of the masses. Epicurus (341-270 B.C.) claimed that myths were only partially released to the masses: "The most sacred names of the gods, the prayers by which their favor could be gained, were kept secret." Perhaps the reason for this was enunciated some three centuries later by Jesus who sympathized with our ignorance: "I have yet many things to say unto you, but ye cannot bear them now."[17] One can only wonder if we are any more ready today, or are we, as the Hindus would have us believe, sinking into a devolutionary quagmire, in the midst of the black age of Kali.

It is in my nature to reject everything which would, in

any way, lower my state of consciousness—today. Unlike the Theosophists, I cannot testify to the distant past, nor the equally distant future, but I know that I exhibit an awareness of the present, manifested in both the subjective and, perhaps to a lesser degree, the objective universes. This awareness, or this state of consciousness, is the expression of my being. Whatever the myths teach others, they taught me that their very scope, both chronologically and in the richness of texture, affirm that man always searched, and will continue to search that elusive straight and narrow path to the celestial realms. The realms of happiness, of Paradise, vary from man to man. For nomads traversing arid desserts, Paradise is adorned with:

"...maidens with swelling breasts, like of age..." [amidst] "gardens underneath which rivers flow... rivers of water unstalling, rivers of milk unchanging in flavour, and rivers of wine—delight to the drinkers, rivers, too, of honey purified... therein to dwell forever."[18]

And for a man blessed with a dozen wives, like the prophet Mohammed, those who enter Paradise " shall hear no idle talk..."[19] Others just dream, as Shakespeare did, of but one woman, *not too mean to be your queen, nor yet too good to be your concubine.* Perhaps Seneca was right when he said that "To live happily, is the desire of all men... but their minds are blind to a clear vision of just what it is that makes life happy."[20]

Or it could be that heaven is just nirvana, the blowing out of the candle of life, the reunion with Brahma, with the attendant cessation of all craving, all desires, all passions. To those whose consciousness resides in a state of warfare, torn amid the battlefields of opposing values, this might mean a state of transcendent peace, a "peace of God which passes all understanding."[21]

**

It is my firm belief, that in spite of the countless religions that came and went throughout human history, each path is always and undeniably an individual path. Perhaps the very richness of the mythological heritage proves this of itself. To share our beliefs is to enrich our lives. To impose them on others is to deny our intrepid fellow-pilgrims the individualized expression of God within their own being. It is to say that our God is better or greater than their God is. Indeed, if there were only one religion, there would be no need for sharing, no danger of imposing. Yet it is the diversity of myths, which breathes poetry into ancient and modern man alike.

God is not in any one of them. But in all. And in many more to come.

Or it could be that Sai Baba, whom many recognize as the present day incarnation of God speaking to his Hindu children from a small, inaccessible village in India, sheds the true light on the enigma of our reality. He says:

There is only one religion, the religion of love.
There is only one cast, the cast of humanity.
There is only one language, the language of the heart.
There is only one law, the law of Karma.
There is only one God, and He is omnipresent.

Perhaps there is only one religion—for the 'chosen'. If not, then I shall be content to accept another statement from the venerable Epicurus: "The gods exist, but they are not what the rabble suppose them to be." But, surely, we are no longer the rabble Epicurus spoke of.

Are we?

***

FOOTNOTES

(1). Campbell, Joseph THE HERO WITH A THOUSAND FACES, (Princeton University Press, 1973; pg. 4)

(2). Ecclesiastes 1:2

(3). Apocryphal Acts of John

(4). Song of Solomon 1:6.

(5). Quintus Horatius Flaccus (65 B.C. - 8 B.C.), Latin lyric poet.

(6). HINDU MYTHS, a Sourcebook translated from the Sanskrit, Intro. by Wendy Doniger O'Flaherty; (Penguin Books, London 1975)

(7). THUS SPAKE ZARATHUSTRA by Friedrich Wilhelm Nietzsche (1844-1900)

(8). John 8:58 et al.

(9). Genesis 1:27.

(10). HAMLET by William Shakespeare. Act III scene 1.

(11). THE HERO WITH A THOUSAND FACES Campbell, Joseph pg. 266.

(12). I refer to them as later sources because they have been committed to paper (or into written word) during the modern area (after the birth of Christ). Before, they had been kept alive by the word of mouth only, although in case of the Vedas, H.P. Blavatsky claimed to have studied secret sources predating any other written scripture known to man, which have been and are still secreted in the inaccessible temples of Tibet. Her book (An abridgement of) THE SECRET DOCTRINE (The Theosophical Publishing House, London 1966), bears witness to this claim. Ms. Blavatsky draws a strong distinction between orthodox Buddhism and the Esoteric Buddhism which is the basis of her studies.

(13). Kali is the black goddess of death and evil, though she embodies some more attractive aspects. She also represents the female principle. The name was originally given to one of the tongues of the fire-god Agni. According the *Gospel of Sri Ramakrishna*, she also carries the title of "The Ferry across the Ocean of Existence."

(14). The original edition of the SECRET DOCTRINE is published in two volumes and 1571 pages.

(15). "The Son can do nothing of himself..." John 5:19. Although Jesus' later affirmation that "I and my Father are one" (John 10:30) does justice to the Roman Church's conclusion. It depends whether Jesus is speaking as his lower (human) or Higher (born of the spirit) Self.

(16). HPB in ISIS UNVEILED Volume 1, *Science*, (Theosophical University Press 1988) adds this footnote: "Brahma does not create the earth... any more than the rest of the universe. Having evolved himself from the soul of the world, once separated from the First Cause, he emanates in his turn all nature out of himself. He does not stand above it, but is mixed up with it; and Brahma and the universe form one Being, each particle of which is in its essence Brahma himself, who proceeded out of himself. (Burnouf: *Introduction*, pg. 118)"

(17). John 16:12

(18). see footnote #49 on the next page.
(19). THE KORAN INTERPRETED, a translation by A.J. Arberry; Simon & Shuster, Touchstone, New York 1955; pgs. 225, 221 and 321.
(20). Lucius Anneus Seneca (4 B.C.- 65 A.D.) From his essay *On the happy Life*.
(21). Philippians 4:7

Chapter 3
Politics and Society

Have you heard the music that no fingers enter into?

Kabir

The **political visionaries** can be relatively easily tabulated into those with a universal vision—a perspective affecting the largest possible number of people, and those who concentrated on aggrandizing their egos at the expense of the world. It would be only fair, however, particularly when dealing with our forefathers, to recognize the relative 'world' in which they lived. The world of Alexander the Great was not as great as is the world of any present-day visionary. Throughout the ages, the measure of the world was directly related to the technology of locomotion. Julius Caesar expanded his 'world', but only as far as his means of transportation allowed. Hannibal's elephants managed to cross the Alps but reinforcements from Carthage had failed him, and he could not take Rome. The peace at Tilsit left Napoleon the master of the Continent, but as with Hannibal, the lack of military support buried his armies in the snows of Russia. Great Britain which had the vision to concentrate on the navy, i.e.: on a mode of transport, assembled the greatest empire, expanded the 'world' to a magnitude never before imagined.

The visions of man grew as civilization empowered them with technology to implement such visions.

To illustrate the point, among men with the broadest social vision are esoteric teachers such as Buddha, Jesus, Mohammed, as well as, though to a lesser degree, Madison and Jefferson, but also Marks and Engels. I am not comparing the ethic of their vision, only its universality. There is one specific characteristic which underscores the universality of a vision. A parochial vision is always at the expense of some other group (nation, organization, religion or business interests). A universal vision draws its power and generosity from the universal source that is, by definition, inexhaustible.

The second, the parochial, category is more variegated than the first. In this league we can include the European monarchs of countries whose interest lay exclusively in the welfare of their own particular nations. Their vision, though not universal, embraces an extensive social mix wherein all members of the group (nation, religious organization, and social system such as kibbutz) can benefit.

Monarchs with exalted egos and members of military oligarchies do not qualify. They belong to the still lesser gods—their visions even more parochial.

They are responsible for centralist governments, for concentrating power in relatively small oligarchies, regardless of the intent of such centralization. Since both Stalin and the magnates of the centralist Detroit Automotive Industry would fit into this category, such restricted vision is not limited to ostensibly political systems. There are also religious leaders who insist on monopolizing the rod of power. In fact, few organizations are as parochial as a number of religious systems, often in direct antithesis to the teaching on which they have been reputedly based. A vision of elitist group's interest is also the driving force of the international conglomerates which, while admitting to solely economic interests (the quarterly returns), wield enormous power over lesser syndicates or cartels. These mammoth organizations often far exceed the economies of many lesser countries. Their vision remains parochial.

Those bring up the tail end of the sociopolitical

visionaries whose sole interest is the titillation of their ego. To this group belong the dictators of Banana Republics, puppet masters at the head of many political parties, the leaders of sectarian organizations within the civil, cultural, and ecclesiastic milieus wherein members are easily manipulated. To these visionaries the wielding of (preferably absolute) power is of greater importance not only over the good of the many but even over the good of the members of their own organizations. The dismal end of these primitive minds belongs to individuals who wish to break down the existing systems in order to enhance their own influence, their personal standing in the society. The many sects with suicidal overtones, the end-of-the-world cults, laic or religious organizations driven by xenophobic neuroses, and some nefarious politically-inspired separatist groups are an example of such state of mind.

One aspect is important to note with regard to all visionaries.

Their visions are unlikely to last unless supported by powerful oligarchies. Great visionaries are harbingers of great changes. Oligarchies survive and subsist on traditions and *status quo*. No empire, no great religion, survived in its original form. All must mutate to survive. Whatever motivated the original visionaries had to be compromised to achieve longevity. Oligarchies led by able politicians are at the root of all compromise. Their motivation is never the protection or the implementation of the original vision; it is simply their own, personal survival.

***

An overview of the evolution of Western Civilization suggest that the reality of various historical eras had been the result of relatively few men inflicting or imposing their vision on the vast majority of people. It is only in recent years that the very imperfect system called democracy allowed for a broader participation in the affairs of state, which to a considerable degree shape the reality of the day. Even so, the American triumvirate of power as well as systems based on the British Parliamentary model are still confined to the controlling influence of a relatively small group of men and women who often suffer from the parochial mindset and the ensuing views of societies.

The formation of visions controlling any society must be regarded in their historical context. What may be obvious to us is only obvious because, perhaps centuries ago, someone initiated a concept which only now came to maturity. Rather like adding yeast to dough and waiting for it to grow. A brief overview of forces swaying the Western Civilizations serves to illustrate this thesis. Throughout the ages there had been men, who, within the amplitude of their talent, opportunity and social standing, exhibited at least a degree of altruistic vision. In the overview that follows I concentrated on the authors of the most influential insights, regardless of their moral, ethical or sociological merit.

I tend to assign the most profound vision of pre-Christian times to Plato (born c. 429 B.C.). It is difficult to assess to what degree his views had been his own, and to what degree they gave expression of his mentor's philosophy.

Plato was a very practical dreamer. He is said to have declared that "he would never consider a political career until philosophers became rulers or rulers philosophers." With some notable exceptions, his vision never materialized. Instead, the rulers became politicians, developing the art of telling an adversary to go to hell in such a way that he would look forward to the trip. This technique qualified them to be called diplomats, whose proverbial tact became little more than the art of straight-faced lying, or at least of never telling the truth. While living in London, England, I have been offered an insight as to why and how Great Britain became the greatest empire. I've been told the story of three diplomats from three nations. The French diplomat was said to seldom tell the truth. The German—to seldom lie. The

English diplomat never lied, and never spoke the truth.

Apparently little has changed. Under the influence of Socrates, Plato "soon grew disgusted with the contemporary Athenian politics".[1] Yet his vision of a Just Society remains to this day and, on occasion influences, or can and should influence, our thinking. Plato's dialogues: the *Republic* and the *Symposium* give ample evidence of the high ethic permeating the vision of his reality. In the *Symposium* he avers that: "Any action which is the cause of a thing emerging from nonexistence into existence might be called poetry". I would suggest that no better definition has been found to define any work of art to this day.

Aristotle (384-322 B.C.), Plato's pupil, having attested to his own vision of the nature of goodness in men (*Nichomachean Ethics*), goes on to inquire, in *Politics*, into the forms of human association which he deems essential basis of the study of politics.[2] One can but wonder how many of our present day politicians share his vision. In his *Metaphysics*, Aristotle shares with us his vision of the nature of vision itself; he writes, "...experience is knowledge of particulars, art of universals". We shall be further reviewing the difference between the particular and the universal visions later. Aristotle's failing was his inability to take full advantage of the insights of Pythagoras (c.582 - c.507 B.C.), whose heliocentric vision was more advanced that Aristotelian geocentricity. Nevertheless, his vision had profound influence on the Arab world and later on Medieval scholasticism.

It is my contention that although Socrates, Plato and Aristotle appeared to have dealt principally with the problems inherent in their immediate society, the essence of the visions of all three had been truly universal.

The vision of Jesus of Nazareth, the Christ, had been and remains by far the most misunderstood of all visions throughout history. Jesus started with a parochial vision: go *not into the way of the Gentiles, and into any city of the Samaritans enter ye not*, and *I am not sent but unto the lost sheep of the house of Israel*, but later expanded his precepts to universal proportions commanding his emissaries to: Go *ye therefore, and teach all nations...*[3] His teaching that heaven is a state of consciousness (*the kingdom of God is within you*)[4] rather than a carrot to be offered in "life to come" for explicit and implicit obedience to the sacerdotal class, was and remains diligently ignored to this day. As such, this most universal vision of all which offered "heaven on earth", left relatively little mark on society. What left an enormous scar on the human psyche is the organization which exploited Jesus' teaching for the purpose of wielding power over vast numbers of people over a considerable period of time.

From the Roman days till the Middle Ages the preeminent minds (Pliny the Younger, Tertullian, Cyprian, Theodosius, St. Augustine) seemed preoccupied with attempts to reconcile their vision of Judeo-Christian teaching with the exigencies of the State. (The concept of the separation of Church and State remained a vision of distant future). Perhaps the contemporaries forgot that the teaching on which they based their arguments dealt with a "kingdom *not* of this world". Reconciling fire with water seldom gives desired results. From the sociological point of view, had they considered giving Caesar what is Caesar's and God what is God's, they might have met with greater success. Politically speaking, they were inerrant. Their power grew.

At the beginning of the 5th century, Europe entered the Dark Ages. During this period man's vision dealt, again, almost exclusively with Judeo-Christian ethic. St. Benedict (c.480 - c.543), going against the grain, is recognized today as the founder of Western monasticism. His exemplary life of goodness and sacrifice was held in great contrast to the Germans who extolled the virtues of war. The German vision persisted to the 20th century. Monasticism, to a considerable degree, became an escape from the degenerative trends controlling both the secular and sacerdotal society.

Around the year 610, Mohammed (also spelt Mahomet or Muhammad) began recording his visions in the Koran. Yet it had not been his religious revelation but rather his flight (the Heriga) in 622 to Medina and the subsequent formation of the Mohammedan empire which left a lasting political influence on the world. Nevertheless, since the Koran (+ the Sunna) serve as basis for a judicial system, his teaching continues to control the social lives of many of its adherents to this day; particularly those unable or unwilling to understand the mystical aspects of the revelations explored by the Sufies.

Perhaps this is the right place to stress that high ethical visions of such giants as Moses, Jesus Christ or Mohammed had little to do with the creation of the Israelite, Papal or Mohammedan empires.[5] The *dicta* attributed to Moses and Christ such as "thou shalt not kill", or "love thy neighbor as thyself" never deterred the Israelites, nor the Christians under the auspices and control of the Vatican, from killing. Whereas history of Israel is bathed in blood, all Crusades received Papal dispensation and most had been actually instigated by the Vatican oligarchy. The very same can be said of the Moslem who supposedly not only adopted the Mosaic and Jesus' visions, referring to them as the Book (Bible),[6] but reiterated same in the Koran:

"Therefore We prescribed for the Children of Israel that whoso slays a soul not to retaliate, for a soul slain, nor for corruption done in the land, shall be as if he had slain mankind altogether; and whoso gives life to a soul, shall be as if he had given life to mankind altogether"[7]

It would be hard to imagine that such high moral ground would sanction the rivers of blood which flowed during the formation and the subsequent expansion of the Mohammedan Empire. Little has changed to this day.

Nevertheless, while the Mohammedan influence continued to expand, by the 11th century the bishop of Rome had been recognized as the spiritual leader of all Christians.

The Church also grew to become the generative power of the Western World. In many areas, for centuries, the local bishop filled the position of the governor and pastor. Others formed monasteries. Power was centralized. While Islam looked Eastward, in Europe the Church's vision became the only vision.

The High Middle Ages, beginning around the 12th century, "established institutions and values that were to shape European civilization for centuries."[8] The controversy between Church and State, i.e. the pope and the emperor, had reawakened.

It is more difficult to explain an apparent drive to create a new vision of a Just Society, which lead all levels of government to initiate elaborate judicial systems. The popes and bishops, kings and emperors, lesser barons all the way down to local governments, got involved. Perhaps this drive was in some way inspired by the successes of Mohammedanism, which functioned in a strict legal environment. By the beginning of the 13th century, Pope Innocent III's prevailing vision touched all of Europe. He initiated crusades against the Moslems in the Middle East, against the heretics in southern France, and conducted ideological battles against any kingdom (including England and France) which would question his supremacy. All this he did in the name of the canon law, which allegedly was based on the Scriptures. Pope Gregory VIII's (Innocent III's predecessor) admonition that all Christians: "who desire to reign with Christ are to be warned not to reign through ambition for worldly power"[9] had been studiously ignored. Innocent III's vision while far reaching was anything but innocent. In his attempt to rule the Western world his methods, let alone his vision, were all but parochial.

By the next century the Papacy grew in institutional power while losing moral leadership to such a degree that, in 1324 Marsilius of Padua attempted to limit its domination. In his *Defensor Pacis* (Defender of the Peace)[10] he attacked the theoretical foundations of Papal power. Arguing against the slavishly centralist vision of the Church, he wrote: "...the bishop of Rome has no more of essential sacerdotal authority than any other priest, even as the blessed Peter had no more than the other apostles. For all received this authority from Christ equally and immediately..."[11] In the meantime, the great works of St. Albert the Great and St. Thomas Aquinas, both Dominican monks, offered their visions of the world in such a lofty manner that none of their studious ramblings percolated to the society at large. I doubt if today there are many Catholics who can quote but a single question or reply from Thomas's *Summa Theologica*. Thus, in a practical sense, their visions bore no fruit.

While the Church continued to consolidate absolute power, it was left to the barons of England, to advance the cause of the common man. In 1215 they compelled King John to issue a charter, the *Magna Carta* which became "the most important instrument of English constitutional history".[12] The document was a broad statement protecting baronial privileges against the king's imposition. It also offered a degree of freedom for the English church and customs of towns, protection for the subjects and communities. In spite of future repudiations and re-issuances, the Charter remained a symbol of supremacy of law over king. The vision it represented carried universal consequences.

A bright star in an otherwise dismal period (with the exception of the above) was St. Francis of Assisi. Born in 1182, he witnessed the progressive decadence of Rome. While his vision was the nearest to the vision of Christ, it was too lofty for the masses to emulate. It stood, nevertheless, in direct opposition to Pope Innocent III's pragmatic despotism.

Mid-fourteenth century dates the beginning of 'rebirth' of classical culture. The Renaissance[13] (as the great Italian poet Petrarch called it,) brought the humanists; often erroneously accused of being atheists, to the social if not political forefront. It is difficult to single out any man who's vision brought this rebirth about. Rather, a critical mass of Italian poets, artists, thinkers, have contributed to a modified attitude towards the Church. The Papacy continued to flourish, but no longer to the exclusion of other influences. Rationality gave birth to diplomacy, which began to influence the Church's autocracy of the Middle Ages. Finally in early 16th century, one man's vision left an indelible mark on the new age. It belonged to Niccolo Machiavelli (1469 - 1527). Political upheavals banished him from Florence, which he served in many ambassadorial posts. At his leisure he wrote (*inter alia*) *The Prince*. It became the most widely read book of the Renaissance. It earned many interpretations, ranging from a textbook to a satire, yet by the time of the Reformation, Catholics and Protestants saw it as a rejection of Christian ethics in favor of pragmatic approach to politics. Machiavelli dared to venture, openly, where others feared to tread. He wrote:

"....Alexander VI[14] never did nor ever thought of anything but to deceive, and always found a reason for doing so. No one ever had greater skill in asseverating, or who affirmed his pledges with greater oaths and observed them less than Pope Alexander; and yet he was always successful in his deceits, because he knew the weakness of men in that particular."

What must have enervated Rome was not that Machiavelli wrote what he did, but that he had intended the above words as praise, not as condemnation. Machiavelli justifies such a view further in *The Prince*: "*...for the common people are always taken by appearances and by results, and it is the vulgar mass that constitutes the world.*"[15] One wonders how great an influence Machiavelli's vision continues to bear on the politicians of today. I, for one, do not believe that the judgment Machiavelli passed on

Alexander VI should be understood in a negative light. It is my contention that the pope's vision was the result of his total disassociation from society at large. We see an echo of this condition in John Paul II, who, on his visit to Mexico in January 1999, "announced a new strategy for the church in the Americas: Catholics must struggle against the excesses of capitalism (sic) and the church must try harder to reach the rich and powerful, not just the poor." This 'announcement' suggests that the pope is 'sheltered' by his lieutenants (College of Cardinals?), from the reality of "his people". While he talked about mustering the rich, presumably designed to defray the expenses of his visit to Mexico, his deputies assembled "an all star roster of corporate sponsors... Among the more than two dozen "official sponsors" (were): Pepsi, Federal Express, Sheraton Hotels, Kodak, Hewlett-Packard and Mercedes-Benz." The very, very, very rich international conglomerates. One can only hope the poor have been suitably impressed by this struggle against excesses. The cost of the papal four-day visit is estimated at $2,000,000. A week's stay in a Mexican three-star, seaside resort hotel with all meals and return airfare included is advertised in a range of $879 to a max. of $1,119 in Cancun.[16] The above again illustrates that the visions of individuals are more likely to last if supported by a powerful oligarchy.

Returning to the 15th century, it could well be that Machiavelli's renown had been augmented by the invention of the printing press. Though some assign this honor to Laurens Koster and/or Pamfilo Castaldi, most historians credit Johann Gutenberg (c.1397—1468) with the invention of the movable type (c.1436), enabling thousands to gain access to the written word (ever assuming that thousands could read!) Machiavelli's later Renaissance bestsellers notwithstanding, the 1456 Mazarin Bible, also known as the Gutenberg or the 42-line Bible, typed in gothic type is probably the first book printed by Gutenberg from the movable types in his shop at Mainz. In a recent survey,

Gutenberg's vision had been voted as the most influential of our millennium.

Other visions fuelling the Renaissance had not been confined to paper.
Presage of the Rebirth can be seen as far back as the 11th century when Vikings touched the North American coast. Later, a great deal had been learned about Eastern sociopolitical systems in the course of the bloody crusades discussed above, while the Portuguese Prince Henry the Navigator's vision provided access to the West coast of Africa. But it was the vision of a Genoan, Christopher Columbus, which finally opened the New World to the European influences. We are still in the midst of expanding the Genoan's vision. Men of his character would be ranked among our astronauts. He and men like him refuse to be limited to or by parochial environs.

Yet in spite of great steps forward, the 16th century remains firmly anchored in the Middle Ages. The Papal vision, while showing cracks, continued to dominate the Western World. The Church's vociferous hunger for wealth and power led to a growing criticism which finally culminated in the Reformation. It was Martin Luther's vision which led to a large number of people choosing to think for themselves. In this sense, Luther's vision can be regarded as the forerunner of the so-called New Age of today. Simultaneously, Copernicus' *De Revolutionibus Orbium Coelestium* published in 1543, revolutionized the way we regarded ourselves in the world. Copernican vision is further discussed in the proceeding chapter on *Religion and Science Fiction*.
Nevertheless it was Luther's vision which laid ground for the beginnings of the Modern Period. This new area remained preoccupied with the questions of ethics. The fragmentation of the "one" Church, however, into Roman Catholic, Lutheran, Calvinist and Anglican influences changed the

theological playground. It allowed criticism in matters of religion. This new empowerment, *inter alia*, became known as Enlightenment. It brought new challenges to the stagnant theological conservatism. One could say that the philosophs, as the Enlightenment thinkers liked to call themselves, remained 'fashionable' from late 16th into early 19th century. Francois Marie Arouet, who became known as Voltaire, became quite influential with his relatively libertarian visions. His satiric treatment of the Christian practice of persecution of opposing religious views was typical of the opinions he held.[17] Immanuel Kant's vision, on the other hand, was so immersed in metaphysics and morals that it never influenced the growing pragmatism of his day.

The residual power of the Roman Church can still be seen in the exertions of the Holy Roman Inquisition. Galileo Galilei was forced, on two occasions, to recant his advanced views, and in 1633 the Church authorities imprisoned him. Galileo was seventy-four at the time. Officially, the Inquisition began c.1233, it became established in Spain in 1478, and in 1542 Pope Paul III assigned it to the Holy Office (sic!). While originally the Inquisition resorted to judicial torture, imprisonment and, in cases of some heretics, being burned alive, the vision of the Inquisitors in somewhat milder form persists to this day in matters of faith, morals, heresy, and censorship. In modern times, rather than burning a heretic alive themselves, the Holy Office condemns the delinquent "sinner" to eternal fires of hell. It could be argued that vision of the fathers of the Inquisition survived centuries to act as a model for Stalin's secret police and Hitler's Gestapo.

The nature of Divinity is such that infamy is always balanced with its opposite. Ugliness calls for beauty and in the late 16th century beauty has been provided by the vision of one of the greatest men of the millennium. His name is William Shakespeare. His creativity has affected, continues to affect, and will continue to affect man's hearts and minds for generations to come. Even as a century-and-a-half later

Mozart gave us his vision of heaven, Shakespeare filled all spaces between heaven and earth with undaunted passion. He showed us how very human we are. Yet... the ignorance of the masses as regards Shakespeare's creativity leaves me in awe. I have personal knowledge of people among the so-called "intelligentsia" who have never read any of his plays. Astounding!

The ensuing period is called by historians "the century of genius". Kepler, Galileo, Descartes, Harvey, Huygens, Leibniz, Boyle, Newton, Sir Francis Bacon, Locke and a number of others, add up to as formidable a roster as any in the history of man. Yet their achievements blended almost surreptitiously into our life not because of their lack of vision, only because their genius advanced what was already there to a higher level. If genius consists of five percent talent and ninety-five percent sweat, then it is man's capacity for genius itself which left its indelible mark of this century on the future of humanity.

While the great men went about their business, a witches' brew was stirring in the political cauldrons. The English *Bill of Rights* of 1689 called by the "Convention Parliament" in Westminster, prevented the return to royal absolutism. Its vision would foment until, in time, it would ignite all Europe—indeed—the Western World.

Revolutions are not caused by men.

They are periods of propitious mutations, often cataclysmic, invariably cathartic changes in the social, political and religious affairs. They are the reaction of the masses against the few, a bursting forth of pent up energies held too long under external control. The English political upheavals of the seventeenth century led, if indirectly, to the North American revolt of the British colonies in 1775, the Virginia Bill of Rights of 1776 and finally the Declaration of Independence, principally a vision of Thomas Jefferson. It was Jefferson's ability "to relate abstract doctrines of freedom and sovereignty to the situation of the rebellious colonies which produced the final document."[18] His vision continues to inspire people to this day.

On September 17, 1787 the Constitution of the United States, consisting of a Preamble and seven Articles had been ratified by the convention of the United States. William Rehnquist, the Chief Justice presiding over the impeachment trial of William Jefferson Clinton (January 1999) credits James Madison with the vision that led to the creation of the Constitution. One can but wonder what would James Madison say about the antics of the prehensile rubes of the Republican Party masquerading as 'managers' at Clinton's trial.

In Europe, the 1780's witnessed revolutionary shock waves in the Austrian Netherlands, Sweden, Denmark, Poland, Hungary and to a lesser degree in England and Spain. This brings us to the cataclysmic upheaval of 1789, which announced the French Revolution. On July 14th of the same year Bastille falls. Encouraged by England and the United States, by 1791 the Third Estate now calling itself the Constituent Assembly issues its own *Declaration of the Rights of Men*. But the watchword "Liberty, Equality, Fraternity" carried a hollow sound. "In the revolutionary view of history, the republicans of Greece and Rome had invented liberty, and the mission of France was to bring that good news to all men," writes Professor Hunt.[19] But even as one cannot end war with war, one cannot abolish absolute power by reproducing absolute power. A vision cannot be enforced under the watchful blade of the guillotine. It must be embraced willingly.

Nevertheless, Europe would never be the same again.

The social vision shifted from individuals to a broader base. The recognition of non-aristocrats as human beings, led to a rapid creation of a middle class. In Europe, by the 19th century, Liberalism became the ascendant creed of the dominant middle class. Political Liberalism regarded the English constitution as a model to be followed by other countries. Karl Marks, however, was highly critical of the Liberal theory as regards economics and politics. In collaboration with Friedrich Engels, his vision of "Scientific Socialism" led, in 1847, to the publication of the famous *Communist Manifesto*. His vision, regardless of its merit, had been exploited by parochial politicians until the breakdown of the USSR in December 1991. Over the years, the centralist autocratic approach practiced by its adherents, created oligarchies (parties) which denied individuality of man, resulted in the loss of millions of lives and the destruction of a number of national economies. Notwithstanding Marks dissatisfaction, the Western states increased their intervention in the social relations of their citizen. From 1831 through early 20th century, abundant legislation was brought forward. It included the protection of workers in factories, education, health, compensation (for industrial accidents), social insurance and pension plans, and other reforms. The result of these multiple visions were vastly superior to that of Marks' successors, who imposed rather than proposed solutions.

The year 1859 saw the publication of *The Origin of Species by Means of Natural Selection* by the English biologist Charles Darwin. We have never viewed ourselves in the mirror the same way since. We became intelligent monkeys.

The next great vision affecting the course of humanity was declared across the ocean, on September 22, 1862. The seer was Abraham Lincoln. His vision was expressed in the Emancipation Proclamation. It abolished slavery. It also led directly to the Civil War. It became apparent that freedom cannot be given. It must be earned.

Back in Europe, science, philosophy and religion again crossed swords.

Even as Max Planck's scientific humility led him to explore the relationship between science and philosophy, the proclamation of Papal infallibility at the Vatican Council of

1870 could only have had adverse effect on the self esteem of the vast majority of intelligent people. The proclamation could well be regarded as the epitome of simplistic intellectual pride.

The late 19th and early 20th century celebrated the British Empire as its height. Contrary to most great accomplishments, the British Empire was not the realization of a single person but rather the product of visions of many men in many walks of life. Nevertheless, like all empires, no matter how evil, no matter how great, it came to an end. It's demise had been precipitated, in part, by the Second World War, and in part by the natural evolution of man's self assertion, by men who were no longer willing to be exploited by the autocratic British. R. Buckminster Fuller, the friendly American inventor with a world vision of his own, offers this opinion: "the world came to identify history's most successful world-outlaw organization as the 'British Empire'.[20]

The next drastic tsunami resulted from an Italian political visionary Benito Mussolini. His practice of Fascism fell as short of theory as did Karl Marks's Communism. As with Stalin in Russia, Mussolini's regime was marred with corruption and brutality. He dragged the reluctant Italy into the Second World War as Adolf Hitler's ally, whose parochial vision of a Third Reich came to a dismal end in 1945. The consummate magnitude of atrocities perpetrated in just a few short years, as a direct result of one man's vision is astounding.[21] After all, Hitler came to power only in 1933. In just twelve years he was responsible for more deaths than any man during a comparative period of history.

Yet the war resulted in yet another great vision. It was implemented in the Charter of the United Nations. It was inspired by the heretofore unheard-of cooperation of many nations and the Charter was signed at the San Francisco Conference, on June 26, 1945. It replaced the League of Nations and bore all the markings of world vision. It still continues to develop.

The Twentieth Century ends with two very contrasting visionaries. The first was a man whose vision overcame the greatest empire in modern history. Mohandas Karamchand Gandhi (1869-1948) had proven that water is more powerful than fire. Known as Mahatma (great soul), he offered his people the *Satyagraha* (in Sanskrit—Truth Force) or in English: Non-violent Resistance. It had been also referred to as Passive Resistance, though it was seldom passive, though invariably non-violent. This *Satyagraha* led directly to the proud British packing their bags and going home. Regrettably, his assertion of man's unity under one God fell on deaf ears. The Hindu and the Moslem continued to kill each other, and they persist in doing so to this day.

The second visionary was Mao Tse-Tung. While parochial in his outlook, his parish numbered some one billion people. The very opposite of Gandhi, rather then empowering his people, he subjected them to an autocratic oligarchy and, over the years, became China's absolute dictator. The consequences of his (though based on Marxist theories) vision, are unresolved to this day.

Visions are ideas. Ideas mature into thoughts. Thoughts became reality.

The USA was visualized by the Fathers of the Constitution, even as Canada was by the Fathers of the Confederation. Democracy derives from the vision of ancient Greeks seeking a fair and equitable way to introduce social order into their society. In his "I have a dream..." speech delivered on August 28, 1963, Martin Luther King Jr. enunciated a vision which became a flashpoint in the history of civil rights. This one man's vision continues to inspire world's most powerful nation to aspire to and create a more fair and a gentler society. Likewise, just one man's political vision plunged Europe, later most of the world, into the Second World War. Another individual's vision liberated the subcontinent of India. It is probably true to say that without vision we would be still throwing spears at each other, fighting over the best hunting grounds. It is also true to say that we would not have dropped the atomic bomb on Hiroshima and Nagasaki.

We must always remember that the purpose of studying history is *not* to learn *about* our past. It is to learn *from* our past.

It is fair to assume that none of us are even, as yet, "almost perfect". And until we all become Mary Poppins of our realities, the most to which we can aspire is not to repeat the same mistakes over and over. After all there are so many new ones we can make. Literally, an endless procession of them. We can reach out for new visions, aspire to new ever receding horizons. Ideas form visions. Visions create reality. Reality is the essence of all subjective universes. Ultimately, the greatest visions become shared, objective. The parochial ones die. Dissipate in the ethers. It has been said that nothing is as powerful as an idea whose time has come.

The time *has* come.

Without one man's vision, we would never have thought of loving our enemy. Perhaps this too is an idea whose time has finally arrived.

***

FOOTNOTES

(1). THE TRADITIONS OF THE WESTERN WORLD, General Editor J.H. Hexter (Rand McNally & Co. Chicago 1967)   Hereinafter referred to as THE TRADITIONS...

(2). Further reading in Bertrand Russell's WISDOM OF THE WEST.

(3). Matthew 10:5, and 15:24 though later ibid 28:19. In my DICTIONARY OF BIBLICAL SYMBOLISM I argue that "nations" symbolize thoughts, the vastness of our conceptualizations, and thus Jesus admonished that we must convert *all* our thinking to the universal precepts. If we accept this thesis, then we can still adopt, within our own understanding, Jesus' vision, even if it had been "reserved" for the people of Israel. In the esoteric sense "Israel" symbolizes all men who actively search for the divine within themselves.

(4). Luke 17:21; also The Gospel according to Thomas, logion 3: *...the Kingdom is within you and it is without you.* (THE NAG HAMMADI LIBRARY, James M. Robinson Gen.Editor. Harper Collins 1990)

(5). I would suggest that the subsequent Israelite "empire" has attained power through infiltration rather than peroration, as have most political structures.

(6). THE KORAN INTERPRETED, *The Table*, verse 50 et seq., pg.135.

(7). ibid. *The Table*, verse 35 et seq., pg.133.

(8). THE TRADITIONS... pg.194

(9). THE CORRESPONDENCE OF POPE GREGORY VII translated by E Emerton; Columbia University Press, 1932

(10). MEDIEVAL POLITICAL IDEAS, *Defensor Pacis*. Ewart Lewis, Alfred A. Knopf Inc., 1954

(11). ibid.

(12). THE COLUMBIA VIKING DESK ENCYCLOPEDIA William Bridgwater, Editor-in-chief, Viking Press, New York 1968

(13). Latin: *Renascentia*, new birth.

(14). Peter Riesenberg writes in THE TRADITIONS...: The renaissance pope... famous for his patronage of the arts and sciences and also for the worldly life of his court and his skill in handling the Papacy's political and diplomatic problems.

(15). THE HISTORICAL, POLITICAL, AND DIPLOMATIC WRITINGS OF NICCOLO MACHIAVELLI, translated by C.E. Detmold; Boston 1882

(16). data regarding the Mexican trip gleamed from the Montreal GAZETTE, January 23-25, 1999.

(17). vide *Toleration*, PHILOSOPHICAL DICTIONARY by Voltaire, J.P. Mendum, Boston 1836.

(18). writes Franklin L. Ford in THE TRADITIONS.

(19). Hunt, Lynn POLITICS, CULTURE, AND CLASS IN THE FRENCH REVOLUTION (University of California Press, Berkeley 1984) pg.28.

(20). Fuller, R. Buckminster, CRITICAL PATH, (St. Martins's Press, New York 1981) pg.58

(21). Historians' estimates hover around 20,000,000 deaths. But it is the manner and circumstances in which his opponents died wherein the real evil lies. His concentration camps left a legacy of depravity for generations to come.

Chapter 4
Religions and Science Fiction

Silver and gold have I none:
but such as I have give I thee:
In the name of Jesus Christ of Nazareth
rise up and walk.

Acts of the Apostles 3:6

Science Fiction is to science what Myths are to religions:
Inspiration.

Science Fiction is based on a hypothetical, though not necessarily correct, premise followed by a logical development. Religion is based on an unknowable (thus not necessarily correct) premise, followed by a logical development. Nobody expects infallible logic from a premise, but if development is illogical, the system is doomed to failure. This is the problem the religions face in today's world. As we know from the preceding chapter, the Roman Catholic Church attempted to rectify the problem at the Vatican Council of 1870 by declaring the pope infallible, but it was too little too late. By then science developed a firm grip on the domain of logic. And what is more, the scientific society while also littering its history with countless mistakes learned relatively early not to affirm them to its adherents. Or at least not to impose them. Or at the *very* least, not to aspire to infallibility.

Over and above the religious visions discussed in the previous chapter, history is replete with struggles between the religious interpretations of various revelations, *vis-à-vis* new revelations based on new visions backed up by keen observation and the use of man's intellect. While in recent years religious revelations seem to have waned considerably, visions in the realm of Science Fiction continue to inspire its adherents. There are a number of cases wherein *bona fide* scientists, unable to contain their vivid imagination within the prescribed parameters of science, took to fiction. Theirs the true inspiration of the future. Of any ilk, of any discipline.

Yet until fairly recently, the literary gender of Science Fiction has not been recognized as literature, let alone a source of non-religious revelation. A closer examination will quickly dispel this impression. Karl S. Guthke, Kuno Franke Professor of German Art and Culture at Harvard University, in his book *The Last Frontier*,[1] gave us a fascinating insight into the visionary process which moves science forward. The book's subtitle: *Imagining Other Words From the Copernican Revolution to Modern Science Fiction*, gives an indication of the author's attitude towards Science Fiction. By integrating words Science Fiction into the subtitle, he calls our attention to the fact that when Copernicus' *De Revolutionibus Orbium Coelestium* was published in 1543, it was recognized "as highly" as Science Fiction has been some years ago and continues to be by many today. Throughout the pre-Copernican time knowledge derived from religious Revelations took precedence over any and all scientific observations. Any deviation from traditional 'science' has been recognized as little more than fancies of not very serious people.

The scientific establishment has afforded equal contempt to any and all supporters of wild raving that dared to oppose the Aristotelian geocentric view of the universe. Such a view has been recognized and firmly supported by the Roman Church. It may have been his belief in the plurality of inhabited worlds derived from Copernican theories which cost Giordano Bruno his life. The Holy Inquisition burned such dangerous advocates at the stake. We can only thank divine intervention for saving Copernicus from a similar fate. His famed treatise (*De Revolutionibus...*) had been banned by the church only in 1616, fully 73 years after its publication. One can only imagine that the members of the Inquisition had been too stupid to understand its purport sooner. Even today many regard the belief in extra-terrestrial intelligence as Science Fiction. It is difficult to climb down from the geocentric Olympus and face reality.

Almost a whole century later the Roman church still felt threatened by Copernican 'heresies'. On publishing his dialogues on the two systems of the world in 1632, the Holy Inquisition forced Galileo to abjure his belief that earth moved around the sun.[2] Again religious revelation took precedence. Or at least its conservative if not regressive, certainly fundamentalist, interpretation.

It is my contention that there is an interpretation of the Bible, and virtually all other esoteric scriptures, which in no way negates scientific discoveries.

All revelations, be they religious or secular, originate from the same source. The scientist and the mystic visualize the workings of the world but neither competes with the scriptures. To quote a cleric who defended Galileo against the Catholic Church: "The purpose of Scripture is to teach how one goes to heaven, not how heaven goes." Unfortunately both visionaries see these concepts, rather like Mozart, as complete *gestält* images. To transpose them into linguistically structured communication often shrouds them in symbolic mists. To perceive the truth is a lot easier when it is illustrated with pragmatic observations. Or as the very same Galileo wrote in his essay on *Two New Sciences*: "...sight can teach more and with greater certainty in a single day than can a precept even though repeated a thousand times..."[3] But it might be a grave mistake to classify Galileo as a "celestial voyeur". Milton, the author of *Paradise Lost* (published in 1667) called Galileo the "Tuscan artist with his optic glass."[4] I stress the word *artist*, because it is Galileo's *vision* which

Milton admired. Not his gazing at the stars and planets. While all revelations may well point in the right direction, the scientists, once they demystify the symbolism, make it understandable to the masses.

A case in point is the Hindu belief that the universe derives its being from the breath of Brahma. God's expiration, His/Her breathing out, initiates the centrifugal action which results in countless eons of evolution. The intake of the divine breath will eventually result in the centripetal motion, leading to the collapse of the universe into, presumably, a cosmic egg.[5] A few thousand years after this 'religious' thesis was proposed, our illustrious scientists are still engaged in a frantic search for sufficient mass within the observable universe to prove the Hindu theory. We know, reputedly from observation, that all galaxies and solar systems are moving away from us (and each other), and continue to do so since the initial momentum gained during the explosive birth of the universe, known as the Big Bang. According to the astrophysicists' vision, the universe must contain sufficient mass to halt the outward movement resulting from the Big Bang, and initiate reverse direction prompted by the gravitational pull. Rather as though attached to a long elastic, or a yo-yo in the hands of an expert child. Each year the physicists make progress in this endeavor.

Probably the most famous theoretical physicist living today, Stephen W. Hawking,[6] visualizes a universe littered with innumerable primordial tiny black holes (the mass of a large mountain) which came into being at the early stages of the formation of the universe. I would venture to suggest that during some twenty billion years since the Big Bang, these thousand-ton-pebbles must have accumulated sufficient interstellar debris to supply a goodly portion of the necessary mass. Other physicists observe "black clouds" which hide heretofore unaccounted for galaxies from our telescopes. Still others propose gargantuan black holes at the center of each galaxy.

Theories abound, rather like revelations did some centuries earlier.

Black Holes are known as singularities. Their uniqueness is assured by the suspension of all physical laws within the orbit of their influence. Their realm seems to lie beyond the laws governing the time-space continuum. As such they could safely supply any amount of invisible matter which would allow the scientist to prove the Hindu vision. Whatever happens, it is the vision, the ability to visualize our universe, which brings us closer the truth of being.[7]

It may have escaped public notice that for many years a number of Science Fiction writers have also shared their *religious* visions with us. There have been, for instance, a whole gender of books inspired by visions of both Utopias and Nightmares. In 1907 R.H. Benson's *Lord of the World* depicts the struggles of the Roman Catholic Church to survive in a society which worships at the shrine of new Humanitarianism. In 1941 Robert A. Heilein's Astounding Stories serial, *Sixth Column*, shows how religion becomes a powerful factor in overthrowing America's Asiatic conquerors. In 1943 Fritz Leiber's *Gather, Darkness!* we learn of an underground movement bringing witchcraft into a despotic, pseudo-scientific religion. In 1952 Kurt Vonnegut's *Player Piano* depicts a post-war America as fully automated; the spiritual poverty of such a society leads to the inevitable revolt. In 1953, one of the giants of Science Fiction, Arthur C. Clarke, gave us *Childhood's End*, in which alien Overlords are the prelude to man's evolution into a finer type of being.

Religious themes have inspired stories on the evolution of robots and androids. In 1948, Robert Moore Williams (aka John S. Browning) wrote *Burning Bright*, in which a group of robots are in search of a Creator. In 1954 E.C. Tubbb's *Logic* we find that robots are in need of a form of worship to preserve their sanity; a religion suggesting that a robot becomes a man after death is introduced. In 1959 Robert F. Young's *Robot Son* tells of a machine god which attempts to construct a machine Christ. In 1967 John Brunner's *Judas* we meet humans who are worshipping a seemingly omnipotent robot. In 1971 Robert Silverberg's satirical *Good News from the Vatican* tells of a robot being elected pope.

And then there are Star-gods, Galactic Creators, gods who are good and not so good, stories on how aliens would view God, what happens when *The Nine Billion Names of God* have been uttered (Arthur C. Clark, 1953), questions on what happens to your faith when you find out that *The Star* of Bethlehem (also Clark's in 1955) was a nova which destroyed a great alien civilization.

These are just a few examples gleamed from *The Visual Encyclopedia of Science Fiction*[8] to show that Science Fiction does more than inspire science. It is also a source of religious inspiration, wherein visions belong in the present or the future, rather than in the misty, unknowable, often distorted past.

There is a unique crossroads at which Science Fiction and Religion seem to wink at each other. In 1950, L. Ron Hubbard after a successful career as Science Fiction writer, brought out *Dianetics*. He refused to treat it as Science Fiction, and instead put it, perhaps unwittingly, into the domain of fringe cults. It has been suggested that his motivation may have been to gain a tax-exempt status for his 'research'. When this attempt failed he left the United States and developed Scientology, which he affirmed as... religion, and thus not subject to taxation. I am told that he has gathered a considerable following among the Hollywood dilettantes.

And then there are Religious Visions.

While the source of inspiration is One, religious visions are also a subject in their own right. In spite of considerable progress in ridding humanity of superstition, religious visions remain by far the most powerful notions known to man. It is symptomatic of our evolutionary status, that just three major religions: Hinduism, Judeo-Christianity and Islam gather under their gargantuan wing one-half of the population of the world. Fully three billion people prefer to rely on ancient revelation than on the *dicta* of pragmatic science. It is reasonable to assume that Buddhism, Confucianism, Taoism, Zoroastrianism, Sikhism, Theosophy, Shintoism, Spiritualism, Christian Science, Ba'hai to mention but a few, shall take care of the vast majority of the remaining human race. I am not talking about the original myths associated with great avatars who gave humanity pointers regarding our true potential, only about the organized religions created and maintained for the explicit purpose of political and social control of the masses. I draw a very distinct line between faith and religion.

Faith is always an *individual* vision. Religion is an imposed regiment.

The vast majority of believers wouldn't hesitate to give preferential allegiance to their faith rather than accept the latest "revelations" of their scientific community. On closer examination, however, I found that those same faithful are equally as ignorant about the origins (myths) of their own religions as they are of the latest advances in science.
Ignorance remains bliss for the vast majority of the human race.[9]
And then there are the practical implications. I have personal knowledge of people who live exemplary lives, yet, due to their religious conditioning, regard themselves as worthless sinners. If they cannot visit a confessional to rid themselves of their imaginary transgressions against some vindictive deity they created in their own mind, they became depressed, even suicidal. Such is the power of autosuggestion resulting from years of brainwashing. I recall, as a child, I shared a similar heritage.

The Hindu religious cast system imposes on the whole population a precondition of limitations. The lower casts, defined by the work they perform, cannot rise above their "station" in life to which they have been born. The Untachables, the lowest cast, are relegated to sweep the streets, clean the public lavatories of human excrement by hand, and perform all tasks which the "upper" cast would not deign to do themselves. When the Untouchables refuse to perform their assigned duties, they are physically abused, beaten, forced to prostrate themselves on the ground and beg for forgiveness. If they refuse, they are shot or hacked to death by the upper classes, with apparent impunity.

This serves to illustrate the power of religious revelation over not only scientific but also social progress. Since Mahatma Gandhi initiated the process leading to the elimination of the cast system, the Indian government has outlawed "cast" discrimination. This relatively new law is completely ignored by the "believers" who insist that treating the Untouchables as much less than human is their God-given right. This preposterous depravity is so widespread that the government is helpless in their attempts to eradicate it. And this absurdity is all the more incredible when one learns that the Untouchables comprise over one fifth of the population: over 200,000,000 people. It seems that the oppressed have been conditioned to accept their religiously inspired limitations rather than rebel *en masse*. It is of some interest that the germinal initiative to balance the scales is in the hands of women. Men are more apt to adhere to the chains of the past. Particularly the self-imposed chains.

The Judeo-Christian religions also tend to specialize in self-imposed suffering.

In the present day Israel, the tribal conflicts have risen little above the Hindu cast system. Their recent history shows that the struggles for power among Israel's different tribes, nowadays often called parties, are at least as unforgiving in relating to their Palestinian neighbors. The olive skin working class, the fair-haired wealthier and the ultra-religious in their black suits and fedoras bark at each other for greater influence, for a greater chunk of power. "Each group thinks they only have to worry about themselves. Extremism is growing," said Orthodox Rabbi Yehuda Gilad.[10]

Over thousands of years, the Jews have been conditioned to dwell in their bloody past, the older the better—the bloodier the better, preferably connected with some suffering or at least inconvenience. I find it of some interest to briefly examine some of their feasts and festivals. Like their Christian successors, the Jews managed to misinterpret their *Sabbath* by relating it to the creation of the world (see chapter on *Creativity*). Fundamentalist interpretations *always* results in paradoxes. The Sabbath originates, of course, in the Ten Commandments. The very first one states: "...the seventh day is the Sabbath of the Lord thy God: in it thou shalt not do any work, thou nor thy son, nor thy daughter, thy manservant, nor thy maidservant, nor thy cattle, nor thy stranger that is within thy gates."[11] Some fifteen hundred years later, Jesus pointed out the silliness of taking the Bible *á la lettre*. He asked: "What man shall there be among you, that shall have one sheep, and if it fall into a pit on the Sabbath day, will he not lay hold on it, and lift it out?"[12] And since the Christ realized that men are not ready to understand the inner meaning of Sabbath, he added: "The Sabbath was made for man, and not man for the Sabbath."[13] Nevertheless, according to fundamentalist interpretation, the Five Books of Moses ordain absolute abstention from work.[14] So much for progress.

The *Passover* celebrates the exodus from Egypt. A commemoration of running away. Rabban Gamaliel used to say:

> "Whoever has not said the verses concerning the following three things at Passover has not fulfilled his obligation: "Passover, unleavened bread and bitter herbs." "Passover," because God passed over the houses of our fathers in Egypt. "Unleavened bread," because our fathers were redeemed from Egypt. "Bitter herbs," because the Egyptians embittered the lives of our fathers in Egypt."[15]

It all sounds rather bitter to me.

Shabuoth commemorates the day of the encounter at Sinai, resulting in the Ten Commandments. As we all know, the Ten Commandments place a heavy accent on the shall *not* aspects of our behavior pattern. We shall see in the later chapter dealing with *Negative Programming*, that this is a psychological no-no. The best example can be observed from the universal non-conformity to the commandment "thou shalt not kill". In spite of a further admonition (in Leviticus 19:18) to "love thy neighbor as thyself", the ancient Hebrew specialized in killing everyone in sight, and continue to do so with the Palestinians and Lebanese. [The Christians later developed mass killing to a fine art as can be seen in Hiroshima and Nagasaki]. It is interesting to note that 3,500 years after the encounter on Mount Sinai, not just killing but also adultery, stealing, lying (bearing false witness), and greed, are all alive and well.

Sukkoth is the last of the "pilgrim" festivals. It is a way of remembering the forty years the Jews have wondered in the desert after leaving Egypt. Speaking as a goy, it is a period I would make every effort to forget, while the Jews appear to prefer to continue walking in religious circles. On the other hand, Johathan Eibschutz (1690-1764) a master of all fields of Jewish learning (including the cabala) so advises his people:

"On Sukkoth, the end of the Days of Repentance, the Torah advises us to accept the exile and to consider all the world as void, as a shadow. ...we are strangers on the earth, without permanence, and (that) our days are like a shadow lasting a night, blown away by a wind."[16]

This is a fascinating interpretation of Sukkoth, reminiscent of the Hindu concepts of maya, illusion. Jesus echoes this sentiment with the seemingly plaintive: "The foxes have holes, and the birds of the air have nests; but the

Son of man hath not where to lay his head".[17] I would suggest that this is not a doleful cry of despair, but a statement of the nature of reality in which Jesus chose to live. After all, his kingdom was not of this world. It seems that once we leave behind the fundamentalist interpretations of the scriptures, all religions could teach us the very same truth.

Alas, only if we are ready to face it.

In direct opposition to Johathan Eibschutz's interpretation of Sukkoth, the evolutionary trends of Western civilization laid grounds for the creation of a Jewish state. Albert Einstein had this to say on the subject:

"I would much rather see reasonable agreement with Arabs on the basis of living together in peace than the creation of a Jewish state... my awareness of the essential nature of Judaism resists the idea of a Jewish state with borders, an army and a measure of temporal power, no matter now modest. I'm afraid of the inner damage Judaism will suffer—especially from the development of a narrow nationalism within our own ranks".[18]

Rosh Hashanah begins the annual cycle of the Jewish religious year. The ten days that follow this festival are known as "Ten Days of Repentance," within the context of God's judgment. Nevertheless, the punitive stick is softened by assurances that God will forgive a contrite heart. This hopefully brings some light to what would be an otherwise gloomy period.

Yom Kippur is the Day of Atonement. On this "festive" occasion Jews are allowed to neither eat nor drink anything at all! They are obliged to spend all their waking hours in prayer. "On Yom Kippur, eating, drinking, washing, anointing with oil, wearing of sandals and sexual intercourse are forbidden."[19]

So much for fun and games.

I defy any man, woman of child to spend all their waking

hours in prayer. If this definition includes the conscious realization of God, then I would aspire to ten, perhaps twenty minutes. After that my mind starts wondering. Perhaps the Jews know a great deal more than they are willing to share. But to me, the strangest enigma of the Judaic festivals is that in 3500 years they found nothing more to celebrate. Their glory seems tied in the their distant past, their sentiments and religious significance seems as outdated as their liturgy. The only more recent remembrance they have added to their history is the memory of the Holocaust. Not the sort of thing I would choose to celebrate.

Furthermore, according to the book on Judaism referred to above, suffering seems an integral and indispensable component of Jewish destiny. Their God metes punishments for whatever transgression the believers commit, rather like those administered by the Islamic Allah. The religious Jews are expected to accept their punishment with stoic resolution and continue to praise their God. Nevertheless, once we go past the ultra-orthodox fundamentalist factions and their interpretations of the Torah, Judaism offers a broad spectrum of edifying truth, best summed up in the Latin expression *imitatio Dei*, the imitation of God. It is a dictum which compels man to live in constant awareness of the Presence of God.

Christianity is, of course, a continuation of the Jewish tradition.

Regrettably, Jesus' assertion: "Think not that I am come to destroy the law, or the prophets: I am not come to destroy, but to fulfill"[20] seems to remain obscure to all the Christians I've ever met. The origins of Christianity can be traced to the vision of one man originally known as Saul of Tarsus who became known as Saint Paul. Paul was brought up a Pharisee, educated in Jerusalem at the feet of Gamaliel, a celebrated Rabbi.[21] As a Roman deputy, he was overtly against the incipient Christian teaching. Paul was converted in A.D. 38, some years after Jesus' death. His teachings inspired by his interpretation of the vision of a Master, whom he had never met, led to the creation of an organized religion.

Christianity is founded, therefore, on myths surrounding the life of Jesus, who is recognized by the majority of Christians as God. To complicate matters, Jesus is only one of the three divine manifestations, the others being God-the-Father and God-the-Holy-Spirit. The interrelation of the three has been subject to many interpretations and controversies throughout history of the Christian religion. Finally, to maintain cohesion among the faithful, the church introduced the concept of Dogmas, which imposes on all its members articles of faith regardless of personal convictions. Anyone disagreeing with the dogmas was expelled, anathematized or later, burned at the stake.

The other means of maintaining uniformity was derived from the concept of sin.

Once the faithful became convinced that they were all inherent sinners, the religious powerhouses found it easy to instill an insidious suggestion in the minds of their faithful, to accept "their lot", to bend their back and to "bear their crosses". As discussed in some detail in a later chapter on *The Problem with Karma*, once St. Augustine invented "original sin" in the 4th century, the rest was relatively easy. The church became the sole intermediary which could guarantee salvation by baptism. Not even the cheapest Science Fiction paperback would ever accept such an inane premise. Not only the readers would reject a postulate without any proof, but they would equally dismiss the premise of having any and all rewards for decent living deferred till after death, while the enforcers wallowed in luxury. Such paradoxes can only be maintained in a religious field, where logic is replaced by fear. Also, such abuses of human propriety are never based on any, even vaguely verifiable, myths.

They are inventions of power, not of love.

Once the visions embodied in Reformation (1500-1563) discussed in *Politics and Society* failed to straighten the rudder, the course for disaster had been set. It is of little wonder that the ensuing social environment eventually spawned communism, socialism and national-socialism of the Nazis, to overcome the fallacious propaganda. Had the mass psychosis not been permitted to weaken man's resolve, none of the secular/materialistic systems could possibly have taken root. All three systems drew their power not from the implied contradictions of the original revelation, only from the abhorrent distortion of those revelations by the ensuing Christian religions.

Nevertheless, in direct opposition to the very essence of the original teaching as embodied in the Bible, the Church continued to inspire and even encourage its members to suffer, promising retribution after death. Rules and regulations placed the faithful under continuous scrutiny. This pathological masochism continues to be promulgated by the sacerdotal conclaves which had been and continue to be blind and deaf to the biblical assurances of great joy being bestowed on all believers. A vision of great delight and felicity depicted in the Bible has been reduced to a whimpering, sinful, suffering existence under a self-imposed cross. The Good News had been totally lost. In Science Fiction the premise or hypothesis is a means to an end. It is that which inspires towards greater knowledge. The same was true of early Christianity. Under persecution, symbols of the original concepts served to ignite the heart and soul of the believer. A fish stood for wisdom. A cross for the meeting of the visible and the invisible reality. The earth symbolized materiality. Egypt—limitation. And so forth.[22]

These were symbols designed to help in the creation of one's reality.

Then the symbol replaced that for which it stood. The 'body' of Christ, meaning his teaching, became a symbolic consumption of a wafer. No one cared about the teaching anymore. The 'blood' of Christ that once symbolized his secret knowledge, became a sip of wine. To my knowledge no one teaches the faithful what any of the symbols stand for. No one teaches them the essence, the substance, the meaning behind the word. In time, symbol replaced the substance.

Roman Christianity slowly metamorphosed itself into a 'symbol' for sacrifice, suffering and penance. Then—even symbols lost their meaning.

The religion became an empty shell.

Finally we come to Islam.

Since the religion is based on the Koran (or Qu'ran, or Qor'an), with claims of having been dictated by angel Gabriel to Mohammed, who in turn dictated it to his scribes, the word of Allah is beyond dispute. Unfortunately the *interpretation* of the word is left to the mystic and the inept in equal measure. In addition, Mohammed recognized the Judo-Christian scriptures to which he referred in the Koran as the 'Book'. However, as the Koran had been dictated in Arabic, there is a scholarly consensus that any translation is *per force* only an interpretation. It is said to lose a great deal in any 'translation', and thus its knowledge is inaccessible to the Western scholar.

Islam means submission, surrender, and utter obedience.

The consequences of rebellion against the teachings of Allah as embodied in the Koran and dictated by angel Gabriel are painful, terrible, fiery, vengeful chastisements by an All-forgiving, All-clement, All-compassionate God. Never was the paradigm of the carrot and the stick so pronounced as in Islam.[23] But even the form of the Koran came under heavy criticism. R.A. Nicholson, in his *Literary History of the Arabs*, writes:

"The preposterous arrangement of the Koran is mainly responsible for the opinion almost unanimously held by European readers that it is obscure, tiresome, uninteresting; A farrago of long-winded narratives and prosaic exhortations, quite unworthy to be named in the same breath with the Prophetical Books of the Old Testament".[24]

It is evident that that Nicholson is not versed in Arabic.

As such the poetic quality attributed to the Koran by Arabic scholars may have eluded him. The translation by A.J. Arberry from which I offered some quotations in the chapter on *Myths and Reality* is said to be the nearest to the intent of the original. Alfred Guillaume quoted below states: "There are many translations of the Quran... A.J. Arberry, *The Koran Interpreted*, is the best." Nevertheless in his own book *Islam* (Penguin Books) Professor Guillaume adds his reservations:

"The Koran is one of the world's classics which cannot be translated without grave loss. It has a rhythm of peculiar beauty and a cadence that charms the ear. ...read aloud or recited it has an almost hypnotic effect..."

John Alden Williams, the editor of *Islam*,[25] supports this motion. He states that the "Muslim have always deprecated and at times prohibited any attempt to render it (the Koran) in another language." Professor Gibb describing the language of the Koran writes: "No man in fifteen hundred years has ever played on that deep-toned instrument with such power, such boldness, and such range of emotional effect."[26] I must conclude that I am not competent of comment on the music of the Koran.

It is of some consequence, however, that Mohammed counted Jesus of Nazareth among the Messengers of God. In fact, the Prophet of Islam wrote: "Say: People of the Book, you do not stand on anything, until you perform the Torah and the Gospel, and what was sent down to you from your Lord."[27] Nevertheless, it is my opinion that Mohammed found much greater inspiration in the Mosaic "eye for an eye", than the ensuing philosophy of love some fifteen hundred years later.

Yet, as it seems usual with the great religions of the world, there is the ever-present diversity of interpretation. While the fundamentalists derive authority from the Koran to administer most barbaric punishments and mutilations on their own believers, Jalal ud-Din Rumi calls upon the Koran and the Prophet Mohammed many-a-time. And the Persian poet Rumi is said to be the greatest advocate, indeed champion, of love since Christ. A mystery? Rumi claims that there are seven levels of understanding the Koran. I am tempted to believe this. It took me over twenty years to begin understanding the inner symbolism of the Torah and the Gospels. Twenty years of daily study to understand that which to Moses' and Jesus' contemporaries must have been self-evident.

Tempus fugit.

It is probably fair to say that unless one is fully aware of the environment in which Mohammed received his vision, one is not in a position to judge their content. The aftereffects of it, however, are as unfortunate as those of Christianity.

***

The one byproduct of religions for which we can all be grateful is their immense contribution to the cultural heritage of the human race. From Lao Tzu through the aboriginal shamans, to the great avatars, to the latest prophets endeavoring to share their vision with the world—they all have contributed to the diversity that is truly human. Without them our poetry, literature, music, architecture, painting, sculpture, theatre, and other aspect which enhance and enrich the texture of our lives would not exist. The only problem is that there are always people who, lacking their own vision, aspire to exploit the visions of others for their own ends.

More often than not most religions fall pray to such moral paupers.

***

As I already mentioned, there are many other religions which influence man's vision of reality. In addition to those discussed, religions can also be categorized into the metaphysical or materialistic, depending on whether we believe in a tangible or an intangible deity. The teachings of Engels and Marks had prompted many to offer their lives for their 'cause'. No more can be expected by or from any religion. By this definition, communism had many saints or at least martyrs. As did even the bane of Nazism.

What of reality?

Reality, like beauty, is in the heart of the beholder. No religion is wrong for the simple reason that all systems of belief are products of the vision of man. They are as real to their believers as the ancient miracles to the Christians. And the Flying Saucers are as real to Science Fiction enthusiasts as the cosmological phenomena in Fatima to the Roman Catholics. What is wrong is the application of an individual vision to a larger group of people. All visions are intensely personal. The realities they create are thus intensely subjective. What we must all learn is to draw from other people's visions that which applies to, implements, and enriches our own. We are all unique individuals. We must all develop our unique visions.

By the beginning of the next millennium, six billion souls shall be incarnated into six billion physical entities. I would that there be six billion religions.

Each praising the very same One God.

Each in its own, individual way.

***

FOOTNOTES

(1). Originally published as DER MYTHOS DER NEUZEIT, 1983. English translation by Helen Atkins, Cornell University Press, Ithaca and London 1990

(2). Galileo Galilei DIALOGO DEI DUE MASSIMI SISTEMI DEL MUNDO.

(3). Galileo Galilei DIALOGUES CONCERNING TWO NEW SCIENCES, translated by Henry Crew and Alfonso de Salvio (Evanston: Northwestern University Press 1950)

(4). Clark, Kenneth CIVILISATION (BBC and John Murray, 1971). Pg. 218.

(5). NB.: The Hindu universe was never restricted to the puny, geocentric vision of Aristotle and the Roman Catholic Church. Their cosmic cycles are measured in "units" of 4,320,000,000 years.

(6). Hawking, Stephen W., A BRIEF HISTORY OF TIME, (Bantam Books 1988) pg.97.

(7). In BEYOND RELIGION Volume II (Inhousepress 2000; Smashwords 2010) I explore other visions of the universe in two essays entitled: *Cosmos* and *A Little Bang*.

(8). Ash, Brian (editor) THE VISUAL ENCYCLOPEDIA OF SCIENCE FICTION (Harmony Books, New York, 1977]

(9). I would suggest that ignorance springs from indifference. This trait is particularly surprising among Christians in view of the phrase in Revelation 3:15/16: "...*thou art neither cold nor hot. I would thou wert cold or hot. So then because thou art lukewarm, and neither cold nor hot, I will spue thee out of my mouth.*"

(10). Kaplow, Larry THE TRIBES OF ISRAEL, *Cox News Service* (The Gazette, Montreal, May 7, 1999.)

(11). Exodus 20:10

(12). Matthew 12:11

(13). Mark 2:27.

(14). Hertzberg, Arthur (edited by) JUDAISM, (George Braziller, New York 1962)

(15). ibid. pg. 125-6.

(16). ibid. pg. 133.

(17). Matthew 8:20.

(18). Gleamed from an article by Mordecai Richler published in the Montreal Gazette on 15 Feb. 1998

(19). Mishnah YOMA 8:1

(20). Matthew 5:17.

(21). Young, Robert, LL.D,. ANALYTICAL CONCORDANCE TO THE BIBLE (WM.B. Eerdmans Publ. Company 1980)

(22). Kapuscinski, S. DICTIONARY OF BIBLICAL SYMBOLISM (Inhousepress 2001; also available as eBook)

(23). Kapuscinski, S. BEYOND RELIGION Vol. 2. *Submission*. (Inhousepress 2000; Smashwords Edition 2010)

(24). Nicholson, R.A., LITERARY HISTORY OF THE ARABS (Cambridge University Press)

(25). Williams, John Alden, Editor, ISLAM (George Braziller, New York 1962)

(26). Gibb, H.A. R., MOHAMMEDANISM (2nd Edition, New York 1953)

(27). THE KORAN INTERPRETED, *The Table*, verse 72, pg.139.

Chapter 5
Groups and Traditions

*Do you know that you are God's temple
and that God's Spirit dwells in you?*

1 Corinthians 3:16

Perhaps the Hindu myths are right. Perhaps we are in the process of an inexorable tumble from the Golden Age, the Satya Yuga, into a dismal degenerate existence under the auspices of the black goddess Kali, the mistress of death, evil and destruction. Perhaps we do already live in a world where power—surely the opposite of love— rules to the exclusion of all nobler instincts which once guided men on their journey. If it is so, then traditions are of little use to us. The only way to save our souls is to break with the past and start all over again. All over again...

It is indeed sad to note that traditions do not seem to enhance an individual, but invariably serve to magnify the power and influence of a group. All organizations, regardless of their initial noble visions, invariably twist the original constitution to benefit the organization, even if the original intention was to protect an individual. The chapter on *Visions* offers ample examples of this thesis. It is a fact of life.

Yet such is the process of evolution that that which is simple becomes more complex. That which is One becomes the many, becomes embellished in cosmic diversity, only to eventually realize and affirm its allegiance to the One.

It is a long journey. As long as time itself.

When atoms combine into molecules, they initiate a process which grows in complexity. In other words, the rise in quality necessitates an increase in constituent numbers. This law came into being at the time of the Big Bang, and it continues to manifest today. It is as though God became greater for the sum of His parts.

At the other end of the spectrum we have a strange biblical saying "Where two or three are gathered together in my name, there am I in the midst of them."[1] Although both initiatives appear to advocate a tendency towards the formation of groups, in fact they are diametrically opposed. We may safely assume that whatever is conducive to the welfare of the material universe, is probably at odds with the subject matter of scriptural teaching. Even as 'evil' is said to be the opposite of good, matter is the opposite of spirit. Yet, as we shall see in the chapter dealing with *The Problem with Karma*, there is no evil. Even as there is no matter without spirit. Nevertheless, within the context of subjective reality, what is good for one may well be derogatory to another.

It doesn't take an Einstein to observe how relative the worlds are...

The biblical quotation given above deals with the conversion of the subjective to the objective reality. A person who has an idea cannot share it, until he or she meets someone to share it with. If the two find agreement, become of like mind, (meet in "my name" or nature) the idea becomes objective. That is why only two or three are needed. Any larger numbers while perhaps desirable, are not necessary. They simply contribute as spectators. They would not participate in the creative process but merely take advantage of an accomplished fact. Thus, from the spiritual point of view, large groups are redundant. The concept of an ecclesiastic "one church" unifying all the worlds nations under one religion is not only a psychological, phenomenal and even a conceptual impossibility but it is a distorted and misunderstood idea driven by very profane, materialistic and mundane ambition. We must indeed aspire to unify all 'people' or 'nations', but these, in the biblical idiom, always symbolize 'thoughts'. Our *own* thoughts within our own psyche. The bible never intended us to impose our dissolute interpretations of "divine" revelations on others. All revelations are divine. There is no other Source.

On the other hand, we need an endless stream of tiny groups of "two or three", for the creative process to continue. There is an infinite number of ideas, from the limitless Source (heaven), which we can bring out into the objective reality for all to enjoy. While we all invariably create subjective universes, there are points of contact, points of overlapping. Those points are the exchanges of ideas, the binding glue of all humanity into the eventual *awareness* of Oneness. Some millions of years from now.

Perhaps a little longer.

Finally, the groups must be inevitably limited to two or three for the simple reason that the chances that more then this tiny number would agree on anything is too remote to contemplate. To the extend that we, humans, are individuals with an infinite potential, we are, *per force*, extremely unlikely to agree on anything, let alone a new idea. History shows that it takes 20-25 years for any discovery to wend its way to general application. Yet the ideas are as disparate as the creation itself. It is safe to assume that the divine Oneness manifests Itself through infinite diversity. Not by imposing uniformity on intelligent beings.

Although they will vehemently deny it, members of groups are not yet fully developed individuals. The lower the life form the more it finds its expression within a group. We can hardly conceive of a single virus or bacterium. The difference between the lowest forms and the still nascent but relatively advanced units of consciousness is directly proportional to the awareness of their environment. A bacterium is aware only of the immediate environs controlling its survival. A mammal is aware of a much larger territory. Yet members of all groups recognize only the group's milieu as friendly environment. The world outside its influence is the enemy. Most of us are not yet ready to rejoice in *differences* of opinion. How sad. Imagine a world in which all people agree on all things. How incredibly dull! Isn't it just possible that God "gave" us individuality for a reason? Conversely, it took nature millions of years to evolve our differences. Yet there are many group leaders—political and religious alike—who wish to melt us in a single cauldron of conformity. Should they succeed, we would be easier to control, but we would also be no longer human.

Robots conform, humans rejoice in diversity.

Groups are the archetypes of the "us and them" syndrome.

From the spiritual point of view, groups of whatever species, organization or persuasion, are always an expression of a lower, less developed state of consciousness. Their dictum is "strength in numbers". They invariably place their own welfare above that of a competing organization. As long as groups exist, strife, conflict, exploitation, and wars will continue to flourish. All these may consolidate the "survival of the fittest", but do naught for our spiritual development. To gain and sustain power the constituents often form oligarchic bands, such as governments, churches, armies, international conglomerates or trade unions.

Among these, the religious organizations have proven to be the most tenacious.

Yet even the Roman church's apparent attachment to the values of the past demonstrated elastic morals. For many centuries, there have been papacies that claimed to support ancient traditions. In at least one respect, this policy came to an abrupt end in early 1500s. Although religious oligarchies invariably tried to destroy all who dared to question *their* established traditions, their leaders have never exhibited any such compulsion within their own domain. In the early 16th century, pope Julius II (1503-1513) decided to destroy, literally raze to the ground, one of the largest and most ancient churches in the Western world, in order to build a bigger and better and more splendid testimony of the church's temporal power. The old basilica of St. Peter was certainly the most venerable church marking the place where St. Peter was supposed to have been martyred.[2] No matter. The new St. Peter's was certainly more pompous, acclaiming greater secular power, more impressive to the sheep.

So much for traditions.

Julius II evidently suffered from the "do as I say, not do as I do" syndrome. Nevertheless, we can be grateful to Pope Julius for bullying three men of genius—Bramante, Michelangelo and Raphael into submission. Without them, (and coincidentally without Julius' magnanimity with other peoples' money), we would not enjoy today the *new* resplendent St. Peter's, nor the ceiling in the Sistine Chapel, nor the frescoes in the papal apartments. Spirit may lead us to heaven, but money, strength and shear brutality of vision overrides any considerations of traditions. Although the new basilica had been completed only a century later, it befell the sovereign pontiff to start a new tradition of what is commonly described as the decadence of the papacy.[3] Not in the development of their international contacts, civil service and increasing wealth, but in all things holy.

Renaissance men had little time for religion.

Likewise, the later oligarchies, such as the Communist Systems, created for the explicit purpose of enhancing the quality of life of the masses, degenerated to serve but the few at the top of the 'party'. There are published reports of the magnates atop the Detroit Automotive industrial groups who sacrifice human lives by willfully concealing life-threatening mechanical defects, if it proved cheaper to pay compensation to the surviving family members rather than recall their product and correct the deficiency. The Tobacco industrial groups offer ample evidence that poisoning human, preferably youthful pulmonary and cardiovascular systems, on the one hand, and perjury on the other, is a lesser evil than risking diminishing quarterly returns. Pharmaceutical Conglomerates poison millions, torture and mutilate experimental animals, cater to the medical profession's ignorance, all in order to line their bottomless pockets. Cosmetic industries rely on stupidity of women and, like their Pharmaceutical colleagues, on lamentable and grievous torture of innocent animals in the name of a false image and skin-deep, Barbie-doll type beauty.

So much for the Titans of our civilization.

As for an example of the degeneration of our political groups, I recall a period spanning part of 1998 and early 1999 during which the United States of America's Republican Party wasted public money on an abortive attempt to dethrone their President William Jefferson Clinton. Both, the House of Representatives and the Senate gave a performance of such stupidity and degradation that average citizens of their great nation publicly expressed their disgust. Gabriel Garcia Marquez, the renown Columbian author (*One Hundred Years of Solitude, Love in the time of Cholera, et al.*) and the winner of the 1982 Nobel Prize for Literature, so cites Clinton's fundamentalist enemies and their ignominious cohorts:

"*...his inquisitors came up with evidence against him, for Puritanism is insatiable and feeds on its own excrement. It has been a vast and sinister conspiracy of fanatics aimed at the personal destruction of a political adversary whose stature they could not abide. The method was the criminal use of justice by a fundamentalist prosecutor called Kenneth Starr, whose fierce and salacious questioning seemed to excite those fanatics to the point of orgasm.*"[4]

It is of some interest to note the shear scope of political depravity. The ineffectual vote on impeachment of their President took place in the Senate 386 days after the preposterous soap opera began. The president's alleged dalliance has been documented by a $50 million investigation, 445-page referral by Starr, nearly 60,000 pages of grand jury testimony, and 36 boxes of videos and tapes. Why? Because Clinton had reputedly lied about having been unfaithful to his wife. How incredible! I can only imagine that most men in both legislative assemblies would have bragged about it.

Perhaps the last word on the subject belongs to another Nobel Laureate, the African-American author Toni Morrison: "They treated him like a black president".

Another example of a group mentality is the case of the Canadian Senate. The senators enact laws which place them above those very laws. Due to their countless abuses, thefts of public money, refusal to work, to resign, to tell the truth, to abide by any code of decent behavior, they have become the laughing stock of the citizens who pay their exorbitant salaries and pensions. And why? Because all senatorial positions are sinecures offered by the elected politicians in order to be reelected, i.e.: for essentially and nauseatingly partisan behavior.

Yet another recent example of group decadence is provided by the members of the Olympic Committee, who like the Canadian senators, had placed themselves above the law. The committee is responsible for the enforcement of the "very highest ethical standards", while taking bribes and lining their own pockets with lucre. An athlete who's urine sample shows a trace of an ingredient found in an over-the-counter flue medicine which is forbidden by the Committee, is instantly disqualified and forced to return a medal won after years of sacrifice and arduous training. A member of the Committee who accepted but did not actively seek bribes, is... "reprimanded", whatever that means.

The examples could fill voluminous tomes.

I know of no groups or organizations in which graft, corruption and abuse of power do not abound. In any organization, in any country of the globe, at any time in history or the present. Not one.[5] It is evident that creative visualization belongs to individuals. The groups, all groups, appear to exercise their talents in a purely destructive capacity. Even groups which were originally created with "good intentions", such as the non-profit, charitable or religious bodies, more often than not sink to an equally despicable level. The media abound with reports of exorbitant salaries, 'imaginative' bonuses, expensive automobiles, padded expense accounts all derived from the donations of widows and widowers contributing their humble tithes.

Due to the inherent weakness of component members of any group (clan, clique, crew, gang, mob, camp, sect, faction, nation, race) autocratic leaders often head such organizations. Parochial interests invariably hold sway over more universal values. As the group is their sole power-base, the bigwigs invariably place the welfare of the organization as a whole before that of its component parts. In fact, the leaders will even sacrifice the lives of their own members for the affluence, prestige or the survival of their organization. This is particularly evident in the manner in which wars and military conflicts are conducted. The leaders who initiate such murderous games seldom become involved in situations in which their own lives are at risk. Yet they conduct their mass murders in the name of a group such as a nation or a clique which they claim is aspiring to become a nation. The recent history of the Balkans is a case in hand.

Others seem to act for either purely selfish reasons, or in the name of dire stupidity. When asked to offer a reason for their behavior during the above mentioned impeachment proceedings, a number of senators replied "Why not? It will be all forgotten by the next elections." A formidable reason indeed. Perhaps they suffer from congenital boredom and filling their time with senile tantrums is their sole source of amusement.

How can an individual protect himself against such lunacy?

For as long as we choose to delegate our responsibilities, we shall have to put up with groups and their inherent foibles. Our governing systems, both aptly yet misleadingly called democratic, are in fact conducted by only those elected officials who respond most judiciously to the popularity polls conducted at their bidding.[6] Others are either expelled, or assassinated. Physically or politically. All's fair... Yet I recall a wise journalist who once said that bad governments are elected by good people who don't vote. The problem is that the term "good government" is an oxymoron. After all, it relies intrinsically on compromise. The 'compromise' so exulted by politicians is little more than a degradation of morals, principles, ethics, honesty, responsibility or even the most basic human decency. Those aspiring to power invariably avow judicious compromise. They never compromise on their personal incomes or pensions. Perhaps one day we shall choose to live in an enlightened anarchy, wherein individuals will care more about one another than about the group they once belonged to.

Quite apart from the above, the human consciousness continues to develop until it reaches a paradox. When it eventually attains relative maturity, it is in a position to impose its will on the less developed members of society with the greatest of ease. Yet, by then, such form of exploitation is abhorrent to it. Becoming an individual is synonymous with gaining enormous respect for the nascent potential of other life forms, including and particularly, human. There follows a complete inversion of attitude. Rather than sacrificing others for the welfare of the group, they are prepared to sacrifice themselves to help even one other individual.

It is the coming of age.

Though we affirm to the contrary, most of us resent others being different from ourselves. Our need for belonging, perhaps our hunger for Oneness, takes the form of a xenophobic fear of non-conformity. We think of 'individuals' as odd, peculiar, perhaps abnormal, yet we hoist them onto the pedestals of the heroes. We raise them there, then we resent them, we learn to fear their individuality, and eventually, usually sooner rather than later, we destroy them. Yet the price of freedom from these fears seems to lie in learning to find joy in diversity, in a profound respect for individuality, and in discovering that which we all have in common. We must remember, once more, the adage about the mutual attraction of the opposites. We must remember that it is the individuals who reach out for the unknown, the new. The traditionalist is almost invariably fundamentalist in his nature and thus attitudes. Fundamentalism never unfolds. It clings to the past, finds strength in numbers, remains stagnant, passive, like dead memories. Its adherents live in the past, they feed on dead things, dead ideas, or as Gabriel Garcia Marquez put it, fundamentalism "feeds on its own excrement."

What holds those misbegotten effigies together are innumerable traditions. Only they hold them together, mindless bodies, reliant on other people's achievements. Groups cannot survive without traditions, and traditions are maintained exclusively by groups.

I've heard it said that every nation is proud of its heritage. To protect our legacy, we go to war. We sacrifice our lives to protect our heritage. We do not fight for the present; we fight for what is already in the past. We fight for that which made us different from each other. We parade our differences as though the very fact that we are different has any bearing on the merit of that which sets us apart. On that which separates us. We—the good, versus them—the bad. We are always right. They—wrong.

Watching various groups bloating their meager cumulative chests, one hears the word *pride* used often. Again, they declare *pride* in their past. *Pride* in the accomplishments of those who went before them. *Pride* in being proud. "My father knew Lloyd George", said a nobody. "I am proud of being a female", asserts a feminist who just burned her bra and hates anyone who didn't. "I'm macho, a *real* man," echoes her moron counterpart, flexing his steroid muscles. I am proud of being a liberal, conservative, democrat, republican, communist, anarchist, any member of any group seeking power. I am proud of whatever it is that sets us apart.

I need to be proud of... anything?
I need... to belong.
Anywhere...

That's *our* tradition, declares everyone needing support. Note, there is no such thing as *my* tradition. Traditionalists also need praise. In the absence of any individual accomplishment, others' achievements make them proud. We also like to refer to our faltering pride as *dignity*. We are to be accorded human dignity, and then we are to die in dignity. Many traditions call for funeral caskets being displayed to the morbidly curious public. What dignity is there in the corpses being bled of the last drop of blood and then filled with formaldehyde to hide the putrid smell of decomposition? But such are our traditions.

Pope John Paul II often speaks of the dignity of the common man. The Dalai Lama echoes the Holy Father's sentiments. Mother Theresa assures that people die with dignity. We hear that dignity is a basic human right. Workers have dignity. People strike with dignity. We are reminded of the dignity of a mother, a woman. A child. Just about everyone has pride and is dignified. Dignity makes us feel important, importance make us feel proud. That's our tradition.

Vanity of vanities, all is vanity, counters the Preacher.

***

It is not easy to renounce one's past. It seems anchored in our genes. It is a part of us. Krishnamurti, whom Henry Miller called *one man of our time who may be said to be a* *master of reality*, once said: "You can renounce a few cows, a house, but to renounce your heredity, your tradition, the burden of your conditioning, that demands an enormous inquiry".[7] The burden of our conditioning. But are we not more than Pavlovian dogs? If we must be proud, shouldn't it be of being endowed with a free will? Or are we all slaves to this insidious brainwashing we call traditions. The same sage, Krishnamurti, mused: "Freedom comes when the mind experiences *without* tradition."[8] Freedom! Surely, a word all but unknown to all steeped in traditions.

Again, the shackles of conditioning.

Conditioning requires a conditioner. One who imposes a condition. One who imposes that which *he* needs to lean on, to prop *himself* up against, lest *he* falls flat on the non-accomplishments of *his* own.

What if we decided to be proud only, *only* of our own accomplishments, our own visions? If we stopped being proud of the great composers or painters, or philosophers who, by an accident of birth, had been spawned from a particular womb, in a particular country. Yet, there are no accidents. Nature disposes her greatest gifts not where most deserved (nature knows no national boundaries) but where most needed. Show me a nation where the creative spirit manifested itself in greatest abundance and I'll show you a nation capable of the greatest depravity. Nature restores, or endeavors to maintain, balance.

Traditions are barriers that set us apart.

No truly great man or woman ever recognized boundaries. Great avatars, saviors, prophets, artists and scientists—they all gave to the world. Always, the *whole* world. Barriers are created by children of a lesser god. And those who create them are worshiped by immature owners of fragile egos.

I do not believe one must renounce one's heredity. But I do believe that being proud or ashamed of one's heritage is of no consequence. If we were to take pride in racial or national accomplishments, we would also be compelled to assume responsibility for racial or national crimes. All nations have skeletons in their cupboards. Mass murders, religious conversions at the point of a sword, persecutions of minorities, national cleansing, expropriations, usurping of land and its riches, theft on international scale. As already mentioned, Buckminster Fuller called the British Empire the world's most successful world-outlaw organization. History's heroes carry the burden of holocausts of every description. We build them monuments, adorn their brow with garlands of lotus leaves. We seem to forget that there are no proud nations. There are only proud people.

By choosing individuality, we choose freedom. And if—as fish—we are a tiny bit smaller, our chauvinistic pools of yesteryear have already expanded to a mighty ocean of unparalleled proportions. Joseph Campbell holds that community today is the planet, not a bounded nation. Buckminster Fuller calls the planet a global village hurling through space on the good spaceship Earth.

We all carry some bias. We are children of tradition. I hope mine will die with me. I hope you will shed some of yours.

***

FOOTNOTES

(1). Matthew 18:20.
(2). Clark, Kenneth CIVILISATION (BBC and John Murray, 1971). Gleamed from pages118-121.
(3). ibid 119
(4). Translated by Alastair Reid, Distributed by *The New York Times*, in *The Gazette*, Montreal, on February 7, 1999.
(5). They may exist, particularly at the initial stages of development but, after extensive research, I did not come across any in which the higher echelons did not usurp a disproportional percentage of the profits. Nevertheless, I hope there are exceptions, if just to prove the rule.
(6). 'Democratic' from the Greek *demos* meaning people, and *kratein* to

rule. For in-depth definition of democracy, I refer the reader to Prof. Noam Chomsky, who in his book NECESSARY ILLUSIONS, dissects with surgical precision the many misconceptions universally associated with this concept of governance. The present USA model e.g., upholds the premise that those who own the country should rule it. A far cry from the "rule of people".

(7). KRISHNAMURTI, a biography by Pupul Jayakar (Harper & Row, San Francisco)

(8). ibid. [my emphasis]

Chapter 6
Medical View

The medical view of the universe is essentially limited to the human body. While it does not totally exclude the characteristics of our environment, the flora and fauna are there, rather as in the case of Judeo-Christian religions, to serve man. "Be fruitful, and multiply, and replenish the earth, and subdue it: and have dominion over the fish of the sea, and over the fowl of the air, and over every living thing that moveth upon the earth."[1] "And eat them till your bodies are distended, and use them for the fun of killing, and amputate their appendages in steel traps, and poison them with the poisons you have developed, and torture them in your laboratories that your own excesses might be cured," one might well add. The two visions seem made for each other.

The ecosystems, let alone star configurations are of no consequence. Nor are the wonders of nature, the finer arts or the needs of the soul. In this respect the medical view has long been a very narrow one. Alas, things are a-changing...

Slowly. Very slowly. Rather like evolution...

In the 'most' modern medicine (literally the last few years) the process of visualization goes under the headings of mind-body interaction, guided imagery and responses, hypnotic and self-hypnotic programming, mental and emotional conditioning, visualization therapy often in combination with meditation, as well as psychotherapy, psychoanalysis, induced daydreaming and—with negative connotations—brain washing. All the above rely on the premise that there is a mind-body connection and that what affects the mind does have an observable effect on the body. The ancient prophets could not have said it better themselves.

In spite of, or perhaps due to, the many recorded cases of success, most of the above methods are used in combination with Standard Medicine, or in combination with alternative medicinal treatments. By Standard Medicine I mean the treatments offered and licensed by the Governments of the various (Western) countries. This particular medical body or organization wields unprecedented power to abuse or ostracize other forms of treatments offered; rather like the Vatican did in matters of religion during the first 1900 years of its existence. What the official body, the Royal College of Surgeons and Physicians in Canada or the American Medical Association forbids—is paramount to law.

There is a fascinating, often reported case illustrating the above thesis.

A Brazilian named Jose Pedro De Freitas, who became known as Arigo, is reported to have treated tens of thousands of people. Arigo became famous in 1956 when a Brazilian senator admitted that Arigo had saved his life by removing a tumor from his colon. Working in a trance, using unsterilized instruments such as rusty scissors, kitchen knives or simply a pocket penknife, Arigo never refused help. He also never used anesthetic, yet patients did not feel any discomfort during the cutting, piercing or probing, nor any adverse consequences from the unhygienic conditions. There were times when Arigo treated up to two hundred patients in a single day. Some had been given instant diagnosis, others were prescribed medicines, but many others underwent surgery, though seldom lasting more than ten minutes. In his twenty years of healing activity there was not a single report of Arigo hurting or harming anyone. Arigo made deep incisions, removed cataracts, removed internal malignant growths, goiters etc.. Whatever he did or advocated, people were helped. Perhaps unwittingly, he conformed assiduously to the Hippocratic oath, seemingly long forgotten by many if not most practitioners of standard medicine. Perhaps this is why the medical establishment expressed their appreciation for Arigo's work by arresting him on two occasions, and having him imprisoned for 'fraudulent' behavior. They should know, they are the experts. After all, Arigo healed people and didn't overcharge them for it. Mostly—he didn't charge them at all. Shame indeed!

Arigo was not alone.

A man called Bruno Gröning received an even worse treatment. Gröning didn't even diagnose his patient's diseases. He neither operated nor prescribed medicine. He merely told people that if they believed hard enough and spent a few minutes once or twice a day "allowing" the spiritual healing energy, or God, to enter their body, they would be healed. He declared that there is no such thing as an incurable disease. A string of inexplicable healings had proven him right. He dared to believe in the healing power of God. He showed tens of thousands of his "friends" how to do it. He delivered on his promise to people on whom standard medicine had given up all hope.

But healing thousands, including the incurable, was not his only crime.

Bruno Gröning committed an additional, final, unspeakable sin. He never, never accepted any compensation for his countless successes. Financial or otherwise. To the medical establishment, particularly to some influential doctors and lawyers, this was the last straw. From 1950 onwards they almost continually accused him of practicing medicine without a license. Invariably they failed. There was simply no evidence that he practiced medicine. He didn't even touch his patients. All he did was to show people how to be healed by the spiritual energy. Had the medical establishment dared, they would have gladly crucified him. To all intent and purpose they did. In 1955 they falsely accused him of causing the death of a girl suffering from advanced stages of tuberculosis. Fueled by complete *lack* of evidence, they dragged the case before the courts for a long time. In the meantime, they procured a ban on his healing. Gröning told his oppressors that if he would not be allowed to help people, he will "burn up inside". In 1959, a mere 10 years after he come to public notice, Gröning died, in Paris, his innards destroyed in an inexplicable fashion. Since his death, circles of people sprung up all over the world, calling themselves "Friends of Bruno Gröning". The healing goes on. Since his death, a Medical-Science Group (MWF) consisting of some 3200 intellectuals, doctors and other professionals have, so far, meticulously verified and recorded over 3000 spiritual interventions attributed to the dead healer.[2]

After Bruno Gröning's death, Dr. Bellanger had said: "The damage in Bruno's body is terrible, it is a total incineration. How he could live so long and without suffering terrible pain is a mystery to me."

So much for the medical establishment.

Yet not all "healers" are treated in like manner.

Mark Kennedy reports in the *Ottawa Citizen*,[3] on a Dr. Allon Reddoch who, just days after being found guilty of unprofessional conduct by the Yukon Medical Council, had been elected president of the 45,000 physicians strong Canadian Medial Association. Mark Kennedy writes:

"The case revolved around Reddoch's treatment in 1995 of *a girl*, who contracted botulism, a rare form of food poisoning. She lapsed into a coma from which she never emerged and died at the age of 17. Reddoch had misdiagnosed her as suffering from acute anxiety, brought on in part by the death of her great-grandmother."

Anyone can make a mistake... providing of course, they are members of a Medical Association. But what amazes me still more is the comment reported in the same article by the girl's father who launched the complaint against Reddoch to the Yukon Medial Council. Speaking about Reddoch he said: "It seems to me that he thinks he's God and nobody can touch him. He seemed to be a changed man from the man I knew before. It was a complete defense from Day 1 when I brought the charges against him. He's never showed one bit of remorse to us."

It is painfully apparent that Dr. Reddoch is no Arigo. Arigo would never aspire to becoming president of any Medical Association. They differ in one other respect. Reddoch will probably also elude jail.[4]

By the way, have you ever heard of a physician who returned money to a patient after failing to cure him? Or put the money in the coffin, to pay for the funeral? And such moral and/or ethical standards are fostered by an illustrious body of standard medicine adherents, who, as I've recently read, fail to teach the medical students to wash their hands between touching successive patients. Perhaps they are all inspired by Arigo. Perhaps they all imagine they possess Arigo's gifts. If so, they'll all end up in jail.

In spite of the traditional rejection of methods of treatment untested by the official medical establishment, the mind-body connection is winning daily converts to its cause. Physicians, who even a few decades ago would rely exclusively on chemotherapeutic treatments, now tend to agree that the attitude of mind has a definite healing effect. Dr. Andrew Weil's book championing a marriage between standard medicine and alternative systems of healing has achieved the #1 bestseller status in the New York Times. Dr. Weil is a strong advocate of the mind-body connection, and ventures even into the mind and spirit affiliation.[5] He is by no means alone in his views.

As far back as 1962, Dr. Joseph Murphy in his enigmatically entitled book: The *Amazing Laws of Cosmic Mind Power*,[6] cites copious cases in which the efficacy of spirit-mind-emotions-body connection is illustrated. He follows with examples wherein the desirable emotional and mental attitude, reinforced with prayer, resulted in not only spontaneous healing but in extended if not permanent remissions. He further illustrates that the 'right' mental attitude can bring spontaneous results in other, non-medical areas. I have personal knowledge of members of my immediate family who can attest that the systems he advocates—work.

The TV programs, particularly the public educational channels (PBS), regularly sponsor physicians who advocate the mind-body connection. The concept of psychosomatic diseases, once espoused by few, is now gaining wide acceptance. The principle underlining this new awareness, apparently *new* only to the medical profession, is that even the diseases attributed to viral if not bacterial invasion, may well be anchored in psychosomatic roots. The theory gaining ground is that a well-balanced 'body', i.e. a body that is not subjected to inordinate or excessive stress, is endowed with sufficient self-healing ability to counteract the viral and/or bacterial effusion. In other words, our immune system can take care of us,[7] even as it takes care of the vast and varied fauna, throughout the earth. What we, humans, must stop doing is abusing ourselves by overeating, excessive ingestion of alcoholic beverages, substituting sucrose for glucose (or eating too many sweets or sugars and sugar additives), leading unnaturally sedentary lives and finally abusing our lungs either by smoking in any form or by exposing ourselves, on a continual or prolonged basis, to high levels of air pollutants. This last includes living in heavily populated areas, working in buildings which offer insufficient air-changes in their air-conditioning systems, or working in any environment which places undue stress, be it mental, emotional or physical, on our immune system.

I shall draw the line at quoting numerous books on the subject before this shall become a book review. Anyone can visit the nearest bookstore and pick up a dozen self-help books, advocating similar advice. One other author, however, deserves to be mentioned. His name is Deepak Chopra. His many books are as forceful in advocating the mind-body connection as any I've read. Dr. Chopra enjoys a considerable following thanks to his successful series of programs on Public Television (PBS). In his book *Ageless Body, Timeless Mind* he not only elaborates on the mind-body connection, but questions the very reality of time itself.[8] He introduces medical implications of relativity in terms of our perceptions of aging. Dr. Chopra differentiates between the chronological, biological and "real" age. The last is the true perception resulting from the way we live and act rather than from the norms established in the past, as to how we should or are expected to act at any particular age. I remember that in my native Poland, society expected people over sixty (if not younger) to behave in "an orderly (meaning sedate) fashion", that is to say not to create an impression that they are (still) young. A sexagenarian would not ride a bicycle let alone enjoy inline-skating, would not run the parkways to keep fit, God forbid run along sidewalks to get to the park. Such behavior would be considered deviant; one would expose oneself to laughter and ridicule. Sexagenarians would generally dress in darker suits or dresses, walk with a measured step, and in general conduct themselves in a dignified, imposing and stately manner. While there are some exceptions, the vast majority of people conform to the 'morals' imposed by the society. No wonder people truly age quicker and die earlier. That is the reality they are expected to visualize. And they do.

They conform and subject themselves to the power of black magic.

What the wiser physicians are rediscovering is the middle path, akin to the path advocated by Buddha 2500 years ago. We can eat what we like, but not too much. Wine, in moderation, is good for us. We should not exaggerate in anything. If we have a heart operation we should not curl up and wait to die, but should initiate, as soon after the operation as practical, an extensive program of physical exercise. We do not have to stay in bed when feeling under the weather—but also we should not dip into the nearest pool. We should avoid putting undue stress on our body, mind, and perhaps even emotions.

Periodically we hear about the return-to-nature syndrome.

We are told that our immune system is a magnificent machine, developed over millions of years, and we should give it a chance to serve us without testing it to the limit. Such perceptive breaths of fresh air linger for a while then, unsupported by the medical establishment, dissipate in the ether like the memory of Greek muses that we have long outgrown. The medical establishment finds it more rewarding to cooperate with the pharmaceutical industry and continue to fill us with pills. One color for every day of the week. Like quarks only much, much bigger. Big enough to result in a profusion of unpleasant and often dangerous side effects.

Poisons are like that.

But there are some, all too few, physicians who advocate a more natural approach to life. Reduce stress, they say. Stress, not money, is the root of all evil. I think they are right. They even reach out tentative fingers to dabble surreptitiously in alternative medicines as if venturing into a secret garden of Allah. Rather than poisons, the steroidal or the anti-inflammatory concoctions, they advocate green tea and the Chinese mandrake. Others make millions on Ayurvedic remedies. It's not much but it's progress. Anything to break down the degenerate system.

Why this sudden interest in such "ancient sciences"? In the wisdom of the East?

My only answer is that we, as the human race, are coming of age. We are on the verge of achieving a critical mass that will place man face-to-face with his ultimate, or at the very least a very heightened, potential. We shall no longer rely on the hordes of doctors, priests, pedagogues, lawyers and other professionals making a good living out or our ignorance. For the foreseeable future some of us will remain under their power. But those who *wish*, whose desire and will are strong enough, will make their spirit-mind-body connection on their own. We might still call on a professional physician for assistance in moments of weakness. Or perhaps to procure some natural medicament which the law prohibits from making it accessible to all. We might even take advantage of their specialized knowledge, particularly in the various fields of surgery. But we alone shall make informed decisions based on their diagnosis. We shall no longer act as guinea pigs for the biochemical conglomerates making billions of dollars out of our ignorance.

Finally—our time has come.

Millions of years of evolution employing an arduous process of trial and error have fitted us with a superb brain. For countless generations we managed to survive by reacting to our environment. Finally, we can begin taking *conscious* charge of our future. Finally we have come to realize that our brain is little more than a calculating machine—rather like a superb computer—and, as such, it is subject to the maxim: "garbage in—garbage out". All the brain's calculating capacity is directly related to the information which we feed it. The data storage is preserved in our subconscious mind, which manifests corresponding components in the physical brain and the genetic system. Injuries to a particular part of our brain can result in the loss of a particular corresponding memory. But even then our brain is known to compensate, on its own. Yet even if we learn to differentiate between the mind and the brain, (the latter being an effect, the first—the cause), we still must remember what a wise man once said: "mind is a wonderful instrument but a terrible master."

We are neither our brain nor even our mind. We are that which is using both for the purpose of affording Life a mode of expression. Power of faith conjures up within the subconscious images of healing. It is those images which in fact heal. It is my contention that it is not just our belief in them but the actual images, an amalgam of concept and desire, which result in a new reality.

Perhaps the best way to understand the healing process is to realize that the body is not a solid mass but an array of atoms in constant movement. Matter is discontinuous. The atoms arrange themselves according to a program that is set for them in the subconscious mind. The process of feeding the subconscious with a program, or amending the present program, is the process of visualization. The medical profession is slowly emerging from the middle-ages of tradition to accept this premise. This truth has been known to the ancient Hindus, the Egyptians, the Hebrews and many succeeding religions. They did not have, however, a scientific language to convey this wisdom to the masses. First, the vast majority of the populace had always been illiterate. Secondly, their expression of the mind-body connection had been limited to maintaining mind and body together. Even as wild animals spend most of their wakened hours fighting for food, procreating or conserving energy, until fairly recently, and with the exception of the elite, the human animal differed little from all fauna in this regard.

It has been said that once the stomach is full, culture will follow. And the concomitant of culture is invariably knowledge. Today we have finally reached the evolutionary stage in which we can convey the ancient knowledge to the masses, and the masses have conserved sufficient energy and acquired sufficient linguistic skills, to take advantage of it. This leads us to the concept of the information age. It is not only the acquisition of knowledge but also its vast dispersal through the written word, including the mass-media and particularly the Internet, which, for the first time in history, gives vast numbers of people access to self-help.
A scan of the Internet titles speaks for itself:
With some trepidation I "clicked" the Netscape searcher

to identify '*medical self-help*' subjects. I have been rewarded with 1,990,541 references. Scanning the first hundred of them I found a plethora of references to practically all diseases imaginable, an equally abundant and well documented concern for our physical, mental and spiritual (sic) well-being, references regarding the maintenance, prophylactic methods, rehabilitation, nutrition, sex, support groups, self diagnosis and every other imaginable subject dealing with our health, all the way to "self inflating coronary sinus perfusion.... with self inflating balloon" whatever that may be. Even allowing the number of references offering insurance, the magnitude of remaining services is staggering.

Next I "clicked" again, this time asking the Netscape to search "medical self-help publishing". We shall never run out of reading matter. The number of references offered came to 2,249,653. You will forgive me if I do not review the publications listed. This book is not intended to teach anyone how to treat himself or herself. It is intended to discuss who and what we are, and, most of all, what is our present potential. Whatever conclusion anyone reaches will lead him or her in the direction right for *him or her*. We are all different. We all travel our own individual paths. I would no more suggest that you follow my path than anybody else's. What I do hope is to inspire you *to move*. Not to stay put in the stagnant pool of tradition and *status quo*. The future belongs to all of us. It is today that we build our tomorrows. And even if tomorrow doesn't really matter, there is inherent joy in the act of building, the act of creation. Each one of us can best visualize his or her own universe. I merely hope that we shall all make a *conscious* effort to participate in the individual process of creation.

The human race has finally reached a critical mass necessary to take a giant step on the evolutionary scale. Whether the medical profession will assist us or hinder us in this endeavor remains to be seen. If they help us, we shall leap faster and further. If they do not, it is they who will be left behind.

But there are glimmers of hope.

In my home which at present is in Quebec, Canada, we live in an age where the medical profession is undergoing a massive reorganization. Perhaps, it is time. As I write this chapter, people, young and old, are dying in the hospital corridors of emergency departments, while waiting for an empty bed, or even empty space in a room. As I write this chapter, Quebec has 11,500 bureaucrats administering 12,000 doctors.[9] The politicians, as elitists always do, enter by the back doors and have themselves and their families treated. One of the recent provincial premiers resorted to medical treatments in the United States, since he did not trust the medical establishment he runs and controls in his own province.

This is where we stand today.

The remainder of Canada's provinces differ little from Quebec. Even the wealthy United States, sporting the proudest physicians of them all, are in the middle of a strife between the exorbitant insurance premiums they have to pay and the fees physicians and particularly the specialists are forced to charge to cover them. The American judicial-system-gone-mad forces the insurance companies to continually raise the premiums to survive against judgments demanding millions of dollar for "maltreatment" of patients, who during their entire life and in perfect health would never earn one tenth of the amount figured in judicial awards.[10] It is as if the system was designed to fail. It was. It is only a question of time. Uranus will do its job. The Age of Aquarius is the age empowering individuals, not groups or organizations. The medical, judicial and all other groups living at the expense of others will gradually decompose until they collapse under the weight of their own greed. There are always exceptions. There are always Dr. Schweitzers who will forsake their own lives to help others. But the vast majority will perish—in time.

What do we do in the meantime?

We can go back to the old ways. We can pour billions of dollars into the Health System and continue to plug the leeks, to fix the symptoms. The efforts will prove futile. It has been reported that the retirees increase at a rated 14% faster than the labor force. Since the aged already utilize up to 80% of the "heath-care" resources, there will never be enough money to sate their needs. Peter G. Peterson, former Secretary of State of the United States proposed rationing medical care.[11] But even that will not suffice. Not until we start killing off our old and infirm. No one will propose that. Not for any moral or ethical reasons (there are neither morals nor ethics in politics), only because as the aged population swells, they will reach unprecedented power. They will be the controlling majority in any political election. Their vote will decide.

We can do worse.

We can emulate Great Britain and most of Europe who proudly display their nationalized Medicare systems which converted physicians into a bunch of unionized public servants. These government-sponsored civil servants are now offering equal opportunity for everyone. Equal opportunity to be poisoned by irresponsible government employees who feed us toxins to alleviate symptoms. Perhaps the epitome of irresponsibility is the medical profession's use of antibiotics. I know from personal experience of people being given frequent doses of antibiotics for ailments which the physicians admitted were of viral origin. Even the medical doctors know that antibiotics do not combat viruses. The explanation given for the misuse was that they administered these precious medications *in case* the patient acquired bacterial infection due to some (completely unforeseen and unfounded) complications. In the meantime the bacteria, due to the constant supply of antibiotics, has become immune to them. We now have specialized bacteria residing exclusively in hospitals, where the abuse of antibiotics is most prevalent. The good doctors unwittingly and witlessly developed a new strain of microorganisms which do not respond to any treatment.

Is this called healing?

The medical profession cares little for our health. Less for healing. Some even try hard but their hands are tied by traditions. Had the medical profession remained in private hands the physicians would have been held accountable. Now, the governments change, the civil service drags on.

And on. And on.

Now, at the end of the millennium, in Canada we have a chance. We can try to patch-up what doesn't work. Our already excessive taxes will rise yet again; our standard of living shall descend even lower. We can draw billions of dollars from taxing the tobacco companies which make us sick, lose countless millions on administration, and pass the residual amount to the Health System to make us, supposedly, better.

Or we can turn a new page.

Dr. Weil, in his excellent book mentioned before, *Spontaneous Healing*,[12] allots a whole chapter to medical pessimism. Then he goes on to ask:

"Look at our National Institutes of Health. Really they are National Institutes of Disease: the National Cancer Institute, the National Institute of Allergy and Infectious Disease, the National Institute of Arthritis and Skin Diseases, the National Institute of Diabetes and Digestive and Kidney Diseases, The National Institute of Neurological Disorders and Stroke, and so on. Where is the National Institute of Health and Healing?"

Dr Weil is a physician. Perhaps he is the sign of a new trend. But don't hold your breath. He sounds more like John the Baptist crying in the wilderness. And we all know what the establishment did to him.

So if we do attempt to resuscitate our ailing "Health" system let us call it by its true name. The National Disease

System. After all, it hardly heals anyone. It might extend the vegetative state of the biological existence of some people a little longer, but it will not enhance its quality. It is a very sick system. It does not deal in health. It deals in sickness. In death. It always did.

Life is up to us. Individuals.

***

FOOTNOTES

(1). Genesis 1:28.

(2). These figures assume a strange meaning when we consider that the Roman Catholic church requires one 'miracle' for beatifications, and one more... for canonization. Bruno Gröning, of course, did not call his healing powers miraculous.

(3). Gleamed from an article in THE GAZETTE, Montreal, Monday, April 26, 1999. [I withhold the name of the patient for obvious reasons]

(4). It maybe of some interests that on October 15th 2004, CBC (6 p.m. News) reported that "medical errors", kill 24, 000 Canadians/year.

(5). Weil, Andrew M.D., SPONTANEOUS HEALING (Ballantine Books, New York 1995)

(6). Murphy, Joseph D.D., D.R.S., Ph.D., LL.D..THE AMAZING LAWS OF COSMIC MIND POWER (Parker Publ. Co., Inc. West Nyack, N.Y.. 1965) It should be noted that Dr.Murphy is not a medical practitioner though very much a man of letters.

(7). By setting off an autoimmune reaction.

(8). Dr.Chopra's AGELESS BODY, TIMELESS MIND (Harmony Books, div. of Crown Publ.) might serve well as introduction to his philosophy of healing.

(9). Josée Legault, THE MONTREAL GAZETTE, *There are ways out of health mess.* Nov. 20,1999.

(10). Though I hold little compassion for the tobacco companies, the absurdity of the USA legal system is illustrated by a compensatory award of over 80 million dollars for the estate of a *janitor* who started smoking in his teens and died at 67.

(11). Interview by Charlie Rose on the Vermont PBS on February 16, 1999.

(12). See footnote 109 above, pgs. 65-6.

Chapter 7
Scientific Perspective

Physician, heal thyself.

Luke 4:23.

There was a time when science and religion had been one. Then, after humanity decided that the learned priesthood held too much power invariably exercised with the attendant exorbitant exploitation, the bright among our predecessors turned their backs on religion. This in no way diminished the benefits that organized religion brought to humanity. After all, were would we be without the beautiful churches, the priceless works of art adorning the Vatican, without the magnificent music commissioned and paid for by the scarlet princes of the church. In equal measure the Byzantine treasures, the Hindu and Buddhist temples, the Taj Mahal contributed to the creative glory of mankind.

All thanks to organized religions.

Unfortunately a time has come, when the sacerdotal oligarchies have amassed such formidable treasures that their protection took precedence over all other considerations. Traditions overtook drive for discovery; *status quo* became so comfortable that its protection became paramount. But since stagnant societies are bound to shrink, the sword has provided the means of expansion. It has been disguised under the misnomer of Apostolicity, or spreading the faith. By force.

As mentioned in the chapter on *Visions*, individuals, later an infantile scientific society, raised its curious head, humbly, cautiously, and if they were lucky they kept it from having it chopped off or being burned at the stake by the priesthood jealous of power.

Now we have turned a full circle. While the astrophysicists continue to wonder if there is enough mass in the universe for the Big Crunch to occur, their comrades in arms poison our atmosphere with unprecedented pollution, nuclear radiation, biochemical issuance and possibly with biological, genetically altered constructs. It looks as though we, the simple folk, cannot win.

Or can we?

It seemed that our fate had been sealed at the end of the 16th century. As discussed in the chapter on *Politics and Society*, we can all blame Copernicus for raising the ugly head of reason with the publication of *De Revolutionibus Orbium Coelestium* in 1543. He discharged his pragmatic theories into a sea of metaphysical speculation. Within a few years the fledgling scientific society realized that thinking was allowed, providing one did not advertise it within the hearing distance of the voracious ears of the Holy Inquisitors. This new awareness was directly responsible for the eventual unfortunate but expedient separation of philosophy and science. In very broad terms, philosophy continued to deal with the Cause, while Science dedicated itself to the study of the Result. For now, God remained the (Prime) Cause, while the Universe—God's masterpiece—became the sole domain of pragmatic observation and experiment. Nevertheless, it could be argued that science attempted to study the Cause by studying Its creation, while philosophy continued to predict the results by attempting to visualize the Cause. Centuries later, after a long divorce, the reconciliation of the two resulted in a new discipline called Theoretical Physics. Regardless of the terminology the modern scientists employ, it is hard to imagine the theoretical physicist dabbling in less than metaphysics. Rather than getting excessively involved in mathematical calculations, they observe the astronomers in their endeavors. They observe the observers. When the astronomers come up with observations which challenge the accepted hypotheses, the theoreticians climb into a hot bathtub and do some serious theorizing. Or as Adam Frank once observed, "Their ideas derive from an intuition about the way nature behaves on its most fundamental level, the kind of 'feeling', or hunch—almost a personal aesthetic that is every bit as important for the good theorist as the ability to solve equations."[1]

There is ample evidence that Einstein was as much a physicist as he was a philosopher. Whether they assume the title of a cosmologist, astrophysicist or theoretical physicist, hardly less can be said of Edward Milne, Richard Feynman, Roger Penrose, Alexander Friedman, and Stephen Hawking or Frank Tipler,[2] both of whom have recently illuminated the masses (that's us) with popular literary efforts.

Things were good when the earth was flat.

When Copernicus destroyed the geocentric vision, he also did something to the egocentric attitudes which drove man up to his day. Yet we seem, as proposed in the chapter on *Myth and Reality*, to move in cycles. While we rightfully credit Copernicus with the departure from the geocentric view of the universe of his day, in fact he reaffirmed the knowledge already promulgated by the heliocentric astronomy of Aristarchus of Samos in the 3rd century B.C., and the Greek mathematical astronomy of the 3rd century A.D.. But as people progress in cycles, in the days of Copernicus humanity was once again ready for the reawakened broader vision. They began to wonder about other worlds, other intelligences, perhaps scattered throughout the universe. Perhaps, they wondered, there were other universes, *cosmi*, beyond the scope of human imagination. The deity who or which created our earth, our sun and some planets in our immediate vicinity, suddenly grew to heretofore unprecedented proportions. If we were created in the image of God who created the earth, what of a

God who created other earths, other solar systems, other galaxies, worlds? Are the other planets also supporting beings in the image of *their* God? How many such planets with their attendant gods are there? In the first verse of the Torah we are told: "In the beginning God created the heaven and the earth." Only the Hebrew word translated as 'God' is *elohim*. If we are to take the Scriptures literally, there are many gods. *Elohim* means gods. Plural. Perhaps they always agreed with the Buddhists, who favor an infinite number of Creative Forces. Perhaps the ancients were right. Perhaps there are many gods...

It may seem inordinate that I bring the scriptures into the chapter on *Scientific Perspective*. If so, let us not forget that the Bible and other Scriptures had been, in their time, the sole repositories of scientific knowledge. If we cannot decipher their symbolism, perhaps the fault lies with us, not with the knowledge they contain.

Today, these are no longer questions posed by monks in moments free from attempting to determine how many angels can dance on the head of a pin. We know that the Torah, the Bible, indeed all the ancient scriptures, employed symbolic idiom to plant in the human subconscious the seeds of knowledge that was yet to come. Yet such questions did not always occupy the minds of the best scientists of their day. In the second half of the 5th century before the present era, the Atomists would envy us who direct enormous radio-telescopes at the stars, awaiting a message from our galactic neighbors.[3] One thing is certain: as we revise our vision of the world, we revise our concept of God. The deity grows exponentially together with the universe which continues to expand at a staggering velocity to this very day.

To this very day.

If the purpose of science generally and of medicine in particular is to assure survival of the human race, than we ought to, surely, look towards the East. Anyone who regards the Western sciences superior to the Eastern would be wise to remember that the Chinese system resulted in 1.3 billion Chinese walking this earth, and this with one of the most stringent birth-control restrictions known in any part of the globe. And if our illustrious scientists still remain unconvinced, then they might glance at the Indian Subcontinent, which, in terms of population, might well overtake the Chinese.

If, on the other hand, we are to assign a different purpose to science, then we shall dive, headlong, into the awaiting arms of the advocates of Revelation.

It's a tough world!

I believe that there is one limitation of science which will always tend to relegate it to a secondary position in the development of man. While the human race is characterized by an insatiable need to conquer, to reach out for the unknown, to reach out *beyond the limits of knowledge*, science is limited to studying only that which already is. It is as though we produced an immortal work of art and than asked how we did it. The answer seems to be" because we have a vision not of that which is, but of that which can be". As we continue to create new universes, the scientists will continue to study them. Until, one day, they too will attempt to create their own, scientific universe, in which all matter will obey their laws, will fit neatly into their precious equations. But those scientific dreamers couldn't have heard, as yet, about the Chaos Theory.

There are two intrinsic problems with the scientific approach.

First and foremost, science invariably looks to the past. A rear-view is not a vision. It is hindsight. The astronomers study spectra of light coming from the stars which left their origin eons ago. The physicists study matter and energies which came into being in the instant of creation. Other scientists take what is, analyze its structure, then, all too often, forget to put it together again. Perhaps they don't know how. They are so much better at analyses than at syntheses...

Physiologists, biologists, pathologists and many other 'logists dissect thousands of tumorous corpses in search of the origins, perhaps the essence of life.

Dear, dear scientists, *there is no life in corpses*...

At least not the life for which they appear to be searching. The secret of life does not lie in biochemical degradation. It lies in that which wrenches order out of chaos, introduces harmony out of discord. Life is an attribute of that which is perfect, and it attempts to install as much of this perfection in the objective universe as the realm of matter can sustain. It is also that which initiates an ongoing process. Frank Tipler who treats us to a joy-ride in his *Physics of Immortality* has a different vision. He writes: "...'life' is a form of information processing, and the human mind—and the human soul—is a very complex computer program."[4] I would ask what he means by soul. Though he likes to refer to the Bible, he does not specify whether he refers to *nephesh* or *El*. If it is the latter, than I agree with him, but then we cannot call life a program but a *programmer*. If he refers to the first, the *nephesh*, than I agree that soul is a program since *nephesh* corresponds to the modern term the *subconscious*. This matter is discussed in greater detail in the chapter on *Duality*. What I am really leading to is that in spite of Frank Tipler's assurances, perhaps we have not reached, as yet, the final reconciliation between science and theology.

Two pages later Tipler calls on the science of biology to strengthen his argument. He writes: "The biologist Dawkins[5] has reached the same definition of life that I shall use: life *is information preserved by natural selection*."[6] The problem is that Tipler regards the seat of our "information preservation" equipment the human brain, which houses a 'mere' 10 billion neurons. He errs by an enormous factor. Even if we take into account solely our 'biological' memory storage capacity, it adds up to more like 300 trillion, a number that corresponds to *all* the cells of the human body. Each one of them is a complete arsenal of our genetic code, which surely has some bearing on the form of 'life' we inhabit, or, in his definition: are. That's memory storage that surely Tipler should not ignore. I believe he errs in both, the hardware and the software area.

But, notwithstanding the definition of *what* we are, where I really drift apart from Tipler and other physicists is in the determination of *who* is doing the processing of information. If our body is a computer and the information is the program, then, I ask again, who or what is the programmer? Surely, we must be concerned with the programmer not just with the program or the hardware.

Where I do agree with Tipler is that 'life' can choose an infinite number of processors vastly superior to the human body to process the information. The only problem is that life in not a person or a being, as Tipler seems to imply. It is only an attribute of that which has not, perhaps cannot be, defined. It certainly is neither a biological nor a nano-technological infestation. 'It' seems to be as enigmatic as the heart of a Black Hole—of the unknown, perhaps unknowable. We can recognize It by the trail It leaves behind.

Nevertheless, in order to develop a vision of our Self, we must develop a yet clearer vision of life. We seem to search for it in the distant future (as did Tipler or de Chardin) or in the hoary past, gazing at the flickering light of distant galaxies. I need hardly mention the morbid fascination we exhibit with our antiquity, with the dead. Apparently it gives us self-confidence to search, let alone find our roots. It gives us an illusory sense of belonging. This hindsight preoccupation is explicit in anthropology, paleontology, history and many other related disciplines. A wonderful woman in the forefront of her learning reminds me of two statements. The renowned paleo-anthropologist, Mary Leakey said: "All these trees of life with their branches of our ancestors, that's a lot of nonsense." And later, she declared that her discovery of footprints frozen for 3.5 million years in volcanic ash was: "the most important find in view of human evolution."[7]

Perhaps the best time and space to look is, after all, the

present. The present "timespace" as the theoretical physicists would call it.

The second major stumbling block which restricts our scientific search is 'respect' for the past. Science is steeped in tradition. Scientists are *per force* obliged to build on what they already know. In order to do so, they must protect *their* status quo. And the rest of us are just as guilty. Where would we be without our great names in whose reflected glory we all bathe when we talk about the advancement of the human race? *We* did this, that, and the other... *We*, the humans... Is there another way? Paul of Tarsus tells us there is. *I die daily*, he said.[8] Not very scientific, perhaps, but it doesn't leave much room for tradition.

***

Let us review (very) briefly the scientific vision of the universe.

At present, there are essentially two visions allowing for two universes and two architects (or architectural teams spanning centuries) of their scientific vision. The origin of the first (modern) vision could be attributed to Galileo, developed by Isaac Newton, and finally promulgated by Max Planck who advanced the *quantum theory* in which not only matter but all forms of energy could be regarded as discrete aggregates, which Planck called *quanta*. All elements are composed of molecules, which are composed of atoms. To illustrate the scale, let us examine the mass of one hydrogen molecule. Its value has been calculated to be:

0.000 000 000 000 000 000 000 0033 grams.

About half that amount would account for one hydrogen atom. The mass of an electron, in turn, would be about two thousand times smaller than the mass of a hydrogen atom. How the atoms break down into subatomic particles will be discussed later in the chapter *Redefining Self*, when we endeavor to review the vision we hold of ourselves. Here we are concerned not with our "self", but with the environment in which an individual "self" has his or her being.

One way to regard this environment is to think of it as consisting of a virtually infinite ocean of minute invisible particles. To repeat, thanks to Planck, this would apply not only to all matter but also to all energy. The quantum theory holds that an electric charge is as granular in structure as matter. Light is composed of photons, individual particles of light. As mentioned above, since we cannot conceive of particles so tiny, we think of them as groups. As *quanta* which is plural for *quantum*. A light beam is regarded as a *shower* of photons, even as an electron beam a *shower* of elementary particles. Here is how Albert Einstein describes the world of quantum mechanics:

"Quantum physics formulates laws governing crowds and not individuals. Not properties but probabilities are described, not laws disclosing the future of systems are formulated, but laws governing the changes in time of the probabilities and relating to great congregations of individuals."[9]

The second vision belongs to Albert Einstein himself.

If the previous vision could be regarded as concerned with the micro-universe, Einstein was fascinated by the macro-vision. It had its origin in his deep conviction that there is order in the universe. That the world is an expression of an infinite mind. "God doesn't play dice with the universe," he once said. His vision is indeed on Grand Scale. It continues to unfold, continues to be affirmed by many of today's scientists. In as much as the quantum theory breaks up the universe into its incomprehensibly small components, Einstein's paints a vision with broad strokes of the divine brush. It proposes a world of fields and waves, of great sweeping concepts. It reaches out to the very limit of the universe itself.

Before Einstein the vision of the world was essentially mechanical. There were charges and particles of matter which combined to give us a mechanical image of reality. Einstein's considered the fields *between* the charges and *between* the particles as vital to the understanding of how the universe works. This space in-between fills not only the 'voids' between the stars and galaxies, but between the tiny components of the subatomic particles. The "space between" is infinitely greater than the space occupied by matter. And this space is not 'void'. It is filled with magnetic and gravitational forces. Einstein regarded the 'field' as the most important concept since the time of Newton, and essential to the description of the physical phenomena.

His theories came essentially in two stages. The first is known as "the *special theory of relativity* and applies only to inertial co-ordinate systems in which the law of inertia, as formulated by Newton is valid". The law of inertia states that matter at rest tends to remain at rest, and if moving continues to move unless an external force acts upon it. Einstein explains his own theory as follows.[10]

"The special theory of relativity, is based on two fundamental assumptions: physical laws are the same in all co-ordinate systems moving uniformly, relative to each other; the velocity of light always has the same value."

Stephen Hawking's definition:

"Einstein's theory is based on the idea that the laws of science should be the same for all freely moving observers, no matter what their speed."[11]

There is a peculiar byproduct of this theory which seems to be ignored by all the books on physics I ever read. This leaves a *great* many I have not read, but a preponderance of evidence appears to support my concern. Movement and/or velocity of celestial bodies appear to be attributed to the impetus originating in the so-called Big Bang theory. I have grave misgivings with all theories that initiate the Big Bang in a singularity of space. What I mean is that the theoretical physicists appear to regard the original cosmic egg to have 'exploded' some 20 billion years ago in a single 'spot'. How can they talk of a singularity of space when *there was no space* before the Big Bang? Space is a factor of the space/time continuum, and *before the beginning of time* there was no time.

There was no continuum.

And, as cosmological theories go, there is a man in a class of his own. In his above-mentioned book *The Physics of Immortality*, Tipler gives a fascinating performance of scurrilous pride. In a nutshell, he proposes that the human race will conquer the whole universe and do so for 'everafter'. By his own admission, Frank Tipler Ph.D., rubs shoulders with the *crème de la crème* of the theoretical physicists' milieu. This includes such prominent British physicists as Roger Penrose and Stephen Hawking. It is thanks to them that he is enabled (so he writes in his Preface) to draw very deep and very general conclusions about the structure of space and time by looking at the universe in its *totality* in both time and space." How can a veritable walking encyclopedia type of man, and Tipler undoubtedly is, imagine that an insignificant planet, rotating within an insignificant star system would initiate a biosphere which would conquer all of the universe? He completely ignores the fact that as a rather young star, (the sun is calculated to have a mere 5 billion years), with a flora and fauna which no one ever accused of originating further back in history than a tiny fraction of that time, could or would compete with countless civilizations throughout the countless galaxies, all very considerably older than our own trivial and juvenile solar system.

It is not just that he entrusts the spread of 'life', to us, whom he defines as biological mechanisms which may be taken over by nanotechnological contraptions,[12] but he assigns the effort of creating the *universal* biosphere to earth (or 'earthlings'), extends it to the extremities of time and space of a (by then) vastly expanded universe, and then contracts this cyclically oscillating cosmos back to earth again. This vision gives egocentricity (not to say geocentricity) a new meaning. The whole thing would rate as an amusing piece of science fiction if it weren't for the fact that Tipler finds it necessary to back up his musings with over a hundred pages of an "Appendix for Scientists". I must confess that his calculations leave me cold. Not because I disagree with them, only because I don't begin to understand them. But I applaud the critic of the *Esquire* who is cited on the cover of Tipler's book; I quote: "A doozy of a book... it's *2001: A Space Odyssey meets The Divine Comedy.*" I would agree that as Science Fiction the book is above average.

Why so irked? Jealousy? Pure and simple. I am jealous of the man's superior knowledge which he is using towards, what in my opinion is, such an abortive and ludicrous end. Having the scientific background at his disposal, he ought to charge himself in using this knowledge for the expansion of the human understanding, not for bolstering his already inflated ego.

Writing as a non-scientist, I cannot accept that we, the human species, are the sole seed of intelligent life in the universe. As we witnessed in the chapter on *Politics and Society*, we are a primitive people, a very junior member of the thinking species, and judging by our history—considerably retarded in our intellectual growth. When we learn to understand *ourselves*, we may then reach out and search for our rightful place in the universe. But for that to happen, I feel certain, we must lose our parochial attitude. Then we might start our *conscious* growth. Then we might develop sufficient humility to really learn from the universe, not to impose our puerile views on it. The *Physics of Immortality* is a formidable example of man's subjugation of his intellectual prowess to his emotional needs. If we were to regard God as Mind (as the Unity Church does), then there would be some justification in pursuing intellectual solutions. But, as Tipler himself observes, we are mechanical contrivances. We are machines. Or our bodies are.

We are not our bodies.

So much for the aftermath of Einstein's special theory of relativity, with a few world shaking additions. The theory invalidates the old laws of mechanics. And most of all, it postulates a connection between matter and energy. Mass has energy, energy has mass. The famous equation of $E=mc^2$ is a direct consequence of this theory. There are other consequences that while great, do not advance our discussion on the visualization of the universe. And I am not attempting to create a vision for you. I am trying to illustrate the incredible diversity of visions a human mind is capable of. Having said that, there is one consequence of Einstein's vision which does have a direct bearing on the way we 'can' regard the physical universe. We no longer see it in terms of space *and* time as individual dimensions. Instead we regard it in terms of *space-time*.

The next great claim to Einstein's fame is his general theory of relativity. Here is how the genius defines it (in part) himself:

"The general theory of relativity gives a still deeper analysis of the time-space continuum. The validity of the theory is no longer restricted to inertial co-ordinate systems. ...(it) formulates new structure laws for the gravitational field. It forces us to analyze the role played by geometry in the description of the physical world... It regards the fact that gravitational and inertial mass are equal, as essential and not merely accidental, as in classical mechanics..."[13]

Again Hawking's definition:

"Einstein theory based on the idea that the laws of science should be the same for all observers, no matter how they are moving. It explains that force of gravity in terms of the curvature of a four-dimensional space-time."[14]

It gives a vision of an orderly universe. But Einstein's hunger was not satisfied. His theories stressed the importance of field in physics, field: the space in-between. The vastness and the quality of the space itself. But he failed in proposing a theory that would unify all theories, "in formulating a pure field physics". For now, we are stuck with field and matter. So much for Einstein's vision.
What's yours?

Seriously, the search for meaning in the universe goes on. There are those who search for a single vision. This vision, which Einstein found so elusive, is referred to as the Unified Field theory. Some say that the theoretical physicists are getting close. They broke down the quarks into smaller components. They call them *strings*. Little wiggly vibrations which no one has ever seen, no one ever will. They are too small. They are so thin that they "have length but no other dimension, like an infinitely thin piece of string."[15] They are supposed to lead us to the unification of physics. They also say, the hypothetical strings might tell us what happened in the first nanoseconds of the Big Bang.
Wouldn't that be fun?

We, the humans, have come, once again, full circle. We have listened to the revelations, to our silent voice, and then asked the scientists to help us explain them. Today's scientist must become an amalgam of half physicist half mystic. Perhaps a doctor of metaphysics, in the literal sense of the word. The purpose of science will be to translate gestält 'muscular' concepts Einstein talked about into linguistically structured communications. The purpose of this function shall be to share a personal revelation with another person. To find a common language. Until we shall all learn to communicate at a higher level. Until we shall learn to communicate concepts without breaking them down, scientifically, into bland shadows of the original vision.

It will be a while yet.

It is important to understand that theoretical physicists do not spend their time scribbling incredibly complex equations which no one outside their inner circle can understand, and then come up with theories which would back those equations up. Quite the contrary. The scientists visualize a particular universal order, law, condition or even shape, and then they try hard to back those visions with equations, in order to be able to share them with other scientists. There are still scientists today who try to construct equations to prove some aspects of Einstein's visions. The ultimate proof is, of course, in the pudding. But since the universal pudding may take either infinity or upwards of 100 billion years (depending on your definition of time) to bake, it is hard to wait for the final proof. This is why the mathematical equations are so useful. If the pudding works in the field of math, it will work in the kitchen also.

Or so we all hope.

***

While our theoretical physicists continue to hypothesize over ever smaller quanta of matter (leptons, mesons, tychons and finally strings), they do not seem to labor under or harbor a need to get involved on a comparative miniaturization or diminution within the fields of energy. The scientists got to the electromagnetic and gravitational fields and there they got stuck. What about an equation for the velocity of thought (not as streams of electrons but as a pure energy field), or love, compassion and suchlike. Do they imagine that these energies, these fields do not exist? Do they function in waves or fields? Can they be quantified? Can we have a "tiny thought" or just a *soupçon* of love? Perhaps our hard-nosed materialists might even find, one day, a spiritual energy which "works" over vast distances, unperturbed and unhampered by neither matter nor distance. And if they claim that such energies, such fields, do not exist because they can't measure them, let them hypothesize. Let them observe the energy of love by the trail it leaves behind. Like the quarks, or gluons. And if they are looking for infinity, love is a great place to start. It always was, it is and always will be.

And that's a law, which is not relative but absolute.

***

FOOTNOTES

(1). Frank, Adam, MYSTERY OF THE MISSING: DISCOVER mag. Dec.'96. Also see BEYOND RELIGION Volume I. *Celestial and Other Bodies.* [Inhousepress 1997, 2001]

(2). I include Dr. Frank J. Tipler in this illustrious list of names because he, to my mind, represents an extreme in reductionism. The very opposite of his thesis can be found in Mitchell Waldrop's COMPLEXITY, subtitled *The emerging Science at the Edge of Order and Chaos*. My own sentiments gravitate towards the latter.

(3). The philosopher mainly responsible for the development of the atomic theory was Democritus (c.460-c.370 BC). The Atomists, as the name implies, held that the ultimate constituents of the universe are indestructible and indivisible a-toms (= indivisible). This theory has been revived by John Dalton in the 19th century and persisted to quite recent times.

(4). Tipler, Frank J., THE PHYSICS OF IMMORTALITY, (Anchor Book, Doubleday, New York 1994) page 124.

(5). Dawkins, Richard THE SELFISH GENE (Oxford University Press 1976)

(6). Tipler, ibid. page 126 (my italics)

(7). More on the subject in S. Kapuscinski's BEYOND RELIGION Vol.1. essay on *Celestial and Other Bodies*. (Inhousepress 1997, 2001)

(8). 1 Corinthians 15:31

(9). Einstein, Albert and Infeld, Leopold: THE EVOLUTION OF PHYSICS (Simon and Schuster, New York 1961) © Albert Einstein and Leopold Infeld 1938.

(10). ibid. pg.244

(11). Hawking, S. W., A BRIEF HISTORY OF TIME (Bantam Books) page 187

(12). Nanotechnology is technology on the scale of an individual atom, i.e. one nanometer or one billionth of one meter in size.
(13). Einstein... ibid., pages 244-245.
(14). Hawking, ibid. page 184.
(15). Hawking, ibid. page 159.

***

There is a state where the mind does not recognize anything.
There is a state in which recognition and experience,
which are the movement of the known,
totally come to an end.
...the whole thing collapses;
there is a different state altogether.

Krishnamurti, J., EXPLORATION INTO INSIGHT
(Harper & Raw, San Francisco 1979; pg. 31]

Chapter 8
Visualizing infinity

There are two aspects of infinity which influence the way we visualize the universe. Together they are known as the space—time continuum. Whether we measure our infinity in terms of space, or time, sooner or later we come to realize that the two are interlocking, part of the same equation. After all, it would take infinite time to cross an infinite ocean of space. And to do 'either' we must tackle the question of immortality.

Since discussing Infinity as pertaining to ourselves, human beings, we must of necessity espouse the concept of immortality—a metaphysical concept at best—I shall limit myself to a brief analysis of the concept of infinity in cosmological terms only, and then you and I can attempt to fit our own selves into the most propitious model.

There are two principle visions of "cosmological infinity", plus one poor cousin. There are a number of subdivisions of both theories, but they need not concern us. We are after a vision, not necessarily after a solution. We know that solutions may be limited in time and space. Visions are unlimited.

The first cosmological model is called the *Pulsating Universe*.

The theoretical physicists tell us that our universe is either finite or infinite in terms of either time and/or space. They call these models the closed or open systems. The closed system is normally recognized as an oscillating or pulsating model. This model is the nearest to those espoused by the ancient Myths. The universe starts from a singularity, from zero point in time and space (neither of which exist as yet). It expands to a specific size which is a function of the mass, momentum and centrifugal force. When it reaches the outer limits, the gravitational force draws it back again, to its original point zero. Here it either rests for an undetermined duration (not time since time doesn't exist in a zero time-space environment) and eventually it expands again only to contract in due course. This cyclic method assures the immortality of the universe, though not necessarily of ourselves. Thus the infinity of time is assured by this cyclic model, though it could be argued that each cycle is an independent unit, and not part of a continuity. If so, the infinity which we have just visualized falls short of an ideal. This model finds its echo in the Big-bang, Big-crunch theories which are favored by most physicists today. Alas, favorite theories seem to oscillate a lot more often than the universe they describe.

Nevertheless, as already discussed in the chapter on *Myth and Reality*, this is a cosmological model on which a number of ancient philosophies including Jainism, Hinduism and the Buddhist religion are based. While the myths make allowances for the continuity of life, the physical model of the oscillating universe makes it rather difficult—unless we assume a "higher form of life" which is not based on either biological or even material existence. Strangely enough, it is the science of physics which would demand an introduction of 'spirit' into the equation, or at least some substance or energy or environment which has its being outside the parameters of time and space. Rather like the environment of Black Holes. Later we shall discuss the Frank Tipler's recent model which endeavors to bypass this need.

But there are further problems.

If the universe continues to expand in relation to the original Big-bang singularity, then the galaxies would continue to drift further and further apart. The spaces between all celestial bodies would widen. Our night sky, over progressive eons, would lose its glitter. Most stars would turn to white dwarfs. If our own sun could last that long, our earth would hang, forlorn in the vastness of "empty space". A lonely, prosaic existence. And this in some 50 billion years, only halfway through the estimated lifespan of the world we live in. Later, during the next fifty eons the universe would contract. But most of the brilliant suns would be long gone now. Just dormant corpses of their former glory would coalesce towards a common grave. Perhaps some would reignite, due to renewed and swelling gravitational forces or due to absorbing hydrogen on their homeward journey. No one knows. No one has come up with a vision.

It is a dismal prospect.

The second model is called *Continuous Creation*.

In his *Brief History of Time* Stephen Hawking claims that in spite of the fact that the Roman Catholic church pronounced the Big-bang model in accordance with the Bible, any model which affirmed a 'beginning' of time smacked too much of divine intervention. Long before Hawkins registered his objections, some physicists, particularly Hermann Bondi and Thomas Gold, together with Fred Hoyle[1] continued to search for another vision. In 1948, together they proposed what was called the Steady State theory, later to be known as the Continuous Creation model.

It is a very different way of visualizing infinity.

Originally it was the distinguished English cosmologist Edward Arthur Milne (1896—1950) who advanced the theory called the *cosmological principle*. This model found considerable support among the scientists when they found that some stars are reputedly older than the universe itself. While today we assign some 20 billion years since the 'big-bang', in Milne's day the universe had been thought to have existed for a much shorter time.[2] In the Continuous Creation vision of the universe, there is no need for a big-bang and therefore no need to date the universe. Many cosmologists liked this theory because it lent itself to the construction of a relatively simple mathematical model. It required an assumption of an even distribution of matter throughout the universe. Einstein liked it as it confirmed his general theory of relativity that wherever the observer observes, he experiences similar conditions. The idea was that as the galaxies moved apart, new matter is continually created in the intergalactic space.[3] Thus at all times one would see a similar density of matter in all parts of the universe.

But infinity is hard to take. We seem to need some boundaries to be able to visualize almost anything. Once again, Einstein supplied the answer. He postulated a universe which could have a *finite volume* but with *infinite* number of galaxies. He seems to have created another problem. Wouldn't the observers at the edge of the universe see an ocean of galaxies on the one side and void on the other? But Einstein was ready for that one. His theory of relativity also holds that an object moving in relation to ourselves becomes shorter in the direction of the travel. As the object (star or galaxy) approaches the velocity of light it becomes paper-thin. Should it reach the velocity of light (away from our vantage-point), its length (or thickness) in the direction of its travel would equal zero.

At least this is how it would appear to us. To the observers *on* the object (say a planet) itself, all would appear normal. To them *our earth* (should it be possible to observe it from such a distance) would appear to be paper-thin. The consequence of this theory is that one would be able to imagine an infinite number of galaxies, all paper-thin as they approached the 'rim' of the world. If you can visualize such a universe, your powers of visualization are as good as Einstein's, and you haven't written a single equation. If not, try to imagine our Earth transparent, and all the Australians walking upside down and peeking under our kilts and skirts.

They are and would, you know! If the earth were transparent.

Anyway, there were objections. There always are.

Perhaps what really matters is the joy of having visions. The joy of visualizing a series of universes, "all your own". Alexander Friedmann comes to mind. He proposed three models; one that expands and collapses, wherein space is bent upon itself like a sphere. Another model that expands forever, with space bent outwards, like a riding saddle. And then there is the third vision wherein space is flat and thus infinite. Take your pick.

I've never seen or met an astrophysicist who was depressed!

As for anyone who harbors a need to reconcile the vision of the Steady State universe with the Hindu myths, all they need do is to transpose the concept of the universe to our (or any inhabited) galaxy. With a gargantuan Black Hole at its heart (as is already proposed by some astrophysicists) and the attendant periodic collapses and explosions, the Milky Way should sate those who need to perceive the Breath of Brahma (see chapter on *Myths and Reality*). If we were to recognize our own galaxy as *our* universe, the Cosmos as we now know it would become not merely a universe of galaxies, but a Universe of universes. Our own 'universal' Milky Way would cater adequately to the needs of even the most discriminating mythologists.

But then there is the *Hyperbolic vision.*

Hyperbolic universe is not oscillating but it does last forever. There is a price to pay. It begins as a thinly spread, omnipresent gas, perhaps hydrogen. Slowly the quanta of matter coalesce into bigger and bigger clamps of matter. Stars and planets slowly come into being. Then we do. We inhabit the universe for a brief instant of time. An accident? Soon the stars die, collapse and innumerable white dwarfs are formed. They litter the whole universe. The universe persists forever in this unchanged condition. For ever.

Perhaps astrophysicists can get depressed. At times.

Finally there is the universe of Frank J. Tipler.

As already mentioned, in 1994 Tipler wrote a 'popular' book: *The Physics of Immortality*, in order to spread the good news that we are immortal, that we shall all end up in heaven and that we shall all be resurrected, atom by atom, in the scientifically foreseeable future. His book reads like a who's who in physics, with a rich admixture of ancient and present day theologians and philosophers. Tipler (rightly) assumes that religion is fueled by emotions, while science by reason (or should be), and thanks to his theory (according to him) "the divorce between science and religion, between reason and emotion, is over."[4] His *a prori* assumption is that the sole purpose and motivation for cosmology, and by inference of all science, is to confirm our immortality. I do not contest this thesis. What I find difficult to accept is that he seems to bend the universe to accommodate *his* emotional needs. To me the taste of immortality is a transcendental experience, requiring no scientific confirmation whatever. Frank Tipler obviously attempts to sate his own emotional hunger by intellectual prowess. He might benefit from the biblical story of the Four Horses of the Apocalypse which I review in the chapter on *Universal Laws*. He seems to be riding high on a black horse, flaying the poor beast with a red crop.

A sort of scientific flogging of a black horse.

Nevertheless Tipler is the first to admit that physical eschatology is a very young science.[5] Having said it, he offers us six testable predictions of his Omega Point Theory. Had there been 600, I would have been none the wiser. I have a less than hazy understanding of anyone of them. He does develop, however, 'theological' implications of his theory as pertaining to omnipresence, omniscience and omnipotence[6] and later some others, which I shall endeavor to share with you. Bear in mind that any attempt to simplify or abbreviate Tipler's theory would be a disaster. I recommend all interested parties read the original, and hopefully understand some of it. It might not advance their vision of the universe, but it will do a world of good for Mr. Tipler's bank account.

His vision he called the *Omega Point Theory*.

As near as I can gather in Tipler's 'theo-cosmology' (that's a word I coined to simulate Tipler's attempt to marry theology with cosmology with theoretical quantum-relativistic-physics with theoretical mathematics and philosophy thrown in) he more or less defines God as a computer in the far distant future, which sports infinite memory storage capacity with infinite programming potential. This memory storage would retain information on the activity and characteristics of virtually every single atom throughout the history of the world. This ability to store *all* information, backed up with the program to do so, with whatever He/She (that's the word Tipler uses for the bisexual or androgynous Computer/God) empowers He/She to resurrect us in the far distant future, atom by atom, whether we like it or not. Presently we (you and I) are defined as "life" because we have a certain, albeit minimal, data storage ability, which is situated in our brains. Soon (on the cosmological time scale) we shall be replaced and superseded by computers which will vastly exceed our present computing ability. Nevertheless, this metamorphosis into a nano-technologically-advanced computer will save our lives. We shall construct a biosphere (which will not actually be bio) which will spread all over the cosmos. My own impression is that we (that's again you and I) are little more than holographic projections from a far distant future whence we are in fact all sitting comfortably in heaven.

Will an ameba be eventually resurrected to live happily ever-after? It seems that it will. How? Well, it appears that 'life' will be a little different in the ever-after. In Tipler's vision a copy which cannot be told apart from the original, is the original. He calls such a copy: emulation. But why bother to create such a copy? After all, if you are a Super-program in a Super-computer (that's He/She God) and can at any time in any coordinates create such an entity, than why bother to limit yourself by creating it? You might well continue to enjoy your (theoretical) "life" as memory storage data. You might call it *virtual life*. Tipler argues as follows:

"...an emulation of an entity *is* the entity. An emulated human will be made of emulated human cells, make of emulated molecules, made of emulated atoms, made of emulated electrons, quarks, and gluons. No experiment using any experimental apparatus which will fit inside the visible universe can distinguish between the emulation and the original. The emulation and the original *are* the same."[7] [Tipler's emphases]

Beam me up, Scotty![8]
I do not question that, in time, we shall develop technology to "beam up" our "quantum emulation", a tri-instrument of our consciousness consisting of body, mind and emotions. This will enable our consciousness to find equal expression through equal tri-instrument. What Tipler is missing is that same consciousness can manifest through completely different tri-instruments, as in fact happens in 'real' life (as against the world consisting of physics alone). The case of Sai Baba discussed in the chapter on *Visions* is a point in hand. He described in detail the characteristics of his previous incarnation to such a degree that skeptics gave up on him completely. The emulation of the body is *non sequitur* to the discussion. Emulation of the *spiritual* body is unnecessary since it is immortal. Tipler deals with soul as defined by the Hebrew *nephesh* discussed in the chapter on *Duality* i.e. the repository of memory patterns. He erroneously equates it with *El*, also a Hebraic concept and the only one understood to be of immortal nature. For a physicist to understand the true nature of immortality one would have to invoke the concept of a singularity (a Black Hole) which, by definition, is outside the laws of physics.

Tipler argues that since one cannot tell apart (nor is it theoretically possible to do so) the emulation from the original, i.e. a body with all its appurtenances resurrected from perfect available patterns, the original and the emulation is one. Furthermore, he says that if they act the same way they are the same. I agree completely. The problem is that what Tipler 'resurrects' is not the "human being" but the envelope in, or through, which Soul finds its expression. One cannot play the violin on a piano. The same keyboard is set at Its disposal. Soul can only manifest its Life through the instrument that is available. Thomas Aquinas said that "Whatever is received, is received according to the nature of the recipient." Note that the moment Soul leaves this magnificent original *or* its emulation, it (the emulation) is as dead (inactive) as the pattern from which it will have been "resurrected". A human being, or any animal, or any technological construct is only alive to the extent to which the 'breath' of Life imbues it with Its presence. Whether this breath is biological, electrical, or otherwise is another discussion. I refuse to place limits on Life, or on God. Infinity is not divisible.

Furthermore, the Spirit or the *El* is well capable of recreating an image (perfect emulation) of Its tri-instrument, its body-mind-emotional envelope, even at a considerable distance. Father Pio is an excellent though by no means unique example. Father Pio, better known as Padre Pio, was a Capuchin monk who projected his seemingly "solid body" over vast distances, while remaining in his 'original' body in or near the monastery of San Giovanni Rotondo, near Poggia, Italy. He had been seen as far away from Rotondo as Uruguay, South America.[9] There are many accounts of the monk's bi-locations, all equally as impressive. Among the best known is the case referred to above, when Padre Pio promised Monsignor Damiani that he would visit him, in Uruguay, at the moment of the Monsignor's death. Twenty years later, in 1942, the Archbishop of Montevideo was told by a Capuchin friar to visit the dying Damiani. On arrival at Damiani's deathbed the archbishop found a note saying, "Padre Pio came". Some years later the archbishop visited Italy and met Parde Pio whom he instantly identified as the Capuchin friar who had brought him the news of Damiani's plight. Padre Pio was known not to have left Italy at any time. There are other stories of Padre Pio such as saving a general from suicide,[10] as well as diverse accounts of enigmatic cures experienced by people who swore the Capuchin monk had visited them.

There are many other substantiated bi-locations, among them those of St. Anthony of Padua, Alphonsus Liguori of Arezzo, and Ignatious of Loyola.[11] Neither time nor space nor any laws of quantum mechanics seemed to affect them. All cases were much too well documented to be relegated to hallucinations.

Conversely it could be argued that a single consciousness might manifest itself through completely different bodies. Cases of *possession* are "religious" examples, while in psychiatry there are many well-documented cases of the so-called *split personalities*, wherein different states of consciousness appear to occupy the same body. To reduce man to the sum of his physical components is *reductio ad absurdum*. Those who dismiss the concept that the Whole is greater than the sum of its parts I would describe as reductionists.[12] One wonders, which of the *split personalities* would the reductionists propose to resurrect?

Nevertheless, the author of the Omega Point theory assures us that: "...immortal soul is no longer necessary for individual immortality".[13] Well, you ain't gonna miss what you ain't got. However, the author of the theory seems to forget that the word "individual" comes from Latin word meaning *indivisible*. And what of Christ's assurance that "...whosoever liveth and believeth in me shall never die."[14] Jesus follows these words with a question of his own: "Believest thou this?" Evidently, the modern science (or the scientist in question) does not. Or are we talking about some other sort of life altogether?

Soul is One and indivisible. Soul is an attribute of the Infinite.

What reductionists talk about is personality (a common error), which indeed in *not* immortal and, I am sure they are right when they argue that it could be emulated by future computer machinations. On the same page as the quotation above Tipler confirms my suspicions by the title: "A Later Emulation is Identical to the Original Person." Since the author eliminated immortal Soul, the residual elements must define his concept of a 'person' i.e.: body, mind and emotions, or our tri-instrument *used* by Soul to manifest Life. A very different kettle of fish.

On the one hand, since God has no being other than in a mode of being, the reductionists give God a truly magnificent mode of being. On the other, many will accuse them of trying to sate their emotional desires by creating a physicist's God. I rather think that Einstein was trying to read the mind of God. A reductionist is attempting to create a God whose mind he can read. He offers us a universe in which God, Holy Spirit, Heaven, Resurrection of the body are all mathematical equations. So be it, if that is what makes him or her happy. He might draw freely on the Judeo-Christian scriptures to back up his own vision. Why not? Any half-intelligent man or woman can find quotations in the scriptures to back up almost anything. Look at the Southern Baptists. *Their* "first man" Adam was created "fully blown" in 4004 B.C.; the sun is presumably still rotating around the earth; man and woman are one flesh doubtless like Siamese twins; Jesus is about to descend from heaven to sit on a throne in Jerusalem for a 1000 years—that's any minute now, while the earth will be mostly destroyed in the process. People who live in the past or the future can find substantive texts in all the scriptures of the world to substantiate their drivel. That doesn't make it right.

What is right is living in the present. When you live in the present, you are in the presence of God.

The real problem is that the author discussed has a formidable mind. He doesn't drivel but he does seem to waste his superb analytical ability on theology. Like all brilliant physicists, he deals exclusively with (real or imaginary) effects. It cannot be otherwise. Theologians progress from belief to belief. Physicists from effect to effect. They cannot see the cause for the forest of effects. The entire physical world, the "scientific cosmos" is an effect. It is a shadow cast by God's mind. It is transient, ephemeral, of relatively little consequence. And that is why Tipler is trying, desperately and brilliantly, to make the effect immortal. It is as though he equated the immortality of a Rembrandt painting with Rembrandt himself. But this wouldn't help either! Rembrandt's body, mind, hand, were each as much an instrument of Life, or which Life used, as were the brushes, the canvas or the palettes of oils. The immortal Life that manifested through Rembrandt will remain immortal even if not only Rembrandt but also all his paintings fall into dust.

A vision of infinity is more than a mathematical symbol. The future is more than a chronological projection. The ongoing improvement, 'vertical' amelioration, accumulation of wealth, is not the only way to evolve. It is only the materialist's way. Not the spiritual, or even mental or emotional way. Tipler's "perpetual amelioration"[15] is linear. Always upward towards the single point, the Omega Point.

The universe can expand in different directions.

It can expand laterally. Eternity can be lateral as well as vertical. One can be a wonderful painter who is neither better nor worse than a wonderful sculptor, violinist, healer, astrophysicist. What matters is diversity of life not a vertical trip from dust to riches. No matter now beautiful life becomes in the future it might not match a rose of today. But it might offer a new, fresh beauty. Again, neither better, nor worse. But *just as* beautiful. Beauty is beauty—by any other name. There are no opposites in heaven. There are just diverse expressions of infinite attributes of God. Not of a computer.

Is Tipler wrong?

Not at all. We all create our own universes. It's the name of the game. I hope he'll be happy in his virtual heaven. Or perhaps, he will be virtually happy teaching virtual mathematics in a virtual university. Only he knows for sure—if anyone. And so it should be. The reason why I take so much time discussing his theory is that it epitomizes materiality while usurping the realm of the divine. And it does so brilliantly, with just two major errors. One, he interprets the Bible literally in a truly fundamentalist fashion, and two, his *a priori principle* is wrong: he equates a human being with "mind and body". He is dangerous because he uses his considerable scientific knowledge and, once past the initial errors, superb logic to baffle, stun and convince the less erudite by default.

The quagmire of fundamentalism has been mentioned in the chapter on *Groups and Traditions*. Normally, people who treat the scriptures generally and the Bible in particular literally, are regarded as fundamentalists. I go past such limitations. I propose that anyone who regards matter or anything in the material universe as *real* is also a fundamentalist. Such people know (or should know if they express their views publicly) that the world is not what it seems, but they prefer to lie to themselves and pretend that it isn't so. In the chapter on *Redefining Self*, I shall prove that we, you and I, are mostly empty space. Not by metaphysical trickery, but by the tools offered and developed by the physicists. The same is true of the illusion of the book you hold in your hand. It is less true of a Neutron star, and probably not true only of the heart of a Black Hole. But the universe which you can perceive with your senses, observe and/or measure with the most advanced technological devices, is essentially *empty space*. Or at least empty of matter. Not the space between the stars, but the stars themselves. They are all an illusion. Maya. To ignore this fact is to be a fundamentalist. To believe in that which you know is not true is to be a fundamentalist. To take the Bible literally is only the beginning because it leads directly to duality. The material universe is *by nature* dualistic. Otherwise we would suffer from the extremes of final entropy. We would suffer from complete inertia within the bounds of an absolute zero, a temperature at which no molecular movement, and thus biological life, is possible.

People claim to believe in the 'infinite' God, but they trim God's powers to suit their inability to understand infinity. This problem is particularly pronounced in the principal Western religions: Judaism, Christianity and Islam. All three assign power to both, good *and* evil. They all acclaim that God is one, all merciful, yet... he 'allows' evil to rein. All three religions create a dilemma with their concept of infinity that cannot be solved within a fundamentalist structure.

The foremost Dominican philosopher and theologian St. Thomas Aquinas (1225-74) has exposed a fascinating insight into the Christian philosophical cocktail. His *Summa Theologica* is generally recognized as the greatest work of Christian medieval philosophy. He writes:

"Is seems that God does not exist; because if one of two contraries* be infinite, the other would be altogether destroyed. But the name God means that He is infinite goodness. If, therefore, God existed, there would be no evil discoverable; but there is evil in the world. Therefore God does not exist."[16] [*The contraries of good and evil]

Notwithstanding the above perfectly logical argument, only a few sentences later, St. Thomas proceeds to offer us five proofs for the existence of God, known as the Five Ways. The 'ways' tell that God does, nevertheless, exist. The proofs offered are the argument of *motion*, argument from *efficient causality*, from *possibility and necessity*, from the *degrees of perfection*, and the argument taken from *the order which governs nature*.[17] This evidently overshadows his abortive search for infinity in the dualistic context. The whimsy of the arguments seems to have been lost on his contemporaries.

Notwithstanding the intellectual giants of the past or present, I, in all humility, do not agree with many a Titan of the scientific community (nor with St. Thomas, for that matter). I admire their erudition, imagination, perspicacity and ability to sell an idea. Yet... well, I am not buying. The scientists, as already mentioned, seem to deal only with results. I am concerned with causes. More specifically, the Prime Cause. I do not mean the Big-bang. The big-bang was the result. I am concerned with what no scientist *can* answer. By their own definition, their big-bang originates from the mother of all Black Holes. The original singularity of the universe. They do not know what happened within it. They can't know. It cannot be learned by observation. It does not lend itself to pragmatic experiments or analyses. It can be observed, rather like its microcosmic counterparts, by the trails it left behind. We cannot even speculate on the nature of the original Cosmic Egg; apparently, it is as much a theological as a scientific concept—the Original Source of the *physical* universe. What we can do is to observe how matter and energy behaves in the vicinity of the original singularity's distant echoes, hidden in the Black Holes which, according to Hawking, may be spattered throughout our universe. There are scientific hypotheses that place such Black Holes at the heart of every galaxy. As I mentioned, they cannot be observed because they are, by definition, black. Not just to the visible spectrum but to other forms of radiation. Due to their gargantuan gravity no form of light escapes them.[18] They are chunks of infinity suspended in space. They may be more numerous than the visible stars in our galaxy.[19] Fragments of mystery dotting the infinitude all around us. They swallow matter and make it disappear. They clean up the universe from all unwanted debris. They are the opposite of creation. And yet? What happens, ultimately, with their insatiable appetites? When this question is answered we shall know also how the universe came, and continues to come into being.

The concept of infinity continues to occupy great minds to this day. A British philosopher and mathematician Bertrand Russell teases us with, what he called, the Tristram Shandy paradox. When Shandy set out to write his autobiography, it took him two years to describe the events of his first two days. He complained that the material accumulated at a faster rate than he could write it down. Russell showed that, if Shandy were immortal, no part of his autobiography would remain unwritten.

Such are the paradoxes of 'linear' infinity. And yet the mathematicians insist on linear reasoning.[20] Spiritual perception is holistic: it embraces All simultaneously. It does not chop the universe into tiny pieces, quanta, even as we do not admire a beautiful woman by analyzing her molecules. We are concerned with images, perceptions, with *visions*. To this end we are admonished to be like little children,[21] who are capable of holistic perception, at least up to the point when parents break up their 'gestält' vision into, what Chopra calls, a linguistically structured communication.[22]

Mathematicians, physicists and other scientists deny us this privilege. It is, again, because they are concerned with results—not with cause.

Another concept of infinity that preoccupied the human mind throughout history is heaven. Again, the fundamentalists of all Western religions acknowledge heaven as a *place*, probably in the far distant future. They seem completely oblivious to Christ's assurances that heaven is a state of consciousness, here-and-now.[23] Likewise, they find it convenient to forget that the Roman Catholic Church only invented the resurrection of the body in the 7th century. Before that time, the Latin creed read: the resurrection of the *dead*. Dead, in Christ's idiom, always symbolizes a state of consciousness: "he who believeth in me, though he were dead, yet shall he live."[24] Not one day in heaven, but right now. Today. This minute.

There are a number of aspects of infinity that will affect our efforts of visualizing our own, personal universes. The physical universe reflects but one part of our nature. The other that gnaws at the human entrails is the concept of immortality. Not of the universe, but our own. Yours and mine.

At the individual level, cyclic theories are reflected in the concept of reincarnation. The idea is as old as the world itself.

I do not question Tipler's expertise as a physicist. Nor do I wish to cast doubt on Theilhard de Chardin's good intentions. Tipler obviously rides with the best in his field. The problem with Tipler and de Chardin on whom, with some apparent anguish, he styles (amid ardent denials) his philosophy, is that they both visualize a far, far distant future in which we shall all unite in a mega-organism—Omega Point—via a sort of biospheric Noosphere. This is Science Fiction in reverse. They both start with the end product, and then look for a way to back them up their visions, with either arguments or intricate calculations. It is my contention that we are and always have been a single "organism". A single Entity, if you like. What is evolving is our awareness of this fact. One might suggest that our being is and always remained within the Cosmic Egg, an incomprehensible Singularity, and the expanding universe is an expression of Our expanding consciousness through the process of individualization. The breath of Brahma has no other purpose then has a dawning of a morn. To rise and shine, to gather experience, to *live*. I shall reveal a mystery though it was never really obscured, never intended to be hidden from our understanding:

THERE IS NO PURPOSE TO LIFE
OTHER THAN LIFE ITSELF.

Life is the purpose in Itself. Any attempt to read into Life a purpose other than the act of being leads to an inevitable disenchantment. Steven Weinberg, the Nobel Prize winning physicist wrote: "The more the universe seems comprehensible, the more it also seems pointless..."[25] This is the consequence of looking for a purpose, or an end, in that which is Infinite. By definition, the Infinite has no end. It is the Potential in Being, and the Bliss of Becoming that makes us what we are.

We are the manifestation of Life Itself.

When Jesus tried to explain this fact to his illiterate audience, apparently as illiterate as many Christians appear to be today, he said: *I am Life*. It is the identification with not just the Potential but *with the Process Itself* that unravels the philosopher's stone. Jesus continued to say that he who believes in this simple fact shall never die. And until he believes, it is as thought he were (still) dead. But if one loses touch with this knowledge and then rediscovers it, if one becomes aware *again* of this simple truth, he or she shall live *again*. Resurrection was always intended to mean just that. To rise from a dead state into life. To live again. After all, no one can really die. We are immortal.

We are gods.

"Nothing is hidden that shall not be made clear".[26] The only problem is that of allowing new wine to enter our awareness. That is all. After all, our true being is within the Singularity. It is beyond time and space, or time—space, and thus beyond being born or dying. We are not eternal because we shall never die, but because we were never born. We are an individualization of a Single Consciousness, the eternal, unchangeable Omega Point, which IS. The Infinity in which we find our true being is not measured in duration or in light-years, or even in mathematical equations.

It is experienced in the Eternal Present.

As we grow in awareness of this truth, we approach our own, personal, individual Omega Points. Again, I repeat, the Omega Point IS. It is not becoming. We are becoming. We are becoming aware of our true nature.

We are Life.

In spite of all of the above, other hypotheses persist.

There is one pertaining to the concept of resurrection which is supported by scientists who, in the interest of science, accept the ultimate concept of a cyclic universe. This hypothesis partially supported by many ancient religions and presently by the oscillating universe theory (big bang—big crunch) holds that time, like everything else, is subject to reversal. Under such conditions, the cannibal will release the atoms of the priest from his entrails, to form a perfectly good—pre-eaten clergyman. In other words, wherever the atoms of the dearly departed are, including those who departed some billions of years ago, will be resurrected. Speaking for myself, I have absolutely no desire to "ease back" into my body, and eventually into my mother's womb. A real reversal of time would also entail a reversal of all identical events. The horror of this concept led Nietzsche to his aberrant philosophy.

***

My own concept of evolution comes in two parts. There is an evolution of an individualized consciousness that is *reflected* in the evolution of matter or the universe. In the strictest sense the two are one. The first is the cause, the latter—the result. The result, is all that the scientist can study. Apparently unbeknownst to them, they also embody both, the cause and the result. This is the duality of our nature in the material universe. Not our true nature, but that nature with which we choose to identify—for now. The scientists visualize nature in her plethora of biological life forms, in the unfolding of the cosmos, in the ever-present cycles. The *effect* of the creative process is their sole reality. Their ideas remain subjective until such a time as a critical mass of people becomes informed and then the theory becomes objective. An objective reality, a reality shared by a number of people, nevertheless, may well change, when a better idea occurs to someone who allows it to run its course of becoming objective. Under such circumstances I am convinced that nature or spirit, or life (guided by an ever higher awareness) would discard the human body if it found a better organism into which to embody itself. I found support for this thesis from quite unexpected quarters. Charles Darwin in his *Origin of Species* (1860) writes:

"Judging from the past, we may safely infer that not one living species will transmit its unaltered likeness to a distant futurity."

David Raup strengthens this hypothesis by affirming that not one in a thousand of all the species that evolved on Earth still exists.[27] Joseph Pearce even questions our brain capacity as an aid to survival: "Our enormous brain is not a 'survival mechanism.' The cockroach is far older than man, obviously 'better adapted', and will probably be around long after we are gone."[28] It would be foolish indeed to identify even with such a magnificent animal as we embody, as our true being. What if the next month, or next year, a meteorite changes our climate by, say, twenty degrees either way. Do you imagine that the human specie would survive? And what of God? Would He or She or It die with us? A student of esoteric Buddhism was asked by his master, what did he visualize he became during his last meditation. "A rock," the student replied. "It is not a bad way to be," said his master. The master knew the *true* nature of his student. He knew that any form of becoming is a transient state.

As I shall repeat many times throughout this book, we must decide not only what we are, but also *who* we are. We must discover our quintessential nature. Until we do, we remain part of the effect. So far most of us believe that we are men and women endowed with a soul. In the chapter on *Aging and Longevity*, we shall learn that we are (also?) a

mass of swirling atoms, micro-universes of energy and information.
Or are we more than either?

***

FOOTNOTES

(1). Who later discarded his own long-held steady-state theory.

(2). The cosmological longevity of 20 billion years assigned by astronomers is banal to say the least. It is directly related to the 'visible' universe, or determined by our ability of seeing the most distant galaxies receding from us. The latest proposals threaten to increase our telescopic efficiency to 13 billion light-years, i.e. to increase the diameter and therefore the lifespan of the universe to some 26 billion years. I'm sure the time and the diameter will expand in due course.

(3). It takes billions of years for the distance between galaxies to double. Time enough, writes Isaac Asimov in THE UNIVERSE (Penguin Books 1971) for "matter to be created at the rate of one atom of hydrogen per year in a billion liters of space, and such a rate of creation would be far too small to be detectable by any instruments we possess."

(4). Tipler, Frank J., THE PHYSICS OF IMMORTALITY, (Anchor Book, Doubleday, New York 1994) pg.338.

(5). ibid. page 146.

(6). ibid. pages 153-4.

(7). ibid. page 223.

(8). The method of recreating a complete human being from patterns is not Tipler's invention. It has been the favored method of transportation over a number of years on countless TV episodes called *Startrek* and the *Startrek Next Generation*. Both series were confined to science-fiction. Scotty was the chief engineer on the starship Enterprise, and an adept at using the 'transporter'.

(9). Greenhouse, Herbert B., THE ASTRAL JOURNEY, (Avon Books, New York, 1976) page 74.

(10). Spencer, John and Anne: WORLD'S GREATEST UNSOLVED MYSTERIES, (Headline Book, London) page 55 *et seq*.

(11). Greenhouse, ibid. page 72-73

(12). The author readily claims the title for himself if defining it, roughly, as one capable of describing all physical phenomena... by physics. Tipler, ibid. page 294.

(13). Tipler, ibid. page 235

(14). John 10:26.

(15). Tipler, ibid. page 217

(16). Aquinas, St. Thomas, SUMMA THEOLOGICA, Part 1, Question 2.

(17). ibid, Part 1, question 2, answer 3. Gleamed from CATHOLICISM Edited by George Brantl, (George Braziller, New York 1962) pages 30-32.

(18). Hawking, Stephen, W., BRIEF HISTORY OF TIME (Bantam

Books1988). Hawking proposes that "black holes are not really black after all: they glow like a hot body, and the smaller they are, the more they glow; page 97.

(19). ibid., pg. 95.

(20). Tipler, (ibid. page 248-9) describes another tidbit from a German mathematician David Hilbert called Hilbeta's Hotel. The hotel has an infinite number of rooms, all occupied. When another guest arrives, the clerk offers to put the new arrival in room 1, by moving the present occupant to room 2, the one from room 2 to room 3, and so forth. When 100 new guests arrive, he offers them the first 100 rooms, by moving the present occupants by 100 numbers each. Then as an infinite number of new guests arrive, he puts the first person into room 1 by moving the present occupier to room 2. The person from room 2 he puts into room 4, the person from room 3 into room 6, and so forth, thus freeing all the odd room numbers. Infinity takes a long time to fill.

(21). Matthew 18:3

(22). Chopra, Deepak AGELESS BODY, TIMELESS MIND (Harmony Books, div. of Crown Publ.)

(23). Luke 17:21; The Gospel According to Thomas, logion 3.

(24). John 11:25

(25). Weinberg, Steven THE FIRST THREE MINUTES (Basic Books, New York 1977) page 154.

(26). Matthew 10:26; Mark 4:22; Luke 8:17, 12:2, et al.

(27). Raup, David M.: EXTINCTION: BAD GENES OR BAD LUCK? (Norton, New York 1991)

(28). Pearce, Joseph Chilton EXPLORING THE CRACK IN THE COSMIC EGG (Washington Square Press, Pocket Books 1975) page 65.

Chapter 9
Apports and other Phenomena

"The higher one climbs on the spiritual ladder, the more they will grant others their own freedom, and give less interference to another's state of consciousness."

Paul Twitchell

Within the growing field of research known as Extrasensory Perception, there is one peripheral contingency which is of great interest to the students of reality, particularly as it bears on the subject of the creation of one's own universe. This fascinating application of the creative energy is a process called Apports.

The word 'apport' comes to us from Latin via the French language *apporter* meaning *to bring*. The *Encyclopedia of the World's Greatest Unsolved Mysteries* defines apports as "the spontaneous materialization of objects without known origin". The Oxford Dictionary prefers: "production of material objects by supposedly occult means at spiritualist séance; objects thus produced". The Webster Dictionary refuses to commit itself. Not surprisingly. After all, hundreds if not thousands of witnesses gathered randomly in the open air can hardly be described as a "spiritual séance". Yet we are dealing with just such cases.

For many years we had no idea how the prophet of Nazareth managed to materialize food to feed thousands of people from—apparently—thin air. Our forefathers have been so baffled by such feats (not to mention other 'miracles') that they promptly defined Jesus' traits as divine and declared him God. The fact that Jesus himself never claimed such unique distinction is beside the point.[1] Considering the circumstances, such reaction is hardly surprising.

In recent years, with vastly improved methods of communication, of printing and distribution of information, it has transpired that Jesus was not alone in these particular abilities. A Hindu saint known as Sai Baba is said to have apported enough food to feed hundreds of people (at a time) "including hot foods and sticky, honey-like substance called *amrith*."[2] To me, this substance is reminiscent of manna, served at the instigation of Moses to the Hebrews in the wilderness some 3000 years earlier. That Sai Baba (Sai means saint, Baba—father, the name he adopted from his previous incarnation) apported or manifested from thin air countless other articles including jewelry such as gold rings and statues, $100 bills (US), photographs and images of himself and particularly a "healing ash" called *vibhuti* is beside the point. What is of interest to us here is his method. When asked how he managed such feats he replied that he imagined or visualized the objects and then brought them out from a place where they already existed. One can but wander if this is the technique that Jesus employed some 2000 years ago. Baba did affirm, however, that the process required power from God. While it is not my intention to minimize Baba's power nor God's intervention, I always held that *all* power we use originates with or from God. To me, there never was any other source. I doubt that Sai Baba would contradict my contention.

A scientist, Professor Arthur Elison, offers this opinion of Sai Baba: "I really do think that Sai Baba understands the nature of physical reality and he can alter his thought forms wherever he wishes, and does so".[3] I repeat that what is important to us is neither the frequency of apportation (witnessed by the vast majority of his visitors), nor the objects which appear out of thin air, but the *technique* of apportation on which Sai Baba sheds light. It is evident that visualization is the imperative ingredient necessary to alter reality, as we know it. There is ample evidence that reality can and has been altered throughout the ages. Reports of apports were not limited to Moses, Jesus nor Hindu saints, but have been extensively reported on over the years. While the ability is not common, John and Ann Spencer offer examples of Mrs. Agnes Guppy (formerly Agnes Nichols), a British medium, apporting a variety of objects and large numbers of flowers, including a six-foot sunflower which appeared out of nowhere on the table in front of her, "complete with roots and clods of earth". A French medium, Madame Elizabeth D'Esperant is said to have apported a golden lily some seven feet tall.[4]

Our concern is with the how.

There is one particular Sai Baba story which sheds more light on the possible technique or perhaps the 'logistics' of apports than any other. I found it on the Internet which offers hundreds of sites dedicated to Sai Baba. The story concerns the apportation of a Rolex watch. Apparently an Australian skeptic wanted to catch Sai Baba on a slight of hand. Since Sai Baba normally asks the devotee what he or she would like him to manifest, the Australian knowing that all Rolex watches carry an exclusive serial number, asked for such a watch. With the usual wave of his hand, Sai Baba offered him one. On his return home, the Australian traced, by the serial number, the store in which the watch had been purchased. He then asked the owner of the store if he remembered when the watch had been bought. The owner replied that he kept accurate records, and anyway, he could hardly forget. It is not often that he sold Rolexes to Indian gentlemen clad in orange robes and sporting oversized fuzzy hair. A fairly exact if unique description of Sai Baba's appearance.

The Rolex watch had been purchased *on the exact day and at the exact time* it was manifested or apported for the Australian visitor in India. Sai Baba had been present, simultaneously, in two places at the same time. It seems clear that apports and bi-locations also discussed in the chapter on *Visualizing Infinity* are incontrovertibly connected. Once we accept one, the other seems less miraculous. And vice-versa.

***

Some advocate that the ancient/modern evidence of apports should be examined in the same light as various aspects of extra-sensory perception (ESP). If we choose to follow this route, we might bear in mind the inimitable observation of Joseph Pearce: "An extrasensory perception is no more 'extra' than any symbolic formation. It simply generates at a further step removed from ego awareness."[5] More about the ego versus the universal awareness later.

Llyal Watson in his intriguing book *Lifetide* notes that "Paranormal phenomena are part of the normal repertoire of human behavior and can be produced on demand, at will, given the right circumstances. Anyone can learn."[6] While I rejoice in Dr. Watson's assurances, I find that paranormal activity does not seem to find laboratory conditions the "right circumstances". Yet, there is a growing body of literature on the paranormal and related subjects, pressing with growing resolve against the sacrosanct envelope of the scientific establishment. It is only a question of time before the bastions of pragmatic science will tumble under the sheer weight of evidence supporting the so called 'paranormal'.

To illustrate the scope and diversity of related subjects, I list a few of them:
Altered States of Consciousness in which subjects lose all sensation of time and seem capable of performing feats otherwise deemed impossible. *Auras* that surround all living matter including humans, animals, plants and trees. There is evidence that with practice most of us can learn to detect these. *Automatic Writing* which is a name given to the ability some people have to 'channel' prose and poetry of unknown

origin. These writings are usually characterized by inspirational nature and are often written in characters and/or writing style different from those normally used by the exponent.

Next we have the whole range of *Crisis Apparitions* so called because they are normally associated with some crisis, such as visual messages received from people far away at the moment of their death. A book by E. Gurney, F.W.H. Mayers and R. Podmore titled *Phantasms of the Living* (published in 1886) lists 701 accounts of such occurrences.

Then we have a broad range of paranormal disciplines connected with health and healing. They include *Crystals* which are said to have healing, calming, stimulating and protective powers. They are also used in divination, dowsing, and in the enhancement of psychic powers. In her book on *Healing Energies*,[7] in the chapter on New-Age therapies Mary Coddington lists Acupuncture, T'ai-Chi and Acupressure, all three designed to stimulate the flow of the life force *Chi*; Reflexology (practiced for some 5000 years in China); Reichian *Therapeutics* which according to the psychiatrist and natural scientist Wilhelm Reich utilizes *orgon* energy, "a mass-free primordial power that operates throughout the universe as the basic life force."[8] *Chi*, or *ki* in Japan, appears to corresponds to the Hindu *prana*, the Reich's *orgone*, the Ba Sothos' *moya,* the Hebrew's *neshamah* or *ruach*, the Greek's *pneuma* or the Christian's spirit; Coddington also lists *Transcendental Meditation* which, as shall be discussed in a later chapter on *Relaxation*, appears to have considerable influence on our metabolism at the cellular level. These energies, or perhaps better said: this energy under any other name is recognized by neither science nor by the proponents of the so-called standard medicine.

Continuing with the list, there are the *Doubles and Doppelgängers* which have been extensively recorded in literature. These deal with the apparitions of living (as against dead) people. They may have some connection with bi-locations (also discussed in the chapter of *Visualizing Infinity)* and with the Out-of-body-experiences (the OBEs). Herbert Greenhouse discusses the latter at length in his book on astral projection.[9]

And then we have multiple reports on *Dowsing* (including map dowsing), reputedly invaluable in searching for water, minerals and precious metals; it is also known to have been used by healers to identify areas in patients body requiring treatment.

Other witnesses testified on seeing *Ectoplasm*—a vaporous substance exuding from a medium and assuming various shapes. There are also many recorded cases, recognized by various church authorities, requiring *Exorcism*. Elsewhere we read of medically inexplicable cases of *Firewalking* witnessed and photographed by thousands of people in India and elsewhere; of numerous *Ghostly* appearances apparently determined to aid or deter people in need; of multiple cases of *Incorruptibility* of corpses over long periods of time; of fantastic feats of strength or equally baffling ventures into memory recall under *Hypnosis*.

We read of various forms of *Mediumship* for whatever purpose; of inscrutable omens often indicative of foreboding events in the future; of mischievous and noisy *Poltergeists*; of demonic and angelic *Possessions*; of psychic and spiritual *Healing*.

There are a great many reports by advocates and skeptics alike, dealing with psychokinetic (PK) powers ranging from theatrical performances of dubious veracity to controlled experiments by J.B. Rhine at Duke University in North Carolina. The Criminal Investigation Departments (CIDs) throughout the world use, or surreptitiously try to employ, people gifted with *Psychometric* ability in their police work. Psychometry consists of the ability (of a medium) to determine at a distance the future or present location or the activity or condition of a person by holding an object which used to be in the missing person's possession.

And then we hear of the mind-boggling *Savant*

Syndrome.

Men or women of relatively low intelligence (IQ of 40 to 70) are able to perform extraordinarily complex mathematical calculations almost instantaneously in their head, or name the day of the week of any date hundreds or thousands (sic) of years into the past or future. We also hear of *Shamans* who are the modern-day sorcerers among the native people from Alaska to Hawaii, to Siberia to Australia to the inaccessible crags of Tibet.

And then there are the *Stigmata*. According to John and Ann Spencer, there are an estimated 300 people, from St. Francis to the present day Padre Pio who carry the marks of the suffering of Jesus Christ. The medical profession can neither cure them nor explain them. And finally we have literally countless documented cases of Telepathy, Clairvoyance, Clairaudience, in addition to Apports and Bi-locations discussed previously.

To mention but a few...

***

The field of the paranormal would increase greatly if we were to include in it the whole range of UFO sightings and associated experiences; Crop Circles seemingly appearing out of nowhere, particularly in Southern England; a variety of religious experiences including weeping Madonnas and other lachrymose statues; an assortment of hexes, jinxes, voodoos, charms and enchantments, spells, evil-eyes and assorted cauldrons of black and white magic. People who find such matters of interest can consult the Encyclopedia of the World Greatest Unsolved Mysteries and a number of other books in your local bookstores.[10]

We all live in subjective universes. The truth for one is hysteria to another.

The range of reported paranormal cases increases as people shed their fear of ridicule by reporting on their personal experiences. Many ESP phenomena, Lourdes and

Fatima come to mind, are repeatedly witnessed by vast crowds of people. Yet the scientific establishment regards none of these events as anything other than hysteria or hallucination. This ostrich syndrome reminds me of a contemporary of Galileo, a man named Cesare Cremonini, who refused to look through Galileo's telescope because he *knew from pure reason* that whatever Galileo claims to have seen through his instrument was just a hallucination. For the same reason Cremonini dismissed all the mathematical support of Galileo's claims. All this would have been of no consequence if it weren't for the fact that Cremonini had been Galileo's senior at the University of Padua.

So much for 'pure' science.

As discussed above, apports deal with the production or manifestation of something out of "nothing". I say this because, in terms of scientific reality, anything which cannot be looked at through either end of a telescope (or other inept instrumentation) does not exist. At our present evolutionary level, our science does and can only deal with the manifested universe. After all, it is the only universe which, as of now, lends itself to pragmatic testing. Furthermore, until such a time as even the observable data can be tested they remain in the realm of hypotheses or theories. And even then the 'proven' data or events remain 'real' only as long as they are not disproved by a new theory.

It sounds very much like the Wheel of Awagawan.[11]

We create a universe, we test it within the present limitations of our science. The universe changes and we start all over again. In case of astrophysics we observe that which took place some billions of years ago. The nearest cluster of galaxies, the Virgo cluster, is 60 million light-years away. Since, however most cosmologists hold that the universe came into being some 20 billion years ago, and since nothing can travel faster than light, it is normally assumed that the visible universe is about 20 billion light-years in diameter. We have no way of knowing what happens at the heart of distant galaxies today. We don't even know much about the hub of our own Milky Way.

However, science and metaphysics do agree on one premise. Even as "nature abhors a vacuum" so apparently does God, and thus we accept that He/She is Omnipresent. In this context apports are not manifestations of something out of 'nothing', but, at the very least, out of fields not as yet tested (nor discovered) by science. Notwithstanding healthy opposition from physicists or professional skeptics, many apports have been well documented—even as some six billion reincarnated people populate the earth, each endowed with *invisible* minds, *immeasurable* emotions, often *unpredictable* desires, and mostly *unexplained* dreams—this moment. Soon, barring cataclysmic events, which hordes of psychics continue to predict with such passion, there will be many more of us.

As a species, we seem to put quantity ahead of quality.

All theories considered, it seems a viable hypothesis that the paranormal or extrasensory manifestations take up the middle ground between physics and metaphysics. I would also agree with the recent statements of a number of illustrious physicists that metaphysics will soon be incorporated into the field of physics, though in my view in order for this to happen, the meeting ground shall be in the middle. It could be, for instance, that the next step beyond the string theory, there will be a field called the "omnipresent spirit". I look forward to pouring over completely incomprehensible (to me) spiritual equations attached to philosophical dissertations as "Appendices for Scientists". Those equations shall prove beyond refutable doubt that Spirit is the final and only Unified Field.

***

FOOTNOTES

(1). John 10:34, Psalm 82:6

(2). In the absence of a dictionary definition, I take the liberty to augment the word 'apport' into its kindred forms. Thus I use liberally apport, apported, apporting, as well as apportation etc..

(3). Spencer, John and Anne, WORLD'S GREATEST UNSOLVED MYSTERIES (Headline Book) pg.27

(4). Spencer, ibid page 25.

(5). Pearce, Joseph Chilton: EXPLORING THE CRACK IN THE COSMIC EGG, Washington Square Press 1974; pg.159.

(6). Watson, Lyall LIFETIDE (Coronet Books, Hodder and Stoughton 1979) page 336.

(7). Coddington, Mary, IN SEARCH OF THE HEALING ENERGY, (Warner 1978)

(8). ibid., page 113.

(9). Greenhouse, Herbert B., THE ASTRAL JOURNEY, (Avon Books, New York, 1976)

(10). Spencer, John and Anne: THE ENCYCLOPEDIA OF THE WORLD'S GREATEST UNSOLVED MYSTERIES, (Headline Book, London 1995)

(11). The Wheel of Awagawan can be regarded as walking in circles, or the Sisyphean labours. Those espousing the concept of transmigration of souls claim that during the 8,400,000 reincarnations, only the human form gives us an opportunity to end the cycle and return 'home'.

THE PROCESS

Chapter 10
Universal Laws and Chaos

*Extrasensory perception is no more extra
than any symbolic formation.
It simply generates at a further step removed
from ego awareness.*

Joseph Chilton Pearce

We saw in *Myths and Reality* that our forefathers had been very aware that there are Laws governing our universe, which are as indomitable as taxes. While the ancients differed on the precise nature of those Laws none denied that without them the world would be in a state of Chaos. Some say that Life is the force which brings order to Chaos. It seems evident that the withdrawal of life-force reverts the elements involved to their original state. Therefore we must also discuss the nature of this "original state" to which we shall refer as the state of Chaos.

Nevertheless, the ancients held that it is the Law which is of permanent nature, not that which it controls. Hence the scriptural statement that "Heaven and earth will pass away, but my words shall not pass away"[1] is not a religious avocation, but a statement of fact, particularly as pertaining to the material universe. Later review will also show us that even as the physical universe is controlled by its indomitable laws, so are the realms dealing with our emotions and our minds. It may be wise, therefore, if we agree to address those realms as our physical, emotional, mental and spiritual universes. They might be said to correspond to our physical, emotional, mental and spiritual bodies. The biblical version of this subdivision is discussed in a later chapter entitled *Redefining Self*.

Later we shall also learn that the four realities are co-extant, that they share the same spacetime, with the exception of the spiritual realm, which is beyond not only time and space, but beyond any laws whatsoever. In the spiritual universe freedom reigns supreme. To correspond to this thesis, our four bodies can also be regarded as aspects of our nature, as our attributes, rather as described in the Revelations of St. John, in the chapter dealing with the so called four horses of the Apocalypse. We shall review St. John's 'analysis' later in this chapter.

In the meantime, let us return to the universal laws.

As mentioned, each universe (the physical, emotional, and mental) must conform to its own laws. Although the higher realms control the lower ones, they are never in contradiction to those below, but rather offer a higher understanding of the corresponding laws. This analogy can be illustrated by the difference between the Euclidean and Einsteinian geometries. Around 300 B.C., the Greek mathematician named Euclid formulated a collection of postulates, rules and theorems which form the basis of geometry we use to this day. Among other postulates the Euclidian geometry holds that the shortest distance between two point is a straight line. Some twenty-two centuries later, Albert Einstein had proven that this distance is shorter if measured along a curve. Both scientists are right. It is so because Euclid deals with flat plains whereas Einstein dabbles with the enormity of space wherein the curvature of space (the result of gravitational forces) comes into play. To an architect, Einstein's geometry would be of little use, as would be Euclidian to a galactic astronaut. Both geometries are right within the parameters of their particular context.

The same is true of laws governing the physical, emotional and mental realms.

To illustrate the point further, it is of absolutely no use praying (invoking universal forces or God) to obtain, for instance, good health, if we simultaneously continue to overeat, smoke like a chimney and lead a physically stagnant, sedentary life. Physical health of our physical bodies is subject to *physical* laws, and any tampering with them will only give very temporary relief. I have been asked if the many healing miracles attributed to Jesus, and presently to Sai Baba, are lasting. The answer would only make sense if one would define the word miracle, but at any rate it would depend whether the "miracle-worker" were to heal the physical, emotional or the mental body. If only the physical, the hapless body would obviously soon revert to its previous condition. It would be equivalent to healing the symptom, not the cause of the disease.

There is a reported case of a concerned wife procuring a healing from Sai Baba for her husband, who, hundreds of miles away, suffered from final degenerative stages of cancer. Sai Baba's knowledge of the universal laws brought about instant cure (remission). Following the 'miraculous' healing, the man had been examined by the best physicians of standard medicine and pronounced in perfectly good health. He died a little over a year later of the same disease. Obviously whatever had been the *cause* of the cancer, had not been eliminated. The cause may have been excessive stress, worry about one's job or assumed responsibilities, anxiety regarding results of one's labor rather than joyous participation in the 'process' of living. All dis-eases are ultimately the consequences of 'errors' we commit in higher realms. Religions call these 'sins', whereas they are simply mistakes. The symptoms may also mean that we are doing our job well, but there is still a better way. That we are still missing the mark. Or marks. Our personal best. We are incarnated here to learn, and dis-ease is a welcome sign that we are doing something wrong.

The miracle-makers will seldom tamper with the laws of the higher realms. They might infringe on the universal laws. When Jesus healed someone he had been reported to have said: "...sin no more, lest a worse thing come unto thee",[2] meaning, do not continue in the same vein or you will pay a similar *or higher* price. Thus, in answer to the original question regarding the permanency of physical cures, I know of no reports of any people, men or women, healed by Jesus, Sai Baba, or anyone else, becoming immortal. When the laws are broken, chaos ensues. And one of the characteristics of chaos is (controlled) disorder. And dis-order causes dis-ease. [Even as harmony and order are the precursors of health and beauty].

Total withdrawal of order or Lifeforce means death. Physical death.

Lifeforce thrives on complexity. The greater the complexity the greater the intensity of Lifeforce manifested. The opposite is also true. People of minimal mental acumen manifest relatively little Lifeforce. It is as though they were only half-alive. This is because the Lifeforce thrives not only on physical complexity but on emotional and mental attributes as well. Great minds are vibrantly alive. The great physicist Stephen Hawking, whose physical body is and has been paralyzed for many years, is so alive mentally that when his computerized voice synthesizer "speaks", others hang on his every word. The *Time* magazine reported: "Even as he [Hawking] sits helpless in his wheelchair, his mind seems to soar ever more brilliantly across the vastness of space and time to unlock the secrets of the universe". Professor

Hawking's mental body is throbbing with effulgence of life.

Countless others, in "perfect" physical health, can hardly read or write, let alone contribute a creative thought to humanity. One must ask oneself who is more alive? The proficient use of the complexity of human mind attests more to the presence of Lifeforce than any degree of physical dexterity. The complexity of the mind vastly supersedes the complexity of the body. In a general sense, it can be said that the mind is the cause, the body the effect. It is the mind that is instrumental in providing us with an awareness of order, and thus harmony and beauty. It also gives us awareness of the diversity of creation resulting from unbounded discernment of differentiation.

At the other extreme of beauty and order we find chaos.

Chaos, Greek word meaning "empty space", is therefore a state where there is relatively little differentiation. Webster Dictionary offers also this definition: "a mixed mass without a due form or order; confusion." I might add that the "emptiness" applies to the "practical absence" of universal laws, which though omnipresent, have not as yet come into play (or have been partially withdrawn). During the last few decades, the chaologists have rewritten our understanding of chaos, of the 'empty' space. It seems that Einstein was right again. There is no void. Neither at the physical nor at the mental or even emotional realm. There is evidence that 'chaos' is replete with patterns within patterns, with endless probabilities, enchanting predispositions. It seems that chaos tends towards the *unpredictable* state of order. There is a new branch of science which concerns itself with *fractals* which may be said to embrace the study of patterns within chaos. It also opens a new way of looking at art, at nature, at all aspects of science.[3] It shows that within chaos there is an inherent propensity towards symmetry in diversity. In fact, chaos seems to harbor an Infinite Potential of Possibilities. Rather like Dr. Chopra's definition of heaven or the Unified Field, or even God.

Why? One reason is because chaos is by definition unpredictable. So is God.

But it is an *unmanifested* potential. A potential in a state of search, a constant search for a mode of being. It is as though chaos was filled with sublime desire to become orderly. It is up to the Lifeforce which *we* manifest that the potential becomes realized. We are the means through which chaos becomes order.

In biological life the condition of chaos applies to both matter and energy. Lifeforce arranges the potential inherent in chaos into infinite modes of order. When *order* is disturbed (mostly by the withdrawal of Lifeforce as in the case of a disease), matter tends to revert to its previous (potential) state. In common English this process is known as the tendency towards rotting, decaying, breaking down, corrupting, crumbling, or just degeneration. Some of these adjectives have been adopted by the medical profession. In physics this same trend is called entropy which is the measure of the degree of *disorder* in a substance or a system. Within our universe, entropy increases as the available energy decreases. This is based on the assumption that our universe is a closed system.

But thanks to our chaologists, we shall never again regard chaos as void, nor as confusion, clutter, or disarray without rhyme or reason. We draw our infinite diversity from chaos. And more than anything, the infant science of chaology proves that God in Its potential mode is Omnipresent, even as are aspects of chaos.

Whatever we may believe regarding particular characteristics of the universe, we must accept that it is subject to indomitable laws. If we do not learn them, we shall not advance very far in our evolution. We shall continue to walk in ever diminishing circles, die, be born again, and again, to resume our circular journey, ultimately to be reabsorbed in the ever-open arms of Chaos. We shall be recycled. To continue, to be immortal, we needn't do anything. To be *aware* of our continuity, our immortality, we must learn the Laws. It is to those Laws Einstein referred when he said: "I want to know how God created this world. ....I want to know His thoughts; the rest are details."

Any attempts to create our own universe in opposition or contradiction to the universal laws will meet with failure. Our universe might waver on the periphery of reality for an insignificant while and then collapse, even as a star collapses upon itself, when its usefulness had been exhausted. The study of laws controlling the physical, emotional and mental worlds is the prerequisite of all aspiring gods-in-wanting. Ignorance is *not* bliss. It is a blueprint for disaster. In fact, countless if not all disasters are caused by people attempting to bypass the fundamental laws. Such action punishes the participant and often the ignorant bystanders. For ignorance is *not* an excuse for breaking the Law. It never was, never will be.

According to Sai Baba, there is but one Law, the Law of Karma. If it is so, then this single universal Law applies differently in each of the three universes.

Inasmuch as we wield influence over the state of our subjective realities, our physical body can be said to be the measure of success of our material universe. Its condition, its 'wholeness' is the yardstick by which we can determine whether we are using our physical consciousness the right way. I wonder how many of us are aware that the word 'holy' refers to wholeness. Completeness. The word has since been 'religionized' to assume esoteric connotations. We are offered Holy Ghost, Holy Mother, Holy Father, and Holy Bible. In this context the word holy means sacred, consecrated, set apart for God. We forget, perhaps, that in 1815, the rulers of Russia, Austria and Prussia had formed a *Holy* Alliance to suppress the democratic revolutionary movement in Europe.

Not all that's holy is holy...

...unless we revert to the original meaning. To be healthy is to be holy. To be holy is to be complete. To be complete is to maintain a state of balance which results in a state of order, harmony and beauty. And if we obey the universal laws there is no reason why we should not manifest these traits. It may take a while. The physical universe is just as much subject to karma as the other two. If we inherit 'bad' genes, it is not because our father had disobeyed the laws of nature—but *we* have, in *our* previous life. And if our father (or mother) displays the same or similar physical 'imperfections' it is only because *we* have chosen to incarnate ourselves within an environment in which it will be easier for us to overcome our own shortcomings. Misery likes company. The method of turning misery into a happy state is subject to the laws (or ever the same, single Universal Law) governing our next universe, our 'emotional' body.

In as much as the material universe is essentially the product of the other two, the physical realm does have a limited executive power of its own. While its power is small, the laws which control it are perhaps more adamant than are those of the emotional and mental realities. It is interesting to examine in some detail the vision offered by Saint John in *Revelations* regarding the material reality. I recall trying, some twenty years ago, to understand the often seemingly contradictory 'mysteries' of the Bible, particularly *Revelations*. I would still be wondering about the true meaning of many of the parables if it weren't for Emmet Fox[4] who convinced me that the Bible had been written almost exclusively in a symbolic idiom. Unless one has the key, there is no way one can understand the 'hidden' meaning. Since that time, some fifteen years after my initial attempt, I have compiled and edited a *Dictionary of Biblical Symbolism* which, while still pending publication, has given me the key I was searching for.[5] Below I shall share some of my findings.

Saint John the Divine defines everyone who lives in and/or recognizes the physical reality as the only reality as a rider of the *pale horse*. This rider is allotted relatively little

power:
"...and his name that sat on him (*the pale horse, i.e. physical reality*) was Death, and Hell followed with him. And Power was given unto them over the fourth part of the earth, to kill with sword, and with hunger, and with death, and with the beast of the earth."[6]

In Biblical terms, the material world is paramount to death itself. A man who asked Jesus if he could bury his father before following him had been told brutally: "let the dead bury their dead."[7] The only 'life' Jesus recognized was spiritual. Whoever was not aware of his own spiritual nature, no matter how whimsical his realization, was dead. This is why, using the same biblical idiom, Saint John recognizes him who abides in physical reality as 'Death'. The *Hell* "that follows him" is obviously not some religious shtick with which to punish the errant believers for 'ever-after'. The spiritual realms are always in the *now*. The Greek word for hell is *Hades*, which carries completely different connotations from either Christian or Islamic definitions. Blavatsky offers this definition of Hades: "...Hades signified the inevitable fate of each soul to be united for a time with a terrestrial body. This union, or dark prospect for the soul to find itself imprisoned within the dark tenement of a body, was considered by all the ancient philosophers and is even by the modern Buddhists, as a punishment."[8] While I disagree with Blavatsky regarding the word 'punishment', nevertheless it was a *temporary* abode, obviously designed to restore the balance caused by, or resultant from, negative karma. It is my contention that, due to the dualistic nature of the material reality, such a restoration can be accomplished faster "on earth" than in the 'upper' realms. In this context the 'punishment' is a blessing. The discharge of our karma is, of course, the process of learning. In this context, I rather like the concept of sin and punishment as described by Charles Fillmore who said "we are not punished for our sins only *by* them". This, of course, confirms the law of karma.[9]

As we can see, our power in the physical realm is limited to just a small part of total reality (namely one quarter) and we can kill but the physical body i.e. *with a sword, and with hunger, and with death, and with the beast of the earth*, i.e. we can act as animals do. The hunger is, of course, a reference to spiritual hunger, an unsated desire for "something more" from life, and death refers to the final loss of spiritual awareness. Not much of a universe to abide in, but the fastest to teach us the "errors of our ways".

There is one other interesting aspect of the physical reality. It has to do with time. While all things *seem* solid, time *seems* totally flexible. The very same physical activity can last a very long time, or be over in an instant, depending whether or not we enjoy it. Time drags, or time flies. This too is up to us. We cannot always do what we enjoy, but we can always learn to enjoy what we do. We can make time fly. This factor serves to introduce us to the next reality, that of the world of emotions.

The *Emotional Universe*, or the universe of emotions, harbors its own laws.

One of the measures of success within this realm is our state of emotional happiness. It is essentially the result of the way we use our imagination, and thus this state of consciousness is also referred to as *imaginative* or *astral*. Our emotional body is responsible for the way we 'imagine' the universe. The glass may be half full or half empty. It is up to us. We alone decide. We are gods.

The faculty of imagination can change our perception of the universe diametrically. The same person may regard himself or herself as rich or poor, (relatively) healthy or (depressingly) sick, surrounded by a beautiful world or being stuck in abject ugliness. Those who do not know or understand the laws of this universe will not be able to believe that this reality is a matter of perception. The 'ugliest' baby is beautiful in the eyes of its parents. The 'ugliest' girl is beauty personified to her lover. A retarded child can bring joy to his or her parents who celebrate each minute step their child makes as it crawls up the ladder of intellectual success. A lowly job can bring joy for one who does it for others. A high position can result in anguish and stomach ulcers. A beggar is a king in his own hovel. A king can be a pauper in his castle.

The imaginative world is very relative.

How we perceive it is subject to our knowledge of the universal laws. No one can convince us that our condition is good, bad, or indifferent. We alone must come to our own conclusions. We alone can create our own universe. One of joy or sorrow, one of misery or pleasure, one of wealth or poverty. In this realm, our perception or reality is everything. Professor Hawking, mentioned above, had this to say about himself: "Apart from being unlucky enough to get ALS, or motor neuron (Lou Gehrig's) disease, I have been fortunate in almost every other respect."

Some people have all the luck...

I find it fascinating that in the Bible, our emotional nature is symbolized by a snake, but once redeemed, the symbol metamorphoses into an eagle. It soars towards the upper realms. Saint John in *Revelations* also attributes great power to it, though he is much more ominous regarding its misuse. He offers us this vision of the emotional body, the *red horse*:

"...and power was given him that sat thereon to take peace from the earth, and that they should kill one another; and there was given unto him a great sword."[10]

It is evident that Saint John regarded the "red horse" to be extremely powerful. It is also apparent that in his view our emotional body disturbs our state of mind, our emotions, and has a profound effect on the earth, which symbolizes our physical body. Ulcers have long been known to be a direct result of stress (the absence of peace). And stress is very much an emotional "condition". The medical profession is beginning to wake up to the fact that, in as much as the symptoms are part of the physical body, their causes often lie in the emotional field. This is the power of the *red horse*.

And then we also have the "great sword". All wars, all strife, discord, conflict, contention, disharmony, dissension, division, mischief, animosity, antagonism, antipathy, enmity, hostility, rancor, polarization, and all other manifestations of lack of control originate in our emotional body. We do not start wars as a result of mental deliberations. Not unless we are completely insane. Not unless we are so mentally deficient as to be unable to see the consequences not only on others but also on the karmic load we would have to bear for our "emotional outburst". The laws of the universe demand that whatever aberration we have introduced into the state of balance be compensated. This is not some mythic superstition introduced by misguided religions. Nor is it a punishment for our 'sins'. It is simply the effect of a cause that we have produced. It is simply the Law.

Balance will be restored.

Yet, in a manner of speaking, none of these 'imaginative' states are 'real'. Like the material universe, the emotional realm is part of maya. It is also an illusion. Nevertheless, to us who are emotionally involved in them, they are as real as the noses on our faces. And even this illusion, we shall find out later, has a very different reality than we think at the moment. What is real is only to be found in the spiritual realm. But that comes later. And in the meantime we create all these states, these realities, these universes. We create them with our subconscious. Most of us are so ignorant of the universal laws that our subconscious creates these states without our conscious participation. It doesn't have to be so. We can sit back and visualize worlds of beauty and love and soon, ever so soon, we shall dwell in them. It is up to us.

The universal laws invariably imbue realities with power which can be used and abused to an equal degree. They are equally at the disposal of a saint and a sinner. To a creator and a destroyer. Only the destroyer will have to rebuild whatever he or she destroys.

And then comes the *Mental Realm*.

The measure of success in this realm is the degree of our comprehension. We can imagine ourselves happy, but if our understanding is contrary to the perception of our mental body, all fails. For the physical and emotional worlds to function, we must gain at least a degree of understanding of how they work. The mental world is the highest of the material realms. Its upper reaches are sometimes called ethereal. The ethereal world is the transition between the spiritual and the mental. It is the realm in which the mental picks up inspiration. The intake of Sprit. It is the point of contact with Soul.

The mental body is devoid of feeling. It calculates. The Bible in *Revelations* so describes our mental body, the *black horse*:

"... and he who sat on him had a pair of balances in his hand. And I heard a voice in the midst of the four beasts say, A measure of wheat for a penny, and three measures of barley for a penny; and see thou hurt not the oil and the wine."[11]

It is not good to be devoid of feeling. We must gain control over our emotional body, not obliterate it with cold rationality. If we do, we are apt to sacrifice our happiness, our life's day-to-day joys and pleasures, in order to serve the mind. Mind is a magnificent instrument, but a terrible master. Einstein, still recognized as the greatest mind of the century, perhaps millennium, seems to have committed all his awareness to mental achievement. Instead of sublimating his imaginative body he appears to have coerced it to serve his mental needs. He reached out for the outer universe forgetting to look after his own. His private life, his family—suffered. It wasn't necessary. It never is. The same can be said of the great American architect Frank Lloyd Wright. His superbly disciplined mind introduced radical innovations both in structure and aesthetics. But he allowed the creative power to manifest through his mind to the exclusion of other aspects of his being. Finally, he paid a heavy price in his personal life.

We must always aspire to a state of balance.

It is important to realize that all "miracles" have their origin in the mental realm. People usually associate miracles with spiritual power. All power is spiritual, there is no other. But as we shall establish below, the sole spiritual power is the power of love. If we place our attention on it, miracles ensue, which, however, are never in contradiction to the laws of the universe. They are merely a manifestation of the right application of their efficacy. The cases of producing "something from nothing" or of bi-location described in the chapter on *Apports* are a direct result of deep understanding of the mental reality. As we shall see in the chapter on the *Creative Process*, all creativity is the result of our mental body. This 'body' should never be confused with intellect or with the brain, both of which are the result, not the cause. The Prime Cause, the in-spiration, has its source exclusively in the spiritual realm; the mental realm is a factory, an executive process. The spiritual ideas are always perfect. Their execution often leaves a lot to be desired. It is up to us to learn how to apply the production method. When we do, 'miracles' shall be commonplace.

And this sentiment takes us to the highest realm.

The universe of spirit has no laws. He who sits on the *White Horse* is a law unto himself. There are no laws or bylaws, no rules or regulations in Paradise. Freedom reigns supreme. He who enters the pearly gates is awed by the permanent state of beauty. Saint John had known this when he wrote:

"He that sat on him (*the white horse*) had a bow; and a crown was given unto him: and he want forth conquering and to conquer."[12]

The crown always symbolizes power, in this case absolute power. Yet, as already stated above, a power that does not corrupt as it is derived from love. In order to avoid confusion, I prefer to refer to such power as *Force*. I suspect that the *bow* is borrowed from Greek mythology, wherein it was used extensively by Eros, the god of love in all its manifestations. It is intriguing that the mythology proffers Eros' personal love to be Psyche, which in Greek means breath, spirit or the personification of human soul. Soul is truly the only love of him who rides the *white horse*. It is love which went forth conquering and to conquer. We know that nothing can resist the power of love. It is the force that binds the universes together. It binds us to each other. It leads us to reach out, to help, to share, and to be human. This horse alone is given the crown. No other power has it. Love is the sole force which guarantees to restore balance, the prerequisite for our spiritual maturity.

There is a secret which Buddha discovered long before Christ gave us his philosophy of love. Gautama Siddhartha was born to a noble family. The family inheritance could have kept him in luxury for the rest of his life. He would lack nothing. Yet he felt hunger for what worldly riches could not give. He went in search of the enigmatic, the unknown, the unpredictable, in search of sating his gnawing hunger. From riches he went to abject poverty. He rejected the world he lived in. His hunger remained. Years later, perhaps desperate, perhaps just tired, he sat to relax under the famed banyan tree. There, in a moment of rest, he found enlightenment. There and then he became Buddha. He fond the middle path.

He found balance. The cessation of duality.

And this is the substance of the spiritual realm. It is balance. It is built on that which the opposites have in common. It is the realm of perfection. It is neither in the future, nor in the past. It is a realm that IS. It is beyond any limits, any restrictions, beyond both time and space. It is the field of infinite possibilities which Einstein tried to discover when he searched for the Unified Field Theory. The spiritual realm is the Unified Field. It is One and all-inclusive. And it is not just a theory.

It is the only objective reality there IS.

The various prophets of the Bible advocate us to love God, to love our neighbor, even to love our enemy. It seems so simple yet so misunderstood. A fool can see that once we love our "enemy" he or she no longer is such. They become our friends, lovers. The very presence of love has the power to change realities, to raise us from the physical all the way to the spiritual level. When Jesus attempted to sum up his teaching he said: "By this shall all men know that ye are my disciples, if ye have love one for another."[13] I wonder how many so-called Christians are aware that the counterpart consequence of this commandment is that if they do not love one another they simply are not Christians. No matter how often they attend their religious services.

I've heard it said that there is one law which rules the spiritual realm. They call it the law of love. I disagree. There are no laws in Paradise. Love is not a law—it cannot be imposed. Love is a reality.

Contemporary men have a tendency to classify all data, to make them fit into neat files, slots, which can be easily looked up, and with minimum effort applied to everyday life. Generally, what cannot be filed is promptly discarded. Unfortunately neither the world of physics nor metaphysics works like that. The physical consciousness mentioned above would vary substantially from the envelope (body) which acts as its instrument. One can imagine an incredible number of intelligent species populating innumerable planets in innumerable solar systems within innumerable galaxies. Depending on the appurtenances, senses, perceptions with which the particular body is fitted by the specific evolution, its consciousness will be expressed quite differently. The bodies do not even have to be biological constructs. They can be based on quite different premises which our scientists cannot as yet imagine. The same would be true of their emotional and mental traits.

Thus, not only on earth but throughout the universes the physical, emotional and mental 'bodies' can manifest countless configurations, countless states at great variance from each other. The days of geocentric gods and their attendant religions are over.

This diversity is even more pronounced when dealing with *spiritual* states of consciousness. While the lower states are multifarious though finite, the spiritual, by definition, are infinite. Not only would they differ from specie to specie, but within each consciousness the numbers of 'heavens' must be infinite. What is a "seventh" heaven to some is but a point of departure to another. There cannot be a one-heaven-fits-all state of consciousness, as suggested by some religions. As we think of God being Infinite and His/Her kingdom as heaven, it too must be Infinite.

In scope, diversity in all aspects and attributes.

According to Buddhism, heaven is characterized by the cessation of all desire. I suggest this is contingent upon having all desires satisfied. Since each person's desires vary, so must the resultant states of consciousness. We must never forget that we are spiritual entities and as such our *modus operandi* is and always will be without limits. Perhaps this is what heaven is all about.

There are people who claim to have an allegiance to a "personal God." Others might postulate that "Religions can be based on physics only if the physics show that God *has* to be personal, and further that the afterlife is an absolutely solid consequence of physics."[14]

Why should God be "personal"? God's being is in a mode of being and that's, *inter alia*, in you and me. But we shouldn't limit God's expression to us, intelligent apes [I apologize to all apes who are not yet intelligent]. Each time we perform an act of kindness, God acts through us. Each time we show respect for His/Her creation, we show His/Her respect for us. Each time we offer love to one another, we display God's love for each one of us. The personhood of God is the integral personhood of all intelligent beings throughout the countless galaxies. Since God is Omnipresent, the expression of his Being is Omnipresent. As for afterlife, I've discussed it already. When regarded from the viewpoint of our true nature, we have no more afterlife than prelife.[15] We are immortal beings, individualizations of the Infinite. Of God.

Does such a concept find its expression in physics? If not, perhaps the physics need changing.

In spite of all of the above, we are all free to build our own religions, based on physics or not. Since it is we who create our universes or realities, *all beliefs are true*. Whatever we believe in, that will eventually become manifest in our life. Providing, of course, that our ideas are not contrary to the Universal Laws. That is why learning about those Laws is so vital to the viability of our particular, subjective realities. If we believe that in the physical reality we can fly by flapping our arms up and down, we shall break our necks. It we believe the same in the emotional/imaginative reality, we shall have a wonderful time.

Try it!

A final word.

I have listed the universes from the lowest to the highest. The power they wield works, obviously, in the opposite direction. Anyone who attains the spiritual consciousness controls all the realms below. The same is true of all the other realms—each controls the one below it. When we wish to deal with physical deficiencies, such as overeating, dieting will help. It will also sentence us to weeks, months, perhaps years of, at the very least, discomfort. What we should do is to look in the higher realms for the cause of our overeating. It could be any of a number of things. It could be that as children we were kept hungry and since that time we tried to compensate. It is an emotional condition. Once it is solved at the imaginative level, the physical will follow suit with the slightest of efforts. The same is true of the dominance of the mental over the emotional. I've never heard of an emotional outburst that convinced anyone to change his or her mind. But I have witnessed repeated examples of cool, quiet persuasion calming an emotional outburst.

The mental reality always overrides the emotional, which in turn wields sway over the physical consciousness. Perhaps that is why we can get (physical) ulcers from (emotional) stress and worry, but often having them does not seem to make us miserable. If we do worry it will aggravate further the pathological condition. The three realities coexist in the same "time and space", but they obey their own laws. The spiritual consciousness, as already mentioned, is above limitations. He who sits on the white horse is given a crown. A right to wield absolute power. No matter what the various religions might tell us, we must earn it. We must knock. If we knock long and hard enough, the door will be opened. For you and for me.

And then you will come face to face with yourself.

***

FOOTNOTES

(1). Matthew 24:35.
(2). John 5:14. The word *sin* is a translation of the Greek word *hamartano*, which is derived from archery. It means missing the mark.
(3). Briggs, John FRACTALS (Simon and Schuster, New York, London, Toronto etc., 1992).
(4). Fox, Emmet ALTER YOUR LIFE (Harper & Row Publ. , New York. © by Emmet Fox 1931—1950) Emmet Fox has also authored: *The Sermon on the Mount, Power Through Constructive Thinking, Find and Use Your Inner Power* and other books of considerable value in unraveling the Bible.
(5). *Dictionary of Biblical Symbolism* (Inhousepress, Montreal 2000; now also available as eBook)
(6). REVELATION of St. John the Divine 6:8
(7). Matthew 8:22
(8). ISIS UNVEILED Vol 2, *Theology*, (Theosophical University Press 1988) pg. 145-6 (footnote)

(9). Charles Fillmore was the co-founder of the Unity School of Christianity. He is said to have been an innovative thinker and a pioneer of metaphysical thought.

(10). REVELATION 6:4.

(11). ibid. 6:5-6.

(12). ibid. 6:2

(13). John 13:35.

(14). Tipler, ibid. page 327.

(15). Reincarnation concerns itself with our Personality, not our unchangeable Individuality.

Chapter 11
The Problem with Karma and Reincarnation

One went to the door of the Beloved and knocked.
A voice asked, "Who is there?"
He answered: "It is I."
The voice said,
"There is no room for Me and Thee."
The door was shut.

After a year of solitude and deprivation he returned
and knocked.
A voice from within asked, "Who is there?"
The man said, "It is Thee."
The door was opened for him

Jalal ud-Din Rumi

There is a little bug, so small that it's whole universe consists of only one cell. It is an amoeba. This bug lives in the intestine of a particular species of Australian termite. Without it, the termite would die. The amoeba changes the wood that the termite ingests into glucose, so that the termite can digest it. The mono-cellular bug has been thought to be moving along the intestine of the termite with the aid of flagella—long, slender shoots growing out of its sides. Not so. When examined under a microscope the shoots turned out not to be flagella, but bacteria that live on the outside of the single cell and help the amoeba to move along the intestinal wall. In exchange, the amoeba feeds the bacteria with a bit of sugar. The arrangement is profitable for both. In fact for all three. The bacteria, the amoeba and the termite are interconnected.[1]

At different levels of perception, so is the rest of the universe. Everything is connected with everything else. The connection may be physical, mental or emotional. Every action, thought or feeling has an effect on the rest of the universe. This effect, no matter how microscopic, and the restoration of balance that may be upset by this effect is the subject of this chapter.

When creating our own universes we face the problem of Karma.

In the western world, Karma is shrouded in mystery which we tend to associate with everything having its origin in the Orient. Eastern philosophies have never quite penetrated the occidental mind, let alone enriched our vision of the world. So much the pity, since the West comprises only a small part of the human heritage. We know little of eastern religions, of their literature, science or even medicine. This last has begun to make inroads in our society only recently, when our own methods began to fail us. Nowadays we are learning that not only the healing techniques such as acupuncture, acupressure, T'ai-chi, various Ayurvedic and herbal treatments, the so-called Traditional Chinese Medicines, but the very principle of a holistic approach to healing has its roots in the Far East. We are just starting to accept various treatments that affect our body, but hold at bay that which has bearing on our soul. The concepts of Karma and Reincarnation are among them. Yet Sai Baba goes as far as calling the law of Karma the *only* Law in the universe.

Karma, though it has many complex connotations, is essentially the law of cause and effect. We are well conversant with it as regards the physical environment. We know that if we eat poison we shall be sick, perhaps mortally. We know that "what goes up must come down." We know that action is equal to reaction. The Newtonian universe gives ample examples of this law as it applies to the material or physical reality.

The eastern sages take it a step further.
They say that if you hurt somebody, you will, sooner or later, be hurt with an equal or 'opposite' pain. Whether the pain is physical, or consists of mental or emotional anguish, is of little consequence. Action carries it's own reaction. If you hurt, today, the chances are that you are the author of your pain. That at one time or another you have inflicted this pain on someone. You are not being punished. There is no punishing God as promulgated by the Christian or Moslem religions. You have initiated a course of events which will take their usual, adamant course. There is no point avoiding the consequences any more than there is any point in changing your mind about jumping from a multi-story building when you are half way down towards the ground. As the famous LSD experimentalist and father of the "hippie life style, with its heavy accent of drug use,"[2] Timothy Leary, once mused: "If you don't like the song, you shouldn't have let me begin." I mention Leary because at one time he initiated artificial realities that led directly to a psychiatric asylum. Not just for himself but for his followers. "Timothy Leary, robed, beaded, and muttering mystic pseudo profundities about love and LSD, provided a model for thousands of youths."[3] And therein lies the problem. It is much harder to unlearn fallacious teaching than to metabolize even an uncomfortable truth the first time. Thanks to the many religions, we all have a great deal to disregard.

To unlearn...
What we must learn is not just to bear the consequences of our own actions, but to create a universe in which the consequences which our actions create do not limit us in producing other actions. Negative actions impose payable debts on our behavior pattern, positive—maintain our freedom. The shortcut to this end has been offered us in the golden rule "do unto others as you would have them do unto

you." It's as simple as that. Hardly more is required with possibly just one addition. Do unto yourself as you would do to one you love dearly. This simple rule gives meaning to the axiom I mentioned in the chapter on *Visions,* which insists that:

Altruism is not a virtue;
It is an act of self-preservation.

The preservation of your present self, your individuality, or any part of the self you presently are. Remember that Soul is immortal, you and I are not.

The concept of karma with the attendant reincarnation takes care of most mysteries which have baffled the theologians of Christianity for many centuries. In the chapter dealing with *Visualizing Infinity* I have demonstrated how the greatest theologian of the Catholic Church, St. Thomas Aquinas, struggled with the problem of good and evil, or to be more precise, with the problem of *infinite* good and infinite or even fragmentary evil. If God is Good, than how can He/She permit any evil to take place? How can an innocent baby suffer, how can innocent people die in bloody wars, how can the 'bad' benefit from the efforts of the 'good'?

Actually, they don't.

But to try to resolve this problem the *religious* philosophers created a devil. Their effort was not very successful. They invented an extremely intelligent angel called Lucifer, the bearer of light, made him rebel against his own creator, God, and presumably changed his name to Luciper, the looser of light. Why would the brightest of the bright angels be so stupid is not explained to my satisfaction. After all, if Lucifer knew that God is Omnipotent, Omniscient, Omnipresent, Immortal etc, etc, then, if he was so very bright, why did he pick a fight he couldn't win?

To me this is a thoroughly bad theory; so bad, in fact, that the church promptly declared it a 'mystery'. The church fathers are in the habit of declaring as a mystery anything they can't understand, particularly if they have invented the nonsense themselves. They can't change the theory because they have already declared it a dogma. And dogmas, like all the popes since the Vatican Council in 1870, are infallible.

Voilà, a vicious circle.

There are people who react to the law of karma with cowardice. They say that since every action *may* result in the accumulation of negative karma, it is safer to do nothing. To be a vegetable. Well, some people are—almost. To them I remind Jesus' admonition in the parable of the talents. For those of other or no particular faith, as well as for those who don't waste their time reading the Bible, I shall recount a short version of the parable described in Matthew 25:14-30. "A rich merchant entrusted his three associates with different amounts of money (talents) in the hope of getting some return on his investment. On his return from a trip, the merchant found that two of his aids took the necessary risks and doubled the amounts entrusted to them. The last man, being scared of losing his share, secreted his money for safekeeping. The merchant complemented the first two for their diligent labor and investment, allowing them to keep the amount they made. The last one had wasted his opportunity. The merchant disappointed with the man's cowardice and lack of enterprise took back his original amount leaving the man with nothing."

The investments of money are illustrative. We are all entrusted with special talents. Some of us may have more than one. Our gifts are intended to double our pleasure, our joy of life. And above all, the greatest gift we have been given is life itself. You might call it "an investment" God made in us. We should at least try to manage it well, and show a good return. We must play the game. If we do nothing with our abilities, whatever they are, they will atrophy. The old adage: "if you don't use it—you lose it," corresponds to this biblical parable. It is infinitely better to try and lose than not to try at all.

If we lose, we can *always* try again. After all, we are immortal.

***

Contrary to the solons of Wall Street, in the final reckoning the results are not the most important. By the time they manifest we may be long dead. What really matters is the trying, or to put it more bluntly, it is not how you die but how you live that counts. What matters is the *process*. Two thousand years after the above biblical parable had been promulgated, an American named W. Edward Deming has rebuilt, almost single-handedly, the war-torn Japanese industry by teaching them to concentrate on the method, on the process.[4] The results will take care of themselves, he said, if you only look after the quality of production. He was right. Japan recovered faster than any other country.

To do nothing is to be less than human; it is to remain a part of the 'result' rather than the 'Cause'. It is to waste the talents with which we have been individually endowed. It is vital to understand that every person on earth is entrusted with a *unique* ability, *unequalled by any other person*. It is up to us to discover what our particular talent is. Then, it is up to us to double (or better) our endowment.

In *The Revelation of Saint John* we are further admonished against being placid, tepid, indifferent. The words are rather forceful: "I know thy works, that thou art neither cold nor hot. I would thou wert cold or hot. So then because thou art lukewarm, and neither cold nor hot, I will spue thee out of my mouth."[5]

We are to live fully. Vibrantly. To fill our cup to the brim.

There is one other aspect of karma that needs stressing. There are people who think that by living off the efforts of others they can avoid karma. They pray and they pray and they pray. For our sins, no doubt. Nothing could be further from the truth. We all should reserve a quiet period, every day, to listen (pray). But the purpose of such *extremely important* "time off" is intended to recharge our batteries and return to active life with renewed vigor. Not to become a remorseful, apologetic, contrite, penitent vegetable.

After all, aren't we created in the image of God?

We can easily eliminate most if not all of the Judaic-Christian-Islamic "mysteries" if we espouse the concept of karma and reincarnation. Let us again assume that there is an Omnipotent, Omniscient, Omnipresent, Immortal etc, etc. God who is also Infinitely Good and Compassionate. How can we reconcile such All-Powerful Goodness with evil in the world? Well, it's rather simple:

THERE IS NO EVIL.

Goodness is self-sustaining, living, conscious and indestructible. Rather like Soul. Good and God are synonyms. Evil is a temporary and *imaginary* absence of good. It is a void, a non-existence. Why imaginary? Because God (Good) is *Omnipresent*. There is no room left for evil. Thus the intangible 'evil' is not self-sustaining. If left to itself, it dissipates by itself like anger, like desire for revenge, like hatred and other traits that separate us from experiencing the omnipresence of Goodness. To give evil artificial life, *man must be involved.* (Note, there is no 'evil' in nature). There is a particularly sad example of this involvement in the case of the so-called Holocaust. Its memory, no matter how painful, is artificially kept alive by a faction of Jews who, at great effort and expense, impose and prolong the reality of man's horrendous inhumanity to man. The Holocaust of the 2nd World War consisted of inhumane torture and destruction of some ten million Russians, six million Jews, three million Poles and another million men, women and children of other nations. Yet only the Jews are bent on keeping the memory of such unprecedented *man-created* evil alive. It is true that by referring to the Holocaust they invariably ignore the "other" fourteen million gentiles, but they refuse to let evil die its natural death. The other day I had an opportunity to see on my TV an academy award winning film *Schindler's List*. From the very start it was filled with such unimaginative horror that after ten minutes I switched it off. Yet a man named Halsey Minor who is apparently responsible for the "holocaust memorabilia" on the Internet, proudly introduced the film with words: "Holocaust is one of the most catastrophic events in history—one that must never be forgotten." I agree with the first part of the sentence. The second I consider most opprobrious. I can easily imagine substituting the word "Titanic" for "Holocaust" and making as much cinematographic money from that disaster: The sinking of the "*Titanic* is one of the most catastrophic events in history—one that must never be forgotten."[6]

Keeping evil, or the memory of evil, alive is among the worst perversions.

It is my deep belief that that which we remember should be conducive to raising our consciousness, not dragging us down into the cesspool of human depravity. Some will argue that the film also served to illustrate the courage of one man, Oscar Schindler. To that I shall answer that a million courageous men do not justify even one human life being taken.

Not one.

I am also deeply convinced that the Jews would be much happier physically, mentally and emotionally if they concentrated on the good of today instead of on the evil of yesterday. There are some that do. I have personal knowledge of some that invariably delight me with their joyful disposition. Others, judging by the media, might benefit greatly from the wisdom of another Jew, Jesus Christ, who said: "Sufficient unto the day is the evil thereof," and "...resist not evil."[7] Or, if they reject the teaching of the their own prophet (they usually did), they might drink from the wisdom of their very own Solomon, the son of David, king of Israel:

"An ungodly man diggeth up evil: and in his lips there is as a burning fire."[8]

The Christians, following in the ideological footsteps of their elder brothers, got stuck in the same perverse rut. Rather than celebrating the memory of Christ's teaching with the ancient symbol of wisdom, invariably (and originally) represented by the shape of a fish, a few centuries after Jesus' infamous death they have selected his tortured body nailed to a cross as their symbol. The symbols of wisdom—as has his teaching—all but disappeared. The symbol of suffering became immortalized in every church, in every Christian school. The pernicious effigy, in all shapes and sizes, dangles from golden chains on the necks of bishops, nuns, superstitious sportsmen and prostitutes alike.

The religious interpretations of evil, like those of Original Sin, the Sacraments, Heaven and Hell, Last Judgment, resurrection, are all inventions of man, and are mostly contrived to facilitate control over masses.
Let us examine them one by one.
Original Sin in *not* mentioned in the Bible, neither the Old nor the New Testament. As mentioned in the chapter on *Religions and Science Fiction*, St. Augustine (354-430), Doctor of the Church, invented the concept sometime in the 4th century presumably to increase church's control over people who saw no point in being baptized. The new theory became: "No baptism—no entry into heaven." To make this threat work, heaven had to be re-christened as a place of reward for "ever after-death", rather than anything which might benefit the believer during his or her present stint on earth, such as a raised state of consciousness as taught by Jesus. Saint Augustine probably borrowed the concept from the Eastern philosophies, some of which purport that the so-called "seed karma" is supposed to "kick-start" our material existence. I find it equally as illogical. The very fact that we became covered with "coats of skins",[9] i.e. incarnated in

physical bodies, makes us subjects to a dualistic reality in which the opposites serve to teach us discrimination. We need neither original-sin nor seed-karma to learn from the interaction of opposites. It becomes a simple question of survival. However, since the *sacrament of baptism* has been and continues to be administered almost exclusively by the sacerdotal classes, the financial benefits to the church have been and continue to be self-evident.

The same is true of all the other *Sacraments*, which tied a firm knot around the necks of the faithful and kept them insidiously under the influence of the church. In most cases the essence that the Sacrament represented with the intention of influencing the state of consciousness of the partaker or the recipient of the rite, has been long forgotten under the heavy shroud of mystery and symbolism. The sacrament of the *Holy Eucharist*, for example, is being presented as the body and blood of Christ. It is self-evident that the Roman church is not advocating cannibalism. Under the circumstances, the onus is on the church to provide an explanation of what the wafer and the wine symbolize. I submit that an average Christian knows what the sacrament commemorates, but not what it symbolizes.

The sacrament of *Confession* is a very positive psychological aid to people who are apt to dwell on their past misdeeds, rather then getting on with their lives. However, in my own past experience, I have found that the church fails to drive home the karmic portion of the psychological regeneration. Among the five indispensable conditions of 'absolution' (good confession) is a "strong resolution not to commit the same sin again" and 'atonement'. I suggest that the vast majority of the faithful either does not know about these conditions, have forgotten about them, or they have chosen to ignore them. One can but wonder how many of them would continue in their allegiance to the church, had the priests insisted on these two conditions being met.

I suspect that to the vast majority of the church members,

Confirmation and *Last Rites* (*sanctam unctionem*), like most other sacraments are a 'mystery'. Finally, the church wedding rites have been obfuscated by the traditional (as expensive as possible) wedding receptions.

And so on...

Hell, as discussed further on in the chapter on *Negative Programming*, is a mistranslation of Greek and Hebrew words of quite a different meaning to those given by the ensuing religions. The concept of hell supplied the sacerdotal classes with a much needed stick to balance the carrot of heaven. To increase their power, the priesthood converted the Hebrew and Greek *Sheol* and *Gehenna*, respectively, into a sort of fire-and-brimstone free-for-all, one eternal-suffering-fits-all perversion. In fact, heaven and hell are states of consciousness. At a personal level, heaven depicts the effulgence of divine glory, a profound awareness of an affinity with God, while hell the opposite. In an abstract sense, heaven is an ocean of infinite possibilities, a state of consciousness which rejects all limitations. It might be interesting to note that since hell is a state of separation from God, those who are separated are hardly aware of what they are missing. To those functioning at the level of spiritual consciousness, the concept of hell represents an unrequited desire for unity with God—'hell' indeed. For those 'in' hell, the absence of good is normally beyond their ability to appreciate. One must be aware of what one is missing in order to miss it. Few people are. They are quite happy to continue their dark existence, their pseudo-life for one reincarnation after another.

The *Last Judgment* is an oxymoron.

What would happen after the *last* judgment? All activity would have to cease since any action requires a decision and decision means judgment. One can only imagine that we would all became little monkeys in the heavenly gardens which see nothing, hear nothing, and do absolutely nothing. A profoundly dull sentence for eternity. But, as in the case of any good stick, the idea of Last Judgment scared the primitive, ignorant faithful into submission. Even some greatly admired minds remain scared to this day which may explain the preoccupation of the presiding pope with eschatology (the Last Things), in which the Last Judgment plays a staring role.[10]

The best fantasy of them all is the religious concept of *Resurrection*.

How can one be resurrected if one never dies? If Soul is immortal, what is the point of de-immortalizing It only to re-immortalize It again? As Einstein assured us, God does not play dice with the universe. He/She also does not create contradictory, illogical, nonsensical ideas. People do. Saint Paul claimed that "if Christ has not been raised, then our preaching is in vain and your faith is in vain."[11] I have utmost respect for Paul's insights but this is ridiculous. How can the message of Christ be any less whether he did or did not appear in his astral body after he left his physical envelope? The two subjects are completely *non sequitur*. Paul, like all his followers tended to confuse the message with the messenger.[12] It is of some interest that most scholars recognize St. Mark's gospel to be the earliest, yet in its original version there was no mention of a risen Christ.

The human race was always in need of heroes, paragons to be emulated, but mostly in whose glory we could bask with vicarious pleasure. The early Christians had been no different from their succeeding generations. They must have been well aware of the handy ancient rites of the resurrection of Osiris, Adonis, Bacchus and other slaughtered sun-gods to draw on. Perhaps early Christians found it necessary to emulate the old myths in order to inspire their few followers. To me, Christ's 'saving' is *in his message*, in the *Good News*, not in his personal life of which we know very little. Is Mozart's prolific creativity any less for the foibles of his personal character? Are Einstein's theories of lesser value because he left his wife? And how much greater the teaching of Christ who exhibited no weakness that we know of? If resurrection consists of leaving ones body and appearing in diverse places, than we need look no further than Padre Pio. (See previous chapter on *Visualizing Infinity*).

***

The Orientals have a philosophy called Yin and Yang. Literally, *yin* symbolizes the passive-female principle of the world, and *yang*, the opposite: male and active. As already mentioned in the chapter on *Visions*, the same principles are embodied in the Hebrew religion in the name YHWH, the incommunicable name of the God of Israel, which the Jews pronounce Elohim. The Hebrew letters *Yod*, *Hé*, *Wau* and *Hé* combine into a tetragrammaton which represents the Universal Male and Female Principles. Thus referring to God in English as *He/She* is an accurate progression from the Chinese and Hebrew roots. These same principles which are later reflected in the name Israel where the syllables *Is* stands for the *yin*, the passive-female principle, and *Ra* corresponds to *yang* the male-active principle. The last syllable of Israel, the *El*, is translated as "the mighty God", and stands for the *Unifying Principle*, or the divine presence within a person who actively pursues the search for perfection. Elsewhere the Bible assures us that the Universal and the Unifying principles are one and the same. (If not in a quantitative, certainly in a qualitative sense).

We find here a fascinating continuity from China, to Israel. The New Testament teaches the very same essence, though the Christian religions have chosen to ignore the parallel. Christ's words "I and my father are one", have been reserved to apply only to Jesus himself, in spite of Christ's pointed reference to the psalmist that "...*all* of you are children of the most High" (my emphasis).[13]

Regrettably, the yin-yang philosophy has been considerably diluted. The premise that there is only One source embodying *both* the male and female principles has been split into *two* forces affecting reality. This resulted in philosophical dualism, intellectual dichotomy, and explains our inherent need to judge. This, in turn, led directly to naming one force good and the other evil. Incredible though it may seem, this primitive depravity also accounts for associating the female principle with evil, while arrogating the good-positive aspect as the domain of men. Henceforth, the priesthood remained male, the temptresses—female.

Obviously, nothing could be further from the truth.

Evil, if it were to exist, would have to have been created by an All-Good-God. This obviously is illogical. Karma places all actions, whether *we* judge them good, bad, or indifferent at the feet of the perpetrator. At your and my feet. We cannot say: "the devil made me do it" unless we are referring to our own lower nature. We are the only agents, or agencies creating and judging our realities. And I say *we* judge them, because "my Father (God) judges no man."[14] All misinformation disseminated by the various religions that God might punish us for any errors in judgment we may commit is utter nonsense. It would also be completely unnecessary as the law of karma takes care of all such eventualities. Furthermore, (the Father) "hath committed all judgment unto the Son."[15] If the scriptures are right [and scripture cannot be broken[16]]—the Son, or the Higher Self, is your and my higher nature. You and I must practice constant vigilance and discrimination in thought, action and even in the emotions we allow to enter our consciousness. We alone create karma that will follow us until perfect balance is restored.

And this is why we have the law of karma—to restore balance. God is said to be "that which the opposites have in common". A great Sufi poet once said, "beyond doing right and doing wrong there is a field—I'll meet you there." That is where God resides. Where time stands still. Where all is One.

So—there is no evil.

Is black evil and white good? Or which is better, high or low, up or down, left or right, red or green. They are all contrasts. Opposites. Yet surely we all know that if we combined all colors together they would add up to white. A single merging of all is just white light. The symbol of knowledge.

The reason "evil" such as pain, theft, lust, murder or whatever juxtaposition to the golden rule we may come up with is recognized as negative because it carries negative karma. The reason juxtaposition of opposites exists is because we are here to learn. We can learn fastest by observing the effect the contrasts impose on each other. Don't get me wrong. If we make a wrong choice we shall pay for it. But we don't need presumptuous laws, prosecutors, prisons, police, armies or... imposed religions. Karma will take care of it all. It will restore the balance. Perhaps this is why an inspired prophet wrote: "To me belongeth vengeance and recompense; their foot shall slide in *due* time."[17]

In due time.

And anyway, all opposites are illusory. If left alone they dissipate under their own insignificance. So does 'evil'. Its presence is an illusion. Like everything else in the material universe. And this leads us directly into the concept of reincarnation.

While the Law of Karma assures Infinite Justice, Reincarnation confirms the principle of the Infinite Goodness and Mercy. A paradox? Only in the Judaic-Christian-Moslem religions.

What is reincarnation?

It begins with a postulate that we are immortal beings, souls if you like, which having left the land of milk and honey, Eden, are exposed to a dualistic reality in order to accelerate the learning process towards the manifestation of our infinite potential. While True Reality continues to have

Its being "in the middle", straying from this straight and narrow (middle) path exposes us to innumerable opposites. By comparing the antipodal appearances, functions, behavior, usefulness, etc., we enable ourselves to learn quickly the advantages of sticking to the middle path. In fact, ideally we should be detached spectators, learning, absorbing, participating to a degree, but never allowing the events of the dualistic reality to get under our spiritual skin.

Easier said than done...

But it does get a little easier when we realize, easier still when we fully metabolize the idea, that *we are an indivisible part of the Whole*. The attribute through which the Whole individualizes itself is called Soul, with a capital S, to differentiate it from 'soul', which is an expression given to our subconscious mind and emotions. Soul, like all attributes of the Whole, is not limited in any way, and can only be regarded in terms of the Infinite. (Refer back to chapters on *Visualizing Infinity et seq*.)

Nevertheless, the concept of a path to the true reality has been hammered down our collective throats for millennia. Lao Tsu's Tao, Buddha's middle path, Christ's straight and narrow, are all facets of the same philosophy. To understand it we must not deny the reality of the dualistic world, only to place it in the right perspective. We must learn, metabolize the idea into our genes, that the *opposites work in common*. Once we master this simple axiom, the rest become a lot easier.

While the Western churches either reject or continue to straddle the fence on the subject, Buddhism and Hinduism have long accepted the concept of reincarnation. In spite of growing evidence, the scientific world continues to ignore it, just as it ignores most aspects of paranormal evidence. Nevertheless, a discussion on reincarnation belongs in this book because our previous lives have a great and direct bearing on the type of world we shall be able to create in our present lifetime or, at the very least, on the environment in which we shall commence our cosmic endeavor.

While the law of karma takes care explicitly of the problem of justice, reincarnation makes it pragmatically possible. Karma has nothing to do with good or evil. It deals exclusively with restoring the balance. As implied in the relatively new Theory of Chaos, we can think of karma as acting and reacting to constant feedback. The negative and positive feedback enable birds to fly in constantly adjusting patterns without drifting apart nor ramming into each other. The negative and positive feedbacks maintain our earth in orbit. If the cosmic balance were to be disturbed beyond certain parameters, our earth would spiral into the sun—or else it would careen into the freezing vastness of space. The centripetal and the centrifugal forces must be constantly adjusted to maintain their state of balance. Likewise, no matter where we run, no matter *how long we run*, the law of karma will restore the balance in our own, private, personal universes. The universes which we continue to create with every thought, every emotion, every action and reaction. To satisfy the aspect of "how long we run", the concept of reincarnation is indispensable. In this sense, the law of karma is the law of protection, ultimately the law of Infinite Love, designed to last beyond a single life, beyond a single construct of our subjective universe.

Isn't it strange how Infinite Love comes back on us?

We can also think of reincarnation in terms similar to our genetic inheritance. So while the genetic hereditary characteristics deal only with our physical body, reincarnation is concerned with our emotional and mental inheritance. All three can be "good or bad", giving us certain predispositions such as a weak immune system, or superb physique, or an ability to learn easily or face stumbling blocks designed to teach us to overcome the seemingly impossible. It is seldom known that many very successful people overcame hurdles which have resulted in other peoples' downfalls. Scanning a report on the forthcoming Conference on *Learning Disabilities Association of Quebec* (LDAQ), I learned that

Albert Einstein and the renown author Virginia Wolf were unable to speak until they were three years old. As a child, the sculptor Auguste Rodin was so inept at reading and math that his parents and teachers discouraged him even from his passion for art. The multimillionaires of the entertainment industry, Tom Cruise, Cher, Whoopi Goldberg and Henry Winkler are dyslexic (unable to grasp the meaning of that which is read). So were Leonardo da Vinci and Winston Churchill. Louis Pasteur had problems with math while George Washington couldn't spell.[18] The problems these people faced were theirs to be overcome. And they have been.

Conversely, there are many fascinating examples of 'inherited' *talents* for which only the concept of reincarnation gives satisfactory explanation. Some are reviewed below, in the course of answering questions I have been asked most often about reincarnation. Here are some of them:

What of children born maimed?

There are two distinct factors at play here. If in our previous life we have maimed a child, we have an excellent chance to be born maimed. Again, it is *not* in punishment. It is only to restore the middle path. We and we alone, are the judges and the executioners. After all, the scriptures say we are gods, and the scriptures cannot be broken. And the reverse is also true. Mozart composed his first symphony at the age of four. Did he play the piano in his crib? No. Did he have a voice operated computer? No. He had no formal schooling. (By the way, nor had Einstein). Did he inherit his talent from his previous life? What do you think? Was he the only wonder-child?

Yehudi Menuhin played solo violin with the San Francisco Symphony when he was seven years old. At eleven he made his debut in Carnegie Hall playing Beethoven's violin concerto, opus 61 in E—the concerto requiring very mature musical insight. The young Menuhin earned raves. When Einstein heard him play in 1929 he said: "Now I know there is a God in heaven!" Yehudi was thirteen at the time.

Johann Gauss was correcting his father's mathematics before he was three; John Stuart Mill and Baron Macauley started writing almost before they could walk.[19] There are others. Many others. Accidents or reincarnations? Or, perhaps... a mystery?

There are no mysteries. Not... once we fully understand our true nature.

And the second factor is that we are *not* our body. We are spiritual entities which design, build and occupy a body to satisfy and expedite our thirst for learning, our need to restore the balance upset by our own inadequacies, our longing to find our way back to Eden. When we finally do get there, we shall no longer be innocent but useless entities with no experience. We will have created countless worlds, countless realities which we will have tested by the most stringent law of all. The Law of Karma. When we no longer produce effects which have to be rectified, compensated, our work here shall be done.

But... there are other worlds...

So much for the law which takes care of Infinite Justice.

But what of Infinite Love? In religions these two are invariably incompatible.

As mentioned above, this again is explained by the simple fact of reincarnation. No matter how many errors we commit, how many times we miss the mark, how often we shall stray from the straight and narrow, no matter in how many *lifetimes* we repeat the same errors, we, the individualizations of the One Life shall be given another chance. There is no death penalty in heaven. Perhaps, as already mentioned in the chapter on the *Universal Laws*, that is why the word 'sin' is also so misunderstood. In the New Testament the Greek word *hamartia* or *hamartano* originates from the sport of archery. Its literal meaning is "missing the mark".[20] Throughout our lives we all strive for the best. No one sets out to be hateful, evil, nasty, selfish—no one unless they are deeply sick. Such miscreants need help, treatment—

not prison. When we don't quite "make it" we are said to have committed a sin. We missed the mark. We don't go to hell for it; we are not sentenced to eternal damnation. We make up for the error and try again. This second, thousandth, or innumerable chance is the manifestation of Infinite Love. No matter what we do, no matter how many times we err, we are allowed to try again.

And... again.

For as long as it takes.

Sometimes we send ourselves to a prison which we construct through our stubbornness. Fat people imprison themselves in fat, cumbersome bodies, only to continue eating too much and to die prematurely from heart attacks or other debilitating diseases. No one punishes them—they inflict their own punishment, by themselves. The smokers continue to smoke until only cancer may be painful enough to teach them the lesson of not abusing the body which, to quote the Bible, is created unto the image of God. Again, their own doing. The thieves continue to steal until they are caught. If not in this life, then in the next, or the one after that, but eventually they will return every single cent they have pilfered. With interest.

Can we suffer for the mistakes of others?

Yes, we can. But only *by our own choice*. Sometimes we take on other people's negative karma to help them. It is a concomitant of great love. "Greater love hath no man than this, that a man lay down his life for his friends."[21] We think of wars as unspeakable horrors. Yet, the opposites work in common. It is during wartime that we witness countless examples of the "greatest love"—of one man giving his life for another. For friends? Often for strangers... perhaps for one's neighbor. Yet, obviously, neither wars nor taking on other people's karma should be encouraged. After all, we all learn best from our own mistakes, not those of other people. When we do begin to learn from the errors of others we make a gigantic leap on the scale of spiritual evolution. It accelerates our learning process enormously. But this requires us to enter a *mode of conscious living.*

Can we lose what is ours through greed or dishonesty of others?

Never. All possessions we have are states of consciousness. Whatever wealth is part of our inner being we cannot lose. Even if we should be shortchanged by events or some people who don't as yet know better, it would be a very temporary condition. What is truly ours, what we have earned in an honest fashion, we cannot lose. After all, the material world is only a manifestation of higher realities. What is ours in our soul and mind must be reflected in the physical universe. It cannot be otherwise. (Conversely, we can never keep what is not truly ours. Not for long.)

And what of pain, physical pain—does it not collide with Infinite Love?

Whenever we experience pain we can count it as a blessing. I neither justify nor advocate masochistic perversions. Pain is our body's means of communicating to us that we are doing, or have done, something wrong. That if we continue to do it, we shall get sick. That we shall bring upon ourselves a karmic debt. If we learned to listen to our bodies, daily, we would learn to overcome all causes of pain in quick succession. We are not to "enjoy" pain by continuing in the same vein. We are to discover its cause and get rid of it. Not by resorting to the removal of symptoms. By going to the source. Once we discover and remove the real cause, then we can get rid of the symptom, though the chances are that by then the pain will have disappeared on its own. After all, we are here to learn, not suffer. Heaven is within us. We are supposed to discover its environs.

There are Christians who stagger under the weight of their 'crosses'; men and women who are convinced that to be a Christian is to suffer, to partake in their own private Golgotha (to their heart's content). This is an absolute perversion of the Christian ideal. It derives, like most perversions, from utter ignorance of the teaching. Jesus said: "My yoke is *easy*, and my burden is *light*;" and elsewhere: "I bring you good tidings of *great joy*."[22] Doesn't sound to me like much suffering. Like any suffering at all. And if there are circumstances when pain is unavoidable, such as when helping another, there is still a way out. We can *all* eliminate physical pain from our lives by the simple process of diverting our attention away from the cause of pain. Few people, if anyone, can think of two things at the same time. By diverting our attention *fully*, we lose our awareness of pain. This principle is also evident in the mental practice of self-hypnosis. It takes a few weeks to learn, perhaps at the expense of gossiping with friends or watching TV. That's all. Just a few weeks. It is that simple. But most people I know, in spite of their ardent denials, *prefer* to suffer. Though they will never admit it, their predilection is obvious to any detached observer.

It is so obvious it hurts.

I have personal knowledge of wonderful people who suffer from osteoarthritis. Dr. Jason Theodosakis writes: "Excess weight can cause secondary osteoarthritis specifically of the knees. The problem may be due to the extra weight alone or perhaps to obesity related metabolic change. But by reducing your weight... you can either prevent the development of osteoarthritis of the weigh-bearing joints or dramatically reduce its symptoms".[23] Dr. Theodosakis should have said: "extremely painful symptoms." My good friends prefer to eat excessively than to stop suffering. But even then, there is another way: "Keeping your body in motion raises your basic metabolic rate and burns calories faster then before—even when resting!"[24] All my friends must do is to keep their bodies in motion. A few hours walk per day. Just a few hours—to stop pain.

Do they like suffering? I dare not ask.

One other thing. The "healing power" is *not* the domain of the select few. It lies dormant within every one of us. To some it comes inherently, through karmic inheritance, others can come by it through other means. But it is there. It always amazes me how very few people ever attempt to see if they are blessed with it. Many would be extremely surprised. Some even scared. To all that recognize 'inner' powers such as healing as "divine", I offer my favorite textbook. A true heavyweight in the healing business once said: "...He that believeth on me, the works that I do shall he do also; *and greater works than these shall he do...*"[25] (my emphasis). This statement might be hard to swallow by those who deify its author.

In the context of reincarnation, can we 'lose' our soul?

Yes. Unfortunately we can. By that I mean that we can lose all awareness of the divine potential, the divine Presence within us. It is not *our* soul, of course. It is Soul. The individualization of the Infinite. When we manage to 'metabolize' a universal trait, incorporate it into our personal nature, such a trait becomes also part of our Spiritual body. To that degree that the portion of our personality, or individuality, also becomes immortal. Each divine trait is, of course, indivisible and infinite. That's what makes it divine. But that is also why there is an infinite number of ways to manifest it. Our 'way' remains forever 'ours'. Each time when we reincarnate into yet another 'life', we hope to add to this spiritual entity, to spiritualize or immortalize another portion of our individuality, until eventually our full consciousness is spiritualized. This is known as being saved. No matter what others will tell you, this saving process cannot be done by somebody else. It is our job, and if it takes eternity less-a-day, so be it.

But what happens when during a whole lifetime (a particular incarnation) we have neither perfected nor improved on any universal trait acquired during our previous incarnations? Then that particular lifetime is lost. No part of that particular personality shall be incorporated into that 'you' which enjoys immortality. As mentioned in the *Introduction*,

Jesus called such people "the dead". Spiritually dead. And spiritual life is the *only* definition of life Jesus recognized. When we come down from *samadhi* we take on our imperfect mental and emotional characteristics left behind from previous tries. We continue to do so until we have succeeded in translating the particular (ourselves) into a perfect vessel for the Universal.

Thus, by accepting the concept of karma and reincarnation, we eliminate the problems which plagued the greatest minds of Christendom and many other religions. The "downside" is that karma places full responsibility on our own shoulders. We can say a thousand prayers to a thousand saints... which is fine if it makes us feel better; we can lie prostrate in abject humility for hours, days, months, in any church or temple—but we still remain responsible. We can no longer blame the governments, politicians, economists, pedagogues, priests or even parents. We cannot count on a messiah to come, die for us, and pay off our karma. What the Messiah does (and did) is to *show us the Way*. All we must do is follow it—of our own free will. But we all have to do our own walking. Once we fully understand the concept of karma we have come of age. And there are absolutely no exceptions. Paul of Tarsus put it in an nutshell: "whatsoever a man soweth, that shall he also reap."[26]

It there no end to the cycle of reincarnation?
The brief answer is yes. The cycle does run its course. But for most of us the cycle is so long, it seems to go on forever. The Orientals call it the wheel of Awagawan, the coming and going. Nevertheless, when we become a perfect mirror for the universal, our cycle comes to an end.

Would we ever have to be reincarnated again?
When we complete the cycle of reincarnations we become as gods. We can do anything we wish. We will have become perfected embodiments of Divine Love. When we

reach the level when the particular (we) become a perfect channel for the Universal, when "I and my Father become one", I am sure that we shall reincarnate wherever we can help the most. On earth, in the vicinity of one of the stars of Andromeda, or within the furthest galaxies billions of light-years away. Or in different realities altogether. Wherever we can do the most good. After all, we are One.

So we wouldn't have to stay in "heaven" forever?

People who externalize God, externalize heaven. Those people also talk about "afterlife". There is no such thing. Life is Life. Neither before nor after. It just IS. It is an attribute of the Universal, Immortal, Ineffable that we call God. As for heaven, in every practical way that can do us any good at all, heaven is a state of consciousness. In other words we cannot be *in* heaven. Heaven can be within *us*. But to answer the question directly, gods don't *have to* do anything. They are almighty. "Staying in heaven", to me, sounds pretty boring. Staying in heaven means to become integral with the Infinite Potential. You'd be conscious of the universe, all the universe, but you would not participate in anything. Remember that God has no being other than in a mode of being. The universe is the mode in which God chose to have His/Her being. You and I are part of this mode. Enjoy it!

And supposing none of the above is true—what do we stand to lose?

Nothing that I can think of. We shall have learned to obey the golden rule, we shall have stopped suffering, we shall have stopped worrying, we shall never entertain any fear of death, we shall still try to do the very best we can with every moment of our lives. We shall still continue to create our universes as though nothing has happened.

Isn't this what life is all about?

***

FOOTNOTES

(1). The termite story has been gleamed from Dr. Ric Dickerson from the book by Paulson and Dickerson REVELATION: the Book of Unity, page 124.
(2). Toffler, Alvin FUTURE SHOCK (Pan Books London 1975) page 282.
(3). Ibid. page 280.
(4). Walton, Mary DEMING MANAGEMENT METHOD
(5). Revelation of St. John 3:15-16.
(6). In the course of writing this book Hollywood did in fact produce a movie entitled "Titanic." In my view, such films could be compared to grave-robbing. Also see chapter on *Art and Creativity*.
(7). Matthew 6:34 and 5:39.
(8). The Proverbs 16:27.
(9). Genesis 3:21
(10). refer to Bernstein, Carl and Politi, Marco HIS HOLINESS (Doubleday, New York 1996). Also compare essay on *The Last Things* in BEYOND RELIGION, volume I (Inhousepress 1997, 2001) by the author.
(11). 1 Corinthians 15:14 (RSV)
(12). I believe the scholars are now unanimous in crediting Paul of Tarsus with the creation of the Christian Church, not Jesus Christ.
(13). Psalm 82:6
(14). John 5:22
(15). ibid. cont.
(16). John 10:35
(17). Deuteronomy 32:35
(18). Gleamed from Rochelle Lash article in the Montreal Gazette, March 17, 1999.
(19). Watson, Lyall LIFETIDE (Coronet Books, Hodder and Stoughton 1979) page 322.
(20). Kapuscinski, S., DICTIONARY OF BIBLICAL SYMBOLISM (Inhousepress 2001, also available as eBook)
(21). John 15:13
(22). Matthew 11:30 and Luke 2:10, respectively. (my emphases)
(23). Theodosakis, Jason M.D., M.S., M.P.H.; Adderly, Brenda M.H.A.; Fox, Barry Ph.D. THE ARTHRITIS CURE (St.Martin's Paperbacks 1997) page 159.
(24). ibid. page 160.
(25). John 14:12
(26). Galatians 6:7

Chapter 12
Aging and Longevity

*You can't help getting older,
but you don't have to get old.*

George Burns

Few visualization processes are as pronounced, as immediately apparent, as the process of aging. I met literally dozens of senior citizens (some of them not so senior), who assured me, repeatedly, that at their venerable age they can no longer be expected to remember, think straight, absorb new ideas, understand a computer, be responsible for their actions and generally function in a fashion we normally associate with a reasonably intelligent human being. Should I venture to suggest that they suffer from the it-is-all-in-the-mind syndrome, they smile condescendingly murmuring: "You'll see, young man, you'll see..." I was sixty-six at the time they shared their doubts with me. I've also heard the same tune when I was fifty-six, and younger.

What is worse, the "aged people" (I am at a loss how to call them without being offensive yet portraying *their* reality), translate and impose their imaginary deficiencies to their physical bodies, disabling them from performing in a fashion for which they have been designed. Once people attain the age of sixty or so, they seem committed to acting old. They visualize themselves slowing down, mentally and physically, and gradually their *vision* becomes true. Strangely enough, many of those same people affirm that they are in personal possession of an immortal soul, that they are subject to an almighty God who, nevertheless, is incapable of designing for them neither mind nor body which would last as long as they do. It is not as if the soul wanted an experience of being repeatedly incarnated in a dysfunctional physique. If this were the case, it would have already gathered abundant experience in any of the previous reincarnations.

What is true, however, is that in the same way that our physical bodies are made up of countless atoms and molecules with specific characteristics, there are other traits inbred into our genetic code; traits which we have deposited there on our own. It is we, not some eternal or external deity, who continually contribute to the cumulative imprint on our gen.[1] We record on our memory cells what we believe to be true. We also record every other bit of information in case it turns out to be 'true'. Our genetic code is particularly concerned with preserving all traits which we visualize as being necessary for our *physical* survival. The totality of our visualization process shapes our reality. It extends well beyond our genetic code. It leaves a seemingly indelible imprint on our psyche, establishes our viewpoint, and controls our relationship to the world around us. Unbeknownst to us, we have created the subjective world we live in. Each one his or her own. Only we did it without conscious participation. With few exceptions, we have all set our creative process on automatic. And the process itself is near-identical to the workings of a computer. Garbage in—garbage out. Our genetic code cannot function in a manner other than that in which it has been, and continues to be, programmed. It regulates our lives more surely than could any absolute dictator.

Is there a way out?
There is always a way out.

As stated above, we maintain our form, our mode of being, through a matrix or a program we have put together over millions of years of evolution. This program is automatically and continually updated. It is subject to continuous feedback, which adjusts it minutely on a second-to-second basis. If we do not question (by a conscious act) the efficacy of previously acquired traits, then such traits not only remain but also become reinforced. In addition, new data temporarily stored in our subconscious, later become ingrained in our cells for future reference. Since the program has been subject to such a long and arduous period of trial-and-error experiments, it is protected by automatic safeguards from external interference. New ideas, no matter how beneficial, are rejected until proven by the same trial-and-error method to be of value. As we know from our discussion on the subject in *Scientific Perspective*, the scientists call this method "information preserved by natural selection."

If natural means automatic—then I agree.

Such a system is oriented, *like all organized systems*, to the protection of *status quo*. The principle follows the dictum: "if it ain't broke, don't fix it". Unfortunately under such circumstances the program is renewed at a pace of somewhere between dead slow and dead slow, which is the way the British scientist James Burke describes the pace of evolution.

To check the above theory note that the older we are, the less likely are we to tolerate changes. Any changes. We might complain (usually continually) about the countless things which do not please us: about a mountain of aches and pains, about the way we are treated, about the food, room temperature, the political system, the local ladies' association... whatever. But God forbid anyone should ask us to do anything about it. Any such suggestion is met with: "...better a devil you know than a devil you don't know," "...things could be worse," "...mustn't rock the boat," "...mustn't offend anyone," "...if I say anything they will take it out on me," and, the worse of all: "...surely, you don't expect *me* to do something about it!" As we age, we become profoundly dissatisfied spectators. We no longer participate in life. Through our thick lenses, we watch life pass us by.

We are no longer fully alive.

In my essay on *Aging*[2] I suggested that there is a direct correlation between the use of our faculties and their eventual atrophy. The old premise that "if you don't use it—you lose it" applies as much to our mind as to any part of our anatomy. Contrary to some advocates (in some respects Dr. Chopra among them), it is not enough to *know* how to program our health, agility, and ability to counteract the aging process. Having acquired the knowledge, *we must act as though the program really works*. Someone once said that to be a Master one must act like a Master. It is equally as true that we expect a healthy person to act in a healthy way. If it were otherwise, then all the couch-potatoes would be Olympic athletes.

When searching for a location which could serve my parents who were in need of regular nursing help, I had occasion to visit a number of "Old Peoples' homes". Over the years, I've noticed that the residents, often referred to as "patients" in such establishments, are deprived of all initiative. Their time is organized for them, with an evident considerable concern for the patients' welfare. Furthermore, the main preoccupation of the para-medical staff, the visiting doctors, nurses and sisters, is the patient's *physical* well-being. While some effort is made to supply the residents with mental distractions (chitchats, movies, excursions, occasional concerts), such are provided without the least effort on the part of the resident. In other words, the resident becomes exclusively a recipient of attentive TLC, (tender love and care) from others without the least *mental* effort being expected of them. Kindly, angelically clad sisters (nuns) told me that "they (the elderly) deserve to do nothing, to have everything done for them." They might as well have said, "they deserve to be vegetables".

The consequences are staggering.

The residents deprived of any opportunity, not to say *necessity*, to exercise their minds, reach a vegetative state in a matter of months. Men and women, who on entry to the "senior citizens'" establishment had been still coping reasonably with the majority of everyday challenges, promptly lose their ability to make any decisions, to face let alone solve any problems. All matters requiring the slightest mental effort are delegated to the staff, who, with an amazing measure of equanimity, perform them. On an average day, the residents' efforts are limited to a trip, three times a day, to the cafeteria, and then to evacuating the masticated, reasonably healthy diets in their semi-private toilets. Once a week they are washed, even as I wash my dog. But this is the only comparison with my pet animal.

In every other respect, the residents are expected to perform considerably less than any animal must perform to remain alive.

This dotting type of love results in the mental death of the residents, long before they vacate their bodies. The residents who had a perfect right to expect their last years to be truly golden, are promptly relegated to the status of "patients", whose vegetative existence is dragged out for as long as possible. We pride ourselves on being members of a society which looks after its old and infirm. We don't. We look after their bodies. We do little for their minds, let alone souls. We sequester them where we do not have to see them, nor witness their expeditious deterioration.

There is one other aspect of aging which bears attention. Some people never develop a desire to fathom their "inner nature". They skim along the surface of most issues, relish the joyride, and quickly turn their eyes to greener though equally ephemeral pastures. Most blame lack of time for any meaningful research. Their time allocation is dedicated to non-participatory sports (watching professional semi-clad millionaires run after a ball), social engagements (parties, dinners, guests, entertainment and the cultivation of multiple 'friendships'), cultural commitments (TV, theatres, ballet, opera, concerts). Such people never find time to do justice to the Socratic admonition to "know thyself". Such people, contrary to their innermost conviction, remain shallow in body, mind and spirit. When they age, they invariably live in their 'past'.

Yet, there are others well capable of profound research, of detail analysis and synthesis of the elements comprising their *true nature*. I am not referring to navel gazers, closet philosophers, or to intellectual dilettantes. I am talking about people who live with their eyes wide open, and who make a *conscious* effort to live consciously. It is with those few that I am most concerned; because they too seem to lose their talents, their ability of paying attention to *detail* when growing older. I believe this to be an emotional reaction to "what can I possibly do at my age" syndrome. This is a syndrome to be avoided at all costs. The adage that "doing anything is worth doing well" does not and should not fade with age.

The deeper we dig, the more fascinating the lode.

I remember a most wonderful couple who did (and continue to do) more for their "neighbor" than most people I know. They are both in their seventies. While still preoccupied with what they can do for others (which is probably the single greatest recipe for keeping young at heart), they both suffer from arthritis. As mentioned in the previous chapter, some time ago I came across a fascinating book entitled *The Arthritis Cure*.[3] The three authors of the book purport on over 250 pages that they discovered "The medical miracle that can halt, reverse, and may even cure osteoarthritis." Overjoyed I grabbed the book and drove to my arthritic friends the same week. They were very glad (as always) to see me but declined the book, waving before me a single sheet of paper which, they claimed, was the 'synopsis' of the book. I didn't impose, but I felt sorry. What reading the *whole* book does is to saturate one, over say some twenty-five hours of reading time, with an indelible confidence that the book works. Its chapters are constructed in a manner to help you visualize yourself in a healthy, cured condition. The two nutritional supplements the book advocates (on which my friends place their whole reliance) are almost coincidental. I am deeply convinced that what really cures is the new image of oneself the book builds, page by page, over its entire length. This is what I mean about skimming over and not delving deeply into matters which can truly help us.

Until people *of all ages* are actively taught to visualize their dreams, to mobilize their desires and imbue them with a vision of reality, the old will remain old, regardless of their physical age. If we really are individualizations of One Soul, we are ageless. We are therefore also immortal.

All we must do is to realize it.

During the last few years a notion has been introduced by Deepak Chopra that we exhibit characteristics of different time modes.[4] Theoretically when asked how old we are we should ask whether the questioner is referring to our chronological, biological or real time. The chronological time merely stipulates how long ago we were born. The biological age can be calculated in relation to life expectancy in terms of *average* deterioration. The real age, however, is the only age that really matters.

If we are given the averages regarding certain mental and physical dexterities, such as sporting achievements, feats of strength, power of endurance—such as sustaining a good speed over a long walk, climbing mountains, swimming a few kilometers, etc., then we can evaluate in what 'physical age group our performance will place us. This 'evaluated' age group might well have nothing to do with our chronological age.

Likewise, we might wish to evaluate our mental agility.

We might try to assess how long does it take us to learn a poem by heart, how good is our memory recall, how well do we (still) play a musical instrument, whether and to what extend we keep up with the latest developments in technology—science, how conversant are we with (local and global) cultural activities, how good is our game of chess... such an evaluation might help us to determine what is our mental age. There may be some amongst us who never exhibited great physical skills but excelled in complex crosswords. On the other hand, some people's metal abilities might not have been developed as well as they, perhaps, should have been. No mater. We can compare our present age *with our own* previous abilities. Not those of others. We might be a very healthy and happy "dodo". Or a genius who seldom leaves the couch. What matters is that *we* control, or at least have some influence on our destiny. That we are more than just puppets responding to the statistics compiled by insurance companies.

The concept of flexibility of time is not new.

St. Thomas Aquinas proposed three types of time. *Tempus* concerned the "temporal" or earthly time. It measured the duration of changes taking place on earth. The second type of time Aquinas called *aevum* or time affecting changes in or of mental processes. It did not concern material changes but rather changes in metal states. It also applied to all that is incorporeal, to angels and to states of consciousness. The third type of time Aquinas called the *aeternitas*. It concerned the divine. While it was the domain of God, it also embraced our ability to experience infinity or immortality in a single instant. It is the time that permits the present and infinity to be one.

In science, Aristotle and Newton measured time unambiguously as the duration between two events. They believed it was *absolute time*. Then, as discussed in the chapter on *Scientific Perspective*, Einstein destroyed the misconception that time is absolute. In his theory of relativity he married the concept of time and space into a single idea of space-time. According to the physicist Stephen Hawking, the distinction between space and time disappears completely when using *imaginary time*; time measured using imaginary numbers. There is no difference between going forward or backward in imaginary time. We can also go in any direction in space.[5] Other scientists took up the banner and came up with different definitions of time responding to different qualities and/or events of past, present and future. Another (previously mentioned) Professor of mathematical physics, Frank Tipler, offers us an elaborate menu of different 'times'. He measures duration in terms of *proper time*, as measured by our clocks in the present astrophysical environment. Using this definition, time and space is measured in the same units, i.e. if time is measured in years then distance is measured in light years. He also computes in *conformal time*, which is measured in terms of a specific scale factor. We don't have to worry about it because, as far as I understand, it is used only to calculate the behavior of light rays. Then there is the *entropic time*, which "is a more physically significant time-scale than *proper time*." It is used to measure the amount of entropy that exists in the universe at a specific proper time. Next is the *subjective time* defined as the time required to store irreversibly one bit of information. Rather as in the speeds of computers. Finally the theoretical physicists use the *York time*, so called after the American physicist James York, which simplifies mathematics of the field equations.[6]

Quite a choice...

Once science broke down the rigidity of time, the universe became fluid, relative. So did we. We can no longer claim the privilege of age. Someone might ask us how old we are in conformal, subjective, entropic, *aevum*, biological or absolute time, to mention just a few... Frankly, I no longer believe there is such a thing as *real* time. It would probably be just somebody's vision of reality. Yours and mine might be different. Let us make sure we know the answer to the question regarding our age. Or we may have to learn to enjoy the privileges accorded senior citizens because of our contribution to society. Not because we are old.

Alternatively, we might choose to live in the present.

So what can we tell our retired citizens packaged into "institutionalized residences"? We can no longer regard them as 'old' in terms of 'real' time. There is no such thing. All is relative. We simply don't know how old they are. We don't even know how to measure their age. Perhaps Chopra's definitions would be of some help. But are our retired citizens willing to undergo such scrutiny? Is there a way to protect them from the illusory wiles of tradition?

Perhaps.

We cannot, we must not, be afraid to allow the *aged* to participate in, what is normally referred to as *hardships*. Solving problems, particularly mental problems, is what sets us apart from other animals. Surely we have earned the privilege to solve problems more complex than those allotted to the rest of animal kingdom. Problems reaching beyond keeping our body and soul together. Until problems are treated as challenges, until we learn to rejoice in the new, the unknown, we are no more than the dilapidating shadows of our own pasts. We created our subjective universes and now, in our "old age", we watch entropy dissolve them.

I, for one, refuse to participate in such scurrilous farce!

It is my contention that old age is the most glorious age of all.

In India, among some casts, there is a custom that when a man assures a reasonably safe future for his wife and children, he is free to retire to pursue spiritual life. We, in the West can surely offer the very same opportunity for both sexes, for men and for women. It is the time in our lives when we can apportion the majority of our time to the study of Self. We can finally do justice to the admonition: Know *Thyself.* I've never discovered any endeavor more fascinating. Apparently, nor had Socrates.

As for longevity—this matter is of no consequence. It simply doesn't come into the picture. What difference does it make whether you live long if your life is filed with misery?

Alexander the Great, Jesus of Nazareth, Wolfgang Amadeus Mozart, Felix Mendelssohn, van Gogh all died before they reached forty. Can anyone of us claim that we achieved more by living longer then those few? Albert Einstein achieved his greatest insights when we was twenty-six. Which of us got smarter than he did—by living longer? Is length of life the measure of success? Some scientists tell us that we might attempt to measure duration of our lives by the frequency and quality of our thought impulses. If we don't think much we might live a long time.

I wonder why? What for...?

There is now evidence that the human life-span can be extended by genetic manipulation.[7] Will it also enhance our will to overcome new, ever more challenging problems associated with critical overpopulation of our poor spaceship Earth? If we live longer, shall we be smarter, or shall we only prolong our stay in the Florida doldrums, packed like sardines in multi-story condominiums with rationed water consumption?

In the Book of Genesis it is written that Abraham (In Hebrew his name means *father of a multitude*) had been 'awarded' with long life. He had to be—to sire such a multitude.[8] We are told that Abraham lived to be 175 years old. But his "longevity" pales when compared with biblical accounts of Adam who lived 930 years (Genesis 5:5 *et seq.*), Seth 912 years, Enos 905 years, Cainan 910 years, Mahalaleel 895 years, Jared 962 years... If we are to take the Bible literally, didn't God shortchange Abraham rather than award him?

I've recently discussed the matter of longevity with a nonagenarian who still sparkles with good humor and perspicacity of mind. We both wondered whether long age is a reward or a punishment for a life of limited accomplishment.

I still wonder.

Life is whatever we visualize it to be. Not just in terms of duration, but in terms of achievement. If we think of length only, we may have to dilute our vitality, our capacity for adventure, our hunger for new horizons over a longer period of time. Are we sure we would want that? Isn't intensity more satisfying than a semi-vegetative state in a comfortable, but dull retirement? If our true nature is immortal, must we insist on staying in the same physical enclosure, use the same senses, brain, nervous system, which being material, surely, must have its temporal limitations?

It is up to us. We can visualize any type of life we want. Perhaps not in this reincarnation but, by the time the two thousand years of Aquarius are up, you and I will be watering our own, individual gardens with great joy and contentment.

Good luck.

***

FOOTNOTES

(1). Alternatively, *we are* this external, eternal deity.

(2). BEYOND RELIGION Volume II. (Inhousepress, Montreal, 2000)

(3). Theodosakis, Jason M.D., M.S., M.P.H.; Adderly, Brenda M.H.A.; Fox, Barry Ph.D. THE ARTHRITIS CURE

(4). Chopra, Deepak AGELESS BODY, TIMELESS MIND (Harmony Books, div. of Crown Publ.)

(5). Hawking, Stephen W., A BRIEF HISTORY OF TIME, (Bantam Books 1988) pg.134. To calculate histories, one would have to use negative numbers. To avoid it the scientists multiply negative numbers by an imaginary number to achieve a positive answer to the equation.

(6). Tipler, Frank J., THE PHYSICS OF IMMORTALITY, (Anchor Book, Doubleday, New York 1994) gleamed from pages 348, 402-403, 266 and 106 respectively.

(7). Briefly, an enzyme called telomerase, discovered in 1984, can repair the damaged telomeres which are responsible for cell's ability to divide, and thus renew itself.

(8). Students of Biblical symbolism know that the "multitude" refers to the richness of his thoughts or ideas, not the efficacy of his loins.

Chapter 13
Art and Creativity

*It is the supreme art of the teacher to awaken joy
in creative expression and knowledge.*

Albert Einstein

The **fine arts,** among them painting, sculpture and music are particularly useful in understanding the process of visualization. We are told, for instance, that Mozart 'visualized' or in his case 'heard' complete compositions, including whole symphonies, before he began committing them to paper. That is not to say that he heard individual notes, as they would sound later when interpreted by an able conductor and a well-versed orchestra. He visualized them in his mind's eye, in his 'inner' ear, as integral, complete, whole works. It was as if he heard all the arias of Don Giovanni, or the musical phrases of the Brandenburg concertos as single complex chords. Apparently his "visions" had been so complete, that the mere transposition of them to music-paper were for him so dull that he asked his wife to read a novel aloud while he did the transcribing.[1]

It is my contention that we all have artistic visions.

Walking in the park, gazing onto the reflections in the pond, washing dishes after a sumptuous meal, our minds wonder, sometimes inspired by what we see, sometimes escaping the physical reality. But we all have visions. What we are missing is the ability to distinguish those visions from the "background noise" which permeates our minds—the subliminal "roof chatter"—to let them solidify into, what Einstein called: "muscular shapes". [This inability to separate individual thoughts, or blocks of thoughts, from the stream of consciousness will be discussed further in the chapter on *Relaxation*]. But even if we could, this is only the first stage of the creative act. In order to share our artistic visions with "the world", we must learn to translate these *gestält* images into a "laterally" structured expression. We must learn to transform the single integral image, to break it up through hard, painstaking labor into individual lines, strokes or dabs of paint, individual notes, words, phrases, or strokes of a sculptor's chisel... and then to bring those images together, again, as close as we can to the original creative vision. The first and the last are art. The hard work, the pain, the struggle between the two, is the process of creativity. We all have an inherent ability to regard and visually appreciate a painting at a single glance. Just as it is true of a particularly breathtaking landscape. We drink it all in a single gulp. We inhale it. With practice, we absorb it whole, as a complete work of art in the instant we face it. In that instant we share the artist's original vision. Then, at a second glance, we follow the artist's labor, his hours of work to share his vision with us.

It is a quite different matter with music. Or poetry.

If we were presented with all the notes of a symphony, or even of a simple song, in a single chord, we would register it as unbearable cacophony. The same is true of the written word. Imagine cutting out the individual words from your favorite book, mixing them in a bag and emptying them on your table. You would hardly enjoy the turn of phrase, the poetic lilt to some visions that the writer had skillfully unfolded for your pleasure. It may sound absurd, but when a poet or even a writer of a novel sets out to put his vision on paper (today on a computer screen), the overall vision is already extant in his or her mind. It is true that in the case of a novel, in later chapters the characters take off on their own.

But the overall, the complete, the cohesive vision must remain firmly in the author's eye. Otherwise the book would not have integrity, a musical composition—would have no coherence. Both, the book and the musical composition would be an aggregate of features, of bits and pieces, not an integral whole. The composer, the poet, the writer must sublimate his or her ego, and let the vision unfold as it would.

And this is the secret.

We can all be creative if we pay the price. The price is the sublimation of our ego. The artists often pay dearly for this sacrifice. When they leave their studio, their work finished, they are often accused of just the opposite. They are accused of suffering from an exulted sense of self, of what others regard as unwarranted pride and self-centered vanity. It may be true, sometimes, but mostly it is only the evidence of balance being restored. When partaking in a creative act, the artist loses himself in his work. He loses awareness of the world in which the rest of humanity move, work, have their being. He, or she, for many hours at a time, is not aware of his or her existence. A mother absorbed in the process of giving birth seldom expresses her interest in the people around her. Likewise the artists become instruments through which a vision, a divine act, is translated into physical reality. It is an act of transposing the Universal into the Particular. It is often said to be a painful process. Perhaps. But painful or not, it is certainly absorbing beyond any awareness of one's inconsequential, paltry self.

Later, with some artists, after long periods of creative endeavor, this very ego suppressed so insidiously screams to be recognized. As already said, balance must be restored. As for the rest of us, I firmly believe that it is not lack of vision which limits the scope of our creativity—it is our inability to translate a subjective vision into objective reality. It is the direct result of our inability to sublimate our little self; to curb our innate laziness, to devote many agonizing hours, often years, to creative pursuit. It has been said that genius is five-percent talent and ninety-five percent of work. I believe this to be true.

We, on the receiving end of the vision, expect to be spoon-fed word by word, note by note, in a lateral or linear fashion. The most we are prepared to accept is to be given notes modulated into chords, and words into intensity of expression. Imagine being taken to the Grand Canyon and then, rather than facing its splendor in a single, overwhelming, breathtaking instant, we were permitted to view the panorama a few inches, millimeters, at a time, always from left to right, from the top downwards, in narrow strips of visual images. And yet this is exactly how we absorb Mozart's visions.

A note at a time.

The great painter sees the finished painting in his minds eye before he begins. The great sculptor claims that the sculpture is already extant within the block of marble, and all he must do is to remove the unnecessary debris. What the artist attempts is to visualize the work of art, he tries to reproduce his inner vision as close as his techniques allows him. We might say that he attempts to visualize his vision. What we must try, as the listeners or viewers, as the recipients, is to see or hear *the original vision* that inspired the artist. If we do, we partake in the creative process. One could almost say, we help the artist.

Alas, so few of us succeed in this endeavor. So few even try.

Perhaps this is why the majority of people seem to ignore the "fine arts". To be a recipient of a divine act is a responsibility. It takes an effort. It often means study, it demands that we rise to the level of those who sublimate their egos to become channels for our joy and pleasure. As Aristotle had said: Art is the knowledge of the universals. The domain of the divine. Or in the words of the renown art critic, perhaps better said, unfettered art lover, Sister Wendy: "So many people live in a prison of daily life with no one to tell them to look out or look up. If you don't know about God, art is the only thing that can set you free. It satisfies and challenges the human spirit to accept a deeper reality."[2]

How empty is the life of him who knows neither art nor God.

Art is the evidence of miracles.

The word miracle comes from Latin *miraculum*, which derives from *mirari* to wonder at, and finally from *mirus* meaning wonderful. This is where art and miracle congeal into a single meaning. Both testify to the invisible being made manifest in the visible, the material realm. But the nature of both remains tied to its roots. Both are wonderful.

There are 'artists' today, who seem driven by what is new. They are not concerned with beauty, with harmony or even order. They are not concerned with life. Yet for art to be art it must be imbued with life. It must bear witness to a greater reality, it must attest to the human potential, it must enhance the life of the recipient, at least attempt to raise him or her to a higher level. Not by promulgating some great truths which have already been proclaimed and promulgated for thousands of years. Not by preaching its own righteousness. It must reach out directly for our hearts. The mind calculates, the heart feels. So does Soul. It absorbs by direct perception. When we encounter a great work of art we are often speechless—or should be. Time seems to stop. There is no need to discuss it, to praise it or to express one's relation to it. All has been already said in color, or shape or music. All that's left is feeling. The partaking in the echo of the divine.

I do not object to artists crossing new horizons. I encourage it. The new, the unknown, is the dynamic of life. It is the essence of progress. But what art must bring into the world is new *beauty*. Or perhaps a new way of looking at beauty. After all, beauty is a divine attribute, it has no boundaries. Art must not, nor can it, bear witness to ugliness, to the banality of "life" of those who are still dead. It has been said that it is the artist's job to chronicle his or her era for posterity. Ugliness has no posterity. It has a barren womb. Let the dead take care of the dead. Ugliness is to be fast forgotten; never to be repeated, never to have its reality extended by our acceptance. Ugliness, noise, smut are the opposites of beauty, harmony and poetry. They who dabble in the first three, let alone make money by disseminating such among the masses, will pay dearly for their folly. A time will come when such false apostles will hunger for a vision, for contact with the upper realms, and they will be denied. Not forever, but until they restore the balance they have upset by their base greed and irresponsibility. And by the way: true artists are they who can find beauty where the rest of us see only the mundane. God is everywhere, and so is beauty. But only the greatest amongst us can see it. The artists.

They are the messengers of God.

An artist's responsibility, his or her job, is to raise those who provide other necessities of life to a higher level. To "make us look up" as Sister Wendy has said. They must not only enjoy their talent; they must share it with us.

***

The film industry has long lost its vision. They show no love of art; at best they saturate us with anemic melodrama.

To illustrate: an actor is accompanied throughout his, say, urban exploits by the blaring strains of a grinding organ, piercing screech of burning tires, and the deafening sirens of police cars in hot pursuit. The dialogue is so insipid, so feeble, spoken is such bad English that little is lost other than the acuity of our eardrums. A fully-fledged symphony orchestra follows our intrepid hero-actor into the verdant jungle in the heart of Africa, to the murky depth of the Pacific Ocean, across the silent dunes of an arid desert. The babel they play will be forgotten together with the film. They no longer aim at quality; they serve the gods of numbers. The more films the better. Never mind art. Never mind vision. Money? "Give me the money" is their favorite password. Millions of dollars for a *single* role, for providing a hilarious laugh, an amusement, an entertainment, while watching and hearing thousands scream while dying on the fateful Titanic. What happened to the soft whisper of the wind, the gentle wash of the ocean on a deserted beach, the song of the nightingale? What happened to poetry, to elocution, to the wondrous strains of a trained voice delivering an immortal soliloquy? If one is past the teens one is past one's prime. A cult of youth? Or total disregard for artistic training?

One cannot mention film without mentioning television.

If the film industry, for the most part, lost its vision, than I might argue that the TV and particularly the televised news media never had one. The 'news' does not have to be new to qualify, but it must be virtually limited to the destructive. The headlines are only headlines if they deal with (preferably mass) murder, flamboyant explosions, devastating hurricanes or earthquakes, passenger train derailments, airplane crashes... all cast in beautiful color, directed by the best directors, produced by the best producers. After all, the reporters do not 'report' on the news, they perform it! All news must be bathed in currents of blood, pain, all presented in dripping, gory details. It is abundantly apparent that if no one got murdered, raped or at the very least cheated out of their lifetime savings, the news media would close shop, unable to provide any 'entertainment' for their faithful listeners. After all, we must get good ratings. Let us throw in a few more good murders. If there are none homemade, perhaps we can find some corpses in Japan, or Sri Lanka, or perhaps in Kosovo?

No one would listen to "good news".

But this pathological face of the TV news and its pushers, who spend as much time advertising themselves as embellishing the news they are paid to deliver, have a peripheral quite accidental side effect. When the bland faced reporters, often unable to deliver a single sentence without stammering, errr'ing and aaah'ing every second or third word, display their gory videotapes, a strange subliminal lesson is fed, unwittingly, to the unsuspecting public. The small, intimate screen shimmering in the comfort of our living rooms shows the close-ups of people often thousands of miles away. And the screens show that the expressions on the faces of mothers mourning their sons and daughters dying from the NATO righteous bombs, and the mothers of the Kosovo refugees whose husbands and sons had been murdered by the Serb unrighteous soldiers are exactly the same. But the real shock comes later. The next week the gleeful reporters show new close-ups, this time of mothers mourning their children murdered by deranged youths in a mid-American High School. And again a strange thought invades the unsuspecting viewer—or it will soon, suddenly, during some hot summer night... a strange, lingering thought that the faces of mothers in Littleton, Colorado and the faces of other mothers in Belgrade, and those of mothers in Kosovo were so very similar. Perhaps they were all united by the very same expression. Perhaps they are related...

And then the horror of it all hits us with an overwhelming force. The mothers with their stunned, vacant faces *were* all members of the same family—no matter what the politicians say.

We kill each other's children.

But there is reason in the news-barons' madness. Why did I choose to expose the lack of vision in a book about vision? The full import of the effect of the dismal newscasts shall become visible in the next chapter which deals with *Programming*. Suffice to say that thanks to the somber reporting fewer people listen let alone view the prevalent negativism inherent in all the news broadcasts. In spite of a necrophilous appetite of many humans and beetles alike, fewer and fewer people waste their time looking at the events of the past, at *that which has happened*, and concentrate more on their lives *in the present*. And so, even in depravity there is some, albeit unwitting, reason. Even as there are hidden patterns in the midst of chaos.

Unbeknownst to them, by sinking below the tolerable levels of decency, the newscasters are releasing masses of people from their depraved grasp. People are growing tired of death. The same is true of the Hollywood film business. The lower they sink, the more people will choose to be active, to shed the long-induced, media-exploited couch-potato lifestyle and start *living*. Not vicariously, on the screen, but within their own enticing realms.

They will busy themselves with the creation of their own, vibrant universes.

So much for the creative media. Nietzsche was right. The gods are dead; they took their muses with them. The media are barren of any human values. Hollywood is barren of music, barren of art, barren of the sounds of nature. Unless, of course, the sound is that of a devastating cataclysm tearing our earth from its foundations, augmented by thousands of amps in a stereophonic nightmare.

And the filmmakers are not alone.

Covering canvass with paint does not an artist make. A chimpanzee can do it, often with better results. Compounding discordant noises, drowning them with amplified percussion, does not add-up to music. It is still only noise. Loud noise. So is the rush-hour traffic, the screams of beer-bloated fans in a football stadium, the clucking of ten thousand hens pecking on a chicken farm. And the smell is similar, too.

Surely we are meant to reach higher. Aspire to greater deeds, live greater dreams.

The first spark of divinity within us is manifested by our ability to open ourselves to our own inner vision. To become aware of being more than what we seem to be. A vision that defies limitations opens us to the unknown. There is but one reward for a true, aspiring artist: Immortality. When thousands of years have passed only the best will have survived. If we are amongst those few, they shall embrace us with awe, love and gratitude. They'll pay us homage. They will recognize us of yore as the messengers of gods.

Art is the vision of the gods immortal.

***

To sum up, art embodies the culmination of order, harmony and beauty. Anything which does not include these three is not art. I am not saying that a discord or conflict cannot be used in a composition to accentuate the beauty of harmony. Nor am I disputing the value of contrast in visual arts to enhance that which expresses the opposite. What I am saying is that the use of discord *in lieu* of harmony is not to be confused with art or a vision of art. Such misuse of divine resources is the denial of art—even as power and indifference is the denial of love.

We live in a transitional period.

The ancients knew, and we are learning fast, that we cannot pour fresh wine into old skins.[3] The present set of values will be destroyed to make room for the new. As students of the Zodiac know, the beginning of the Age of Aquarius is under the powerful influence of destructive forces. The planet Uranus, the god of the sky, symbolizes them. The Greek myth tells us that he, Uranus, had been wounded by his own son Cronus. His blood fell onto the earth producing the Furies and the giants; but from the drops, which fell into the sea, arose Aphrodite. Aphrodite—the goddess of love, fertility and beauty.

So not all is lost.

The darkest scourge of the present age is noise, both aural and visual. Noise is to our eyes and ears what confusion is to the realm of physics. It is the absence of order, of harmony. It is most dangerous when the 'beat', or its ugly sister the blinding glitter, override our senses to the exclusion of an intelligent thought. Noise, today, is so prevalent that the next generation of children, of youths, is rapidly losing their ability to use their two primary senses. They are growing deaf prematurely, their eyes grow weaker sooner. The omnipresent television and radio are filled with programs wherein the voice of the actor, the speaker, the announcer is obliterated by the foreground noise erroneously styled as music, whereas the viewers' eyes ache from the frequency of explosions, outbursts, eruptions, flare-ups, and a variety of flashing visual excesses.

Are we killing our children?

Perhaps this is all necessary.

Perhaps this is all necessary in order for us to lose our ability to use physical senses and pay more attention to the inner body, the inner vision, inner hearing, inner perceptions. Perhaps as we grow deaf and blind we shall open our senses to greater, higher art-forms.

Perhaps we shall visualize a new and better world.

How can we learn to tell art from the modern excesses masquerading as such? Is there a way to distinguish 'real' art from other decadent forms of visual or aural distraction?

The first and foremost is exposure.

If we visit art galleries, exhibitions, on a regular basis, if we attend symphonic concerts, if we spend time with and listen to the discreet sounds of nature... we shall learn discrimination. It will creep slowly upon us. It will wend its way into our soul, claim us as its chosen victims. We shall become prisoners of the gods, before becoming gods ourselves. And then, gradually, we shall learn discrimination. Whatever survived a century or two, there is a good chance that is has qualities which might, just might be immortal. If so, they qualify. We can also visit museums, walk through the silent hallways, then come back and stop at our most favorite exhibits. There we can spend some time in gentle communion with the artist. If we are lucky, he will invite us into his studio, and there, vicariously, we shall partake in the creative process. Time will stop, our painting will develop an aura, such as saints are depicted as having around their heads.

It is the aura of vision.

And then there is poetry.

All written word suffers from inherent limitations. It is bound by its language. Language imposes national boundaries, universal ideas held in the vise of parochial limitations. But there had been those who traversed those boundaries. Their vision refused to be contained by the imposed conditions. Is Shakespeare an English or a universal poet? His poetry hovers on the very verge of music. And poems last forever. The poems I have learned as a child I can still recite by heart. The poets left their imprint on my soul. I hope all parents will enable their children to partake in such joy.

As for music—it is, surely, the greatest of all art forms.

It is not reduced by the limitations of any language. It is truly global, recognizes no boundaries. It is the most universal of all creative endeavors. There are good composers living today, of this I am sure. But only time will tell if any of them will become immortal. Before we pass judgment on them, let us be sure that we are well grounded in beauty. That we have already tasted of that which has survived a long while. When we are attuned to divine vibrations we shall know the difference between music and noise—the scourge of our present era.

Some children of a lesser god compose music which suffers from chauvinistic overtones. Others have not been constrained by such limitations. And those others will survive long centuries, surely they will become immortal. Some already have. Some already gave us the food of the soul. Some shared with us their divine vision.

Aren't we lucky?

***

FOOTNOTES

(1). This subject is discussed in broader terms in BEYOND RELIGION Vol. II, essay on *Wunderkind*.

(2). Sister Wendy Beckett, born in South Africa, now living in a trailer in Norfolk, on the grounds of a Carmelite monastery, became a renowned art critic and commentator thanks to her inimitable powers of observation.

(3). Matthew 9:17, Mark 2:22, Luke 5:37.

Chapter 14
Health and Healing

In recent years more has been written on health and healing than at any time in human history. The bookshelves in our many bookstores are sagging under the ponderous volumes, each offering the bewildered sufferer a way out of the recurrent recalcitrant maladies which seem to be increasingly testing mankind. Most of us are vaguely aware that we poison ourselves with the chemical cocktails placed at our disposal, but few would dare to refuse the scientific-sounding concoctions. Few of us seem to realize that half of all the antibiotics produced are fed to the animals which are fed to the humans, which are fed to the bacteria which develop superb immunity to the said antibiotics. I am confident that there are international biochemical conglomerates which are in the process of inventing poisons to combat diseases which have not as yet been invented.

The self-help books usually start with voluminous advice on diets, weight loss, exercises subdivided neatly into anaerobic and aerobic which I shall discus briefly in the following chapter, and range all the way to many prophylactic methods all but guaranteed to keep us fighting fit, even if we have no one to fight.

During the last few years the West has been swamped with the East. Our pragmatic medical regimen of Standard Medicine is in direct competition with the so-called Alternative Medicine systems. Dr. Andrew Weil, mentioned in the chapter on *Medical View*, in addition to his own inimitable cocktail of self/assisted healing avocations (for which I have the highest respect), lists competing medical trends in an alphabetical order. I took the liberty of adding a few from other sources:

Acupuncture, Acupressure, Anthroposophy, Ayurvedic medicine, Bioenergetics, Biofeedback, Biomagnetic techniques, Body work, Traditional Chinese medicine, Chiropractic, Guided Imagery and Visualization Therapy, Herbal medicine, Holistic medicine, Homeopathy, Hypnotherapy, Naturopathy, Orthomolecular medicine, Osteopathic Manipulative Therapy, Religious and Psychic Healing, T'ai-chi, Therapeutic Touch.

Why so many alternative systems? Could it be that an average patient can no longer pronounce let alone understand the labyrinths, skeins and morasses of the so-called "standard medicine"? We are no longer independent units of consciousness endowed with any residual free will, but rather represent the Standard Medicine's vision of ourselves. A random look in our telephone book will reveal to a suffering patient more departments than body parts. Here are some of them:

Behavior therapy, Birthing center, Cardiac clinic, Colposcopy, Comm. mental health center, CT Scan-tomography, Dentistry, Dermatology, Diabetics, Diagnostic, Endocrinology, Endoscopy, Epdemiology & Biostatistics, ERCP clinic, Family medicine, Gastro-enterology, Geriatric, Gynecology, Hematology, Infectious diseases, Immune deficiency, Internal medicine, Intensive care-Medical, Intensive care-Neurological, Intensive care-Surgical, Lifeline Rotary-RVH, Lupus, Medical clinic (sic), Medical imagining, Medical oncology, Metabolic day center, Nephrology, Neurology, Neuroradiology, Neuroscience, Neurosurgery, Nuclear medicine, Obstetrics, Oncology, Ophthalmology,

Orthopaedic, OTL clinic/ENT, Pain clinic (sic), Palliative care, Pediatric consultation center, Physiotherapy, Psychiatry, Public health, Radiation oncology, Respiratory diseases, Speech pathology and audiology, Surgery clinic, Tropical diseases, Ultrasound, Urology........

Yes, there are others, many others.....
And we haven't mentioned as yet the really specialized fields such as Psychology, Psychotherapy, Gestalt Psychotherapy, Psychoanalysis... nor medical jurisprudence, forensic, sports and even (!) preventive medicine... I find the list alone is in grave danger of making most of us sick.
Very sick.

And then there is an array of quasi-religious 'systems' which, while not strictly religious, nevertheless rely on our belief systems to respond to the healing energies emanating from, if we are to believe their advocates, an incredible number of sources. I know of people who bathe in incredibly polluted waters of the Ganges to procure a physical and/or spiritual healing. I know of others who dip their dirty fingers in cesspools of pollution known as "holy water" placed astutely at the entrances to many churches, and then touch their foreheads with those same damp fingers spreading disease from one to another. Similar "holy waters" which may have been stagnant for extended periods of time are sprinkled by priests on moribund believers. If the disease doesn't kill them, the germs in the water will.

I've heard of people traveling thousands of miles to places where miracles occurred, in ardent hope of a repeat performance. A sort of religious instant replay. I've heard of others who lie prone, their faces on the cold marble of a church floor, to obtain a healing. I have read that there are people who believe that walking on their bare knees up a steep concrete stair will have a positive effect on their infected lungs.[1] Such devotees believe that pain and sacrifice has curative properties.

While I am more than willing to concede that I am guilty of omitting a number of healing techniques advocated among the many cousins of the various systems enumerated above, the ones listed should suffice to prove that the human race is in an incredibly bad shape. That God, Nature or the Evolutionary Forces must have veered somewhere from the straight and narrow.

Are so many systems of healing necessary?
Depends for whom....
If so many medical systems exist, can you imagine how many thousands of, surely, honest people are making millions, ney billions of dollars from our simplistic credulity? How many people are amassing fortunes from our inability to cure ourselves? And after all this, have you heard of anyone who, in spite of the impressive if scary list above, did not die? Sooner or later? And therefore, if the "medical" systems are there only to extend our misery, why do we put so much faith in them?

And most of all, didn't nature equip our bodies with a superb immune system which managed to assure our survival for countless millennia *before* the medical systems had been invented?

And then we have the incredible array of poisons to which the hapless bodies of the human race are subjected. I am not talking about air-pollution or the acrid effluent from the pernicious factories, but the spurious rain of poisons with which the pharmaceutical industry inundates our gullible gullets. I am reminded of a saying: *"Not that which goeth into the mouth defileth a man; but that which cometh out of the mouth, this defileth a man"*.[2] But this wisdom will not stop the pharmaceutical combines from trying. Dr. Weil in his book mentioned above adapts this biblical thesis to the art of healing. He writes: "Treatment originates outside; healing *comes from within.*"[3] It is evident that the effect of whatever we ingest is tempered by our faith in its efficacy. If we take a pill and we don't believe it will help—it will not; or at the very least its remedial result will be vastly impaired. According to the innumerable positive results obtained with placebos, the reverse effect is true also. Placebos give substance to the biblical creed: "According to your faith be it unto you".[4] In the western world, the power of visualization had been known for, at the very least, two millennia. The learned researchers of today are just beginning to rediscover it's potential. If we only stopped treating the Bible as a religious dissertation and studied it for the scientific knowledge it contains, our "standard" medicine would be vastly more advanced.

In the misguided footsteps of medieval alchemists, it is apparent that, as a rule, standard medicine relies on poisons, known toxic concoctions, to remove symptoms without ever attempting to heal the cause of the disease. Many of these toxic "remedies" are known to have dangerous side effects. Linus Pauling, the twice Nobel Prize winner,[5] cited a label adorning some medicaments:

CAUTION: Children under 12 should use only as directed by a physician. If symptoms persist or are unusually severe, see a physician. Do not exceed recommended dosage. Not for frequent or prolonged use. If excessive dryness of the mouth occurs, decrease dosage. Discontinue use if rapid pulse, dizziness, skin rash, or blurring of vision occurs. Do not drive or operate machinery as this preparation may cause drowsiness in some persons. Individuals with high blood pressure, heart disease, diabetes, thyroid disease, glaucoma or excessive pressure within the eye, and elderly persons (where undiagnosed glaucoma or excessive pressure within the eye may be present) should use only as directed by physician. Persons with undiagnosed glaucoma may experience eye pain; if this occurs discontinue use and see physician immediately."[6]

This caution is not posted by a mad scientist working for a dictator with visions of world domination, but apparently by a 'responsible' pharmacist over a 'healing' drug. Linus Pauling also had this comment about prescription for treating colds and other respiratory ailments: Instead of the warning "KEEP THIS MEDICINE OUT OF REACH OF CHILDREN" carried by cold medicines, I think that they should say "KEEP THIS MEDICINE OUT OF REACH OF EVERYBODY! USE VITAMIN C INSTEAD!"[7] Dr. Pauling was a strong advocate of maga-doses of vitamins which, according to him, enhanced and assisted our immune system in doing its work.

Dr. Pauling was not alone in expressing grave reservations about the amount of poisons our pharmaceutical industry is determined to administer to their unsuspecting buyers. Earl Mindell whose Vitamin Bible had, by 1985, over two million copies in print reports the following example (one of many):

More than ever before, Americans are gulping down drugs.... What people don't realize is that a lot of these medications... ...are taking as much as they're giving, at least nutritionally.
... ingredients found in common over-the-counter cold, pain, and allergy remedies actually lowered the blood level of vitamin A. Since vitamin A protects and strengthens the mucous membranes lining the nose, throat and lungs, a deficiency could give bacteria a cozy home to multiply in, *prolonging the illness the drug was meant to alleviate.*[8]

Is it possible, just possible, that we are going the wrong way?
It is now becoming apparent, that all the medical systems or disciplines have something to offer. There is no profession, however, which can tell us which offers what that is best for us. Not best for the various systems but for us. We and we

alone can make this decision. We may have to conduct considerable research before we accept anyone's diagnosis, let alone their recommendations for any cure. And we must never forget that which the practitioners' of Standard Medicine appear to have long forgotten: "treatment originates outside; healing *comes from within*."[9]

Whatever our decision, we must at the very least stop interfering with the natural healing process. This, the most important aspect of restoring health is up to us. Not up to any medical or quasi-medical system. We can no longer pass the buck.

We have come of age.

Can you visualize a universe in which there are no physicians? In which people are born healthy, and live in the protection of their magnificent immune system developed over millions of years of evolution? Rather like animals which live in the few areas not yet affected by man's paranoia—by man's need to dominate all at all cost? Go forth and multiply! Why? Isn't six billion enough?

Can you imagine Eden?

***

FOOTNOTES

(1). Such feats are practiced to this day on the many flights of stairs leading to Saint Joseph's Basilica in Montreal, Canada.

(2). Matthew 15:11

(3). Weil, Andrew M.D., SPONTANEOUS HEALING, pg. 6. My emphasis.

(4). Matthew 9:29

(5). 1954 for chemistry, and 1962 of peace. He's also the recipient of over 40 honorary degrees from colleges and universities.

(6). HOW TO LIVE LONGER AND FEEL BETTER by Linus Pauling, Avon Books, New York 1987; pages 323-4.

(7). ibid.

(8). Earl Mindell, VITAMIN BIBLE, [Warner Books, 1985] pg.262 (my emphasis)

(9). To repeat Dr. Weil's admonition: Weil, A., SPONTANEOUS HEALING, page.6. [my emphasis].

Chapter 15
Visualization in Sports

*I swear by Apollo the physician, and Aesculapius, and
Health, and All-heal, and all the gods and goddesses that,
according to my ability and judgment
I will keep this oath and this stipulation...*

*...I will follow that system of regimen which,
according to my ability and judgment,
I consider for the benefit of my patients...
With purity and holiness I will pass my life and practice my
Art.*

Hippocrates c.400 B.C.
THE OATH
[part. Translated by Francis Adams]

On **Monday, March 15, 1999** it had been reported that a Stephon (sic) Marbury agreed to a $70,900,000 (that's 70.9 million U.S. dollars) six-year contract with the National Basketball Association's New Jersey Nets. Assuming a forty-year earning life of non-basketball players, that's approximately 70x more than a lifetime income of an average citizen of the United States. It is also 35x more than the top ten percent of people.[1]

Do the basketball players know something we don't?

After the announcement Marbury said: "The thing I can

say to pretty much sum this up in one is that this is the day I've been waiting to come since I was a child. Through all we want to accomplish in life it's all coming true. It's a dream."[2]

It's a dream.

Disregarding for a moment the image of a baby Stephon lying in his oversized cradle, rattling his rattle while dreaming of $70.9 million contract, I cannot help wondering how many people remember the words of a song from South Pacific: "If you don't have a dream, you cannot have a dream come true." Dreams are the factories of universes, of subjective realities. They seldom affect the lives of others. You are unlikely to be successful in dreaming up fortunes, talents or successes for your friends. You can have some results by the so-called powers of white magic (see chapter on *Programming)*, but usually it would take much too much effort. Also, if you succeed, you will bear the karmic consequences of your actions. Good or bad. A risky proposition. On the other hand, dreams as pertaining to your own universe are automatically self-perpetuating. In some respects, you must be careful what you dream about. It might well come true. And you will be stuck with the results, like it or not.

Dreams are built in your subconscious. Your emotional body fuels them. Of course, you must believe in your success. "If you have faith as a grain of mustard seed, you shall say unto this mountain, Remove hence to yonder place: and it shall remove; and *nothing shall be impossible unto you.*"[3] But this is only an allegory. In fact, with this technique Soul builds whole universes. The emotional reality is also called the imaginative body. It is not a body you imagine, it is a body which imagines. And which translates images into physical reality. All you must do is to visualize your dream—then leave it alone. Let the factory do its work. Your subconscious will guide you to success (or failure). The only part of the biblical statement which is *not* an allegory is the assertion that:

NOTHING SHALL BE IMPOSSIBLE UNTO YOU

This part can be taken literally. Your only constraint is your faith. And, of course, the universal laws. Even God cannot create a stone so heavy He/She couldn't lift it. I doubt God would want to. Nor would you. This will be discussed in detail in a later chapter on the *Creative Process*. And this Process has been used, often unwittingly, throughout history. Now, we seem to be losing awareness of its power. Except in one particular arena that is the domain of the young. It is the arena of sports.

We can watch them and learn.

There once was a time, when the success in sport had been thought to be the result exclusively of training, diet and discipline. Athletes have been guided to lift progressively heavier weights to build up their muscles, to run for long distances to develop strength and stamina of their cardiovascular and pulmonary systems, to practice sprints to enhance their speed. All these remain of vital importance. They result in attributes which offer the athlete the means. They add up to the equipment that an athlete can use to accomplish his of her dream. But the actual success comes from within. It is comparable to the healing processes discussed in the previous chapter: treatment (training) originates outside; healing (visualization of success) comes from within.

In no discipline is the visualization process so accepted, so widely practiced as in sports. With more stringent rules, and particularly their rigorous enforcement, the professional sportsmen can no longer rely on steroids which brought so many East Germans to the victory podium in past Olympics. A Canadian sprinter's World Record and his Olympic gold medal had been revoked, because a 'forbidden' substance had been found in his blood. With the reputedly harmful chemicals being outlawed, we could say that visualization, or the mind-body liaison, has been forced on the athletes of today.

Apart from the years of arduous training, hours upon hours of repetitions, an athlete still needs an edge. This edge is no longer found in additional physical activities. What has been found is, that if an athlete spends additional time visualizing his (her) body functioning in a perfectly coordinated manner, if he can see in his mind's eye the whole race, step after step, if ultimately he can visualize his chest breaking the tape at the end of the race, his chances of wining are greatly enhanced.

Visualization is no longer the domain of stage magicians, yogis and gurus, or sinister characters on the periphery of our society. It is practiced by athletes whose annual income exceeds, by far, the lifetime earnings of most other mortals. Yet, this method, the art of visualization is not limited to the rich and famous. In fact, it is the only discipline of 'medicine' which is absolutely free. And you don't even have to leave home to do it.

Isn't it time we all took advantage of this system?

Every record ever broken on the athletic field had been first broken in the mind of the athlete involved. We are all programmed with limitations. We all tend to visualize the impossible. We back our negative vision with armadas of excuses. "I'm too old, too weak, too tired, too busy, too lazy, too stupid." The chances are that only the last two are true. But we don't have to be. *It is always up to us.* Great spiritual avatars of the past did their utmost to dispel our limitations. They all worked to convey the message that the spirit to mind to body connection is the way to achieve results. This applies as much to sports as to any endeavor. On May 6, 1954, at Oxford, England, Roger Bannister (later Sir Roger) ran a mile in 3 minutes 59.4 seconds. Until that time, four minutes had been regarded as an impossible barrier for the human potential. Bannister convinced himself that it isn't. He had to deny the conditioning which limited *all* the runners to-date.

Once he broke the *mental* barrier, the physical one became a natural aftermath—a consequence, an effect. And the best way to break the mental barrier is to visualize oneself doing it. There are other methods which aid one in crossing new horizons. Some are called affirmations, various other techniques dealing with autosuggestion, but they all deal with the future events. "I *shall* do this or that. I can do it, I shall do it, I am capable of doing it."

But in visualization *we see ourselves actually doing it*.

It becomes a *fait accompli*. When we approach the playing field we are no longer facing the impossible which we "believe" we can overcome. We face an event that we already performed in our mind's eye. We repeat in physical life what we already accomplished in our imaginative body. We no longer face the unknown.

The same process is now universally employed in virtually all sports. At almost every athletic meet, men and women break their personal bests. Why haven't they done it before, in training? Why wait to better your own capability when under great pressure? Surely, it would be even harder to break one's own barrier while stared at by thousands of people. The answer is that training is meant to supply one's imaginative body with the equipment, with the means of accomplishing the seemingly impossible. You cannot break a record sitting on a couch. The laws of *all* the universes must be obeyed (see *Universal Laws*).

Have you ever watched a high-jumper ready himself for his next leap? There is tremendous concentration on his face. He measures every single step in his mind's eye. He sees, feels, visualizes his lean body approaching the bar, springing up into the air, and clearing the new, the heretofore impossible, height. Only it is no longer impossible. He had already cleared it. In his vision. He now must simply recreate the conditions which he'd seen in his dream. Every step, every step....

... something is still missing. Ah... yes. In the dream there was the roar of the crowd gradually dying out. Then there was rhythmic clapping. The athlete raises his hands above his head and initiates the sound he heard in his dreams. The crowd responds. The next moment the athlete clears the bar. It was so easy...

The athlete chose to leave the 'ordinary' reality. He or she had to transport his or her body into the realm of the dream. Completely. For a moment, minutes or seconds, the dream reality became the only reality. And the dream materialized practically as an afterthought. It became an effect.

The cause is always within, the effect without.

If Shakespeare was right, than we are all players. Be it in sports, on a stage—in any arena of any endeavor. It might be wiser if we weren't to take our lives so seriously. We could treat life as a good sport. Both can be competitive, be a source of great pleasure, and provide us with an opportunity of enjoining really hard work. It can also bring great rewards, great satisfaction, fame and fortune. With the exception of an athlete, perhaps his family and a circle of friends, no one really cares deeply if any particular record will be broken. The sun will still rise, lovers will continue to search for the unknown fruit; artists will remain lost in a reality shrouded by their muses. The world will continue to unfold itself, as it should.

Perhaps we should all try a little less hard to improve others, a little harder to improve ourselves. No sportsman or sportswoman can make their best friend break a world record. It is as personal an achievement as is his or her soul. We alone can create a reality in which we are world-record beaters. Only we must not leave it to chance. We must learn to do it consciously. The creative aptitude is a factor built into our genes. It lies within the heart of every man, woman and child. All we must do is to supply it, our potential, with the greatest equipment we can, with the widest possible means our talents allow. We supply those means by hard work. We must never forget that genius is five percent talent and ninety-five percent sweat. Ask any successful neighbor. But after we provided the means, we must leave our dream alone. Let our inner self, the creative factory, do its job. We can do the training but our inner self does the record breaking. At the right moment, we just stand by and watch. Watch the moment of glory.

We have been given unimaginable powers. It is up to us to muster our potential. Not really for the sake of fame or fortune. Just for the shear joy of living.

***

FOOTNOTES

(1). The Montreal Gazette. $(70900000 \div 40) \div 70 = \$25,321.43$ average annual income over 40 years. Please note, these are 1999 dollars.
(2). ibid.
(3). Matthew 17:20 [my emphasis]. Compare Luke 17:6.

CREATING YOUR OWN UNIVERSE

Chapter 16
Redefining Self

Four hundred years before the birth of Christ, Socrates summed up his advice in just two words:

KNOW THYSELF

Towards paying my homage to Socrates, in this and the next chapter, I shall attempt to review some of the consequences of my observations of reality I have shared with you so far. I shall also repeat some of my conclusions, while, as always, leaving the final judgment to the reader.

All who took the trouble to analyze the factors discussed in this book so far can no longer suspect that the universe we inhabit, the universe of which we are aware, is an environment which we detect solely with our senses. For some of us, whatever we cannot see, smell, hear, touch or taste is not part of our reality. People who ascribe to this form of perception often proudly avow themselves as atheists, never having taken the trouble to define what it is that they actually don't believe in. Suffice to say, the intangible has, in their opinion, little or no bearing on their well being.

This stance is perfectly acceptable, providing the adherents to this reality define themselves as physical entities, endowed with the five, reasonably well functioning, senses. They must also concede, however, that they have not (yet) risen above the animal level, which I define as being capable of abstract thought.

All animals think. Few think in abstract terms. Those which do, I define as human.[1] The assumption of an intangible reality requires abstract thought patterns. Nevertheless, every saint, spiritual teacher, mystic, prophet, savior and the majority of philosophers, have proposed this assumption. As we have seen in the chapter on *Scientific Perspective*, our pragmatic scientists have joined the bandwagon. They also forcibly challenge the 'materialistic' viewpoint. In their view, the very 'solidity' of the 'solid' universe has crumbled. According to theoretical physicists, the tangible universe in which we find our being is not at all what it seems. In many respects, it is no longer tangible at all.

Can anyone really pretend that all of them are wrong?

Before Einstein "unified" matter and energy, the two had been recognized *by our senses*, as separate entities, separate manifestations of reality. Although even the most obdurate materialists will probably concede that while the evidence of our senses is no longer reliable, the cumulative input of our imperfect impressions does result in a certain viewpoint, a certain mindset, to which I refer as a *State of Consciousness*. I like to think that this State is the cumulative effect of our awareness of our existence, and that it defines and describes our relationship and perception of reality. This "cumulative effect" results in a growing awareness of our selfhood, and our relation to the environment. Since our experiences vary, our individualized States must, *per force*, also represent unique views of reality. It is to this uniqueness that I would like to address myself.

This unique view I define as our *Subjective Universe*.

In like vein, since our sensual perceptions rely on the interplay of opposites, it is reasonable to assume that our reality is of a dualistic nature. If the materialists are still with me so far, they now face the reality of a "state of consciousness" which they cannot define in either sensory or physical terms. This realization leads us to think of ourselves as also exhibiting a dualistic nature: that which is visible, sensory, and that which is invisible and beyond the detection of our senses. While our physical bodies enjoy physical states of consciousness enhanced by the five senses, we also exhibit an inner nature, an inner State of Consciousness, variously described as spiritual, Higher, or Soul body, which exists in parallel to our physical nature.

Next we must face the chicken and the egg dilemma. Having established that the quality of our State of Consciousness is the result of the input of our senses, I shall now attempt to show that the State of Consciousness has its "being" regardless of and independently from our sensory inputs.

The ancient visionaries recognized three principal aspects of the human entity. As discussed in the chapter on *The Problem with Karma*, these have been symbolized by the word ISRAEL, wherein the IS represents our feminine or passive-nurturing nature, the RA our conscious-positive awareness, and EL the Divine Presence. It is fascinating to observe that the first two, the IS and the RA have been derived from the Egyptian mythological science, i.e. from the nature goddess Isis and Ra the sun-god, chief among all deities. It is of further interest that the Hebrew EL supersedes the RA.

We would be wise to remember that in the ancient days there had been no defined division between religion and science. The priests had been the curators of all knowledge of any and all medical sciences and physiological advancements. We shall soon see, perhaps with a dose of irony, that humanity made little progress in the latter field.

As already discussed in the chapter on the *Universal Laws*, the last book of the New Testament, the Apocalypse or Revelation of St. John the Divine, further breaks up our nature into four separate forms of expression. This quadruple-nature is symbolized by the four horses (of the Apocalypse), each representing one aspect of our disposition (character of personality). To recapitulate, the four are the white horse, symbolizing our spiritual aspect, black—the mental, red—the emotional and the gray horse—our physical nature. It is of vital importance to remember that it is the single entity, our true Self, which can choose which horse he or she rides. In other words, the spiritual nature explores the various aspects of the lower or animal nature, while being able to remain in its own realm: upon the white horse.

In more recent times various psychologists attempted, perhaps a little less clearly, to break down our nature into the various components. The renowned Sigmund Freud is responsible for the introduction of id, ego and the superego. His model of the psyche, however, places all three components of our self within the realm of the 'unconscious'. Margaret J. Black[2] describes Dr. Freud's primary constituents of the mind as follows:

"The id 'is a cauldron full of seething excitations' of raw, unstructured, impulsive energies; the ego is a collection of regulatory functions that keep the impulses of the id under control; the superego is a set of moral values and self-critical attitudes, largely organized around internalized parental imagoes."

Freud's repugnance towards religion[3] precluded his recognition of our spiritual nature, an aversion not shared by his contemporaries, including Carl G. Jung, whose concern for spirituality contributed to his break up with the father of psychoanalysis. Jung's awareness of the symbolic nature of the Bible, is seen in his essay: "The importance of dreams,"[4] in which he discusses the animals symbolizing the four Evangelists, relating them to the vision of Ezekiel[5] and its analogy to the Egyptian sun god Horus and his four sons. Jung was the first among the modern scientists, who acknowledged the scientific value of visions, and recognized that the communication between the unconscious and the conscious mind is often shrouded in profound symbolism. In other words, for us to understand our inner self we must learn the manner in which it communicates with us.

Equally as interesting though perhaps a more complex suggestion of redefining our true self if offered by Carol Pearson.[6] She suggests that we find expression of our nature through assuming or equating our personality with six (rather than four) archetypes. Ms. Pearson borrows the concept of archetype from Carl Jung, the concept of hero from Joseph Campbell (*The Hero with a Thousand Faces*) and evolves an interesting amalgam. She claims that once we leave Eden, wherein we manifested the nature of an *Innocent*, we will find our expression by identifying with the following archetypes: *Orphan, Martyr, Wanderer, Warrior* and *Magician*. The names of the five archetypes, somewhat suggestive of their *modus operandi*, manifest different needs, aspire towards different goals, exhibit different responses to, and methods for, overcoming problems (slaying-the-dragon), possess diverse spiritual needs, emotions, etc.. The world of each hero (that's you and me) symbolizes and is colored by different hues inherent in the perceptions of the various archetypes. We embody, according to Pearson, these dominating traits of character in a cyclic manner, until finally we merge the *Magician* again with the *Innocent*, our place of origin, only to eventually leave Paradise once more in search of new adventures.

Pearson's heroes fall one short of seven which, in most esoteric writings, is the number symbolizing perfection. The Hindu esoteric doctrine does not regard the human body merely as flesh and bones, but rather as *linga chakra* or subtle body, represented by a system of energy centers and interconnecting channels. In Hindu the energy centers are called *chakras*, and contrary to biblical symbolism are numbered from the seventh—lowest, to one—highest. The seven *chakras* are connected by *nadis* or tracks through which the 'neural' energy travels. The object is to unite the latent vital force residing in the lowest, seventh *chakra* with the power of thought, which dwells in the brain.

I shall not list all the *chakras* as this is specialized knowledge presumably of relatively little interest to the general reader. Suffice to say that the symbolic object is to unite the female and male principles in our subtle body to achieve enlightenment. When the goddess Kundalini the "coiled one", whose seat is in the lowest, the *muldhara chakra,* rises to meet her Lord at the *Sahasrara*, the *chakra* of the thousand-petalled lotus, a superphysical mating of Siva and Sakti takes place uniting the female and male aspects of the creative power. It could be said that the Hebrew tetragrammaton YHWH represents just such a mating. It is vital to understand that such mating takes place *within* our being.[7]

In her lengthy exegesis on the subject of Saint John the Divine's *Revelation*, Dorothy Elder bases her explanation of the most intensely symbolic writing of the Christian tradition almost exclusively on the seven *chakras*, equating the Kundalini with the Sprit of God and comparing the *chakras* to the *Seven Churches* (Ephesus, Smyrna, Pergamum, Thyaira, Sardis, Philadelphia and Laodicea) of the second and third chapters of the *Revelation*.[8] The book is well researched but is unlikely to help the reader in his or her day to day struggles. It does provide, however, yet another way of regarding ourselves and even our physical bodies.

A more down-to-earth or less complex explanation of the same scripture, the *Revelation*, is offered by Paulson and Dickerson in the *Revelation: the Book of Unity*. Here the two authors discuss the various aspects of our inner and outer nature, offering us the explanation of the *Seven Churches* in terms of the attributes of our consciousness. They list the Seven Churches as seats of desire, substance or energy, the intellect, the feeling nature, power and authority, love, and finally our power of judgment, discrimination and decision-making. As is the case with Elder, but in a more accessible fashion, the book tends to relate our spiritual, mental and emotional attributes with various parts of our physical body.[9] To each his own. I tend to think that my physical body is a byproduct of the other elements of my being, rather than an entity as such. I find it increasingly difficult to think of a vortex of swirling energy as a 'physical' entity.

Nevertheless, it becomes evident that if we are destined to understand our true nature through a symbolic process, it may be necessary to incorporate such into our mind-body communication or simply into a consciously controlled process of visualization. The second aspect to bear in mind is that since we find ourselves in a world which can be defined as a world manifesting duality, our process of visualization must take this factor into account.

We now have some idea of our complex nature. But in order to understand how we can manipulate reality, to shape it into a 'world' of our own choosing, we must face yet another element.

As discussed at the beginning of this chapter, since the Reformation our science has advanced sufficiently to destroy old concepts of our material universe. We are still used to thinking of all objects, including the human animal, as solid. With this approach, it is evident that the old sages had been 'forced' to split their reality into the inner and the outer (spiritual and material). They, even as many of us do today, had found it easy to accept that they could change their emotions or ideas, i.e. their emotional or mental reality, at will, but solid objects remained as solid as their perception of them implied. Through revelation they had known that they were more than just material bodies. Through observation, i.e. the employment of their senses, they perceived themselves as material or solid objects. During the last few dozen decades, it was not the first hypothesis which was challenged, but, incredible though it may seem, the second. Science has taken upon itself to challenge the apparent 'solidity' of our universe.

First Albert Einstein succeeded in proving that matter and energy are interchangeable. We always knew that we could convert a log of wood into energy with the aid of a fireplace. What we did not know is that tremendous energy is stored in every gramme of mass. Einstein attests to this hypothesis in his famous equation $e = mc^2$, where e represents energy, m—mass, and c—the velocity of light in a vacuum. This velocity has been determined to be approx. 300,000 kilometers per second. Isaac Asimov calculated that a single gramme of mass "can be converted into 21,500,000,000 kilocalories, a quantity that could also be obtained by the complete burning of 670,000 gallons of petrol".[10] Assuming your car can give you say 30 miles out of a gallon of gas, you could drive it for 20,100,000 miles before pulling up at the next gas station for refueling. And all this distance from a single gramme (1/27 of an ounce) of mass.[11] Since Einstein's equation was promulgated as a new way of visualizing the universe it remained unchallenged.

To do justice to the Socratic admonition "Know Thyself", we should include the view of ourselves as fields of energy. Assuming an average weight of an adult male at say 180 lbs (81.6 kg.), we might convert this to ounces and then multiply it by 27. Our male body would be able to generate the equivalent of [180 (lbs) x 16 (oz) x 27 x 670,000 (gallons of gas)]. This converts to 55,099,200,000 kilocalories, enough to propel the above-mentioned automobile for just under 1563 trillion miles (1.511), seven million times the distance from the earth to the moon. The female galactic traveler conscious of her slim figure could cover approximately 2/3 of that distance, a mere 1000 trillion miles.

If anyone ever tells you that you are full of gas, believe him.

Yet when all is said and done, we must again return to the Eastern sages. There is an occult expression which states: "as above so below". How does it apply to our, Western culture? We notice an echo of this premise in the biblical statement "whatsoever you bind on earth, shall be bound in heaven". While the object of the 'binding' is not specified,[12] we can assume that there is an interlocking relation between our inner and outer nature. There is also the biblical saying that we, the simple folk, have been created unto the image and likeness of God. The fundamentalists immediately reversed this proposal and made their god unto the image and likeness of man. While there is a certain logic in their reasoning, Socrates taught us that although all grass is green, not all that is green is grass. Fortunately there is no likeness of man's ego to be found in the non-ego bound universe. In fact, the universal is the direct opposite of the particular.

And yet...?

And yet there is a direct relationship between the image of God and the image of man. And, to a degree, we can study the universal by examining the particular. Only we must not regard the individual man's ego as the particular. What is comparative is the man's *body*. That's right, a man's physical, mortal, body. Body which is equipped with senses, mind and an imaginative quality. A three in one body. Only to understand this body, we must step out of the Middle Ages and examine the body in the light of today's science. Those of us who are still under the influence of religious conditioning must modify the way in which we regard ourselves. We might assume the following as a working hypothesis:

We are not created unto the image and likeness of God. Our bodies and the way they function *are*.

WE ARE INDIVIDUALIZATIONS
OF GOD HIMSELF.

We are *not* God and never shall be. We are individual expressions of SOUL, a divine attribute that enables the Infinite to experience the finite, the Universal to become the particular. We have the potential to express the qualitative attributes of the Universal. We do not, nor ever shall, express the quantitative attributes of God. God is that which is Whole. When the prophets of various religions stated that God is One, they meant that there is nothing which is outside the concept of God. God is ALL IN ALL. God is also THAT WHICH IS. The Torah calls It: I AM THAT I AM. In other words by God I mean all that has been created *and* all that could be created, i.e. the manifested *and* the unmanifested. In other words, GOD IS THE INFINITE POTENTIAL.

We partake in these qualities. To the extent that we espouse these concepts, we can manifest that which is as yet unmanifested. In this sense and to this degree, we are gods. Until we became aware of even a glimmer of this divine potential within us *and* begin working towards its greater realization, we are (still) dead. Or at least, that is what Jesus called this condition.[13]

At a deeper level of understanding, the "image and likeness" of our body lies not in its shape or form (as most religions would have it), but in its apparent ability to eternally renew itself. Today's science confirms this fact beyond any shadow of doubt. We have our true existence, our being, in the ephemeral fraction of a second between that which was and that which will be. This instant remains always in the present—in the timeless realm of the creative thought. We might think of ourselves as ideas within, and of, the Cosmic

Mind. Your or my physical or material body is the out-picturing or the manifestation of that idea, never the idea itself.

Ever bearing in mind the above, let us examine man's physical structure.

A human body consists of, say, three-hundred-trillion cells (300,000,000,000,000), of which some ten-million are replaced every second.[14] According to Deepak Chopra, every second there are some six-trillion chemical reactions taking place in this assembly of cells, which we call our body. And, again according to Chopra, each cell knows what all the other cells are doing. They are all interrelated, interdependent, integral to the totality of the body they form. You might say that they comprise a single gestält idea. But we must never forget that cells consist of molecules, the molecules of elements, and elements of atoms which are little more than impulses of energy and information.

The number of atoms in an average body is said to add up to 10^{28}, that's ten with twenty-eight zeros. It looks like this: 100,000,000,000,000,000,000,000,000,000, give or take a couple of billion. There is no human language which has a name for such a sum. The story doesn't end there. Baron Ernest Rutherford (1871-1937) demonstrated that the atom consists of a tiny "atomic nucleus" at the center—where most of the mass of the atom resides—and is surrounded by light particles called electrons. The hydrogen atom comes with but one electron but as atoms grow in complexity, more and more electrons orbit the nucleus in ever more complicated patterns. Their orbits are observed as distinctive spectral patterns. The iron atom, for instance, contains twenty-six electrons and produces thousands of lines in the visible range.

The particles of the nucleus itself come in two varieties—the protons and the neutrons, which with hyperons are known as byrons, or the 'heavy' atomic particles. [There are also heavy electrons known as mesons or mesotrons which are unstable particles about 200 times the mass of an electron. They are formed by the disintegration of cosmic rays and need not concern us here]. The mass of a "normal" electron is about 1/1800 that of a proton.

(*Nota bene*: we are still talking about human body).

The shrinking story goes on. All the byrons and mesons are made up of quarks and gluons, which are so small that they have never been seen, will never be seen, as it is impossible to even imagine machinery or cameras small enough to capture their size. We know they exist, and can observe them, by the trails they leave behind.

And here 'things' get really amusing...

Quarks come in a number of varieties. They come, perhaps, in six "flavors" which are called *up, down, strange, charmed, bottom* and *top*. Each flavor has (sort of) three 'colors': red, green and blue. Only they are not really flavors and are certainly not really colors. They can't be. They are too small to have *any* color. They are much smaller than the wavelength of visible light and so they can't have any color. But... protons and neutrons are made up of up and down quarks, three each, one of each color... A proton is made up of two up flavors and one down flavor. A neutron the other way round.

We are made up of quarks. They blink in and out of existence. Like you and I do.

Quite a lark, this quark. It's all James Joyce's fault.[15]

If you still doubt what you really are, let us again discuss the question of size from a different standpoint. An atom, as a whole, i.e. including the space taken up by the orbit of its electrons, has a diameter of say a hundred-millionth of a centimeter. The diameter of a sub-atomic particle is more like a ten-trillionth of a centimeter. To arrive at a diameter of a single atom, we would have to lay out, side by side, say 100,000 sub-atomic particles.

The volume of an atom is 10^{14} (100,000,000,000,000) larger than a single sub-atomic particle. Isaac Asimov put it in a nutshell:

"Since even the most complex atom contains only a little over 300 sub-atomic particles, it can clearly be seen that the intact atom is largely empty space, held in its wide-open structure by the electromagnetic forces that kept a few electrons moving through wide spaces about the tiny atomic nucleus at the centre of the atom."[16]

WE ARE LARGELY EMPTY SPACE

We are made up of minuscule impulses of energy and information held together by electromagnetic forces in, what is largely, empty space. How did it all come about? How is it sustained? Could all this have happened by shear accident? It seems that physics have invaded the domain of metaphysics. What of biology? How does it all work?

Our body operates on a divine principle.

We, individualizations of Soul, conceive of an idea. The unconscious mind translates this idea into a "proto-material" or protoplasmic form. From this protoplasm the subconscious draws elements necessary for the formation of individual cells. In other words, the *gestält*, whole or integral idea (image of God) is translated into a magma which contains all the elements necessary for the formation of individual cells ("...and the earth was without form").[17] This stage of the *spiritual* creative act (confirmed by recent embryonic research) is echoed in the formation of stem-cells, which have the potential to become any of the 210 specialized cell types our body requires. Every phase of spiritual manifestation is reflected in its material component. The occult law states: "As above—so below." We are the living proofs attesting to the veracity of this law. When a cell begins to acquire specific traits to serve a specific purpose, it is guided in the process by the subconscious mind. This part of our psyche is the storage of all the information acquired over millions of years of evolution. Think of a computer with millions of gigabytes

(GBs) of memory and you'll probably still fall short. The information from the subconscious is not only stored in our brain, but in the genes which give each cell its specificity. When science unravels the genetic code of man, it will unravel millions of years of evolution.

But then again... cells are made up of atoms which are impulses of energy and information. Whenever we think of matter, any matter, we must learn to think of it as fluid. As transient, adaptable, as malleable quanta, of an unmanifested idea made manifest. I repeat, matter is transient, its solid form is illusory. The Eastern sages call it maya. An illusion. The same is true of our physical bodies. As we walk, every hour our body sheds around 1.5 million skin flakes.[18] New dermal cells are created to take their place. The same is true of other cells in our body. Over the period of one year, new cells replace virtually all the cells in our body. The same, only much more so, is true of the sub-nuclear substance of which our bodies are made up:

At the subnuclear level, the quarks and gluons which make up the neutrons and proton of the atoms in our bodies are being annihilated and recreated on a timescale of less than 10^{-23} seconds; thus we are actually being annihilated and replicated—resurrected—10^{23} times a second in the normal course of our lives.[19]

We are in a constant state of appearing and.... disappearing. Even at the "gross" biochemical level we are *completely* different beings we have been a year ago. At the nuclear level the same is true, great many times, of every second. We are ephemeral flashes of light. I am again reminded of Sai Baba's affirmation: *"The light is you. You are the light."* The real you.

Physically, we are but shadows cast by our mind.
Shadows of light...

No cell is more fascinating than any of the ten thousand million cells (10^{10}) in our brain. While throughout our body cells come in all shapes and sizes, the brain cells display a characteristic of a truly inspired nature.

"Protoplasm in cellular form maintains a precarious electro-chemical balance and, like an explosive, can be fired by a trigger-action. Firing causes the cell to discharge (with an emission of impulse) and at the same time to reload and to re-cock the firing mechanism. ...the number of shots it fires is not determined by the length of time the trigger is pressed but by the force, the intensity, with which it is pressed just once..."[20]

I have given this information not to blind the reader with my research prowess, only to suggest that *we are not what we seem on the outside*. That we must regard ourselves in a slightly different light, even when we think of our bodies. That we must never confuse our consciousness, the divine Presence, with Its *effect*, namely with our body. With our microcosm.

Let us recap.

Each cell consists of molecules. Each molecule of atoms and of subatomic particles. Think of the numbers... We already know that our body, in terms of energy it can generate, is the equivalent of 21,500,000,000 kilocalories. These, while finite numbers, have a divine ring to them. Our mind can hardly conceive of what we truly are. But our mind is part of the created body. It is not the creator, it is the executor of the creative impulse of Soul.

You are light, said Sai Baba.

VISUALIZE YOURSELF AS LIGHT.

Imagine yourself as light radiating with the power of twenty-one billion kilocalories. Now do you believe the prophet who said: ye are gods?

Any man facing such energy would be burned to a cinder. Vaporized in a fraction of a second.

***

FOOTNOTES

(1). There is strong evidence that some simians as well as dolphins have this ability. If so, they find themselves in a higher evolutionary category than the "not quite yet" human.

(2). FREUD AND BEYOND by Stephen A Mitchell & Margaret J. Black, Harper Collins publ. 1995.

(3). ibid. pg.21

(4). Jung, Carl, G. MAN AND HIS SYMBOLS, (Dell Publishing Co., Inc, New York, 1964)

(5). Ezekiel 1: 4 et seq..

(6). THE HERO WITHIN by Carol S. Pearson Ph.D., (Harper Collins Publ. 1998).

(7). For amateurs of Hindu Yoga systems I recommend YOGA EXPLAINED by F.Yeats-Brown, (Victor Gollancz Ltd, 1937, London).

(8). Elder, Dorothy REVELATION FOR A NEW AGE [The Aquarian Age] (DeVross & Co. California 1981)

(9). Paulson, J. Sig / Dickerson, Ric REVELATION: The Book of Unity. (Unity Books, Unity Village, Missouri 1976)

(10). THE UNIVERSE by Isaac Asimov, Penguin Books 1971; pg.126. To the uninitiated, petrol is the British word for gasoline, or gas.

(11). In physics, *mass* is the quantity of matter a body contains as measured by its acceleration under a given force. It is determined by dividing the weight of the body by the acceleration due to gravity.

(12). The sacerdotal interpreters like to limit this "binding" to the rites of marriage, although Jesus speaks of it only in connection to Peter's understanding of the Truth. See Matthew 16:19

(13). Matthew 8:22.

(14). Weil, Andrew M.D., SPONTANEOUS HEALING (Ballantine Books, New York 1995) pg.74

(15). The word 'quark' was coined by James Joyce in *Finnegan's Wake*. N.B.: Quarks have been examined under the imaginary microscope of theoretical physics. In the latest theories, they are composed of 'super strings'. The physicists hope that the 'strings' will lead them to the unifications of physics, or the elusive "unified field theory".

(16). Asimov, Isaac, THE UNIVERSE (Penguin Books 1971) pg.180; a number of other facts have been gratefully gleamed from the late Dr. Asimov.

(17). Genesis 1:2. Analysis of the creative process is reviewed in BEYOND... Vol.1, *Genesis,* with extracts from the chapter on *Creative Process.*

(18). This subject of Life is review from a different standpoint in *Life*, see BEYOND... vol 1.

(19). Tipler, ibid. page 236.

(20). THE LIVING BRAIN by W. Grey Walter; Penguin Books 1961.

Chapter 17
Reviewing the Elements

A lamp am I to you that perceive me
A mirror am I to you that know me

Apocryphal Acts of John

We visualize that which we cannot see with our physical senses.
We visualize that which we desire, which we dream of, to which we aspire. We visualize in order to create a better, a more desirable reality for ourselves, for those close to us and, if we are sufficiently advanced, for humanity. Nevertheless, the reality we envision for humanity always remains subjective to a considerable degree. We can visualize a world in which all people are kind to each other, are good and honest. This will not change all people to make them reflect our mode of behavior. But, amazingly though it may seem, if our vision is powerful enough, we shall notice that people in our immediate vicinity, people with whom we deal on a day-to-day basis, seem to be kinder, better, more honest. There is an Oriental law which states that "like attracts like". In order to attract people of a certain character, we must become that character. Then others of similar ilk, of similar vision will tend to gravitate towards us and we towards them. When Will Rogers averred that he never met a man he didn't like, it didn't follow that all men he met were likable. It did mean that all men were probably likable towards Rogers, and

if not, perhaps Rogers could see the goodness within all men he met, goodness that other people could not see.

I cannot stress too strongly that all visions are always individual, personal, subjective. The chapter on *Society and Politics* bears ample proof that *all* visions intended for other people have undergone considerable if not total degradation by those who attempted to implement them. There is a long-standing dispute whether history makes men, or men make history. As with most surrealist *dicta*, the truth lies in the middle.[1] History produces a propitious environment in which those who are ready can create history. Under such conditions, empires have been built and sunk into oblivion. Organizations, political systems, movements, religions, in fact all attempts to popularize any personal vision or to impose it on others *always* resulted in eventual abysmal failure. Those who aspired to impose other peoples' visions, have invariably degenerated into agencies which attempted to adapt great ideas into instruments of power, thus progressively sinking into conscious or unwitting corruption.

While most people are aware that political, military and social visions suffer from inherent disintegration, few seem aware that religious visions meet equal fate. I call them "religious" although the visions (with the possible exception of Islam) on which religions are supposedly based, never intended to be 'religious' in nature. Buddha never built a single temple. Moses (1571-1451 BC.) though he reputedly lived to be 120 never attempted to centralize his power under a mantle of religion. It may be argued that only in the "Promised Land", the future Israel, such an organization could have been fashioned, but this would also have been a bastardization of the concept of the inner temple of God which Jerusalem was intended to represent and inspire. Finally Solomon who had been crowned over 400 years after Moses' death, sank Moses' vision to its lowest level. He built the first temple. The 'temple' throughout the psalms (attributed to David) was always intended to be your heart. Within you. King David knew this, but his son, Solomon, was a politician. He needed grandeur to flatter his own ego. He brought to Judaism what pope Julius II finally did to Christianity. Yet both Solomon and Julius II secularized intangible concepts. Solomon's hundreds of wives, concubines, his unheard of riches all attest to the same. Vanity. We know nothing of Pope Julius' love-life, but his yearning for secular power is well documented (see chapter on *Groups and Traditions*). There was no room for God within either of the two man's visions.

Their potential became externalized.

A thousand years had passed since Solomon's digression, before Jesus reminded his people that "heaven is within you." Jesus reinstated the original teaching, *saved* his contemporaries from distortion, vanity, misunderstanding. His truth had been intended to set men free, not to subject them to the iron-fist of ensuing religious organizations. While Jesus, like Moses and David, did not build a single church of brick and mortar, his successors could not conceive of a "kingdom not of this world". Just the opposite, the ensuing religion stood in direct opposition to his teaching. By centralizing places of worship, the sacerdotal classes advocated displaying religion in public. Jesus called such displays hypocritical. He promised the practitioners greater damnation.[2]

What are we to think of those who do so today? Who kneel in public, make a pretense at being 'religious' but with their hearts as dark as a moonless night? The media are replete with reports of deviants masquerading under religious habits.

Church, Temple, Place of Worship, is always—and can only be—within our innermost being. It is a place where people congregate. Only in the Bible people, hosts, nations, *always symbolize thoughts*. Temple or church is a place where you gather your thoughts, where you commune with the divinity within you. It is not a pile of stones or bricks erected to the glory of man. It is an inner temple; it is our access to heaven, the throne of God. Religions invariably externalize their beliefs. They wish to make heaven objective. Particularly the Christians. Yet it cannot be done.

To repeat again, heaven is a state of consciousness.

If it were possible to impart one's own vision on others, than the Jews and the Christians would have shunned murder centuries ago. They would have adopted Christ's vision, made it their own. But, yet again, it cannot be done. The Christians, as do the members of other religions, continue to kill, lie, swindle, rape, steal... If for 3500 and 2000 years respectively, visions of such spiritual giants as Moses and Jesus could not influence others to improve their moral standing, then how can *we* expect to influence anyone at all? Wouldn't it be wiser to enter our own private, personal church and worship our own, personal God?

Our own personal church.

It is the state of consciousness wherein we create *our* reality.

Whatever *we* imprint on *our* subconscious will sooner or later surface and manifest in *our* conscious material reality. The subconscious has been compared to a phonograph recorder. There is ample evidence offered by many well-accredited researchers that this machine is turned on at all times. It works during our sleep, when we are lying knocked out in the middle of a boxing rink, when we lie prone on table in the operating theatre under deep anesthetic. And it is our subconscious which, in its own time, creates our reality, our universe. We accomplish this act directly. Even as we need tools to perform most creative acts, so we need our subconscious to create our reality. Hardly surprising since its potential is many multiples greater than the ability of our conscious mind, which is but the tip of an enormous iceberg. While we are helpless without our subconscious, we seem helpless to control it. But we can learn. We can finally stand proud at the helm, the rudder firmly in our hands. We can refuse to act like a ship rocked by turbulent waters over which we have no control.

It was a long and taxing journey.

For a while various religions offered some assistance in affirming our grip on the rudder. Then the exigencies of power corrupted the original teaching in order to maintain and control the masses and the attendant inflow of funds. I have reviewed this process in some detail in the chapter on *Politics and Society*. In the case of Christianity the onslaught on the inner teachings of Christ had been accomplished, almost single-handedly, by bishop Irenaeus of Lyons who circa 180 AD. wrote five volumes entitled *The Destruction and Overthrow of Falsely So-called Knowledge*,[3] which concerned themselves, primarily, with combating Gnosticism.

According to Pagels, Irenaeus denounced as especially "full of blasphemy" the document called the *Gospel of Truth*, which starts with the words: *"The gospel of truth is joy..."* This document which "imagined in traditional Gnostic terms (as) a state of wakefulness, a condition of joy and delight graphically contrasted with the nightmarish existence of those in ignorance,"[4] may have been the heretofore unknown gospel discovered in December 1945. In that year, an Arab peasant stumbled across an earthenware jar containing fifty-two tractates, which have been since identified as *Gnostic Gospels*. After considerable delays caused by international scholastic wrangling, already in 1971 Professor Scholer identified some 4000 books, articles and reviews published on the subject of Nag Hammadi texts.[5] This number had grown considerably since. Originally, Gnosticism has been recognized as "exaggerated spiritualism, contempt for this world, and degradation of the body," while having "a more clearly defined doctrine through a personal savior."[6] I would suggest that some aspect of the teaching had been taken out of context, as e.g.: "He that loveth his life shall lose it; and he that hateth his life in this world shall keep it unto life eternal."[7] If you take the trouble to check, you will see that St. John's preceding verse changes the meaning completely.

Later scholars tended to recognize Gnosticism as a viable if mystical philosophy, not requiring excesses, contempt or degradation of the body. Pagels writes:

"Achieving *gnosis* involves coming to recognize the true source of divine power—namely, 'the depth' of all being. Whoever has come to know that source simultaneously comes to know himself and discovers his spiritual origin: he has come to know his true Father and Mother."[8]

In this latter definition it would be hard to think of Jesus Christ as anything but a Gnostic. In the chapter on *The Problem with Karma*, I wrote that the "saving" offered us by Jesus lay in his message. Indeed, the whole message properly understood would add a great deal of joy and pleasure to anyone's life. But the essence of the teaching lies in what the later Christian sects completely misunderstood. It concerns the "name of Jesus" which is a Greek corruption of his Hebrew name. Originally the Christ was called *Yeshûa*, which is a late form of *Yehôshûa*, meaning, "Jah is salvation".[9] So when the Southern Baptist raises his arms and screams "in the name of Jeeeeezus" he should be saying in the name of *Jah* which is salvation. Jah is of course an abbreviation of Jehovah or a corruption of *YHWH* discussed in the above-mentioned chapter. Since the Bible takes great pains to explain that *YHWH*, the Universal and *El* the Personal God are one and the same, the plot against the Gnostics thickens.

Bishop Irenaeus clearly noticed that if people were to realize that the Savior to whom the church claimed exclusive rights had been and always will be within the consciousness of every living man, woman and child, the church would instantly lose its power. A promising career would be over, the source of income evaporate into thin air.

A sad prospect.

Unfortunately for Irenaeus, Jesus is said to have also said

while praying in his last days: "I in them, and thou in me, that they may be made perfect in one."[10] Perfect? You and I? Weren't we told that we are miserable sinners? I suspect that according to bishop Irenaeus, Jesus too was indulging in blasphemy. And that's in addition to his words: "Behold, the kingdom of God is within you....!"[11] Some damage was already done. Rome had already recognized the gospels of John and Luke, and now the Gnostics were the last straw. Probably, from the bishop's point of view, the worst of the Gnostic gospels was the *Gospel According to Thomas*. It consists of 114 sayings of Jesus and starts with an ominous and potentially disastrous assertion:

WHOEVER FINDS THE EXPLANATION OF THESE WORDS WILL NOT TASTE DEATH.

What if you don't understand?

It is self-evident that this sort of statement could not go unchallenged by a fledgling organization which worked so hard to insert itself as an intermediary between men and God and the attendant immortality. Irenaeus mobilized all the church's resources to stamp out this dangerous 'heresy'. Mostly he succeeded. Furthermore, Thomas in the third logion wrote: "heaven is within you *and* without you," (my emphasis). This not only offers the 'personalization' of heaven, but also defines it as *the only reality*. All else, as the Orientals claimed for thousands of years, is maya—an illusion. It appears that in order to see the true reality it is necessary to be... a Gnostic.

Now Irenaeus was really stumped. His universe was dissolving...

But, to quote Einstein yet again, God does not play dice with the universe. In hindsight, it is abundantly evident that the human race had not been ready for the 'real' teaching of Christ. By the present century any resemblance between the Roman Catholic Church and the original teachings of Christ is purely coincidental. Symbol became a permanent substitution for the "real thing". The other protestant sects did little better—not much.

And then came *Nag Hammadi*. While The Nag Hammadi findings had now been completely translated, most of it is of little use.[12] Over the years, and thanks to the two Arabs who originally intended to use the books to stoke their fire, the more esoteric gnosticism had been decimated, tarnished and became fairly incomprehensible. *The Gospel According to Thomas* survived almost intact. As did the *Gospel of Truth*. My commentary to the first of the two reveals the secret promised in its first verse.[13]

Irenaeus, eat your heart out!

Yet, while the destruction of Gnosticism was an evil in itself, destroying the mysticism within the Gnostic thought was the real crime. The Mysticism which internalized divinity rather than regressing to the inaccessible Olympus by different name. Orthodox Christianity did not destroy paganism but merely substituted their own names, feasts, rites and gods in lieu of the previous ones. Only Gnosticism attempted to veer away from this rut.

It is evident from all the above that the only savior Jesus envisaged was the savior within, or what we refer to nowadays as our Higher Self. It is the exact equivalent of the Hebrew *El*, the immortal spark, the indivisible yet individualized Soul, an aspect of God. This was and is the essence of Christ's message. He endeavored to free his people from the shackles of the established religion and its minions, only to fall pray to yet another organization which took advantage of the esoteric nature of his teaching to twist it into yet another means of subjecting and constraining the spirit of man. Christ's message to stop exteriorizing God had been and continues to be diligently ignored. It is evident that Spirit can be constrained in materiality even as light loses its velocity in dense atmosphere. But not for long. As we clear the air, the light will resume its luminal velocity. And light is knowledge. Two thousand years is but a moment of eternity.

We shall overcome.

The extract from the third verse, or logion, of the Gospel of Thomas quoted above contains more vital information. It deserves to be read in its entirety:

Jesus said: If those who lead you say to you: 'See, the Kingdom is in heaven', then the birds of the heaven will precede you. If they say to you: 'It is in the sea', then the fish will precede you. But the Kingdom is within you and it is without you. If you know yourselves, then you will be known and will know that you are the sons of the Living Father. But if you do not know yourselves, then you are in poverty and you are poverty.[14]

If you know yourselves... remember Socrates?

To repeat, the ancient philosopher admonished us with two words: "Know Thyself". During the last two and a half thousand years we have been learning about our potential. Now is the time to extend his admonition with two more words:

LIVE CONSCIOUSLY

All nature subsists on reacting to its environment. For countless generations, the human animal did the same. It is time for us to stand up and be counted. We know that who-and-what we are, is directly related to who-and-what we believe we are. The *who* is the immortal spirit; the *what* is the universe we continually create. We always become the object of our contemplation. Whatever we implant in our subconscious that, with inexorable certainty, we shall become. It cannot be otherwise.

We are the microcosm created unto image and likeness of the Macrocosm.

For ages the various religions advocated prayer as a means of saving our soul. We already know that they have been referring to *nephesh* the "animal soul" or to our subconscious. Correct prayer [Emmet Fox called it "Scientific Prayer"[15]] is the most efficient method of implanting universal truth into the inner mind. It is truly ironic that while prayer is universally advocated by the sacerdotal leaders of our society, we are seldom explained the reason for the necessity of prayer. Those who do pray, do so either to implore some celestial deity to grant them probably undeserved boons, or to bestow on them or their dear ones an equally undeserved gift of good health. I remember a man smoking two packs of cigarettes a day earnestly praying every Sunday that God might, in his omnipotent mercy, protect him from cancerous lungs.

The Muslim perform their prayers five times a day. They limit their worship to performing bodily prostrations and repeating the same or similar phrases from the Koran. Ubada b.al-Samit reports: "I heard the Prophet say: 'There are five prayers which God has prescribed for His servants in the space of a day and a night. He who observes the prayers had the promise of God that He will cause him to enter Paradise....'"

Paradise? The question is when. After death?

The Muslim are told that it is only permissible to perform the prayers at the assigned times... (zuhr, 'ashr, al-wusta, maghirb and 'isha).[16] One can only wonder why the *ulama* (the learned) or the *fuqaha* (the lawyers) place such restrictions on communication with their God. Other Muslim claim that various religious affirmations are performed (in Arabic) many times a day. Phrases such as "There is no deity but God, and Mohammed is the messenger of God" (La illaha il-lallah, Muhammadan rasul Allah), or "In the name of God the compassionate, the merciful" (Bismillah ar-Rahman ar-Rahim), or simply "Praise be to God" (Alhamdulillah). These may be useful to restore a Moslem's peace of mind, but they have nothing to do with "Scientific Prayer".

Furthermore, the performance of the *Salat*, the ritual prayer, is steeped in ritual. It is defined even more precisely than the wording, with its attendant ups-and-downs (standing, kneeling, sitting, bowing), to which the Catholic Church subjects its believers. The Muslim are told what to do with their hands, head, body etc.. One wonders how can the believers raise their consciousness under such regime. But there again, the Islam has spawned the Sufis, who give every indication of having reached unprecedented heights of spiritual enlightenment.

I cannot attest to the efficacy of the Muslim prayer, but judging by the social and political interaction between many Muslim states it is doubtful if the intention of the prayers is to create a heaven on earth. The same can be said of the present day Christianity. Since these two religions have influence over about a third of humanity, it is indeed sad that so many people are deprived of a state of consciousness which would assure their happiness. It would also go a long way to explain why the birth of the Age of Aquarius is linked to the presence of Uranus which symbolizes destructive powers. Once more one is reminded that one cannot put new wine into old skins.[17] This seems to imply that one cannot make minor or indeed major adjustments to the existing states of consciousness. We really must start from scratch.

It is up to us. We must learn to water our own garden.

***

Finally, a word about the efficacy of religion.

With the exception of the followers of Buddha, all major religions of the world have failed to shed light on the evolution of the human soul. In fact, it could be argued that the religions hindered, rather than aided, those non-religious trends which did aspire to advance the state of human consciousness. That is not to say that the Avatars on whose revelations the religions profess to be based have failed. Nor have failed the great saints whose exemplary lives shed sparks of light on the dark mists of the human psyche. The revelation of Truth cannot fail. Who have failed are the countless exponents of religions, the sacerdotal classes, the theologians, the doctors of divinity, the religious oligarchies which for thousands of years fed their followers their interpretation of other people's visions from distant past. Whether those interpretations had been the result of ignorance or simply to protect their power over the ignorant masses is immaterial. They all failed and continue to fail miserably to protect, unfold and promulgate the divinely inspired message. The message of Truth which would set all men free.

THE MESSAGE OF TRUTH WHICH WOULD SET ALL MEN FREE.

It is not my place to pass judgment.
What I offer are the results of my studies and observations. If religions have been organized to show men the Way, then surely, their road-signs are pointing the wrong way. It seems that more people have been murdered in the name of a pantheon of gods and religions than in any other cause. This cancerous malady seems to be spreading. It continues to this day in Northern Ireland, in Bosnia, Chechnia and other parts of the defunct Yugoslavia, in India and Pakistan, in Tibet and China, in Sri Lanka, Indonesia, Israel, Palestine, Lebanon, in a number of 'liberated' ex-Soviet Republics, in Egypt and Algeria and other parts of Africa. The list goes on. All the children of the One God murder each other in the name of the one god. A horrible, hateful, sadistic god, evidently totally devoid of mercy, compassion or love. It is in the image of this god that those partaking in the slaughter of their brothers have been created. It is in his image that they will die. It is as though they have never lived.
Only to be reborn again. Only to try again.
Perhaps to succeed.
This time.

***

It seems to me that we should attempt to see ourselves as micro-universes within a macro-universe. Once our environment consisted of our village, then a district, a country, continent and finally the earth—once more a global village. But in the meantime, since Copernicus and then Galileo, our physicists have succeeded in changing our horizons. Most of us are now capable of thinking in terms of our solar system, perhaps our galaxy—the Milky Way. But this is only a beginning. Our backyard is growing by the minute. The points of light in our night sky, which such a short time ago stood for stationary sparks placed there by the Almighty Creator—began moving. Now those same dots are speeding away from us at absurd velocities. And even if they remained stationary we could only observe our nearest galaxy, the Andromeda, as it looked 2.7 million years ago. A long look into a far, far distant past. Can we ever hope to visit such distant environs? At 90% of the velocity of light it would take us over 3,000,000 years to get there. The next nearest cluster of galaxies, the Virgo Cluster, is within seventy million years travel at the same velocity.

70,000,000 years of travel at 270,000 kilometers per *second*.

There are two approaches we can take towards the macro-universe.

We can either improve on our longevity by at least 30,000%, say goodbye to our friends and family, and embark on a one-way (shortest possible) galactic journey, or find a different mode of life and transportation. I vote for the latter. Living in the same body for over three million years (not to mention seventy million) might not do justice to our youthful looks. I prefer to rejuvenate myself periodically through the simple process of reincarnation.

It is fun being young again.
And again.
And again...

But I refuse to admit that we were given an awareness of

the magnitude of the macro-universe only to lure us into a permanent state of frustration. If we are aware of the universe, then it is ours to explore. To do so, however, we must change our "mode of being". The least we must do is to advance from the physical to the imaginative or even mental state of consciousness. We must transfer our attention from our physical body to our inner bodies, and then work within the confines of the laws governing those inner universes. Remember that the physical universe is only a congealed shadow cast by the inner states, each drawing closer to Absolute Reality. And if this visible universe is so beautiful, can you imagine the original, the Real Thing?

None of us seems surprised when in our dreams we fly, cover great distances in an instant, traverse time forward and backwards with equal facility. We already know that time is so relative that it doesn't really exist. It is a function of space, physical space. The more we learn about the illusion of the physical universe, the more our "dream-world" becomes real. And we needn't sleep to enter this inner world. With practice, given sufficient interest, conviction, desire and perseverance, we can learn to enter our astral body at will. The other inner worlds are also at our beckoning. Jesus said repeatedly: "my kingdom is not of this world." People take so many of his allegorical expressions literally, yet when he was literal we choose to ignore him. *Our* kingdom is also not of this world. In the four gospels alone the word 'kingdom' as referring to the kingdom of heaven or of God, is mentioned nearly 120 times. Could a single allegory be of such importance as to be repeated so many times? Or was Jesus trying hard to tell us something. Christians are in a habit of deifying Jesus and thus drawing an insurmountable chasm between his achievements and those we might be capable of. But if he spoke of his disciples: "*They* are not of the world, even as I am not of the world,"[18] does this not open the gates for you and me? A blind man can see that to Jesus the inner world had, for him, much greater reality than its shadow, the world you and I live in.

We live in a world of illusion. We don't have to.

We do not have to leave this world to experience True Reality.

We do not have to die; thus we do not have to be resurrected.

We do not have to give up living, suffer, fast, pray for countless hours.

We must simply believe that all things are possible. Then we have to discover our true nature. Then we must start looking towards the Ocean of Infinite Possibilities. Then we must start moving towards it. Then we must make sure we are walking the right way. The road is straight and narrow. Then, when we are ready, we'll get there.

Here and now.

***

FOOTNOTES

(1). I use the term 'surrealist' in the original sense, as that which ensues from the unconscious and is characterized by an irrational or noncontextural abstraction.

(2). Matthew 23:14 et seq.

(3). Pagels, Elaine, THE GNOSTIC GOSPELS (Vintage Books, New York 1981)

(4). From the introduction to the *Gospel of Truth* translated by Harold W. Attridge and George W. MacRae THE NAG HAMMADI LIBRARY General Editor James M. Robinson (Harper San Francisco 1990)

(5). Scholer, D.M., Nag Hammadi Bibliography (Leiden 1971)

(6). McNall Burns, Edward WESTERN CIVILIZATIONS, 8th Edition, Volume 1. (W.W.Norton & Co. Inc., New York 1973) page 229 and 172

(7). John 12:25.

(8). Pagels, ibid. page 44.

(9). Kapuscinski, S. DICTIONARY OF BIBLICAL SYMBOLISM (Inhousepress 2001)

(10). John 17:23

(11). Luke 17:21.

(12). Robinson, James M. General Editor THE NAG HAMMADI LIBRARY [IN ENGLISH] (Harper Collins, San Francisco1990)

(13). THE KEY TO IMMORTALITY (Inhousepress 2001)

(14). GOSPEL ACCORDING TO THOMAS. Coptic text established and translated by A.Guillaumont, H.-Ch. Puech, G. Quispel, W. Till and Yassah 'Abd Al Masih (Harper & Row, © E.J. Brill 1959)

(15). Emmet Fox, ALTER YOUR LIFE, *How to Maintain Peace*.[Harper & Row] pg.168.

(16). Information on Muslim prayers is gleamed from ISLAM edited by John Alden Williams, George Braziller, New York 1962; pages 100-104

(17). Compare Matthew 9:17, Mark 2:22, Luke 5:37.

(18). John 17:16 [my emphasis]

Chapter 18
Duality and Oneness

I fear that you will not reach Mecca, O Nomad!
For the road which you are following leads to Turkestan.

Sheikh Sadi
[Rose Garden]

We learn by comparing the opposites. This realm of opposites which governs the material universe, is known as the realm of duality. The opposites work in tandem; they complement each other. They are two facets of the same coin. Though we employ and abide in this reality for the purpose of learning, our true nature is not of this, the dualistic, world. Our true home lies beyond the concepts of doing right and doing wrong.

Our kingdom is not of this world.

While abiding in the material reality, we exhibit two distinct aspects: one is the product of our subconscious and thus is transient and illusory, while the other is immutable and real and is inherent to the spirit. The first can be regarded as the result, the second as the cause. We must endeavor to learn to align ourselves with the cause.

Since the realm of the spirit is transcendental, i. e. beyond words or even thought, we shall concentrate on a discussion of the illusory reality in which most of us find our being. We shall attempt to learn about the transcendental by studying its results—by studying the trails it leaves behind—rather as the theoretical physicists study the trails left behind by the quarks and other subatomic particles. It could be argued that we shall attempt to combine the science of phenomenology with ontology, where phenomena are events or objects recognizable by our senses, and ontology is the branch of metaphysics dealing with the nature of being or true reality. The present Pope Jean Paul II,[1] probably on the assumption that the transcendental is by definition unknowable and therefore its study would be abortive, has espoused the phenomenological approach.[2] If so, than this approach may be said to date back to Baruch Spinoza, who once said "to define God is to deny God".[3] Spinoza's statement, however, has been profoundly misunderstood. What Spinoza held was that we couldn't *limit* our concept of God (or even His manifestation in Nature) by defining Him. Spinoza held that all being is embraced in a single Substance-God. But he also held that mind and matter, time and everything detectable to our senses is *only a manifestation of* God. Not God Itself. In other words he argued that what is 'knowable' in the universe, or that which is phenomenal, constitutes the results, not the Cause. But in any case, the mystics or Gnostics reject this argument *per se*. They hold that the transcendental is knowable to us, as our real nature is transcendental also.

But that's another discussion.

The paradox that shackles all monotheistic religions is that although they affirm a single deity (One God), they are faced with a universe that exhibits dualistic nature. Since religions invariably assign reality to the phenomenal universe, the many apparent paradoxes become or remain irresolvable. In this light, let us agree at the start that all discussion of our *material* universe is the discussion of that which is the product of our minds and thus it is of an impermanent, elusive and insubstantial nature. In fact, the very opposite of the attributes normally assigned to it.

The material universe has no reality other than that which we decide to assign to it.

As already discussed in previous chapters, our material reality is made up of three principle aspects: the mental, the emotional and the physical. The three aspects combine to create an illusion of the material reality. As such, our physical body, our emotions and our mind are all transient. Our mode of being is maintained by our will or desire to remain in a particular reality. It is important to remember that the human body is not a homogeneous entity, but rather an amorphous association of atoms, which in themselves are fragments or quanta of information suspended in a virtually empty space. What gives them cohesion is the presence of the energy we call: Life. Conversely, when this energy is withdrawn, the atoms revert to their previous (fairly) random condition of chaos. Life is the Creative Force and we are Its individualization. As such *we can choose* to become conscious instruments through which Life can manipulate the inanimate matter. We can consciously participate in the continuous creation of the universes.

Visualization is a vital link in the chain of this evolutionary or creative process.

The key to success in this endeavor is the realization that Life is One though Its form of expression is multifarious. The moment we accept this premise we take a giant step on our individual evolutionary scale. From that moment on, we shall no longer just *react* to unconscious impulses, but begin to take charge of our perception of reality. The prophet Isaiah has this to say about the birth of our Spiritual awareness:

For unto us a child is born, unto us a son is given: and the government shall be upon his shoulder: and this name shall be called Wonderful, Counselor, The mighty God, The everlasting Father, The Prince of Peace.[4]

Most Christians appear to confuse this statement with prophetic allusions to the birth of Jesus, ignoring the fact that Isaiah equates the Prince of Peace with the Everlasting Father, and the mighty God. Jesus laid claim to being a son of God, a title he did not reserve solely for himself but for all to whom the word of God came—adding that the *Son can do nothing of himself, but what he seeth the Father do*.[5] Until we become aware of the birth of our own spiritual consciousness, we are stuck in dabbling in that which we know to be an illusion. Just how illusory is our physical or sensory perception has been amply illustrated in the previous chapter.

What can we do in the meantime?

We can bide our time and... do the best we can.

I've never met a person who did not express his or her concern for his or her state of health. It is regrettable that, like all disciplines of science, matters pertaining to our wellbeing are concerned exclusively with the physical reality. We can apply the laws of visualization to this realm, but must be careful not to work against the dictates of nature (see chapter on *Universal Laws*). We can, for instance, ease the pain of cough caused by smoking by the use of self-hypnosis and visualization. In doing so we can alleviate symptoms which are designed to save us from greater harm of continued smoking. If we confine ourselves only to the reduction or even the elimination of the symptoms (cough, chronic bronchitis, sore throat and suchlike), we might continue smoking longer, inhale deeper, until no amount of self-hypnosis (mind-over-matter) is likely to help. It would be much wiser to use the auto-hypnotic suggestion to heal that which causes the cough, i.e. the habit of smoking itself. The same is true of every medicine or treatment which tackles the symptoms without getting to the root of the problem. Every sensation of pain can be eliminated without the use of drugs. Whether we use auto-hypnotic techniques or others which rely on the diverting of attention, all pain can be eliminated.

With it, with the elimination of pain, we lose access to the greatest communication system our physical bodies developed over millions of years—the reporting system bringing to our attention that we have done, or are still doing, something wrong.

In the chapter on *Health and Healing* it became evident that our standard medicine is no longer equipped to deal with the healing process. It is apparent that throughout western civilizations, a physician is paid exactly the same exorbitant wage whether he (or she) cures his (or her) patients or kills them. This illustrates the illusory nature or the dualistic reality.

Isn't it time we woke up?

Admittedly there are other professions, excluding the one I once practiced myself, wherein such absurd abuses could and do happen. An architect is rewarded for *results* not for presumed *effort*. On the other hand politicians are frequently rewarded not only for ruining the economy, but also for plunging their citizens into devastating wars. Civil disobedience is often the only defense we have against unscrupulous members of the ruling factions. The sacerdotal profession is likewise not paid for results but presumably, for the effort. I know of no priest, parson, padre, monk or any other member of the piously clad fraternity who delivered on his promise. By that I mean that in as much as the physicians fail to cure the body, the priests fail to cure the soul. Here again we must apply the laws of duality and ask ourselves what is the other side of the coin. Perhaps we are to learn to look better after our own bodies ourselves, even as we are also shown that we should rely on our own efforts to look after our soul.

If we open our eyes and ears, we shall soon see that all these apparent dissonances, abuses, and downright lies are there to teach us to take charge of our own lives. They are there to help us to stand up on our own feet.

Buddha is known to have taught the middle path: a way

of life which rejects all extremes, which contends to find fulfillment in a state of balance. Some two thousand years later, George Hegel (1770—1831), a German philosopher, has shown that in order to reach a higher understanding, we must place a thesis in opposition to the antitheses. The resultant synthesis shall lead us towards the middle ground. It is this synthesis which we must achieve when regarding the 'realities' of our world. It is not the extremes for which we must search but the middle path. We must not confuse this admonition with a compromise. We chose the middle path because it rejects compromises. It is the only path which removes us from its necessity. Compromise is only necessary when we take sides. Not when we give way even as a blade of grass gives way to a gust of wind. The grass always returns to its position when the wind passes.

You are a blade of grass.

Duality imposes opposing winds. They are transient, not real. They all pass leaving calm behind them—providing we do not oppose their illusory strength.

It is vital that in the dualistic reality we endeavor to find that which the opposites have in common. The opposites *always* work together to show us the way. The one extreme cannot survive without the other. But *neither* of the extremes is ever right or good, while the other wrong or evil. I find the Chinese yin-yang philosophy vastly superior to the religious concept of good and evil of the western traditions. Yin and yang represent the passive-female and the active-male principles. They show us the left and the right, the dark and the light, the high and the deep. They embody the principle of the *complementary* opposites. They are, however, neither good, nor evil.

In a dualistic reality,
the opposites are always complementary.

They work together. Strangely enough, the old Hebrew tradition gave us the concept of YHWE, which is nothing but the eternal male and female principles of the universe. The *manifested* universe. There is no question of good and evil. As discussed in the chapter on *The Problem with Karma*, there is no intrinsic evil. Like everything in the material universe, evil is illusory. It is no more than an aspect of dualistic, i.e. illusory reality. It is no more than a balancing factor. If we refuse to accept it, it will cease to exist. It has no reality of its own. There is only Life, which finds Its expression in the 'way', the Tao, the Dharma, in a mode of becoming. We can all find our own reality in the careful balance of all factors which enrich the awareness of our existence.

While the physical world is subject to 'physical' laws, we must not forget that the physical world is an expression of a dualistic reality. And all duality is illusory.

It is the creation of our own mind.

The main problem with duality is that unless one is aware of its purpose it tends to cloud its own function. Since the very existence of a dualistic universe is for the purpose of learning, the first thing we must recognize is that all conditions which we have to face in our physical existence are always, and exclusively for our benefit. No matter how difficult problems may seem, no matter what hardships we may have to face, absolutely all events in our phenomenal life happen for our own good. This thesis may be easier to understand once we accept that we and only we are responsible for creating conditions in which we find ourselves. No one bites their own noses to spite their faces. While we may seem to wander aimlessly reacting to the accumulated dross of our subconscious, we remain under continuous protection, an almighty aegis of our own Higher Self. And this fact, this awareness, takes us directly to the discussion of our transcendental, our true nature which is, was, and always will be—Spiritual.

The Spiritual nature is One, Indivisible, Indestructible.

The Spiritual consciousness of every man woman and

child commences with the first glimmer of awareness that each one of us is an individualization of a Single Consciousness, a single Entity we "recognize" as God. The attribute which enables this Oneness to individualize itself we refer to as Soul. Since we already know from physics that all the material aspects of our nature are transient, deprived of essential reality, our objective is to identify with that aspect of our being which is permanent and indestructible. In order to do so, we must define the attributes of consciousness, which are immortal.

The material attributes are always quantifiable. The spiritual attributes are not.

Every material aspect of the universe can be quantified or divided into its component parts. This is true not only of matter and energy but also as pertaining to all emotional and mental concepts. The degree to which we like someone or something is quantifiable. We can derive different degrees of pleasure from associating with various people, partaking in various activities, listening to different kinds of music. Likewise we can understand, enjoy or adopt various concepts, reject others. We can agree—partially, or disagree—to a degree. We can even agree to disagree. There are also degrees of understanding of various concepts, requiring different degrees of concentration, attention, and intellectual effort. On closer examination we can safely say that all mental activities are quantifiable. This ability to divide, to arrange in groups or independent units is the inherent aspect of universal dualism. In a dualistic reality matter, emotions, mental concepts are not only divisible but also relative.

The Spiritual Realm is characterized by exactly the opposite values.

First and foremost, the Spiritual Realm is Indivisible. This is what we mean when we say that God is One. This premise is shared by all the world's major religions, and reaches back to the ancient Myths reviewed in the chapter on

Myths and Reality.

Concepts such as Soul, Infinity, Immortality, Indestructibility, Omnipresence, Omniscience, Love and others are *not* divisible. One cannot be a little indestructible, or ubiquitous only in some areas. Likewise immortality cannot be quantified—one cannot be slightly immortal, or immortal for a while. If one is partially omniscient than one doesn't know all that much.

Contrary to popular assumption, Love is not an emotion, but a divine trait that unifies the universe. If Love were divisible, the universe would "fall apart". It is also That which erases the line of demarcation between you and me. It is That which makes I and my Father, you and I, you and your Father—ONE. Within our spiritual nature, you and I retain our individuality but remain One. Spiritual Oneness is Indivisible. There are emotions which we feel are the *result* of Love even as Joy is the *result* of the marriage between Love and Life, and Wisdom a homology of divine Intelligence and divine Love. Divine Intelligence is that which permeates the whole universe (and thus partakes in all divine attributes), and is the Prime Cause of evolution, which instills the knowingness in each atom and subatomic particle, allowing it to act in a particular manner, without loosing its cohesiveness. By this I mean that each aspect of the spiritual realm is integral to and in full awareness of every other aspect.

This self-awareness is reflected in the micro-universe of our physical bodies.

While we occupy our physical bodies, we are particularly interested in the aspect or the attribute of Individualization. It has been said in some religions that we are all endowed with soul. Some religions also define 'soul' as immortal yet predispose it to spending eternity in Heaven or Hell. If soul is a part of God, as Jesus claimed, than I can hardly imagine God relegating an integral part of Himself for eternity to such dismal circumstances.

Obviously, religions got something wrong.

Luckily for us, and apparently for God, nothing could be further from the truth. The Bible, from which this concept of soul is specifically derived, paints a completely different picture. As already mentioned in this book, when the Hebrew word *nephesh* is translated into English as 'soul', it refers to a *material* aspect of man, namely to our subconscious mind. Mind, being part of material reality, is *not* immortal. By the same token, it is not capable of being subject to *eternal* damnation. The real translation of *nephesh* is *animal soul*, and it is enjoyed by human and non-human animals alike as the subconscious. Our "personal souls", to the extent they acquire spiritual attributes, can be incorporated into our Spiritual Body and thus become immortal. To do so, however, they must cease being 'personal'. The spiritual is always and only universal. Never personal.

Spirit, by definition omnipresent (as is God in all Its aspects) is static. If you already are everywhere, there is nowhere to go. Any movement is quantifiable and therefore outside the Spiritual realm. What is not quantifiable, though is subject to change, is Consciousness. By the process of Individualization (Soul), God enabled Itself to continually enrich Its Spiritual attributes. While Love is indivisible, you and I might give it different forms of expression. Love won't change, the form of expression will. It is this growth in diversity which is the causative principle behind Life.

Life is one, but it finds incredible diversity of expression. Life finds Its mode of being in you and me, in a tree, a flower or your favorite pet... it is all *the same* Life—indivisible, indestructible, omnipresent. What changes is, again, only the form of expression. We, you and I, contribute to Its diversity. And this is the principle reason why every person, every animal, every quantum of flora and fauna are, and must remain different. Nor should any two people think alike. Both must contribute their own (indivisible) individuality to the Whole. To God.

WE ARE ONE

Subconscious is that part of our psyche which enables us to survive *physically*. It is the storehouse of information acquired over millions of years of evolution. Though erroneously translated throughout the Bible as 'soul', it is neither immortal nor indestructible. But it can be sanctified. It can be 'saved'. We, the Spiritual entities, Individualizations of the One God, save those aspects of our subconscious which reflect *universal traits*. All others, for instance those dealing with our personality, are ignored. There is no need for personalities when we are One. There is only a need of ever more diverse expression of the Universal or Spiritual attributes. When we vacate our physical bodies, the attributes of our personalities remain suspended in emotional (astral) or mental realms awaiting our next reincarnation, wherein we shall continue to work on them. Until we make them part of the Whole.

This brings us to the biblical concept of the divine aspect of Soul.

Soul, spelled with capital S to differentiate it from *nephesh or* the Greek *psyche*, is expressed in Hebrew as the unifying principle in the word Israel (see chapter on *The Problem with Karma*). Although not differentiated in English, in Hebrew the word representing the immortal aspect of man is *El*. It is the principle seat of consciousness, of awareness, of knowing that I AM THAT I AM. To individualize Itself means *to remain one*, to remain *indivisible*, from Latin *individualis* and *individuus* meaning indivisible, inseparable. Thus the divine presence within us is not only the seat of our awareness but also the source of all the divine traits available to us. Soul manifests *all* the divine traits i.e.: immortality, indestructibility, omnipresence etc., and as such It is not subject to punitive imaginings invented by the various religions to scare their faithful into obedience and submission.

Just the opposite.

Soul (capital S) represents that aspect of our awareness which is forever free, not subject to emotional, mental or physical anguish. Brad Steiger wrote a biography of the late mystic, Paul Twitchell, entitled "In my soul I am free". What is true of Paul Twitchell is true of every one of us, *to the degree that we are capable of realizing this truth.* Many years ago, Jesus having affirmed that his kingdom is not of this (material, transient, illusory) world, said "Truth shall make you free."[6] It is this truth which we must all face in order to share in unlimited freedom. It is this concept of freedom which we should contemplate, which we should attempt to visualize when practicing our relaxation exercises (see the next chapter on *Relaxation*). As we grow in the awareness of divine freedom, it shall increase accordingly.[7]

Finally, it is fashionable of late to lay claims to the unification of physics and spirituality. A number of physicists purport that this unification is the result of Ontological, Objective or Constitutive Reductionism. Apparently, all three adjectives mean virtually the same thing. Basically 'ontology' means the study of the nature of being and reality. The 'reductionist' qualifier refers to the ability of a physicist to reduce man (and the universe) to his or its quantum mechanical terms. For that to happen, man (and the universe) must be regarded as exclusively material constructs.

By the same logic I have eliminated duality and claim to be an ontological reductionist. I have eliminated all matter from true reality and have defined man and the universe exclusively in terms of Spirit.

Touché?

***

FOOTNOTES

(1). John Paul II authored a book titled *Osoba i Czyn*, later expanded and edited by Dr. Anna-Teresa Tymieniecka and published under the title *The Acting Person*.

(2). Although Martin Heidegger (1889 - 1976) argued in THE BASIC PROBLEMS OF PHENOMENOLOGY that *"Phenomenology is the name for the method of ontology, that is, of scientific philosophy. Rightly conceived, phenomenology is the concept of a method."*

(3). Baruch (or Benedict) Spinoza (1632-77) was a Dutch Jewish philosopher. Under the influence of a pupil of Descartes, he grew critical of some of the dogmas of the Hebrew faith. He died an outcast. Spinoza held, *inter alia*, that evil exists only for finite minds, and dissolves when seen as part of the whole, which is the stand I take in the chapter on *The Problem with Karma*.

(4). Isaiah 9:6.

(5). John 10:34-36 and 5:19.

(6). John 8:32, compare also Romans 6:14, 8:2, James 1:25, et al..

(7). The subjects of *Sanctifying* and *Salvation* are discussed in BEYOND RELIGION, Vol.1. (Inhousepress 1997)

Chapter 19
Relaxation

*It is necessary to note
that opposite things work together,
even though nominally opposed.*

Jalal ud-din Rumi
[Fihi Ma Fihi]
IN IT WHAT IS IN IT

Among the many trends in psychotherapy, there is but one common link. The practitioners (doctors, therapists) all insist that in order to succeed with any form of treatment, the first step is put the patient at ease.

This calls for the art of relaxation.

Few of us are unaware of the proverbial couch on which a despondent patient divulges, in a reclining stance, his or her neurotic secrets and inhibitions to a bored if attentive psychoanalyst. This method may well bear results if you are a millionaire. While I am sure that psychoanalysis has its share of successes, it is known to be conducted for up to one thousand hours, and at $100 per hour (these are 1999 dollars), most of us are forced to seek more accessible methods. We are forced to seek not only alternate methods to relax our mind, body and emotions, but even to overcome mild neuroses, phobias, obsessions, hysterias or compulsions, heretofore the domain of a well paid professional. I am not suggesting that deferring to a trained psychiatrist is not necessary in a number of cases. I am suggesting though that we can do a great deal more ourselves than we are doing at present to achieve a relatively stable peace of mind. Whatever method we decide on, the presumption of relaxation is a *sine qua non* condition, even if in our particular case, as often in psychiatry, it is but a means to an end.

Recently, at the annual meeting of the American Association for the Advancement of Science, Dr. Esther Sternberg of the National Institute of Mental Health (NIMH) said that new research shows that the brain, the immune system and the response to stress are tightly connected.[1] Apparently, the efficacy of the placebo effect can also be attributed to the attendant relaxation. According to Dr. Sternberg, therapies and placebos lower stress causing changes in the brain and the immune system that actually increase our ability to fight disease. It is reasonable to assume that relaxation, even without the use of placebos, will have the same effect. It keeps us quiet and allows our immune system to do its job.

When testing chemical drugs *vis a vis* placebos, a double blind method had been introduced to protect the accuracy of the results; not from the efficacy of the drugs but from the healing effects of the placebo. The reason is that unless the patient and the physician are kept in abject ignorance as to which of the patients are given which pill, too many patients (among hundreds) improved too much with the aid of the placebo. The *expectation* of a positive result was sufficient to destroy the accuracy of the drug test results. The reason was self-evident.

The patients visualized getting better and, as a result, better they got!

While the relaxation of the body is helpful, it is essential to relax the mind. In this context the word "relaxation" only partially conveys the intent. What we must do is to *still the mind* which, unbeknownst to us, is subjected to the constant onslaught or harassment by the "stream of consciousness".

What I mean by that is that innumerable states of consciousness make themselves constantly available to the mind, which acts as a sieve, a selector. At the subliminal level, it is continuously evaluating, adapting and selecting the various options, dealing with past, present and future possibilities, examining the physical and emotional consequences of entering any particular state or subjective reality. This constant activity amounts to a subliminal noise of such magnitude that conscious participation in the selection process is all but impossible. The "roof brain chatter"[2] as Robert de Ropp calls it, must be stilled.

As with all good ideas, the desirability of this cessation of the inner turmoil is not new either. The eastern Yoga systems offer many techniques which are intended to still the mind. The best among them employ the *pranayama*, or a system of "cleansing" breath. While the breathing exercises serve to oxygenate the body, we must remember that, as Dr. Weil puts it "healing system depends on the circulation of blood to bring energy and materials to a malfunctioning or injured area."[3] The energy mentioned is *inter alia* oxygen, which according to eastern philosophies is the integral part of *prana*, or the biological expression of the energy of life itself.

Western science has confirmed that the frequency and depth of breathing can affect our metabolic rate. According to Peter Russell,[4] the practitioners of the Transcendental Meditation techniques obtain the reverse effect of under-oxygenating their bodies by dropping their metabolic rate to around 75% below the basal level. This fact alone should make us careful when indulging in breathing exercises without due care. I have also read of yogis who suspended their breathing altogether for days at a time. It is not the purpose of this chapter to induce the reader to suspend his or her breathing, no matter what level of relaxation might result from it! But evidence remains that elimination of tension tends to lower the heart rate and the attendant blood pressure, as well as reduce any residual muscle tension. Even as imminent danger produces the fright (not fear) reaction, known as the "flight-fight" response, a deep state of relaxation with the attendant reduction of our metabolic rate appears to induce the opposite effect.

Our immediate purpose, however, is to relax our mind to a state wherein we can achieve greater results from visualization. In a relaxed state we can more readily imprint the desired program on our subconscious and thus expedite the process of creating our own universe. I count various breathing exercises among the best methods of achieving a relaxed state of mind and body. Since there are a great many techniques offered by the various gurus, both qualified and not, I shall review some which, I believe, can be of the greatest use to people seeking deep relaxation. There are two breathing exercises which I learned many years ago from F. Yeats-Brown, the author of *Yoga Explained*. It has been published by Victor Gollancz in London in 1937, and I have no idea if it is still available in print.

This first technique is called *bhastrika pranayama*, or the cleansing breath. While it certainly relaxes the body, its principle objective is to cleanse off excessive 'noise' in the mind. It quiets or calms us down. There are the purists who will insist that in order to practice *pranayama*: "Half the stomach should be filled with food, one-quarter with water, and one-quarter should be kept empty..."[5] This indeed is necessary to reach higher levels of initiation wherein very complex breathing techniques are used. For most of us, however, relaxed yet controlled breathing is a means to an end, which is to counteract stress and relax our mind. It suffices to assume a comfortable position, place our attention on the breath and relax. I can vouch for efficacy of *bhastrika pranayama* from personal experience.

The cleansing breath:
Sitting erect, keeping the spine straight on inhalations and bending slightly forward when exhaling, take eleven deep, even, continuous breaths. On the last (eleventh)

inhalation restrain your breath gently. Visualize tapping the air gently downwards, towards the lowest part of your body. Hold the breath as long as reasonably comfortable, and then exhale leaning slightly forward to assure complete voiding of your lungs. Repeat this exercise three times. If you can hold your breath up to a minute you are doing well. Your lung capacity will increase with time. *Never strain.*

When you begin doing this exercise, your breathing should be slow. After a few weeks you can increase the rapidity, which will result in accelerating your pulse. You may experience different 'unusual' sensations but remember the object of the exercise is to calm your mind. If you have time for only one breathing exercise in the morning, do this one. It not only starts the day with the right attitude of peace and calm, but also energizes your body to face the challenges of the day.

Rhythmic breath:

The second exercise I found of great benefit is called *pranvajapa pranayama* or "rhythmic breath". Over the years, I have come across many versions of this technique. The one offered by Mr. Yeats-Brown consists of breathing in the rhythm of 1 to 4 to 2. Again, sitting comfortably with spine erect, you might try inhaling for four seconds, holding your breath for sixteen seconds, and exhaling for eight seconds. You do this by placing your left hand on your lap, while the thumb and the third finger of your right hand are used to block alternatively the right or the left nostril. Your first and second fingers rest on the bridge of your nose. You start with both nostrils blocked with your thumb and third finger. You free your left nostril and inhale for four seconds. You close both nostrils for sixteen seconds and exhale by freeing the right nostril. Continue by inhaling through the right nostril, blocking both and exhaling through the left nostril. And so forth.

As you master the technique (a matter of a few days) you

can elaborate on the 1:4:2 ratio. If you have started comfortably with 4:16:8, you many want to increase to 5:20:10 or 6:24:12. The numbers are up to you, *providing you do not strain*. This exercise should be practiced for fifteen minutes to be of any appreciable value. The idea is to tie your mind into a rhythm or, as you will see: "the mind's attention flows and it keeps your thoughts from wandering." Always remember the purpose of the exercise is to calm your mind, not to add inches to your chest.

Mr. Yeats-Brown offers a number of other techniques but most are too complex for a non-yoga student to attempt with any hope of success. In contrast to the relative complexity of this rhythmic method, Sai Baba, the Hindu mystic mentioned previously, advocates this very simple exercise:

"Concentrate on breathing in one nostril and out the other, then the mind's attention flows and it keeps your thoughts from wandering. Later, choose one point of God to meditate on."

When I began practicing this exercise I never thought that I could inhale and exhale through alternate nostrils without the use of third finger and thumb. Yet in no time I found it amazingly easy. I directed my breath by simply thinking about it. It could, of course, be the result of my previous experience with *pranvajapa pranayama*. As for keeping our thoughts from wandering, it is only the first step, a means to an end. True stillness can be achieved only by the selection of one "point of God" and keeping one's mind's energies on it. The 'point' or any of the attributes of that which we call God are discussed in the final chapter.

Relaxation can also be a direct result of knowing who and what you are. For the more advanced students Sai Baba simply says:

Sit in the light.

The light is you.
You are the light.⁽⁶⁾

For the average person, however, Dr. Andrew Weil offers several simple techniques. He stresses quite firmly not only the mind-body connection, but also the spirit-body interrelation, though not in the context of relaxation. "Until the breath cycle begins, spirit and body are not connected; the fetus and the newborn baby have a vegetative life but are not invested with spirit."⁽⁷⁾ This casts a certain light on the question of abortion, though I choose to leave this matter firmly in the hands, bodies, and minds of women, who may lean on our relaxation exercises to make *their* decision. Nevertheless, Weil's breathing techniques are intended to benefit both the mind and the body. I found he contributes some ideas which are delightful in their simplicity, yet obviously of a tested nature.

In his first exercise Weil tells us to simply observe our breath. We are to remove or loosen any restraining clothing, close our eyes and follow the passage of the air as it enters, sates and leaves our body. We are to be quite passive in this exercise, and are not to try and influence the breath in any way. I found being an observer particularly rewarding. It resonates with my own concept that I am in and around my body, but not the body as such. I found it blissfully relaxing also because it places my attention on the breath, *and thus takes it away* from any aggravating or extraneous thoughts. It is next to impossible to keep one's attention on more than one thing at a time.

Another of Weil's suggestions is to begin various breathing exercises with exhaling. It is his contention that such a beginning will empty our lungs more completely and initiate a more natural and deeper inhalation. I also found it to be true, though more useful in relaxing my body than my mind.

Leslie LeCron, the expert on hypnosis whose preemptive

condition is relaxation, offers a simplified version of the 1:4:2 rhythmic method. He follows a similar technique but changes the rhythm to 4:8:4. I found it easier to do but with less compelling results. When in doubt though, it is better to try something easier than to do nothing at all. Both advocates (Weil and LeCron) claim that the rhythm breathing stimulates not only the lungs and the cardiovascular system but also the entire nervous system. Even sitting down, back straight, and simply breathing slowly and deeply has a relaxing effect. The exercises simply enhance this effect.

Deepak Chopra, some of whose views have already been discussed, claims to have achieved best results with the technique of Transcendental Meditation. The system or technique was devised by Mahariashi Mehish Yoga. In the practice of TM, relaxation, as in the case of Sai Baba, is only a means to an end. Although I do not wish to confuse the messenger with the message, I am a little discouraged by a method taught by a man whose principle interest appears to be making billions of dollars.[8] I can understand, however, that the very same reason might serve as a powerful stimulus to many other seekers. To each his own.

Leslie M.LeCron advocates self-hypnotism as a method of relaxation.[9] While from a spiritual standpoint I find this method has its limitations, I can vouch for its efficacy in relaxing the body, as a prelude to further steps in relaxing the mind. Those interested in the ego-centered results, i.e. self-healing, should find his methods invaluable.

Reaching back for my favorite textbook, the ever-helpful Bible, we find that some three thousand years ago it proposed a formula to "keep still and know that I am god".[10] This thought, or idea, is intended to be of such tremendous magnitude as to exclude all other thoughts, or to still the mind. It expresses the same sentiment as does Sai Baba when he says that "you are light." Elsewhere in the Bible, we are advised not to judge. This avocation is followed by encouragement: "least ye be judged", but in fact the latter qualification, while true of the material reality, is of little consequence when in search of the spiritual realm. The point is that in order to pass judgment we must engage ourselves in a game of balance of at least two possibilities, often many more, and thus we anchor ourselves in a dualistic frame of mind, whereas the purpose of "keeping still" is to achieve Oneness. Later still, the same textbook tells us that when we want to pray, we should enter our closet, shut the door, and only then commune with the divine.[11] The closet symbolizes our inner consciousness, and closing the door refers to excluding the influx of unwanted thoughts. Emmet Fox defines prayer as "practicing the presence of God".[12] In *monotheistic* religions this *should mean* that we discard duality for Oneness. This Oneness is best visualized as residing within "an ocean of infinite possibilities".

Whatever method we employ, the purpose of relaxation is to eliminate anxieties which distract the mind from functioning properly. Dr. Herbert Spiegel, a New York psychiatrist who teaches at Columbia University's College of Physicians and Surgeons, is also known as a most reputable expert on hypnosis. He said:

"When you attach electrodes to your head or listen to a priest in a saffron robe, it is all essentially the same. Call it Zen, acupuncture, TM, bio-feedback, or Mesmer, it taps the same kind of attentive, narrowed inner concentration, erasing peripheral distractions—and it can be very useful."[13]

It is this attentive, narrow inner concentration, erasing peripheral distractions, that we seek in order to succeed in our creative visualization.

***

FOOTNOTES

(1). Michael Smith reporting for *Southam News*, January 25, 1999.

(2). Ropp, Robert de, THE MASTER GAME Delacorte, 1968

(3). Weil, Andrew M.D., SPONTANEOUS HEALING pg.131.

(4). Russell, Peter THE TM TECHNIQUE (Arkana, Penguin Group 1998; pg. 54)

(5). YOGA EXPLAINED by F. Yeats-Brown, Victor Gollancz Ltd, 1937, London. While I have scanned many books of yoga systems, this remains my favorite.

(6). BABA by Arnold Schulman, Simon & Shuster, Canada.

(7). Weil, Andrew M.D., SPONTANEOUS HEALING   pg. 203. It is evident that Dr. Weil equates spirit with self-awareness.

(8). I am referring to the father of Transcendental Meditation, Mahariashi Mehish Yoga, reputedly a Belgian billionaire, who is said to have made his fortune from the sale of Ayurvedic medicines. I have no idea if he teaches the TM for free or not.

(9). SELF HYPNOTISM by Leslie M. LeCron; Signet Book 1970. Also THE COMPLETE GUIDE TO HYPNOSIS by the same author, Harper & Row, 1971

(10). Psalm 46:10

(11). Matthew 6:6

(12). Fox, Emmet ALTER YOUR LIFE *How to Maintain Peace* (Harper & Raw, New York) pg. 168

(13). STRESS by Walter McQuade and Ann Aikman, Bantam Book 1975; pg. 194.

Chapter 20
Creative process

...He maketh me lie down in green pastures,
He leadeth me beside the still waters,
He restoreth my soul.

Psalm 23

Ideas are divine gifts of Light.
In esoteric writing, Light always symbolizes knowledge. An enlightened person always was, and is, a knowledgeable person. To understand this premise we must accept that there are two kinds of knowledge. The first kind we acquire, learn, from others. We read, study, research, listen to lectures, and gradually we acquire *other people's knowledge*. But visiting the world's foremost libraries, memorizing all the encyclopedias, clogging to the brim the Giga-memories of our Giga-computers will not give us the *other* kind of knowledge.

It will not give us the Light.

For convenience, I shall call this other kind of knowledge—Knowingness.

Knowledge comes from without. Knowingness from within. It is this second kind of enlightenment, this inner knowingness, that we seek when attempting visualization. The first kind, the knowledge acquired from outside, is certainly just as important. Our subconscious where the first kind resides is necessary for the *execution* of the idea. The carrying out, but not for its generation. One cannot function without knowledge. We all know how it is obtained. We all train our toddlers in the acquisition of other people's knowledge. We impose on them the old ways, the traditions, the *status quo*, the mistakes of the past. Though we're unlikely to admit it openly, we seem to demand that they do *not* start thinking for themselves. Why bother? Aren't we, the adults, much smarter than they are? Didn't we have to go to school and do as we were told? Why should our children be better off?

But what of Knowingness?

Neither schools nor parents teach them how to acquire the Knowingness from within. Likewise religions soon teach our children to shut off the quiet voice whispering in the inner chamber of their young hearts and listen to the "orthodox" knowledge imposed by others. Nor do we teach the young ones the essence of the creative process. It is as though the adults didn't know that all new ideas come from within. If it weren't so, we would all be walking in circles. Perhaps most of us are. Actually the children could teach us a great deal, if we only listened. But we don't. We are all too smart. Right?

The most ancient analysis of the creative process I came across was 'hidden' in the Bible. The first chapter of Genesis offers us a method which works. We have advanced in knowledge since, but the biblical account is as good as any I can think of to begin with. Those among us, who consider the first chapter of Genesis to be a description of God creating the world in six days, needn't read on. Moses, to whom the first five books of the Bible are attributed, was neither an astronomer nor an astrophysicist. The creation of the solar system was of absolutely no interest to him. He had a vision of how the creative process works. He employed whatever techniques he could muster to convey to his people, at their level of intellectual capacity, his (inner) vision. It couldn't have been easy. He had to employ symbolic language to translate knowingness into knowledge. Even today there are few that take the trouble to try and understand his words. Fewer still succeed.

It could not have been easy for Moses....

Imagine trying to explain the theory of relativity to people who have never heard about Einstein, who can neither read nor write, and have thus never read a single book on physics, astronomy or mathematics. To men who only recently came down from the treetops, or stepped out of their caves. To nomads who traveled lightly. I am not saying that the Hebrew were at that evolutionary stage, but the comparison serves to give some idea of his problems. As I said above, what Moses had to convey has not been understood by us, most of us, for the last three thousand years. Do you still think that I am exaggerating?

The first chapter of Genesis takes us, step by step, relating what happens when an idea first comes to us, out of the blue. Actually the blue color symbolizes a mental state of consciousness, and thus the comparison is not accurate. The idea comes from outer darkness. It comes from 'nowhere'. Until it invades our consciousness it is only a "potential idea". It has not, as yet, found its mode of being. It is we who can, if we so wish, give it life.

Since I have already written an essay on the subject in BEYOND RELIGION Vol.1, *Genesis*, and as neither this book nor the article have as yet been published, I shall take the liberty of transferring part of the article, with only slight elaboration, below.[1]

In the beginning God created the heaven and the earth. (Genesis 1:1)

Two important items of information are given in the very first verse. One, God is always at the beginning of everything; and two, in order for anything to become manifest, to 'happen', to acquire a mode of being, we need to initiate the concept of duality. In 'heaven' every idea is in its potential state. On earth, it becomes concretized. Thus, the two states of consciousness: the spiritual or the potential—'heaven', and the non-spiritual (the mental, emotional and physical)—

'earth'. According to the Bible, before anything at all can happen this concept must be accepted. It is imperative to remember that there is no duality in the spiritual realm; nor, by definition, is there any 'matter'. To successfully convert a spiritual idea into a concrete, material form, we must follow instructions closely.

And the earth was without form, and void; and darkness was upon the face of the deep. And the spirit of God moved upon the waters. (Ibid. verse 2)

Obviously, the earth (matter) was without form; it was void, i.e. it wasn't there! It was only in its *potential* form. It was an *idea*. The darkness simply represents the absence of Light, and Light always stands for knowledge. Since the Bible concerns itself exclusively with spiritual matters, the knowledge it refers to is Divine knowledge, or, in our own adopted idiom—Knowingness. Next, the *face* symbolizes the power of recognition. At this stage there is nothing to recognize thus the face was in darkness. The *waters* symbolize the thought-stream. So we now have an Idea, an incredible potential (the deep), yet without any knowledge of what to do with it! Spirit is attempting to spiritualize the thought-stream. The uncoordinated thoughts (chaos) are the original building blocks of the universe, and thus of absolutely anything within the universe. We must never forget that chaos is only the absence of order, but inherent in chaos is the predisposition towards order. Studying fractals and chaos, Peter Oppenhimer of the New York Institute of Technology writes: "Now I believe that ideas, mathematical concepts, abstract notions, dreams, spirits are somehow more fundamental, and that... physical objects somehow grow out of that. I've come to that philosophy based on my exploration of computer graphics."[2] Moses did not have computers to aid him but he came to similar conclusions. Ideas are preexisting, pre-manifested patterns. They are what atoms were before they became atoms. They are units of information, not yet organized into physical, material patterns.

And God said. Let there be light; and there was light. (Ibid. verse three)

As stated above, light is the source of all knowledge. An illuminated person is a knowledgeable person. To put ideas into concrete forms we need knowledge. But we first need ideas—and they come from within.

And God called the light Day, and the darkness he called Night. (ibid. verse four)

This is a fascinating piece of subterfuge. I have no idea whether it was purposeful or accidental. You never know with the scribes! We recognize the day as time between sunrise and sunset. The Hebrew did the opposite. The Hebrew day started at sunset. In order for an Idea to take root, we must *not* try to think about it but... sleep! The greatest ideas anyone ever had did not take seed in the scientist's labs but at night. There are ample reports of scientists waking up with new ideas. We are reminded here about the true source of ideas and the true "developer" of such. The nearest we get to participate is through our unconscious. So much for our egos!

And God said, Let there be a firmament in the midst of the waters, and let it divide the waters from the waters. (ibid. verse 6)

I confess that I love the King James Version of the Bible. But when, in my favorite edition, poetry and accuracy compete for attention, poetry wins! The Hebrew word *raqia*, translated as 'firmament', in fact means *expanse* or *expansion*. What we are told here is that we must go through the process of sifting our thoughts into the relevant and the irrelevant. As the Idea grows, our thought processes must be concentrated. We must divide them from other thoughts. If we are to develop an idea, we cannot be scatterbrained. Great thinkers, inventors, artists, invariably demonstrate fantastic powers of concentration. The ancients knew that!

The following verse deals with the same subject. It is interesting (verse 8), that *God called the firmament Heaven*. It suggests that the process of expansion of ideas is still a 'divine' process, i.e. it must take place *before* the idea enters our conscious mind. We love saying that we have a marvelous idea. It seems, if the idea is any good, it originated way above the 'we' or the 'I' concept. Our egos take another beating...

And God said, Let the waters under the heaven be gathered together unto one place, and let the dry land appear. (ibid. verse 9)

We made it. Finally dry land. When we gather together our thoughts (waters), *under* the heaven, i.e. in our conscious mind, a manifestation takes place. Emmet Fox, the superb exponent of the spiritual interpretation of the Bible, called this a Demonstration. If we follow the process accurately, if we let God do his work (mostly when we sleep), if we are humble enough to let our thoughts be gathered at our unconscious level *before* we take active part in the process, we end up with a demonstration. If, on the other hand, we are so pigheaded as to think that we, ourselves, with the use of 5% of our brains, can develop an original idea, well, good luck. It would be a first!

The rest of the creative process described in Genesis shows us how not to rush an idea. How to keep checking, at every stage, if the idea is 'good'. This simply means that if our ego takes over, (if a universal idea is relegated to a parochial level), we might channel the idea for our own ends, for our personal gain or advantage. God, whatever we mean by this concept is ONE. It is not concerned with our puny egos but with All. As we grow in Light, in divine Knowledge, our interests begin to reflect that which can benefit the larger number...

My essay concludes that "Genesis, so aptly named, is not

about the 'birth' of the world. It is about the birth of an IDEA." Any idea. For any idea, any inspiration, to become manifest in our subjective reality, it must follow the process outlined above. All ideas are of 'divine' origin and therefore all are 'good'. What dilutes their intrinsic goodness is our inability to follow the method outlined above. We convert that which is universal to that which is parochial. We allow our egos to influence their development. We bear the consequences. We create our own, subjective universe.

So much for the Bible. Hopefully, during the last few thousand years we have made some progress.

There is one other approach to creativity which has been mentioned before but deserves to be examined in greater detail. I have already mentioned that the ideas which invade our minds are *gestält* or whole concepts which only later are broken down into individual thoughts and arranged in, what Dr .Chopra calls, "linguistically structured" communication. Since, as of writing this page, my collection of essays BEYOND RELIGION, Volume II also remains unpublished, I shall again take the liberty to reprint an extract from my essay: *Wunderkind* (with some pertinent additional comments). The essay bears strongly on the question of the creative process.[3]

«As adults, we communicate with each other in a shattered, disjointed manner. We rejoice in every opportunity to cleverly dissect and analyze images we receive with our senses, only to piece them together, again, in an arbitrary fashion, with images familiar to us. Next, we chop our own fabrications once more into countless disjointed fragments, convert the results into words, and finally, with great difficulty, we synthesize them into reasonably intelligible sentences. We might call this process the semantic conversion. It is as useful, as accurate, as a blind man attempting to describe a painting inspired by Beethoven's symphony to a man born deaf. We invariably insist, however, that our description or interpretation of whatever event or concept is the right one, that we have a good handle on objective reality.

The images which our children receive are quite different.

A child is not born with an ability to convert his awareness of the world to a semantically-fragmented interpretation. This comes gradually, at a rate at which the child masters control over his or her language. Like us, the *wunderkind* [4] also employs his senses to define an objective reality, but in addition, he retains an inherent contact with 'Eden' from which he is gradually emerging.[5] In Eden, there are no languages, no words, and no sentences.[6] There are no analytic/synthetic processes which dilute and pervert the intensity and integrity of images which the psyche receives. Jesus did not describe or even visualize the biological processes that the blind man's eye must undergo in order to see, but rather he visualized a perfect eye in lieu of the blind one. A whole, complete, perfect eye. As already discussed in the chapter on *Art and Creativity*, it bears repeating that when Mozart 'heard' a composition, he did not hear it as individual notes. He 'heard' it all simultaneously, in its entirety. Einstein did not 'see' equations scribbled haphazardly on a blackboard, but spoke of visual images, of "muscular" concepts expressing the workings of the universe. Both, he and Mozart, had to spend innumerable hours, later, transcribing or converting these images to a linear interpretation. Words, numbers, even musical symbols are all linear patterns, whereas the Edenic reality is, to say the least, three-dimensional. The images we receive from Eden are non-verbal, *gestält* structures or patterns, symbols or events. They also seem independent of the confines of time and space.

Our culture demands that we convert such integrated realities into linear projections. Perhaps that is why people who have never experienced the 'whole', have great difficulty in accepting its existence. They assign to the concept some mystical, religious values, esoteric mumbo-jumbo, little realizing that as children we all went through a phase of having access to this undifferentiated reality. Then, as now, we need not recognize it as anything special, unusual or sacred. If, as children, we were capable of assigning semantic value to this reality, we would consider Eden our home, our inherent right. And it is.

It is our kingdom.

We, adults, are the creators of the semantic reality. We spend all our efforts in cutting the link our children have with the Edenic continuum. Joseph Chilton Pearce calls this process acculturation.[7] Having lost it ourselves, we demand that our children do likewise, or else... Later, some of us try hard to retrace our steps over this tiny isthmus. Regrettably, there is no way one can put an oak-tree inside an acorn. We cannot *go* back to this state, no matter what we do. It is the 'going' or the 'doing' itself which cuts the umbilical chord between Paradise and us. The best we can hope for is to empty our skins of old wine and do nothing.[8] Nothing at all. We are told to "be still and know we are gods."[9]

Yet there have been, surely still are, people, who retain partial or even more substantial contact with Eden. In case of Einstein, only his intellect entered the field or the continuum, whereas Jesus, when walking on water, or Father Pio, when appearing simultaneously in his monastery in Italy and in South America, or Sai Baba when manifesting an unprecedented accumulation of objects out of thin air, actually entered the field itself. Such examples are usually relegated to 'religious' experiences. I say 'relegated' because religions invariably 'de-mystify' by 'materializing', by dressing the holy in mundane symbols, rather than teaching people how to enter the mystical state themselves.

Apparently, in order to gain entry to Eden, to partake in the field of infinite possibilities, we must be willing, at last temporarily, to suspend the objective reality which we took such pains to create.[10] We must be willing to give up all the accumulated knowledge, all that which constitutes our personality; in a way we must die in order to come to life within the continuum. Jesus tells us that we might succeed if we are willing to be in this world but not of this world.[11]

The reason why we cannot remain in Eden forever is that the prodigy finds himself in a mode of acceptance of the continuum in an open or unconditional way. Only mature individuality such as that of Jesus or Sai Baba can survive in our society while maintaining substantial contact with the Edenic state of consciousness. I suspect the privilege is shared by some Zen masters, perhaps great poets, artists and some child prodigies that have not lost their "innocence". Others sever the link or end up in a lunatic asylum. »

Most of us cannot visualize a state of consciousness on which we do not impose our personality. By that I mean that we recognize reality in the light of our knowledge, in the light of our experience acquired over millions of years. Not just our minds rebel at the prospect of loosing the security of our subjective universes, but also our physical bodies that carry primordial memories of the past. Perhaps this is why Paul of Tarsus declared the necessity to die daily.[12] We need no assurance that he did not refer to his physical body.

Another example of achieving this Edenic state is to "become as little children".[13] Jesus in his reference to little children did not intend us to start having tantrums, become inadequate in the performance of our tasks, in fact to become juvenile. To become like a small child simply means to become whole. As adults we exhibit a personality based on a self-induced dichotomy. In the process of "growing up", we have accepted the duality of our world *to the exclusion* of any other reality. We forgot that the subjective world we live in is a world of our own creation, a world which we continue creating each time a thought invading our mind is impregnated, enlivened with emotion, each time a desire for our own, self-centered ends is allowed to dominate our consciousness. After all, our ends create our universe: subjective, limited, transient.

To quote once again from my essay entitled *Wunderkind*:

"We must stop doing that. We must stop doing. We must be. Every child is a prodigy. A wonder. And within the heart of every single one of us there is a carefree, joyful, trusting child. If we stop shackling it with our conventions, traditions, customs, political and religious systems, perhaps the child will emerge, once again, to play in the field of infinite possibilities."

Perhaps.

We are gods but, at this stage of our evolution, we are errant gods. The great avatars of the past, as well as some walking the earth today, remind us of this. It is up to us.

Up to you and me.

***

FOOTNOTES

(1). History has overtaken me. The collection of essays under the heading BEYOND RELIGION I, has been published by Inhousepress in 1997 and reissued in 2001.

(2). Briggs, John FRACTALS page 91

(3). As luck would have it, the first edition of Beyond Religion II was printed four months before Visualization!

(4). I chose the German word *'wunderkind'* as it suggests not only that the child prodigy is a wonder-child, but virtually a wonderful *kind*, practically a different specie.

(5). I use the pronoun 'he' generically. The exact same applies to every young "she".

(6). In Genesis 2:19, Adam names 'every living creature'. Name in the Bible symbolizes nature. What Adam did was to recognize the nature of that which was before him. It is still the gestält concept that we are dealing with here. Not a chat with Eve who, at this time, was not yet 'created'.

(7). I owe a great deal of the material for this subject matter to Joseph Chilton Pearce, the author of EXPLORING THE CRACK IN THE COSMIC EGG. Washington Square Press, New York 1975

(8). Compare Matthew 9:17, Mark 2:22, Luke 5:37.

(9). compare Psalm 46:10

(10). Eden, Paradise, continuum, the field of infinite possibilities, are all treated as synonyms. They all represent the unchangeable, undifferentiated reality which Jesus called the kingdom of heaven.

(11). John 17:14 - 16.

(12). 1 Corinthians 15:31

(13). Matthew 18:3.

Chapter 21
Programming

*The way to become human is to learn
to recognize the lineaments of God
in all of the wonderful modulations
of the face of man.*

Joseph Campbell
THE HERO WITH A THOUSAND FACES (page 390.)

There **is only one way** to be a Master. It is to act like a Master. There are no shortcuts.

As with every endeavor, in order to succeed we need a plan. In case of visualization I refer to it as programming. When used on others it is called mind-control, and is one of the greatest crimes against a human being one can commit. We often forget that we can influence another person's thinking by our own mental processes. When we do so for what we regard as good, it is called white magic. When we do it with an 'evil' intent, when our influence is for the purpose of doing some harm, physical, emotional or mental, we call such action black magic. While skeptics still believe that only primitive people in the heart of Africa believe in such machinations, the psychologists are well aware that mind control is practiced in all countries of the world under different names.

The best known and perfectly 'legal' (while extremely unethical) method of practicing the magical arts is the multi-billion dollar industry we know as Advertising. We are all subjected to a glut of TV commercials which attempt to influence our, perhaps too gullible, minds to perform acts which we would otherwise be unwilling to do. Promotional considerations in our daily press and periodicals are relegating the news' aspect of the media to a secondary, subservient position. The news, with their "instant-replay dramatizations", seem to be treated as a means to an end. Not as real or true news service for which the public is charged money.

Promotion and Advertising means money—the news is a necessary evil.

While the advertisements of vitamins might be compared to white magic, the millions spent on attempting to induce young men and women to take up and continue smoking, can be counted as the blackest of the black arts. To this day there are countries where the advertising of tobacco is still legal. The same could be said of the International Pharmaceutical Conglomerates that, as discussed in the chapter on *Health and Healing*, amass billions by misleading millions. Selling toxic materials purported to alleviate symptoms without healing the cause of the ailment could be described, at best, as dishonest. At worst, as mass murder. Physical or mental. Carefully worded advertisements aimed at bamboozling the simple-minded buyer into thinking that the poisons will actually help in curing the disease, might not be actually killing the sufferer's body, but it affects adversely his or her mind. As such, once again, it can be included under the heading of black magic.

At the outset, therefore, we must dismiss any thought of resorting to black-magic for whatever reason. And even white-magic, such as practicing mind control in order to help someone, is unethical if done without that recipient's knowledge and approval. To do so we would invade the freedom of such person, and freedom, as we know from previous chapters, is a divine trait. It is unwise to hurt another's body, it is worse to manipulate their mind; it is inexcusable to invade the domain of the divine, or the unconscious.

It will probably come as a shock to most people but it must be said that supplicatory prayer conducted without the permission of the stipulated beneficiary, is a form of white-magic. While it may benefit the recipient body, it is just as likely to affect adversely his or her subconscious, i.e. "their animal-soul". Let us never forget that it is the animal-soul that we are endeavoring to sanctify, not the spirit within us which requires no such effort. Any claims by some religions that a Savior can save our soul do not understand the meaning of the word savior. Your savior and my savior is your own and my own Higher Self, the divine Presence within us.

The only Savior we shall ever meet.

Without we are many, within we are One.

The teacher from Galilee speaking from his higher state of consciousness, tried to explain: "That they all may be one; as thou, Father, art in me, and I in thee, that they also may be one in us..."[1] And then "...behold, the kingdom of God is within you."[2] And then, as cited before, Sai Baba: "Sit in the light. The light is you. You are the light."[3] And then there is this beautiful wisdom given to the Hindus: "I am the Self, seated in the hearts of all creatures. I am the beginning, the middle, and the end of all beings."[4] Talk of programming! Repetition is supposed to strengthen the power of suggestion.

Please note, I am not quoting "religious" sayings. I am quoting the sayings which have been ignored by religions.

There must have been an extremely powerful negative programming polluting the world during the last few thousand years. Powerful enough to practically destroy the essence of all great teaching. *That which saves cannot be an outside agency.* If it were possible, it would deny the One Reality. If we do not discover the divinity within us, what chance do we have to find it in the vastness of the universe? Our animal soul, our subconscious, that which comprises all which makes us different from each other, that individuality can only be sanctified, i.e. saved, by aligning it with universal principles. All else is transient, illusory. All programming must be ultimately directed to this end.

In the meantime....

In the meantime, programming as it applies to our 'little' self is a different matter.

It can be divided into two parts. The first is directed towards the particular. It is intended to benefit our ego, our personality, body, health, wealth or any aspect of our material existence. This would include our social standing, and all matters pertaining to us as individuals.

The second type of visualization (in part described above) is directed towards and by the universal values. To people who are interested in this type of programming, their personal gain is of little interest to them. It is not that they are "goody-goody" merchants, or professional "do-gooders", who care only for others. Quite the contrary. It is that they are completely at ease about their own well-being. They are fully confident that their spiritual body takes care of their own welfare, as individuals, by the indestructible, almighty, Universal Presence within them. Their confidence is such that, to people of a different viewpoint they might, on occasion, appear foolhardy. Zen masters are often accused of, or regarded as, playing the fool. Play-the-fool they might, but perhaps only to hide their wisdom. While such people exhibit enormous confidence in life, they do not escape into the never-never reality of puerile banality and illusion. They make a concentrated effort to live in full consciousness. To be aware not only of their immediate surroundings, but to see every other person, every thing, every event in the context of the Whole.

When successful, they rise above the wiles of everyday life, develop an overview which rewards them with an inner peace. Saint Paul calls it the "peace... which passes all understanding".[5] It results from the elimination of duality from one's consciousness; of perceiving that which the opposites have in common. Buddha calls it the middle path. This state is referred to by some as Samadhi,[6] by others as Sanctifying Grace. It is a state in which the "roof brain chatter" ceases and a sublime, transcendental serenity takes its place. Those who haven't experienced it yet, have a wonderful joy awaiting them. Those who have—will bear witness that we do not have to die in order to 'go' to heaven.

The programming these people seek is to grow in universal vision. This alone is what they seek. They know that by reaching for the top, they might, just might reach cloud nine. All else becomes a byproduct of their principal commitment. They ascribe to the maxim: "Seek ye first the kingdom of God and his righteousness; all these things shall be added unto you".[7] Again the sages knew the formula thousands of years ago.

We are slow learners indeed.

The one marginal exception to the universal aspect of visualization is the programming to 'sanctify' our own animal-soul (*nephesh*), for the purpose of uniting it firmly with the universal. Sanctifying means "making holy", and this simply means "making whole," i.e. the return to wholeness or oneness from the state of duality. Such visualization, however, does not stipulate the means, methods or time parameters. It leaves the execution of the desire to Soul Itself.

Ultimately we cannot do it by just our own efforts. We need help from 'above'. Luckily the 'above' is within us.

From the theoretical point of view, there seems to be a paradox between defining the desired result, when, in the spiritual sense, the end can never justify the means. This is not for any pompous hypothetical reason, but simply because the spiritual life can only have its being in the present moment, and the present is when the 'means' are manifested. Another way of putting it would be that Life takes precedence over death. Furthermore, in the spiritual life there is no end. The spirit, by definition, is immortal. *Endless*.

The desireless state advocated by Buddha refers to the

elimination of desire as pertaining to one's ego. Since we can only experience the divine in the present, the means become the sole expression of Life. Since God has *no being except in a mode of being*, a being as 'something', we are Its expression, regardless of how badly we realize it, how limited our vision.

Yet, in case of programming we are always concerned with the future.

The way to overcome this paradox is to teach ourselves to define clearly our desired result and having implanted it (programmed it) in our deeper consciousness, to ignore it. If we dwell on the desire which is to be manifested later, we shall suspend living in the present and remain in abeyance until the desire is fulfilled. Such are the mechanics of the creative process that such behavior would hinder if not preclude the desire from manifesting itself in the physical (material or manifested) universe. Perhaps the reason is to force us to live in the present.

This technique also teaches us humility.

What we cannot achieve with our conscious effort, is achieved, often quickly and easily, with our inner power. Whether we call it the subconscious, the unconscious or the spirit is of little consequence. As we already know, the divine within us does not operate in a linguistically structured manner. It conducts its business in an integral, whole, or as I like to call it, in a *gestält* manner.

There is one other suggestion which might help us in keeping our attention on the present. As we program our subconscious with the desired suggestion, we should, within our capability, act as though the 'cure' already took place. As I suggested at the beginning of this chapter, the only way to be a master is to act like a master. The only way to be healthy is to act as though we were.

This single most important evolutionary mechanism cannot be stressed too strongly. *We must always work in the present*. We cannot delay our "desired results" to take place in the ever after. People who delay raising their state of consciousness till "after death", miss the teaching of all the great avatars. Jesus assures us repeatedly: "God is not the God of the dead, but of the living."[8] The Christian and Moslem obsession with delaying one's "heaven" until after death is a morbid, destructive, and from the psychological point of view a deeply neurotic interpretation of the inspired philosophies. If you are miserable here-and-now, there are absolutely no guaranties of a sudden change in your state of consciousness later. Some religions teach that we can remain in the wheel of Awagawan, the cycle of re-incarnation, for millions of years.

That's a risk I am not prepared to take.

***

The self-hypnotic techniques can serve to free our subconscious from undesirable misconceptions, as well as to implant concepts which we consider desirable. It is still up to you, the creator of your universe, to decide which concepts you deem desirable. Whatever you decide, it will, sooner or later, become manifest in your reality.

Be careful what you hope for...

If you decide to employ such methods, it is usually recommended that they be applied to one desired effect at a time. The researches found that the subconscious, which is credited with the function carrying out the desire, should not be burdened with an array of instructions simultaneously. This is probably true of programming regarding the particular. Yet Emile Coué who became world-famous for his successes in his clinic in Nancy, France, recommended the exact opposite of the above stated policy. He recommended that those seeking improvement in their condition repeat each day, morning and evening, the following suggestion: "Every day, in every way, I am getting better and better".[9] This non-specific, broadly defined programming seems to fill the gap between the universal and the particular visualization.

In my own experience, I found Coué's recommendation rather slow to bear results. I prefer to add: "...every hour, every minute, each second... I am getting better and better." This brings immediacy to the suggestion and draws us closer to living in the present. What is important in this particular programming is that it stipulates neither the method nor the final result. At least, not specifically. The result might be called open-ended, thus leaving room for constant improvement. While it requires an act of faith in our body's and our subconscious' ability to affect amelioration, it also leaves room for the Universal to do Its work. Others might prefer to think of it as leaving both the method and the result to their Higher Self.

Yet whatever the embellishments, Coué's method still relies on the power of the mind. There is nothing wrong with this approach, but a "spiritual purist" would call any such method the second best. There is an even simpler way that not only heals but sustains a healthy state for thousands of people all over the world. We might refer to it as the late Bruno Gröning's method. Gröning was the German healer about whom I wrote in the chapter on the *Medical View*.

Contrary to all methods requiring mental efforts, in Gröning's "system" we must not think at all. Instead of using our mind, we must learn to use our heart. We must sit straight, hands—palms up—on our lap, (neither legs nor arm should be crossed) and *forget about our diseases*. This is vital. All negativity must be eliminated from our awareness. We can picture a beautiful landscape, our favorite flowers, we can feel ourselves being washed or cleansed with the presence of God. That's all. We must allow the spiritual energy to enter us, to fill us, to do its work. Later, we might experience considerable pain. There may be headaches, cramps, even vomiting. If so, this is the cleansing action of the spiritual energy entering our body.

We sit still for as long as it takes. Usually ten or fifteen minutes at a time, or as long as we feel the energy affecting us. All that the energy does is to restore order. The healing may be instantaneous; it may take days, months even years. Perhaps it took us years to destroy our body. If we believe in its power we shall be cured. Thousands of people were. Including many who have been exposed to deadly radiation in the vicinity of Chernobyl. Including people with 'incurable' cancers. Others open themselves to the flow of the healing energy *daily* to maintain their wholeness. In my case, to stop my mind from wondering, at the beginning of the "sitting session" I like to concentrate on my breathing. I think of the air coming into my lungs as though filling me with the healing energy, while the breathing out as expelling all negativity. But we must never 'outline' the results. The healing process *must* be left entirely to the Healing Energy Itself. It is absolutely vital that we do not define, nor even think about any malady, our own or other people's. We sit and we believe in order, harmony and beauty. It's as simple as that.

But no one can do it for us.

You cannot have a doctor prescribe or administer a daily dosage of spiritual energy. We cannot buy it in a local drugstore. We must sit down and get it ourselves. Once in the morning, once in the evening. We can also reach out for it at any time during the day. We can live in constant awareness of it. After all, God is omnipresent. We are in the midst of It. Or... we can keep complaining and do nothing. Most of us do just that. But whatever we do or do not do, will bear a very specific result, a consequence of our—and only our own—decision. We shall have no one else to blame. The healing energy, the life force, vital energy, chi, prana or the Divine Power by any other name is available to all. At all times. For free.

As are other methods.
And there are many.

In the olden days, our forefathers were well aware of the

tremendous influence programming had on our wellbeing. The ancient method had been called 'prayer'. The ancients had known that in order to influence our environment, including our physical body, we must start with the way we think, with our sets of beliefs at the deepest level. A man or woman whose consciousness rests exclusively in the world of duality and thus who believe in good and evil will have both in their lives. It cannot be otherwise. We are the physical 'out-picturing' of our inner state of consciousness.

Their ancient methods were gradually transformed by religious institutions into begging litanies, lists of requests that had been submitted to some exterior, inaccessible, scary deity, for consideration. This is not what the ancients had in mind. Every mountain, every hill, every high ground in the Bible symbolizes a *raised state of consciousness*. It is in this heightened condition of awareness that we come in touch with our own Higher Self.

This is not to say that we cannot request assistance from the divine spark within us, even for quite mundane things. But we must remember that our requests might very well be granted—we must be careful what we wish for. Emmet Fox recommends the following programming method. He suggests that we select three things we most wish for in our life, and three things or conditions we wish to remove from our life. Contrary to the previously advocated methods, we should "be definite and specific and not vague". Then...

Claim gently but definitely that the Great Creative Life Force of the Universe is bringing each of the first three things into your life in Its own way, in Its own time, and in Its own form. Then claim that the same Great Power is dissolving each of the latter three, also in Its own way.[10]

Fox tells us to do this in a relaxed state, without vehemence or conditions, regularly over a period of time. For best results, we should do it daily. But the vital thing is not to think about the content of our programming the rest of the time. We must get on with our lives as if all the six items had been already taken care of. Note that in spite of the specificity of requests we still leave the "way, time and form" to the Higher Realm.

It helps if we endow our universe with the omnipresence of Divine Intelligence.

***

The absurdity of it all is that the power and efficacy of the spiritual energy has been known to man for thousands of years. Periodically, for a while, it has been usurped by various religions, only to fall into inept misuse—then disuse. When it happens spontaneously, the churches call the healing resulting from its action miraculous. That's utter nonsense. Nothing can be more natural, more proper, more normal and mundane than man regaining his contact with his true self. With the omnipresent energy of life. But this energy has nothing to do with *any* religion. It has to do with the *Universal* energy. It has to do with the Life Itself.

There is one thing that we must repeat to ourselves until it sinks deep into our subconscious. We have always created our own universes. The name of the game is to start doing so consciously. That's all. To do it here and now.

Now is all there is.

***

FOOTNOTES

(1). John 17:21.
(2). Luke 17:21
(3). BABA by Arnold Schulman, [Simon & Shuster, Canada.]
(4). Bhagavad Gita 10:20 [In Sanskrit it means: "Song of the Lord"] Part of Mahabharata, Hindu scripture.
(5). Philippians 4:7
(6). Samadhi is often defined as "concentrative absorption". BUDDHISM

edited by Richard A. Gard, (George Braziller, New York 1962), gives an excellent overview of the philosophy.

(7). Matthew 6:33, Luke 12:31. N.B.: 'righteousness' in the Bible always means "right thinking".

(8). Matthew 22:32, Mark 12:27, Luke 20:38. This phrase also carries a symbolic meaning. Jesus called all who were not born in spirit—dead. To be born in spirit simply means being fully aware of one's spiritual, i.e. divine (as against material) nature.

(9). Gleamed from SELF HYPNOTISM by Leslie M. LeCron; Signet Book, 1970; pg.67,

(10). Fox, Emmet ALTER YOUR LIFE pgs. 4-5

Chapter 21
Negative Programming

The individual is the only reality.

Carl G. Jung
[Approaching the Unconscious]

Our brain is designed in a manner similar to a computer. We can think of it as a mechanical device. We must learn how to operate it as we would any other complex mechanism. And let us make no mistake about it. It is a very complex mechanism. In fact, it took millions of years to develop and it is still being improved—on a daily basis. It is a superb mechanism which relies on constant feedback, like a computer which is never shut off, on which operators continually feed all the new available data.

The neurons, synapses etc., are part of the hardware, the continuous input (and feedback) from our senses represents the software. There are no theoretical limits on the amount of software which can be fed into this biological computer, although it requires special techniques to access some parts of memory. We can design diverse programs telling our electronic brain how to solve very complex problems. But we are not very successful in telling any type of computers what *not* to do. We simply do not design software on *not* performing certain function. If there are functions that we have no wish for our computer to perform, we simply do not program them into our neurons.

It's quite simple really.

The very same logic applies to our minds. We cannot learn *not* to visualize something. The collateral of this is that we cannot program into our "imaginative body" an instruction not to do this that or the other. Our brain (in this case for practical purposes synonymous with our mind) refuses to respond to such negative instructions. If it were otherwise, all hypnotic programs would instantly stop all smokers from smoking, we would program ourselves not to contract any diseases, not to scream at our wives or husbands, not to be an obnoxious child. Alas, neither mental nor electronic computer (in which I include our brain) responds well to such commands.

We must learn to visualize that which we wish to be, to become, not the reverse. We must see ourselves healthy, joyful, intelligent, friendly, rather than not exhibiting the opposite traits. We already know that, in the biological sense, our body rebuilds itself, completely, over a period of a little over a year.[1] All old cells are shed, discarded, dissolved and new, brand new cells take their place. Until recently the scientists thought that this was not true of neurons. Yesterday I heard assurances to the contrary. Our brain cells are subject to the same laws of regeneration as all the other cells.

There is a catch.

Unless told (programmed) to the contrary, the new cells will rebuild themselves *in the exact image and likeness of their predecessors*. The purpose of visualization is to create *a new matrix*, a new program by which the new cells can develop. We do not change the existing cells. Our physical organism will take care of them automatically. What we must take care of is the future, wherein lies our present. After all, what we think of today becomes physical reality tomorrow. Such is the law of the universe.

This may well be the problem with the otherwise sublime wisdom of the Ten Commandments.[2] We are told what *not* to do. We are *not* to kill. We are *not* to steal, *not* make graven images, *not* commit adultery, *not* take the name of the Lord in vain.... A long, long time after Moses smashed his first set of tablets on mount Sinai, another prophet changed the method of instruction. He did not say "do *not* hate thy neighbor, or the devil, or evil." He simply admonished us to love our fellowmen, to love goodness (or God) with all our hearts, souls and bodies. A positive program is a thousand times more powerful than a negative suggestion. Such a method can truly make our subconscious whole. Or holy. Or saved.

No wonder they called him Savior.

Imagine a reality in which the world under the Judeo-Christian influence had been taught just that. Rather than being told *not* to commit dozens and dozens of sins, we would have been taught to love goodness and other people. Nothing else. No complex religious dogmas, no imposing liturgies, no punishments or inquisitions. Just love. For two thousand years....

Don't you think all the 'sins' would have taken care of themselves?

And what of the 'successes' of negative suggestions (i.e. commandments)? We continue killing, stealing; our churches are filled with graven images, adultery is more widespread in today's society than ever although the Christians are admonished to swear by the Lord God at every opportunity: when getting married in a Christian church, when giving testimony in a Christian court of law, taking a major office, or becoming a citizen of a new country. Even the admonition: "Swear not at all; neither by heaven; for it is God's throne: Nor by the earth; for it is his footstool..."[3] has been, and continues to be, completely ignored by the mighty Vatican as well as most other Christian sects. Could it be that the admonition attributed to Jesus had been set in *negative programming*? "...*not at all, ...neither... nor...*" Did no one notice this quotation during the two thousand years?

It is obviously easier to control people kept in perennial darkness. I find it harder to understand the motivation of the faithful to *remain* in abject ignorance of the teaching, when they were the sole losers. Particularly if they knew that Jesus' vision promised them absolute freedom—*here and now*.

Could it be that no one ever took the trouble to find out? Have the Christian masses been so brainwashed as to suffer from anxiety *in case* they found the truth? Could it be that millions upon millions of 'faithful' have been, quite simply—afraid?

Afraid of the Truth?

And yet for the last two thousand years the Catholic Church alone among the countless other churches has had an unparalleled advantage over all other faiths. Instead of asking the countless millions of faithful attending the Sacrament of Confession if they broke any of the 'negative' commandments, the priest could have asked simply: "Did you love your neighbor?" "Did you find a way to show, to demonstrate your love to your enemy? "Did you discover God's presence in every man, woman and child you met since your last confession?"

And if not... how many times?

Returning to negative programming.

It is inherent in human nature to simply ignore negative suggestions. Moses couldn't have known. Jesus tried harder but still, though rarely, employed the psychological no-no (assuming the New Testament reports are accurate). But there again, his positive suggestion to loving one's neighbor did not get very far either. Perhaps it was like seed falling among the thorns.[4] Too much negativity for the positive suggestion to survive. Or, perhaps we were not yet ready. Or, it may be that it takes two thousand years for an advanced idea, a 'universal' vision to mature in our minds. And hearts.

Perhaps only now we have come of age.

A contemporary illustration of the futility of negative programming is supplied by Pope John Paul II. For as long as

I remember[5] he spoke strongly *against* any form of killing. This ardent prohibition includes the death penalty, for no matter what crime;[6] it obviously includes all the bloody conflicts among Christians in Europe and South America; it also includes abortion. Wherever the pope travels, he is greeted by hundreds of thousands of people. The attendance at his open-air masses have surpassed numbers normally reserved only for rock concerts. He is obviously loved and admired by an unprecedented number of faithful. Even "non-believers" grudgingly give him credit for the strength of his convictions. Yet his vision of *non*-killing is completely ignored. Negative suggestions always are.

It is not death that we must learn to hate.
It is life that we must learn to love.

Parents commit exactly the same mistakes with their children. They make up endless lists of what *not* to do. "Do *not* make noise"—rather than listen to the whisper of the wind... a flower unfolding, a Mozart's vision of heaven. "Do *not* smoke"—rather than enjoy the smell of spring, or autumn, or the plants on the window sill—or just watch the intricacy of your breath bathing your lungs with the elixir of life. "Do *not* come back late"—rather than I have a surprise for you, if you come back early. And the worst of all, "Do *not* do as I do, do as I say." The first negative suggestion destroys any possibility of the latter being followed. Example is the most powerful suggestion. I've always been baffled by smoking, semi-alcoholic parents expecting their children to be otherwise. Such poison which parents implant in their children is not (just) into their lungs, nor even their cardiovascular systems, but *into their children's minds*. From the day they were born—and before.

I repeat—nothing is as powerful as an example.

The effectiveness of example is mostly due to the intrinsic power of repetition. Every single time we give a good example, we reinforce a positive vision, a positive suggestion. As for other examples listed above, I am sure that parents are much more competent than I am at making up exiting, positive reinforcements. The word 'no' and 'not' should be abolished from the environment of all children. After all, they are gods in waiting. They can do anything, if shown how.

And that's our job.

Negative programming should not be confused with positive programming of negative traits. Brainwashing is a point in question wherein a negative trait is implanted in the subconscious with a positive suggestion. For instance: "You *will* do such-and-such harm." These, of course, are extreme cases reputedly employed only by the military of dictatorial or oligarchic regimes. I had personal experience with *Hitler Jugend* (Hitler's Youth), a Nazi organization formed before and maintained during the Second World War, which was very successful. Children had been methodically indoctrinated to hate everything and everybody who wasn't German. Members of such organizations practiced the blackest of black magic and are said to carry quite horrifying karma. As they abused the mind, they are said to be reborn with a mental vacuum. They become human vegetables, ostracized by society. What is more common is the everyday occurrence when we all imprint, quite unwittingly, a negative suggestion on someone in the immediate family. Parents, for instance, must beware of how they talk to each other when their children are asleep.

I repeat, *the subconscious never sleeps,* as we shall see in the next chapter.

Leslie M. LeCron's book referred to in the previous chapter offers a number of case histories of negative suggestions affecting peoples' lives for many years. Positive programming of negative traits is equally as powerful and effective as instilling positive traits in our subconscious. As discussed in the chapter on *Myths and Reality*, negative philosophies originating in the Greek myths of Sisyphus and quite recently taken up by Nietzsche, Camus, Sartre or embodied in nihilism, gradually led to Hitler's paranoia. These are powerful influences and unless we make a *conscious* effort to protect ourselves, we may be in danger of falling under their spell. The unfortunate fact is that our subconscious makes impressions of its environment quite unbeknownst to us. Also, as stated above, it never sleeps. It also never judges. It records everything indiscriminately and eventually acts on the knowledge filed in the memory cells. Years may pass before the input is translated into action. But negative action precipitated by negative input will eventually result—particularly in moments of stress—unless we countermand it with positive programming.

There are also inherent symbols that leave their impression on our deepest subconscious without our awareness. Carl Jung calls them archetypes and, according to him, such encoded traits can surface when we least expect them:

"...if archetypes were representations which originated in our consciousness (or were acquired by consciousness), we should surely understand them, and not be bewildered and astonished when they present themselves in our consciousness. They are, indeed, an instinctive trend as marked as the impulse of the birds to build nests, or ants to form organized colonies. ...[contrary to instincts] the archetypes... manifest themselves in fantasies and often reveal their presence only by symbolic images... They are without known origin; and they reproduce themselves in any time or in any part of the world..."[7]

No one knows to what extend our inner self is motivated by archetypes. Some ancient symbols have been imbedded in our subconscious and are only awakened at, hopefully, propitious times of our lives. But we cannot be sure. They hover in the deep caverns of our mind, ever ready to surface. There is a heraldic and religious symbol variously used as a secret emblem but also as an ornament or a pattern to *fill the foot* of a colored window. Hence its name: *fylfot*. Few of us realize that it is also known as *gammadion* which is a cross of four gammas, third letters of the Greek alphabet. We also know it as the *swastika*.

But the most harmful negative vision is offered us by at least three of our major religions. It is centered by instilling in our children and adults alike, the *fear of God*. We are told that God is a Being of Infinite Goodness. Yet in the Old Testament alone, rightly or wrongly, there are at least twelve Hebrew words translated into English as *fear*. "Fright, terror, terrified, and dread" are thrown in for good measure. The Christian New Testament is dotted with the Greek version of fear translated as: to fear, to cause fear, to terrify, to be greatly afraid, to be feared, fearful, terrible... to mention just some translations repeated many times over. Misinterpretations of the Greek *Gehenna*, *Valley of Hinnon*, the unseen world of *Hades*, or the Hebrew *Sheol* all translated and promulgated by the Christian churches as "hell", supplied the sacerdotal classes with the desired stick, but did tremendous harm to generations of confounded and misled believers.[8]

The Islam starts every Sura (chapter or paragraph of the Koran), and there are 134 of them, with the words: "In the Name of God, the Merciful, the Compassionate." And then (The Koran) proceeds to call upon their God to offer mighty chastisements, painful chastisements, evil chastisements, God's anger, God's curses, chastisements of the Fire, assurances that God is terrible in chastisement.[9] In addition, the Koran visions of God's wrath are garnished with truly poetic descriptions of hell:

"Surely We have prepared for the evildoers a fire, whose pavilion encompasses them; if they call for succour, they will be succoured with water like molten copper, that shall scald their faces—how evil a potion, and how evil a resting-place."[10]

All courtesy of God who is All-forgiving, All-merciful, All-compassionate.

As of today, there are some 2.5 billion people who may well have such symbols of fear and 'chastisement' implanted deep in their subconscious. We don't know when these archetypes will surface. But we do know that fear breads fear. We also know that most crimes are committed in, and/or are motivated by, fear. Crimes against our neighbor, our enemy, against humanity. Finally, we know that people confident in their courage seldom resort to violence. This cannot be said of the present day Israel, Palestine, India and Pakistan, and the far and middle-eastern states which are under the influence of Islam's religion. Such powerful negative programming will take many generations to expurgate.

Absurd though it may seem, Marxism was a positive philosophy. What dooms it is the non-recognition of individuality. Marxist's ends justify his means.[11] The adherents of Marxism are prepared to sacrifice others for the good of all; not to sacrifice themselves—but *others*. Yet the principle of evolutionary betterment of many can only be recognized as positive.

One other condition can be held responsible for negative programming.

There are people who identify their own weaknesses, or negative traits, with those they deal with. It could be a husband, a wife, a child or even a close friend. Rather than face their own shortcomings, they choose to live an illusion that an outside influence is responsible for all their misadventures. We all use the immediate surroundings as mirrors of our own selves. Yet we often seem oblivious of the fact that, after all, we are the authors of the realities we live in. There are some amongst us who prefer to blame others for the worlds we have created. As such, we tend to transfer all the unpleasant aspects of our reality onto the nearest person available. *Per force*, it is usually a member of our immediate family.

Little can be done for such people until they decide to take the first step of self-discovery. As for those on the receiving end of the 'transfer', the best advice is not to resist it. One cannot engage in a rational argument against an emotional condition. The book I call my favorite textbook, the Bible, has this to say: "Do not resist evil."[12] The biblical verses go on to quote a series of examples. The gist of them appears to imply that it is better to maintain one's own equanimity, the all-important inner peace, than try to win an impossible argument. No matter who is right. One can protect one's own world by quietly withdrawing from the other person until a later time, when a rational dialectic may do some good. After all, it is the state of consciousness we are attempting to change, not to prove one's gift of the gab.

But it is important to withdraw.

The comforting fact is that most people cannot sustain an irrational, artificial reality for very long. If their intensity or pressure does not meet resistance, it soon dissipates. If we simply ignore e.g. verbal attacks, abuse or any form of adverse criticism, we might well be affected by them at the subconscious level. And subliminal programming can be as dangerous to us as a willful act of visualization. Gentle but immediate withdrawal protects us from this eventuality.

There are case histories of just such negative programming. They can result in mental and/or emotional imbalance, inexplicable aberrations and deviations from normal behavior, as well as in anxiety states such as hysteria, phobias, neuroses, obsessions and other dysfunctions. We hear of cardiologists dying of heart failures, internists suffering from diseases in the treatment of which they are immersed, of psychiatrists committing suicide due to an inner darkness they are unable to escape. And then there is an ever-growing family of diseases to which we refer as psychosomatic. There are some physicians who begin to suspect that most diseases suffer from just such an origin.

Even viral and bacterial maladies can take over our organisms because our loss of inner peace impairs our immune system from functioning as it was designed to do.

We tend to associate those suffering from the psychosomatic diseases as malingering malcontents. Not so. Their suffering is just as real to them as any discomfort from whatever more tangible cause. The well-known psychosomatic symptom of bleeding ulcers bleed real blood—they hurt as much wherever their origin.

The effect of the environment, therefore, is real at the subjective level. If we allow ourselves to fall under its negative influence and do not withdraw from such an environment, we may have to seek outside help. There are experts who specialize in such matters and can offer advice and suggest a regime that will straighten us out. We are "designed" to cope on our own. But we do not live in a vacuum. If we are to love our neighbor, we must allow our neighbor to love us. In many essential ways, every man *is* his brother's keeper. Even though his brother, like himself, is a prince in waiting to take over his own kingdom.

***

The other sector of negative programming results from stripping man of his free will. By imposing one's own will on an undeveloped mind, we retard its growth and impose negative results for which he who imposes his will is fully responsible. It is analogous to teaching one's children to kill, lie, steal etc.. Once the child grows up the damage is done. The "teacher" remains co-responsible.

Responsibility, like all the positive traits, must be taught early.

There is a specific area of negative programming for which we, as a race, continue to pay to this day. The problem arose from the various religions which consistently personified their deities. All anthropomorphic gods invariably limit our potential, impose laws and regulations which restrict the freedom of the hapless ignorant people. The conceptual limitation is unavoidable. After all, anthropomorphism is a direct consequence of anthropocentrism. An analogous transfer.

Belief to belief.

The ancient Hindu, the Egyptians, Greeks, Romans all appear to have suffered from a great need to create gods in their own image. The Christians followed suit in the best traditions of pagan philosophies, not only by creating an anthropomorphic god, whom they depicted (so beautifully) on the ceiling of the Sistine chapel as an Old Man, but misunderstood Jesus' reference to the Father in heaven. The original Hebrew *ab*, meant not only *father* but also *ancestor, source, inventor*. The last three meanings have been diligently omitted from the New Testament, leaving behind the only translation, *pater*, which can be, as mentioned above, personified, in the best pagan tradition. The matter was further muddied by adding the Son and the Spirit and by, in some contorted way, personifying all three. Jesus' reference to his "Father in heaven" takes on a completely different meaning if we substitute the word *Source* for father, and *Ocean of Infinite Possibilities*, for heaven. Just imagine how different would be the development of Christianity if the translation of the original scripture read: *"The Source of my being is an Ocean of Infinite Possibilities deep within my heart."* After all, as I keep repeating throughout this book, Jesus taught that heaven is within us, and the 'father' is within heaven, i.e.: also within us. When I first came to this realization I fully expected to be struck by a thunderous lightening for egomaniacal blasphemy. Gradually my fears diminished, while my sense of responsibility grew—in inverse proportions.

And yet this truth is the essence of the New Testament.

I am I, you are you, we are all one, and that's all there is. The whole, complete, total reality is that which we manage to develop, or become aware of, within our own, individual consciousness. We all, individually, are the Potential and the

Manifestation. Within us—the Cause, without us—the Effect. The latter is limited only by our power of visualization. I am that I am. You are that you are. There is none other, and if there were, it would be of no use to us. We would not, could not, be aware of it. Not unless we made it our own. And then—we would be back to square one.

The negative programming has at its root the inbred ignorance of our potential. This insidious agenda consists of all the negative inputs from our environment consisting of our parents, teachers, politicians, priests, all figures of 'authority', who all conspire (mostly unwittingly) to undermine our faith in *our individual potential*. As our subconscious "never sleeps", the influx of this programming is continuous. Most of us are completely unaware of it. We recite slogans we heard we know-not-where, we refer to authorities we never verified, we subject ourselves to disciplines imposed on us without having checked if such disciplines are really for our good. This is why living consciously is so vital to our wellbeing.

Give me abject ignorance of the masses and I'll give you potential disaster.

Give me negative teaching, and I shall guarantee it.

In the same vein, religious teaching accentuating the reality of suffering, hell and damnation, continues to impose those conditions on the human psyche. The historians declare, in unison, that the last century of the present millennium was the most bloody in the history of mankind. We opened the century with the South African (the Boer) War. The 1st World War declared as the war-to-end-all-wars was followed by the abuses of the Communist and Nazi regimes. In the meantime blood flowed in the Chino-Japanese War, which was followed immediately by the Spanish civil war. The 2nd World War costing humanity some 20 million lives, was followed by the wars in Korea, by war in Vietnam where peasants to this day lose their limbs and lives in the insidious minefields. These were followed by the murderous civil wars throughout Central America as in Nicaragua, Panama, El Salvador ironically named after the 'Savior', by the heinous abuses of totalitarian regimes in Argentina and Chile, by the bloody rebellion of the *Sandero Luminoso* (Shining Path) guerillas in Peru who murdered as many members of the "upper classes" as they did peasants—in whose name they reaped their bloody harvest; by the still continuing mob-rule of the drug-lords in the Northern republics of South America and the Mafia-run Albanian port of Vlorë on the Adriatic coast, by the persistent mass murders of innocent peasants of whom an estimated 2 million have died from execution, starvation, disease or overwork during the rule of the Maoist-inspired *Khmer Rouge* in Cambodia, by the senseless war between Iran and Iraq where children were used on the front lines of the battles, by the subsequent Moslem fundamentalist or just tribally inspired 'cleansing' in Iran, Algiers, Sudan, Ethiopia, Libya, by the continuous genocidal wars still going on allover Africa, by equally vicious politically inspired religious expurgations in many of the newly formed regimes of various republics of ex-USSR, by the invasion of Kuwait by Iraq and the consequent Western military response which hasn't ended to this day, by the homicidal games played by the Protestants and Roman Catholics in Ireland who seem to specialize in the murder of women and children, by the Chinese invasion of Tibet, by the murderous nonsense of Falkland islands, by bloodthirsty ethnic cleansing in the defunct Yugoslavia which reached its ignominious peak in Bosnia, by the Christian/Moslem/Hindu genocidal strife in India, Sri Lanka, Indonesia; by the most recently organized genocidal mass murder and expulsion of Albanians from Kosovo and the brutal response of the western aircraft....

***

Somewhere along the bloody litany I must have lost the chronological order. After all, murder is murder by any other name, in any other time-stream.

And there were so many...

...and these were just a few. The litany never ends. By the time this book is published our honorable leaders will find other excuses to send more sons and daughters to die for their political expediency. For their pride and glory. For the medals.

Posthumous medals.

And these were just a few... I did not research these inhumanities of man to man. I just seem to remember them. They all seem etched in my subconscious.

YOU CANNOT END WAR WITH WAR

No matter what the generals', the admirals', the field marshals', the presidents' distorted visions, *one can only end war with peace*. So why must we wait until so many are murdered?

Negative programming.

We tend to blame the leaders for the crimes, and indeed, the leaders will pay the lions share. But there is no single man or woman responsible for all these iniquities. All the participants, for whatever cause, with whatever excuse, in whomsoever's name—all individual men and women shall pay for every single drop of blood shed in any and all of these perverted conflicts. Such is the law of karma.

I put it to the reader that all the wars which people faced throughout history had been, and continue to be direct results of destructive brainwashing. Had the vast masses of people no matter how simple, how uneducated, had they been told the truth, the politicians would have fought all the wars in their own backyards. The earth, of course, would have become even more overpopulated than it is today. On the other hand, the countless trillions of dollars which the various pentagons and other retarded, degenerate war-merchants had spent on armaments would have been spent on terraforming the nearest planets, asteroids, on building artificial space oases, on developing the vast resources in the depth of the oceans and on the implementation of many other creative visions of the human mind.

Our time is coming...

In the meantime, our millennial history is even more astounding if we realize that most, if not all, of the participants of these barbarous slaughters conducted at all levels of society have been and continue to be members of established world religions.

Yet not only wars were the direct result of negative programming. All visions which tend to enhance the wellbeing of the few at the expense of the many are also a direct product of negative conditioning. We can continue to be inspired by our politicians, our religions, our glib-tongue plutocratic salesmen—or we can take charge of our lives ourselves. No one *who understands* the concept of karma and reincarnation could partake in any war-games organized by any politicians. No one would have the guts. No one would be so stupid!

We do not have to listen to them. To anyone.

We can take charge of our lives. Gandhi showed us the way to do it. So did Buddha and Jesus, and Lao Tsu before them. We all have full knowledge of what to do.

So far we responded to external conditioning at the subconscious level. We all have the potential of living in full consciousness. We are all conscious beings.

Isn't it time to stand up on our own two feet?

***

FOOTNOTES

(1). As we already know from the chapter on *Redefining Self*, at the sub-nuclear level, we are annihilated and replicated 10^{23} times a second in the normal course of our lives.

(2). Exodus 20:3 et seq..

(3). Matthew 6:34-35.

(4). Luke 8:7

(5). As of the first draft of this book, he is in his twentieth year on the throne of the Vatican.

(6). In the United States of America, up to January 1999, over 500 people were murdered (executed) by the various States since the death penalty was reinstated in 1976. Those States which abolished the death penalty showed a marked decrease in the number of homicides.

(7). Jung, Carl, G. MAN AND HIS SYMBOLS, (Dell Publishing Co., Inc, New York, 1964) pg.58.

(8). Kapuscinski, S., BEYOND RELIGION, vol. 1. *The Carrot and the Stick.* (Inhousepress 1997, 2001, Smashwords Edition 2010)

(9). Compiled from THE KORAN INTERPRETED, a translation by A.J. Arberry; (Simon & Shuster, Touchstone, New York 1955)

(10). ibid. Volume 1. *The Cave*, pages 319-320.

(11). The same can be said of the military invasion by the American President George W. Bush of Iraq in 2003, in which tens of thousands of innocent Iraqi had been murdered. This homicidal binge had been quaintly justified as "collateral damage".

(12). Exact wording: "But I say unto you, That ye resist not evil..." Matthew 6:39 et seq..

Chapter 23
Reverse Effects of Visualization

"By virtue of his reflective faculties, man is raised out of the animal world, and by his mind he demonstrated that nature has put a high premium precisely upon the development of consciousness. Through consciousness he takes possession of nature by recognizing the existence of the world and thus, as it were, confirming the Creator.

The world becomes the phenomenal world, for without conscious reflection it would not be. If the Creator were conscious of himself, he would not need conscious creatures."

Carl Gustav Jung

Before attempting to create our own universes, we must be fully aware that the creative power of the mind applies equally to positive and negative effects. A man capable of using his mind can bring upon himself as much good as harm. Hitler, Stalin, Genghis Khan—all empire builders—are prime examples of the latter. No one can deny man's ability when he almost succeeds in destroying the world. Hitler was very close to that. Not on his own, but by the militaristic trend which he initiated. As a byproduct of his vision, the combined destructive power of the world was well in excess of total annihilation. Yet the consequences of parochial or self-serving thinking invariably lead to the same result: Total failure. Conversely, people with limited control of their mind are completely unaware that their *potential* is as great as that which we assign to the few who direct all their efforts towards the realization of their vision. While their creative process unfolds without their hand on the rudder, it does go on nevertheless.

For example, people who constantly worry, who have little faith in the beneficence of the universal creative forces, do not realize that they continually invite disaster. Every thought which we enliven (the Bible calls it 'quicken') with emotion becomes a source of energy which, sooner or later, will affect the material universe. A few thousand people expecting a war to happen will probably cause it to come about. The same can be said of earthquakes, floods, and a whole range of natural disasters. I am not saying that no earthquake would ever happen if people did not actively visualize it happening. The greatest forces which sway our futures are all at the *subliminal level*. We don't *will* the earthquake to happen. We tie our future to earthquakes by worrying about them. This is what I call negative programming. Instead of seeing our world unfolding in perfect harmony, we wonder what would happen if...? People who allow negative thoughts to enter their mind will bring the disasters, personal or communal, upon themselves. In the same vein a mother who continuously worries about her children's welfare, will, sooner or later, bring 'misfortune' upon them.

Thoughts are *things*.

Fear is the fuel of reverse effects of programming.

All thoughts have their potential existence in our material universe. Once the creative cycle has been initiated, the end produce is irreversible. All "thought-things" (objects, ideas, events) find their temporal reality only to become re-absorbed into the matrix of universal forces in due course. Most people, who have outgrown allegiance to a specific religion but are still familiar with the inherited vocabulary, might regard this universal matrix as 'spirit'. While the Christians, particularly members of the Roman Catholic Church, believe the spirit to be part of the Holy Trinity, I do not regard this 'spirit' as something let alone 'someone' very good, or positive, but rather as a *completely neutral force*. The most powerful force in the universe, but one subject to use and abuse alike. As mentioned above, this very same creative force is the basic constituent of all manifestation. We and we alone, determine its impulse on our reality. While the spirit is neutral, it seems to harbor inherent predispositions rather like the latent patterns recently observed by the proponents of the so-called Chaos Theory.[1]

THE SOURCE IS ONE—CREATORS ARE MANY.

You and I, *individually and alone,* wield the power to convert the creative energy inherent in spirit into positive or negative, good or evil, constructive or destructive forces or results. However, spirit can be molded only within the potential and/or limitations of the instrument or entity through which it finds its expression. A tree has no choice but to grow—given water and minerals. The birds must fly, the fish—swim. By the same token the human mind must act as an instrument of creation. It can do so consciously or be as a cork bouncing on the infinite ocean of possibilities. *The benevolence of the spirit lies in its neutrality*, not in subjecting us to its will. *We* are the sole factors which decide if we shall use it for universal or parochial purposes.

Our vision alone will direct it.

My realization of this quality of intrinsic neutrality of Spirit first came to me from quite unexpected quarters. I was reading a true story by Lyall Watson about "a young Englishman who arrived in Africa at the age of sixteen and ventured into the bush alone, on foot, equipped with nothing more than a pocketknife and a plastic bagful of salt..."[2] The young man whose name was Adrian Boshier, explained that only a few days after his arrival in Africa, unable to contain his impatience, he had hitchhiked out of Johannesburg, got out of the car in the middle of nowhere and walked away, "directly into the past."

Evidently, the young man's vision included an urge to escape from civilization. To say that Watson paints a fascinating story is to say the least. Eventually the young man comes across a people who call themselves Ba Sotho and whose word for spirit is *moya*. Boshier learned that the Ba Sotho think of *moya* as the "essence of nature itself". It reminded me of a concept that God is what the opposites have in common. The Ba Sotho regard *moya* as powerful but as "having no will of its own." They place it outside all constrains, outside time (perhaps also space), and suggest that "it may simply exist." As such it can be "used" equally as well for constructive as for destructive purposes. The consequences of the manner in which it is used, however, are borne exclusively on the shoulders of one employing such a force. (The negative effects of programming were discussed in previous chapter). If the Ba Sotho are right, then *moya* or sprit can be regarded as the substratum not only of matter but of all forms of energy, rather like the subatomic particles which appear to have their being as a continuous wave and only manifest a fleeting quantum existence when attention is placed upon them.

When your or my attention is placed upon them.

At the risk of repeating myself, I cannot stress too strongly that most of us carry on as if our lives had been set on automatic. Whatever knowledge we have accumulated in our genetic code and/or in our subconscious memory storage is controlling our lives. Since the subconscious reacts to multifarious sources of uncoordinated programming, the sheer scope of input not only restricts our progress but also is the motive behind our repeated mistakes. The subconscious is designed implicitly to protect the safe, the proven, the *status quo*. To do so, it relies on continuous feedback. While spirit is static, it finds its expression in the ever-changing realm of the material universe. It could be said that change is an intrinsic consequence of omnipresent life force. The subconscious is an instrument facilitating this attribute. However, since the subconscious is a manifestation of the material realm, it suffers, like all material manifestations, from specific limitations.

Here are some of them.

1. *The subconscious exhibits no reasoning power.*

It functions in a deductive rather than inductive mode. It does not originate new concepts. It relies exclusively on data supplied. (Exactly like a computer).

Let us take, as an example, a man who smokes 25 cigarettes a day. Since our immune system is designed to withstand onslaught from a great many quarters for a considerable time, the man (or his subconscious) registers no adverse effects of smoking for a number of years. This very absence of adverse effects establishes a pattern in the subconscious which *assumes* that smoking is good for the smoker. As such, should the man attempt through a *conscious* act to stop poisoning himself, his organism controlled by the subconscious supplies withdrawal symptoms. The idea being that if something which we practiced for a while did not hurt us, it might well be necessary for our survival.

This is an example of the *Reverse Effect* of programming wherein the reactive nature of the subconscious is devoid of any reasoning power. One of the methods we can employ to overcome the withdrawal symptoms, is by a process of re-programming our subconscious. This can be accomplished by self-hypnosis.

2. *The subconscious registers data literally.*

Again, an illustration. A man had undergone a knee operation. While the man is still under an anesthetic, the attending physicians discuss his condition. One of them thinks that the patient might suffer from a slight limp. He remarks that if he is right, the man will have to *learn to live with a limp.* Later, however, the operation is deemed a total success.

Four years later the man is still limping.

On a number of follow-up examinations including X-rays, no pathological condition can be found. The orthopedic surgeons are at a loss why the man is still limping. Here, once again, we witness the limitations of the subconscious mind. The condition (the limp) dates back to the comment made by the surgeon while the patient was still under an anesthetic. The patient's subconscious mind, which obviously had been unaffected by the anesthetic, recorded that he must *learn to live with this condition*. The subconscious interpreted the programming literally; in other words that *should the man lose the limp he will die*. To preserve his life he must learn to live with it. This example is gleamed from actual case files.

In a broader sense, since the vast majority of people still rely on the automatic response to their subconscious programming, they are much more likely to register most inputs in a literal sense. This applies as much to the lack of a sense of humor (i.e. such people take themselves seriously), as to the literal interpretation of the various scriptures. The literal or the fundamentalist interpretation of scriptures is more in "synch" with the 'natural' response to which such people are accustomed. It is of some considerable concern that fundamentalist interpretations produce the exact opposites, or *Reverse Effects* of the original intent. That is why the various religions claim that the scriptures are shrouded in mysteries, and that they cannot be understood until revealed by some self appointed intermediary. Nothing is further from the truth. The scriptures are open to all that take the trouble to understand them not for the purpose of exploitation only for self-improvement. Furthermore, all scriptures teach the same Truth.

What varies is their interpretation.

3. *The subconscious never stops recording.*

As already mentioned, the subconscious records all input from all quarters, at all times, in all circumstances. This includes the time we spend sleeping, under deep anesthetic, knocked out in a boxing ring, drunk-out-of-our-wits, or even in a coma. The effect of this indiscriminate recording system is that what may seem innocuous to us as we discuss matters within earshot of our children may have a positive/negative effect on them many years later. The same is true, of course, of adults. Particular care should be taken when taking within earshot of the "hard-of-hearing" elderly. What their conscious mind does not register through their depleted hearing ability, their subconscious will record, often with very reverse effects of those intended. We should learn to regard our 'inner' bodies with their "inner" senses, as real.

In time we shall discover that... they are.

4. *The subconscious never forgets.*

All sensory, emotional and mental input is filed in memory for possible future use. The retrieval of data can reach back into our infancy, sometimes earlier. Dr. Netherton reports on considerable successes with retrieving data from the "minds" of his patients, often going back hundreds of years. And this is accomplished without hypnosis, and without the patients' belief in reincarnation. By regressing his patients to prenatal memories, Dr. Netherton was able to reveal the causes of many problems and traumas in their present lives.[3]

5. *The subconscious does not pass judgment.*

As already mentioned in Item 1. above, the subconscious has no reasoning power and as such it cannot pass judgment at the time of recording. It evaluates the data stored or recorded only when required in the particular circumstances to which it may apply. The context in which the data had been recorded is not taken into the subliminal consideration. As a result, the latter effects often carry *reverse effects* to those attendant to the original circumstances. This limitation of the subconscious is particularly pronounced when the so-called *instinctive* reaction precedes considered, i.e. conscious analysis. We often act instinctively, in a manner in which we would never act after a minute of thought. Instincts are not based on reasoning power only on the accumulated knowledge, as pertaining to *physical* survival. They serve to preserve the integrity of our physical body, not our 'humanity' or 'higher' aspirations. It is a calculated (not reasoned) response to the data stored over millions of years of evolution. Such instinctive reaction should not be confused with *intuition* which is the faculty enabling us to function in circumstances without precedent. In metaphysical terms, it is the response to the input from our spiritual body, often called our Higher Self.

6. *The subconscious is a machine.*

We must learn to use it, rather than let is use us. As a wise man once said, a mind is a magnificent servant but a terrible master. To learn to use it we must fully understand the way it functions. We must learn to take advantage of the items listed. In the chapter on the *Creative Process*, we discussed the ability of our subconscious to function *inter alia* while we are asleep. To take full advantage of this inherent ability, we can make a habit of committing the 'research' functions of our thinking processes to our sleeping periods. If we cannot remember an item we require, we can learn to program ourselves to procure answers to our problems in the evening, and waking with the desired solutions. The subconscious will research all the data available, the greatest library available to man, and report on its findings in due course.

We must always remember that acting on insufficient data (which is subject to easy or quick retrieval) may well result in *reverse effects*. The adage that little knowledge is a dangerous thing applies here. Luckily, the voluminous evolutionary files are available to us. They function best when left to themselves. By that I mean that if we desire input from our subconscious then we should request it and leave it alone. The subconscious will contact our conscious awareness when the data becomes available. It may be seconds, minutes, hours or even days. If the data is there, it cannot be refused. Remember, the subconscious does not reason, it only calculates. If we continue checking for the answer consciously, we shall interfere with due process. We shall impede the smooth functioning of our built-in computer.

7. *The harder you try—the poorer the effect.*

This fact is often referred to as the Law of the Reverse Effect. It applies equally to trying "too hard" to relax, "too hard" to enter a self imposed hypnotic state, "too hard" to remember anything at all. Mind does not respond well to pressure. If it did, it would have to react instantly to the billions of chaotic inputs per second. When overwhelmed (overloaded), it either refuses to act at all (for the duration) or looses the capacity to function (goes insane) temporarily or permanently. We are all familiar with the expression 'burnout' as pertaining to excessive stress. Since the mind controls not only the calculating (intellectual), but also the physical functions of our body, burnout can actually kill us, or turn us into vegetables.

To counteract this danger of the *reverse effect* of burnout, the ancients have introduced Sabbath, or the concept of Sunday. As we know already from the chapter on *Creative Process*, this 'day' has nothing to do with pious behavior only in allowing our higher functions to do their job. While the mind is still a part of the sheaths enclosing our spiritual body, it is nevertheless the highest material faculty we possess. As such we must treat it with respect and let it function in its proper environment. While we can never eliminate the external inputs completely, the best environment we can provide is to reduce those inputs to the minimum. Hence Sabbath, Sunday, or a good night's sleep. One of the major trouble spot in our routine is, of course, stress. There are ways to reduce its insidious assault on our mind and body.

To all who aspire to take part in the conscious participation of the construction of their universes, I recommend 10-20 minutes "switching off" period in the morning and an equal period, perhaps a few minutes longer, in the evening. The religious teachers, misinterpreting their purpose, assign comparative periods to 'prayers'. We know that prayers in the religious sense of the word (more often than not—supplicatory prayers) do not make any sense: "Father knoweth what things ye have need of, before ye ask him".[4] But the idea of conscious "time out" for the data retrieval and an equal time for programming is imperative. By the way, the retrieval time consists not of "asking for answers", but simply of listening. It is often called contemplation. Strangely enough, the most effective "time-outs" I have experienced were what Emmet Fox called "the Practice of the Presence of God". We all must decide for ourselves who or what constitutes our image of God. If your God were a punitive, zealously judgmental God of the Old Testament or of the Koran, I would discourage your choice for the purposes mentioned.

We would be wise to remember that most great 'discoveries' have taken place during sleep. A number of renowned scientists have reported on waking up with "an idea". The other end of the scale is supplied by Edgar Cayce, who invariably entered a trance in order to provide answers to questions which could not have been answered in the confines of conscious awareness. Others, like Jesus or Sai Baba can draw on the "universal library or data" at will and in full consciousness. The criterion appears to be the ability to exercise this power for others and never for the benefit of self. Sooner or later we shall have to decide whether our reality will have parochial or universal qualities. It is self evident that while there is *no such thing as supernatural* state, there are an infinite number of *natural* states that we have not as yet learned to enter.

There is another, rarely considered side effect of programming.

Most books on the subject of visualization tell us that if

we (repeatedly) visualize anything tangible, such a process will, sooner of later, bring those things or conditions into the sphere of our activity. This is absolutely true.

But there is the reverse side of this premise.

It is the by-product of the already discussed Law of Reverse Effect. If we visualize the *absence* of certain things or conditions, we shall also *attract* them into our life. It seems that what manifests them into our orbit of activity is our attachment to the object of the visualization. Whether we are pulling or pushing, we are connected to those objects by our thoughts. Negative or positive, the link is there. The only way to avoid this effect is *not to think about the undesirable conditions or things at all*. Even better, we should stop worrying about end results and concentrate on the process— on life itself.

Think positive thoughts, and a positive universe you will build.

And then there is a peripheral concomitant of this Law. There is an occult saying which states that "like attracts like". If we hold universal views, we shall attract people with universal visions. If we are a generous person, generous people will enjoy our company. If we are givers, we shall receive a great deal. There is a little trick to this process. Visualize yourself as a magnanimous giver: giving a great deal to a great number of people... and the universe will supply you with whatever you need to be a giver. Only try not to cheat the universe. It is said to be very detrimental to your health.

The Lord giveth and the Lord taketh away.[5] Remember that you are the lord.

You can't cheat yourself.

If you are a taker, you are in mortal danger of loosing everything, including your life. The Law of Reverse Effect takes over. That is not to say that, to a degree, you cannot use the very same universal powers for your own selfish ends. You can. The only problem is that, if you do, the benefits *will not last*. The boon we can all draw on is not ours to keep. It belongs to the Universe which, in its Infinite generosity shares its inexhaustible riches with us. But they are never ours to keep. Even if we don't fully understand this truth, we shouldn't worry. Well, we shouldn't worry too much. We can think of all the hardships, all the "misfortunes", and all the unpleasantness we encountered in our lives and be one hundred percent sure that we shall go through all of them again. And again. If we fail to learn the universal laws in this lifetime, in our next incarnation we can start learning them again.

From the very beginning.

Once again... ...from scratch.

Are you sure you want to do that?

***

FOOTNOTES

(1). Refer to the already mentioned FRACTALS, THE PATTERNS OF CHAOS by John Briggs, also COMPUTERS, PATTERN, CHAOS AND BEAUTY by Clifford A. Pickover [St.Martin's Press, New York 1990]; also ORDER OUT OF CHAOS by Ilya Prigogine and Isabelle Stengers [Bantam, New York 1984] et alii.

(2). LIGHTNING BIRD by Lyall Watson, Hodder and Stoughton Ltd., Great Britain. See also BEYOND... essay on 'Spirit'.

(3). Netherton, Morris, Ph.D. and Shiffrin, Nancy PAST LIVES THERAPY (Ace Books, New York 1979)

(4). Matthew 6:8

(5). Compare Job 1:21.

Chapter 24
The Universal and the Particular

Matter is a form of energy.
Living matter is energy organized in such a way
that it retains its unstable state.

Lyall Watson
SUPERNATURE
[Coronet Books, London 1974; pg.183]

Less than 3% of the population in North America has anything to do with farming. The efficiency of this tiny portion of the citizens of the USA and Canada is such that North America, with but a single annual crop, is a net exporter of food. The African plains South of the Sahara desert are very different—vastly superior. "The growing conditions here are unsurpassed anywhere... Here there is great volcanic soil and the potential for two or three crops per year."[1] Hunger and malnutrition remain rampant in the area. In fact, hunger in Africa is worse now than it was 30 years ago.

Why?

China has expressed firm determination to feed her own people—to become self-sufficient. Mr. Reed, the writer of the report on *Feeding the Planet* in the National Geographic, asked a Chinese nutrition expert, who is also a professor at Sun Yatsen Medical University in Guangzhou, whether the Earth can continue to feed her growing population. "Oh, Mr. Reed," the professor replied, "I've devoted my life to the study of food supplies, diet, and nutrition. But your question goes way beyond those fields. Can the Earth feed all its people? That, I'm afraid, is strictly a political question."[2]

Unwittingly, Professor Ho Zhiquian provided the answer to the African dilemma.

We find another version of this philosophy in the saying: "Give a man fish, you feed him once. Teach him how to fish, and he'll never go hungry." The first gift is an act of charity. The second an act of wisdom, which is a perfect amalgam of love and knowledge. It seems ironic that the greatest gift, the gift contingent on wisdom can be disseminated through political means. Alas, God works in mysterious ways! In this book, however, we are not preoccupied with comestibles. We are discussing the essence of man. We deal with the real, indestructible entity—the individualized Soul.

The individualized Soul 'encased' in the physical entity is also a 'body'. We can think of this body as a union of photons coexisting in perfect harmony. Our physical senses are only a poor reflection of our corresponding spiritual attributes. We are endowed with spiritual vision, spiritual hearing, touch... all the senses and many others to which our physical body cannot aspire. Our spiritual body also needs food. It needs food continuously, more so than our physical sheath.

Religions of the world, at their best, offer charity. A noble, edifying act. A good sermon can quench the spiritual hunger for a while. Perhaps an hour, a day at best. But the next day people will continue to hunger. What the world religions have failed to do is to teach us how to be free. They failed to teach us how to feed our spiritual bodies ourselves. They gave us a fish, not a rod and tackle.

They did not teach us how to stand on our own spiritual feet.

Until people at large learn who and what they are, they will continue to starve. No matter how good the 'volcanic' soil, no matter how balmy the climate offered by the various religions, people will continue to starve. Professor Zhiquian tells us that we can blame the politicians for the lack of food.

Who are we to blame for our spiritual hunger? This latter malnutrition cannot be identified with any particular part of the world.

It is a global phenomenon.

A global phenomenon calls for global vision. A global vision breeds global visionaries. Hence the Universal and the Particular. Though the vision is universal, it is expressed always and solely by an individual.

By a Particular Individualization of the Universal.

So far in this book we have reviewed, in some detail, the characteristics of the universal and parochial visions permeating our history. We went on to discuss who and what we are, or how you and I fit into the scheme of things. Now a word about the relationship between the vision and the visionary. It is my contention that what matters is the vision more so than the visionary. Another way of putting it is to consider the message greater than the messenger. A rather apt example of this thesis is, at least theoretically, expressed is the religion of Islam, where the Koran is worshiped more so than Muhammad himself, who, by his own admission, was the messenger of God, whereas the Koran is, according to the believers, the Word of God. Islam recognizes that the Word is greater than the messenger who brought It.

There is a parallel mostly ignored in the Christian religions. The gospel of John states that the Word was made flesh.[3] The Word, or the Logos, is the ancient symbol for not only the 'word' of God, but also the essence of the word. It is the very substance that parallels the Eternal Source, from which all-that-is ensues. While we have learned in the chapter on *Redefining Self* from various physicists that all things material are transient, ephemeral, the 'flesh' referred to in the Bible is indestructible, eternal. This Eternal Source is always indicative of the Universal, or the *Impersonal*. Yet the only way that the Impersonal can become known within the confines of the human mind, is through the personal or the particular.

Emmet Fox writes: "Your life and mine, our body, our affairs, are the embodiment of our concept of God." And then he adds, illustrating how we personify our understanding of God: "What we understand we demonstrate, and when we understand sin, sickness, lack, and disharmony more than we understand God, we demonstrate those things—we embody them."[4] We demonstrate the Universal within ourselves, the personal. This process of demonstration is ongoing, continuous, subject to change each and every second as our understanding of God advances. One day we shall be "perfect even as your Father which is in heaven is perfect."[5]

Hence the apparent paradox.

Most Christians became so confused by this juxtaposition of the *Universal and the Particular* that they decided to make the Word which emanates *from* God, into God Itself. Jesus, who never referred to himself as God, and often repeated that of himself he can do nothing, became summarily deified. And if that weren't enough, in John 14:29 he stated as clearly as anyone could: "...my Father is greater than I". If Jesus spoke the truth, then his followers who deified him believe in a 'lesser' god, as against a "greater" God who is, according to Jesus, in heaven. As already discussed in the chapter on *Duality*, this is the single greatest falsehood which the early Christians perpetrated on their followers. The later church (the Roman hegemony) evolving into an ostensibly secular power (see chapter on *Politics and Society*) decided to keep this falsehood, in fact to dogmatize it, in order to be in a position to act as intermediary between God and the believer.[6] This single lie gave more power to the church than any other machination of any political body in the history of the world. The leaders of the Church chose to ignore the teaching of the very man in whose name they created a strictly secular organization, leaving the spiritual care-taking to men and women outside their own ranks. The church became the official embodiment of the message and the messenger. The universal *and* the particular.

This, of course, is an oxymoron.

All Universal visions can be defined as Impersonal. There are two little books (little literally: 5 1/2"x 4") the first called the *Impersonal Life*, followed by another called *The Way Out*,[7] which explain this concept better than I ever could. Although both booklets limit themselves to an exclusively Christian perspective, I strongly recommend them to all students of Impersonal life.

The parochial vision, on the other hand, is invariably of a *personal* nature.

We all must allow ourselves a degree of personal and therefore parochial attitude. As long as we inhabit a physical body, we are, in a manner of speaking, an integral part of other bodies. This relationship is comparable to an artist, who during the act of painting becomes one with the object of his or her creation. In order to survive, physically, we must tolerate a modicum of ego in our vision, in our behavior, in our mindset. If we were to give *all* to the poor, we would become poor ourselves and a burden to others. Furthermore, we might well interfere with the karmic consequences of the receiver of our generosity and perhaps even discourage them from creating their own universe, which, after all, is the purpose of our and their lives. We must never forget that we provide the means, or the mode, through which God has His (Its) being. The objective universe is the sum-total of the commonalty of the result. In order not to be relegated to a *result* only, we must make allowances for the transient aspect of our nature (the personal or the particular aspect) at the conscious level. If we do it subconsciously, we do not differ in any way from an intelligent ape.

WE MUST AIM TO BECOME PART OF THE CAUSE.

It seems strange that perhaps the most misunderstood aspect of human evolution is the relationship between the

Universal and the Particular. The average adherents of practically all major religions tend to draw a strong divisive line between the perception of divinity and the mundane. According to the great avatars of the past and present, this is a fundamental error. Neither we nor any gods we can think of can define where the Potential ends and the Manifested starts. As already mentioned, this is mostly because the Manifested thus the Particular or the Personal is in a state of continuous churning, of being constantly created, sustained for the briefest of moments, and destroyed to make room for the new. The universe and all 'things' in it, including our physical bodies, is an enormous recycling machine. Nothing is ever destroyed; nothing is ever created out of nothing. The fundamental substance of the manifested universe is Spirit, of which all things are made. In terms of modern day physics I would suggest that part of this recycling process is carried out on a cosmic scale by the Novae or the Supernovae, whereas the Black Holes provide the universal dustbins, in which matter is purified and eventually recycled as spiritual magma, the substratum of all that is. Religions and science alike recognize the latter transition as the Big Bang(s).

Thus, *the essential world is a spiritual entity*.

As already suggested, the world came into being through the action of consciousness upon spirit. The subatomic particles are not only too small to be observed, but they only become extant at the instant when we place our attention on them. Our physicists tell us that the quarks, the leptons, the strings and so forth, which permeate the physical universe as waves of probabilities within a field of infinite possibilities, blink in and out of existence the instant our attention is placed on them. If it hadn't been for our scrutiny, they would never even have become such ephemeral quanta of matter. Under the circumstances, a religion can no longer be said to be true if the teachers (priests, rabbis, monks et al.) are not fully versed in the latest advances of science. This in no way implies that science is taking over religion. Nor that science is always right. Scientific errors are as profound as the theological ones. Both are committed by men who have not yet reached... perfection. It's just that we can only examine the efficacy of our 'religion' by examining the results. "By their fruit ye shall know them."[8] If the 'fruit' are wars, strife, hatred (crusades, inquisitions) and suchlike, we should beware of such teachers, no matter what their clothing. "A good tree *cannot* bring forth evil fruit".[9] Furthermore, religions dealing with material reality are dead religions. They deal with the dead, with that which has already passed; with that which has already blinked out of the detectable, i.e. objective reality. What maintains the visible universe—its very existence, is our attention. Without us, without our subconscious participation, the universe would cease to be.

We not only create—we also sustain the world we live in.

Armed with this knowledge, we must completely revise, indeed, reverse our way of looking at reality. What *is*, is only the Infinite Potential. At the physical level, we must not be concerned by what "seemingly is" only by what could be. To repeat, every single one of us partakes in a continuous act of creation which sustains that which without us would have never even come into being. We are the Particular through which the Universal manifests Its being. That which is Selfless finds self-awareness through the Self. Throughout the individualizations of Soul. It is our consciousness that gives God His being, because it is through us that God performs the eternal creative act. To repeat, we are the means, the mode, the instruments which the divine evolved in order to sustain, expand, evolve and enhance the creative process. Not through any one particular person, but all of us, together. In his introduction to the Hindu scripture, the *Srimad-Bhagavatam*, Swami Prabhupada writes: "...the Lord is the sum total of all living beings."[10] It is the perception of this unity which leads to the Universal Vision. It also fosters the awareness of the

Impersonal within the Personal, or the Universal within the Particular. You and I, and everyone aware of this truth, is an indivisible and integral part of the Whole.

We are indispensable to God.

Most religions claim the exclusivity of revelation. But it is not a priest, bishop or pope, nor any rabbi nor monk nor any individual seeking anonymity under a cowl, who distributes epiphany. The source is only One—Its manifestation exorbitant in Its generosity and diversity. We can discover God in a single blade of grass, in a wild flower, in the breath of wind, in the twinkle of a distant star, close by, within—our timid heart. Not in churches, synagogues or temples. God is there too, but there He is shrouded in symbols, surrounded by liturgical protocol, hidden from our eyes by the jealous priesthood. The evangelist Matthew so speaks about the sacerdotal casts: "...ye shut up the kingdom of heaven against men: for ye neither go in yourselves neither suffer ye them that are entering to go in."[11] To my knowledge, no representative of any religion ever quoted this sentence from the New Testament, nor any of the damming sentences that follow.

Do not misunderstand me.

It is not the religions I object to. I object to what the religions have become. The original teaching of Hinduism, Buddhism, Judaism, Christianity and a number of other religions provide sufficient information on how to enter the kingdom of God. A straight and narrow path, directly to the One Godhead. There is no substantial difference between a good Jew, a good Christian, a good Moslem, a good Hindu, a good Buddhist. If there is, then they are not... good. Even the Universal and the particular merge, until only the quantitative difference is apparent. Qualitatively the Personal and the Impersonal become one.

The *original* teaching of most religions is available to all that search.

It is not my intention to recommend any specific way of

self-discovery. Some religions claim monopoly on the truth, though truth must be continually rediscovered. Others offer unconditional if vicarious salvation. Still others claim that we can achieve unity with our Higher Self through our own efforts. Others generously recognize that other religions are just as good but theirs is the 'fastest'. The last group must have forgotten that we are immortal.

There is no hurry.

The most selfish reason why the particular would wish to become a perfect channel for the Universal is to share in Its Bliss. This, of course, is no mean reason. But the motivation is always a question of a personal choice. We don't sacrifice anything on the journey of self-discovery. We only gain. But no matter which religion we might choose, we must go back to its roots, to the original avatar that gave up his personal life to become the Word made Flesh.

***

There is one other fundamental difference between the Universal and the Particular. We find it in the act of possession. The Particular, you or I, have and hopefully enjoy certain traits. We possess certain attributes which define our personality. Also hopefully, we display certain aspects of some divine attributes. We love certain people, we acquire certain knowledge, and we display a certain mode of behavior, which make us different from one another. These traits add up to us becoming the 'particular'.

Not so with the Universal.

It cannot be said that God loves us. Nor that God is intelligent, nor just or even compassionate. These adjectives have been used by various religions which had found it necessary to convince their followers that their deity holds power over their lives. The question of free will has been diligently ignored.

While the Buddhist and the Hindu religions made room for the Impersonal or the Universal a long time ago, the western religions persist in their misinterpretation of the teaching of Christ till this very day. Cries of "Jeeezus loves you" echo off many walls in many sectarian churches. Even bumper stickers affirm Jesus' relationship to the driver and all who follow his car.

Nothing could be further from the truth. Jesus never affirmed his love for the fat, egocentric, intolerant, know-all sectarians who impose their will or distorted proselytizing on the even more ignorant masses for a weekly contribution to their bloated coffers. If anything I would suggest, that Jesus wouldn't stand them. He wouldn't give them the time of day. People who claim that they are born-again seldom are. Those who are rejoice in their newly found awareness which is by far the most intensely personal experience which simply cannot be shared with anyone. Anyway, what is a 'new' birth to one, is but a step in the right direction for another. Paul of Tarsus was born 'again' daily.

As I keep repeating, Truth is one, but it must be continually rediscovered.
Daily.
Jesus never affirmed his love for *us*, but he did love some of his followers enough to give his life in order to show them the way. His small group of followers. He called them his disciples. Most of us are not. Most of us have little interest in his teaching. What Jesus did affirm was that he *was* Love. He also affirmed that he was Life, and the Way. And this is the fundamental difference between the Universal and the Particular. Each time you are "born-again", for the briefest moment you no longer love anyone. In the instant of your spiritual realization, you become Love. You become a conscious expression of this Universal attribute. You become a momentary prism of purest crystal which shines with its own light and refracts the divine light into countless hues, into countless traits, all different aspects of the Universal.

When that happens you, the Particular, are reborn in spirit.

***

It has been said that the Messiah is the unique occasion when the Universal finds Its expression through the Particular. According to various myths, such had been Krishna, Buddha, Jesus Christ and quite a few others. There are those that believe that the Messiah will return. How would we recognize him... or her?
    By his or her deeds?
    By the miracles?
    Would we believe the evidence of our own eyes?

I doubt it.

***

There is a man living today... (N.B.: was alive at the time of first printing). He was born some seventy-five years ago. He is of slight stature, has weighed a little over one hundred pounds for the last sixty years. Except for his bushy hair, he's a man you would miss in any crowd. He eats little, sleeps less, if at all. He doesn't seem to need any of the mundane creature comforts. A gentle smile seldom if ever leaves his face. He lives a quiet life. Shuns publicity. Seldom leaves his humble, almost inaccessible village. Perhaps he doesn't have to. Countless thousands come to see him, from thousands of miles away. He feeds the hungry. On many occasions he fed hundreds by multiplying whatever food was available. He heals the sick. He fills the sad with joy. He treats absolutely everybody with the same, uncompromising kindness. He can tell your past, is aware of your future. He is a perfect embodiment of Impersonal Love. He is the eternal giver, refusing any compensation for any of his acts of kindness.
    He is said to have raised the dead. For over fifty years, he has cured countless men and women said to be incurable. He cured their bodies. For other seekers, he raised their state of

consciousness—he cured their souls. He brought them closer to the Universal Vision. Isn't that what it's all about?

He addresses his followers as the "Embodiments of Love." I mentioned him in my *Introduction* to this book. His name is Sai Baba.

He is alive today.

Who is he...?

None of my friends have ever heard about him. They say that when you are ready the Master finds you.

I wonder.

I have never met anyone who believed anything, anything at all, of what I've written in the preceding few paragraphs about Sai Baba, to be true. They've never checked, they just don't believe. On principle. Perhaps they are right.

We are a race of skeptics. Not because we don't or can't or won't believe, only because our hunger is, as yet, not ripe. And because we will not make the slightest effort to search, let alone find the truth for ourselves. Most of my friends own computers. Most of them have access to the Internet. There are thousands of sites dedicated to Sai Baba.

Perhaps my friends simply do not have enough time.

And yet...?

***

FOOTNOTES

(1). Reid, T.R., *Feeding the Planet*, NATIONAL GEOGRAPHIC Oct. 1998
(2). ibid, page 74.
(3). Equally Quixotic is the Roman Catholic Church's dogma of the Holy Eucharist. When Jesus said at in John 6:54 "Whoso eateth my flesh... has eternal life", he was obviously referring the *Word made flesh*, the Logos, i.e. the Essence of the Message. At a misguided moment of history, the Church substituted a symbol for reality.
(4). Fox, Emmet DIAGRAMS FOR LIVING *The Anatomy of Healing* [Harper & Row, Publ. 1968] pg.169.
(5). Matthew 5:48

(6). When I impute secular nature of the Roman Church, I refer to the pope and the cardinal oligarchy. The individual Christians often reached great spiritual heights - not because of the Vatican structure but in spite of it. Probably the best example of this is St. Francis of Assisi whose joyful poverty stood in stark contrast to the profane splendor of Rome.

(7). Benner, Joseph S. IMPERSONAL LIFE, THE WAY OUT (DeVross & Co. Publishers 1987)

(8). Matthew 7:16

(9). ibid. 7:18 (my emphasis)

(10). SRIMAD-BHAGAVATAM, First Canto, interpreted by A.C, Bhaktivendanta Swami Prabhupada; (The Bhaktivendanta Book Trust. Los Angeles, California) page 25.

(11). Matthew 23:13 et seq.

Chapter 25
Creating Your Own Universe

A man came to Rumi and said,
"Please God that I could go to the other world; there at least I could be at peace because the Creator is there."
"What do you know about were He is?" answered Rumi.
"Everything in all the worlds is in you;
Whatever you are hungering for, work for it here by yourself, for you are the microcosm."

Harvey, Andrew LIGHT UPON LIGHT, Inspirations from RUMI, (North Atlantic Books, Berkeley, California 1996; page 53)

Ye are gods.
This statement by the ancient psalmist carries a promise and a threat. It offers us unlimited potential in exchange for absolute responsibility. If and when we taste of the nectar of the gods, we become as gods. If we employ the forces of the spirit, we cannot avoid, elude, escape, nor evade the consequences of our actions.

Beware!

Nevertheless, in spite of extensive discussions regarding many techniques, the intent of this book is not to teach anyone how to create their own universe. It is to convince you, by enumerating overwhelming evidence, *that you are, and always have been*, creating your own universe. And since so far you have apparently been doing so unwittingly, it is time you started doing it consciously. We have an enormous, indeed truly divine power at our disposal. I suggest we begin using it.

In the chapter on *Art and Creativity*, we have discussed some aspects of the Zodiac. Those versed in its mysteries know that our time has come. "The Zodiac is a powerful symbol throughout the Bible. Approximately every 26,000 years, the earth traces an orbit called the Procession of Equinoxes, symbolized by the Zodiac. Each of the 12 signs (spanning about 2150 years) stands for a basic quality of human nature, and during each segment (sign) we are to learn about our relationship to God through the development of that particular quality."[1]

We, the Particular, learn of our relationship to the Universal.

With the onset of the industrial revolution, we entered the Age of Aquarius, the age of personal freedom. The industrial and later the technological revolution have empowered the individual to a degree never before experienced in recorded history. It is as though we have come of age. We no longer have to rely on others to provide answers for us. Likewise, we can no longer blame others for our fate, our lot in life, our health, wealth, our state of mind. We must pickup our watering-can and tend to our garden, the garden of which the Koran speaks so eloquently. The garden of our consciousness. Such is the symbol of the Age of Aquarius; such is the fate of all that enter its guiles. During the previous ages we have been concerned with learning to control our thoughts. The herds of sheep, with which the Hebraic Scriptures abound, always symbolized our thoughts: the innocent lambs, the tumultuous sheep, the negative goats. All symbols are designed to aid men and women in the interpretation of the mysteries that have never been hidden. Not from those who searched. The image of the Good Shepherd, a man in full control of his sheep, was never intended for a single man. Or woman. We are all to be good shepherds; we are to tend our sheep, our thoughts. A good shepherd, therefore, is he, or she, who maintains control over them.

That is the first step.

We, the intelligent animals, are being trained by Soul, the Individualized presence of the Universal within our consciousness. In fact, this Presence *is* our consciousness. Without It, we are dust. Or dead bodies turning into dust.

Our training began in the mists of antiquity. All ancient religions bear some witness to the creative process. Be it Brahma of the Hindus, the Enlightened one of the Buddhists, Allah of the Moslems. The Old Testament, the Torah, gives us the Hebrew version in Genesis. The great teacher during the Age of Aries was Abraham. He tore his people from idolatry and opened their eyes to the One God, to YHVE: the Eternal, the Universal. Next came the Age of the Ram or sheep, during which time, as already mentioned, our destiny was to learn control over our thoughts. Jacob, Moses, David all started as shepherds; looking after their sheep, or gaining control over their thought-stream.

Then came the Age of Pisces.

The great teacher of this age was, of course, Jesus Christ. He taught all who would listen, how to use their thoughts wisely. Pisces or fish always symbolized wisdom. Originally, Jesus was symbolized among his followers as the fisherman. Later, a fish drawn in the sand was their secret sign of recognition. The cross was adopted as an emblem of Christianity much later. In the early years following Christ's death, the cross was an emblem of physical limitation and materiality. Blavatsky gives a more ancient history of the cross. She writes:

"It was adopted by the Christians through the Gnostics and cabalists... who had the Tau (or handled cross) from the Egyptians, and the Latin cross from the Buddhist missionaries, who brought it from India.... The Assyrians,

Egyptians, ancient Americans, Hindus, and Romans had it in various, but very slight modifications of shape."[2]

Before the Romans degraded the cross by using it for inhuman executions, the cross was a mystic sign of life and regenerative power. Since the later Christians implanted a human body on it, namely that of Jesus Christ, it became a symbol of suffering, for the sins of others. Further, the fatal misconception of the original teaching of Christ shows how a misguided visualization can change a vision of life, joy and affluence to one of sinners, sufferers, and poverty, living under the Diocletian sword of eternal hell and damnation. A symbol is a powerful tool in the development of the human psyche. A vision is the means.

Returning to Pisces—a number of apostles whom Jesus picked have been from among fishermen. Even as fish live in the depth of the ocean, so we have been encouraged to look into the depth of the human soul. According to the Bible, therefore, we have progressed from being Shepherds, to Fishermen, and now to being Gardeners.

Gardeners, the inheritors of the Age of Aquarius.

As Gardeners, we are to spend the next two thousand years building, or learning to build our own universes. We shall improve our physical bodies beyond our wildest dreams. We shall "begin to think of the body not as a form, but as a constantly unfolding process which is life itself."[3] We shall conquer diseases, acquire enormous physical strength and dexterity, and vastly increase the efficacy of all our senses. The use of our brain shall grow to unprecedented levels. Today's genius shall be tomorrow's average. And we shall create an incredible diversity of environments. Some will visualize veritable Edens, others will choose harsh, challenging surroundings. Each one of us will create his or her world to a precise specification—to be shared with others but never imposed. We shall cross the oceans of spacetime clad in our physical, emotional and/or mental bodies. There are no barriers we can conceive of today that we shall not overcome during this wondrous age. Two thousand years gives us a lot of leeway. Even today, as we visualize the future, we have begun the creative process. We shall each manifest our innermost heart's desire.

Will it be difficult?

When setting out to create our own reality, we must first decide whether we intend to identify with our spiritual or our material body. Though the first choice may sound farfetched, we have seen it proven, by pragmatic science, that our physical bodies are not what they seem. In terms of the latest physics, we, as solid matter, hardly exist at all. At best we are hosts to impulses of energy and information suspended in, still only partially defined, fields of energy.

Not much of a 'body', as compared to the image we have held of it till now.

We are drawing ever closer to engaging in the conscious process of the creation of our own reality. No two universes are, nor ever could be, alike. We are the creators of each one in direct relation to the input and feedback of our individual process of visualization. It is with reference to this ability to create our own reality that the psalmist referred to us as gods. Some 1000 years BC., King David presented his vision to his people in a manner which, presumably he hoped, his contemporaries would understand. Not surprisingly, 3000 years ago he chose to limit his vision of the creative process to the physical envelope which he and we occupy—his material body. In one of his songs of praise he wrote:

"My substance (body) was not hid from thee, when I was made in secret, and curiously wrought in the lower parts of the earth. Thine eyes did see my substance, yet being unperfect; and in thy book all my members were written, which in continuance were fashioned, when as yet there was none of them."[4]

In his day, David was forced, by the limits set by the

level of understanding of his people, to externalize the creative process. He assigned the function to 'thee', the Lord, as the source of the creative process. A thousand years later, his successor, Jesus, firmly placed this Source of all creation *within* himself. His statement: "I and my Father are one" negated previous assumptions and entrenched the divine potential within our own being. The Lord of King David is recognized today as our Inner Self, the Higher Self or the Spiritual body. This in no way diminishes the magnificence of the power within. As already quoted in the chapter on *Duality and Oneness*, the prophet Isaiah thought in these terms when he described the birth of spiritual consciousness, or the birth of awareness of the Inner Self, in his beautiful, poetic fashion. It bears repeating:

For unto us a child is born, unto us a son is given, and the government shall be upon his shoulder: and his name shall be called Wonderful, Counsellor, The mighty God, The everlasting Father, The Prince of Peace.

There are many who would argue that these were prophetic words foretelling the birth of Christ. For them I would suggest that the prophet of Nazareth repeatedly called us to follow him, to emulate his teaching, thinking, nature. The point I am making is that the 'child' of Isaiah's vision is the birth of an awareness of divinity *within us*, even as Jesus had experienced such within himself. Thus the above words apply to all who accept the teaching of David, of Isaiah and of Jesus Christ. This, at least in theory, would include all the Christians as well as members of the Islamic faith. In other words, as of the day of this writing, some 2,000,000,000 people. Those who find themselves outside this congregation, have little to lose by employing methods discussed in this book.

If it works, don't knock it!

In this light, let us review David's text quoted above. It is my contention that David assumed that before our physical body is formed, a prototype, a *vision* of it already exists in our mind's eye. Not brain's—but mind's. To be more precise, "It was made in secret, and curiously wrought in *the lower parts of the earth*", i.e., the creative process takes place in the unconscious. Furthermore, David claims that "in thy book all my members were written", meaning that the idea or the vision precedes the creative process; and finally that our parts or members are "fashioned in continuance": Our 'members' have not been created once-and-for-all, nor even for the duration of our lives, but they continue to be formed, to be created, "in continuance", i.e. in an ongoing fashion.

Let us examine the same data in the light of our present day knowledge. The biologists assure us that all human cells are continually replaced. The old ones are discarded and new ones take their place. The new cells are recreated in accordance with a plan recorded in our genetic code, and then those basic cells enter a process of specialization, to fit into our various 'members' (organs, skin, bones, etc.) in accordance with the pre-programmed conditions. It appears that King David's powers of visualization have been rather precise. We know today that our physical bodies are in a state of constant flux; six trillion electro-chemical reactions per second play havoc with anyone's image of a stable, material body.[5]

Thus, the new cells are created in strict accordance with programming. It is within our power to affect this programming in a conscious way. Our physical body can be regarded as our universe. A micro-universe created and reflecting the macro-universe. We might regard the nails on our toes and fingers as galaxies of atoms; the electrons swirling around their nuclei as planets in their predetermined orbits. The same can be said of any other part of our body. We are comprised of solar systems and galaxies, and clusters of galaxies, and clouds of atoms in the process of creation. All on a micro-scale. All atoms we can detect anywhere in the macro-universe also exist in our physical bodies.

We, the Particular, are created unto the image and

likeness of the Universal.

And now, finally, we can participate in the creative process consciously. In fact we must. That is the purpose of the Age of Aquarius. We have 2000 years in which to learn to take charge of our consciousness. Only you can decide what kind of universe you wish to build for yourself. It has been said that we are equipped with free will. In some respects it is true. Our physical body reflects the wonders of the universe. Our Higher Self is the presence of God Itself.

In fact, we, in the heart of our awareness, are gods.

And now a word of caution.

I am purposefully repeating in as many ways as possible, the same Truth, stated in as many ways by various scriptures, which immortalized various Ancient Myths. You may or may not have accepted my definition of a human being. In the chapter on *Re-defining Self*, I stated that we are not created unto the image and likeness of God. I said that *our bodies* and the way we (can) function—*are*. I also said that each one of us, through the divine attribute of Soul, is an individualization of God Itself.

If you share my thoughts on the subject then I have no choice but to roil the waters, hopefully without creating too many concentric circles separating you from the center of your being. I still stand by my definition of Self stated above. What we must incorporate into the premise, however, is our concept of God.

In the chapter on *Duality and Oneness*, I have quoted the great philosopher Baruch Spinoza who said that "to define God is to deny God". My comment is a definite, resounding yes and no! If we limit God to *an anthropomorphic Being*, then I agree absolutely. If we limit God to only that in which It is already manifest, the enormity of the universe, then I agree once more. But what if we define God as not only All-in-All of that which Is, but also the All-in-All of that which Is Not, but could be. In other words, as the *Infinite Potential within the Manifested and the Unmanifested*. We would then define God as that which is Undefinable. The Catholic church, while dressing its churches with images of God under different artistic expressions, attempts to express something similar by saying in its creed that God is the creator of the "*visibilium and invisibilium*," the visible and the invisible. This "definition" does not satisfy me because there is a plethora of energies that are invisible to the eye. I would rather state that God is All of that which Is and All of that which Is Not. Whether that which Is Not ever comes into the state of Being, or not. That which Is Not can be characterized as *Potential Being*.

This may sound like a pseudo-philosophical mumbo-jumbo comparable to the medieval conundrum concerning the number of angels dancing on a pinhead. I suggest, obviously, that it is not. The punch line of all the above lies in the word: Being. I reiterate what I have already stated in a number of chapters:

GOD HAS NO BEING EXCEPT IN A MODE OF BEING

As such, it is not only you, the individualization of Soul which Is, but your mind, your emotions, your physical body gives substance to the DIVINE BEING. You are that in which God has Its being. This may help us to understand the words "I and my Father are one". You and your Father are one too. It cannot be otherwise. Without you, God would not have Its fullness of being. It or He would be incomplete.

As Higher Self, our true indestructible nature, we never really leave heaven. As we descend into the illusion of material worlds to examine the results of our dreams, of our visions, we sometimes become (temporarily) restricted or limited by the instrument which we have ourselves created. It could be the scope of its mental dexterity, its range of imagination reached at its present stage of evolution, or even by the laws governing the material universes, which the physicists are so keen on studying.

So we create a new and better vision. We improve our instrument.

We create a greater mode of being. And "greater works than these shall he do" said the man whom many have acclaimed God.[6]

We are the best of both worlds. We combine the two aspects in One. As an individualization of Soul, we retain our infinite creative potential. As humans, we partake in the act of becoming. But at the most basic level, we become the object of our attention. We join, melt, integrate—for the duration. We become One. Even as "I and my Father". Even as you and your Father. This is the heritage of your and my Kingdom.

Perhaps now you are ready to create your own universe. Only let us remember that the subjective universes tend to keep us apart. So let us share them. Not impose them, but share them. We are, after all, endowed with the Infinite Potential. And thus, we can each create an infinite number of glorious universes.

Once we learn how.

There is another aspect of God that bears examination. It has been said that God is a living God. Not just "God of the living" but a *living* God.[7] The divinity does not employ the system of Bingo! It does not, as the fundamentalists would have it, create the world, let alone man, in seven days. The human body is the result of natural selection, acting on random mutations. This is the creative method employed by God. No matter how perfect we are, or become, in our mind and body, the creative process goes on. Should the process described above lead to a discovery of a better result, the present model, that's you and me, would be discarded "without a second (divine) glance." The beauty of the creative process is in the process itself. This is what is meant by the *living* God. God IS immutable, changeless, whole, complete. But in Its *modes of being*, through Its attribute of Soul, it manifests constant change.

Living means changing.

In the manifested universe, the only dead state is that of the absolute zero,[8] though I prefer to call it a dormant state because a tiny fraction of one degree acting upon it would initiate new changes. Not an instant biological 'infestation', but an impulse towards life. Nevertheless, when people aver that they do not like changes they erect a barrier between themselves and the creative force, which subsists on change. People, who do not like changes, separate themselves from the Living God. The God within. From Soul.

By whatever definition.

Sometime ago I attended a seminar conducted by Dr. Chopra, the lecturer mentioned a few times in the course of this book. After the seminar I had occasion to purchase a tape on which Chopra recorded *inter alia* a definition of a Unified Field, as compiled by a number of scientists at the request of Chopra's mentor, Maharaja Mahish Yoga. The tape goes on at some length, but I shall attempt to abbreviate it to the items listed only, without Chopra's commentary. The scientists came up with twenty-five attributes of the Unified Field which Chopra claims are identical with the attributes of Brahman, the source of all creation in the Veda. As I indicated earlier, we must all come up with our own 'divine' attributes, as other people's definitions will only serve to build a "second best" universe of someone else, rather than the very best we can do ourselves. However, for the purposes of an illustration, here are the attributes compiled by the scientists, which I jotted down some years ago. If I am inadvertently inaccurate, I hereby apologize to Dr. Chopra (and/or the group of scientists):

Total potential of natural law, infinite organizing power, pure awareness, infinite correlation, perfect orderliness, infinite dynamism, infinite creativity, pure knowledge, unboundedness, perfect balance, self sufficiency, all possibilities, infinite silence, harmonizing, evolutionary, self referral, invincibility, immortality, unmanifest, nourishing, integrating, simplicity, purifying, freedom and bliss.

I would encourage anyone who is interested in the above approach to contact Dr. Chopra and acquire the tapes on which the commentary on the attributes listed above might be of great help to them. Though I have since mislaid the tape (the lecture was some years ago), I imagine writing to the publisher of his books should bear results.

Dr. Emmet Fox has taken an altogether different approach. Under the title *The Seven Main Aspects of God* [9] he lists the following:
Life (spelled with a capital L, meaning Divine Life), Truth, Love, Intelligence, Soul (again capital S meaning God's ability to individualize Himself), Spirit and Principle.

As in the case of Dr. Chopra, I recommend the reader to purchase the late Emmet Fox's book for a more diligent study. The important thing is, however, to attempt to *produce your own list* of divine attributes, since doing so will clarify your own concept of your own reality. When we define the attributes of divinity, we define our own potential, or, to paraphrase Dr. Fox, "we embody our understanding of God".[10] While the journey may well prove eternal, we are working towards a qualitative integration with the divine attributes we espouse. Creating our own universes is *inter alia*, endowing them with as many divine attributes as we can. Our subjective universe shall grow and expand as our perceptions grow and expand. There is neither end nor limit to this endeavor, but there are stages which we shall observe as we go through them.

***

Our scientists exhibit quite different ambitions. Since the early part of this last century of the second millennium, the theoretical physicists have engaged in an ardent search for a single explanation of how the world works. Or at least, they are searching for a single theory which would unify the various forces which seem to rule our universe. Einstein surrendered most of his last forty years to this search—all to no avail. Perhaps there is no such complete unified theory. Perhaps if we could explain the workings of the universe in a single equation we would limit the diversity of the creative process. In a way, we would place limits on the way God chooses to manifest Himself.

That would place limits on you and me.

As we read in the chapter on *Scientific Perspective*, one of our scientists' latest attempts to solve the mysteries of the universe has been named the String Theory. The strings can be open or closed, no matter, suffice to say that "they seem to be consistent only if space-time has either ten or twenty-six dimensions, instead of the usual four."[11] This sounds like fun! The physicists may not find the answer to the question of how the "manifested God" works, but they will develop a new vision, which will probably broaden our own view of the universes we can create for ourselves. After all, given a few more dimensions we could probably explain (and consciously manifest) psychic and psychokinetic powers, walk through walls and all solid matter, travel through time, in both directions... perhaps forgetting that all these are still manifestations of the *material realm*. It would be a wonderful world—perhaps. Just think of bending space till the distance between us and the most distant stars all but disappears. Perhaps this would be true in the sixth or maybe... the tenth dimension.

We shall see.

But let us never forget that the material universe will always have its limitations. And as we conquer them, we shall create others; in order to have something to conquer. The only real freedom is in Infinite Potential. It is in Spirit. In Spirit you don't have to travel through walls, because you are already there—Spirit is omnipresent. You don't need precognitive powers—Spirit is omniscient. You do not have to travel through time, because as Spirit, as the spiritual-you, as Soul, you are present in all dimensions, in all eternity. Spirit is static.

And this is why God desires to have Being. To be a *living* God.

Living through you and me.

As long as consciousness rises to and remains in Heaven, our feet will forever conquer the earth. And space. And time. And ideas. And all limitations.

When we accomplish and accept the understanding of this concept, we shall have reached phase one. It is often called Self-Realization. We shall know who and what we are. We shall be well on the way to creating a universe, which will reflect as closely our image of 'heaven', as we can make it. We shall have discarded belief in the impossible. We shall have total belief in our own immortality, our potential omnipotence, omniscience.

The next step is one that cannot be defined.

Some call it God Realization. We cannot really know Its nature, and if we could, than we would not be able to express It with words. It is a transcendental state, one beyond the realm of the mind, and thus beyond the realm wherein we can communicate It in the words of any human language. Sometimes we can hear Its echo in the whisper of the wind. But like the quarks on the screen of a cyclotron, we can recognize It by the trail It leaves behind. Sometimes It is a stern trail of our own consequence, like a true mirror. Sometimes It is near-invisible, noticed by hardly anyone. Usually It is a trail of love and compassion.

And divine patience.

And peace.

And an incredible silence.

But mostly—just pure Love.

***

FOOTNOTES

(1). Gleamed from DICTIONARY OF BIBLICAL SYMBOLISM, Kapuscinski, Stanislaw, (Inhousepress 2001; now also available as eBook). For more information on the biblical symbolism of the Zodiac see ALTER YOUR LIFE by Emmet Fox, (Harper & Row Publ., New York. © by Emmet Fox 1931—1950)

(2). ISIS UNVEILED by H.P. Blavatsky, Volume II, Theology. Theosophical University Press; pg. 254.

(3). Paulson, J. Sig / Dickerson, Ric, REVELATION The Book of Unity. (Unity Books, Unity Village, Missouri 1976)

(4). Psalm 139:15-16

(5). A figure supplied by Dr. Chopra in one of his lectures.

(6). John 14:12.

(7). "As the *living* Father hath sent me..." John 6:57. (my emphasis)

(8). In thermodynamics, a point of temperature equal to $-273.15°$ C or $-459.72°$F. A point at which no molecular movement is possible.

(9). Fox, Emmet, ALTER YOUR LIFE, (Harper & Row, 1931-1950)

(10). Fox, Emmet DIAGRAMS FOR LIVING *The Anatomy of Healing* [Harper & Row, Publ. 1968]

(11). Hawking, Stephen, W. A BRIEF HISTORY OF TIME (Bantam Books, 1988) page 162.

How do you know but every bird
that wings the airy way,
Is an enormous world of delight,
Closed to your senses five?

William Blake
(1757 - 1827)

BIBLIOGRAPHY

Aristotle, METAPHYSICS, [ARISTOTLE] translated by Philip Wheelwright (New York, The Odyssey Press 1951)
Ash, Brian (editor) THE VISUAL ENCYCLOPEDIA OF SCIENCE FICTION (Harmony Books, New York, 1977]
Aquinas, St. Thomas, SUMMA THEOLOGICA
Asimov, Isaac. THE UNIVERSE (Penguin Books 1971)
Arberry, A.J. THE KORAN INTERPRETED (Simon & Shuster, Touchstone, New York 1955).
Atkins, Helen (English translation) DER MYTHOS DER NEUZEIT, 1983. (Cornell University Press, Ithaca and London 1990)
Benner, Joseph S. IMPERSONAL LIFE, (DeVross & Co., 43rd. edition 1983)
Benner, Joseph S. THE WAY OUT (DeVross & Co., California 1987)
Bernstein, Carl and Politi, Marco HIS HOLINESS (Doubleday, New York 1996). The book is subtitled "John Paul II and the Hidden History of Our Time."
Bhagavad Gita, The. [Anonymous work] translated by Juan Mascaro (C. Nicholis and Co. Ltd, London 1978)
Blavatsky, H.P. (An abridgement of) THE SECRET DOCTRINE (The Theosophical Publishing House, London 1966),
Blavatsky, H.P. ISIS UNVEILED Volume 1, *Science*, (Theosophical University Press 1988)
Blavatsky, H.P. ISIS UNVEILED Volume 2, *Theology*, (Theosophical University Press 1988)
Booth, Basil & Fitch, Frank EARTHSHOCK (Sphere Books, London 1980)
Brantl, George CATHOLICISM (George Braziller, New York 1962)
Bridgwater, William, Editor-in-chief. THE COLUMBIA VIKING DESK ENCYCLOPEDIA (Viking Press, New York 1968)
Briggs, John FRACTALS (Simon and Schuster, New York, London, Toronto etc., 1992. A Touchstone book).
Campbell, Joseph THE HERO WITH A THOUSAND FACES, (Princeton University Press, 1973)
Chomsky, Noam NECESSARY ILLUSIONS [subtitled: Thought Control in Democratic Societies] (House of Anansi Press Ltd.)
Chopra, Deepak. AGELESS BODY, TIMELESS MIND (Harmony Books, division of Crown Publ.)
Clark, Kenneth CIVILIZATION (British Broadcasting Corporation and John Murray, 1971).

Coddington, Mary, IN SEARCH OF THE HEALING ENERGY, (Warner 1978)

Detmold,C.E. THE HISTORICAL, POLITICAL, AND DIPLOMATIC WRITINGS OF NICCOLO MACHIAVELLI (Boston 1882)

Carter, Mary Ellen EDGAR CAYCE ON PROPHECY. (Warner Books 1968)de Chardin, Teilhard, THE PHENOMENON OF MAN, (Harper & Row, New York, 1965)

Dawkins, Richard THE SELFISH GENE (Oxford University Press 1976)

Einstein, Albert and Infeld, Leopold THE EVOLUTION OF PHYSICS (Simon and Schuster, New York 1961) © Albert Einstein and Leopold Infeld 1938.

Elder, Dorothy REVELATION FOR A NEW AGE [The Aquarian Age] (DeVross & Co. California 1981)

Emerton, E. (translated by) THE CORRESPONDENCE OF POPE GREGORY VII (Columbia University Press, 1932)

Flaccus, Quintus Horatius (65 B.C. - 8 B.C. gleamed from the Internet)

Fox, Emmet ALTER YOUR LIFE (Harper & Row Publ., New York. © by Emmet Fox 1931 - 1950)

Fox, Emmet DIAGRAMS FOR LIVING *The Anatomy of Healing* [Harper & Row, Publ. New York 1968]

Frank, Adam, MYSTERY OF THE MISSING STAR: DISCOVER mag. Dec.1996.

Fuller, R. Buckminster, CRITICAL PATH. (St. Martins's Press, New York 1981)

Galileo Galilei DIALOGUES CONCERNING TWO NEW SCIENCES, translated by Henry Crew and Alfonso de Salvio (Evanston: Northwestern University Press 1950)

Galileo Galilei DIALOGO DEI DUE MASSIMI SISTEMI DEL MUNDO. (gleamed from the internet)

Gandhi, Mohandas Karamchand, ALL RELIGIONS ARE TRUE. (Bharatiya Vidya Bhavan, Bombay 1962)

Gard, Richard A., Editor. BUDDHISM (George Braziller, New York 1962)

Gibb, H.A. R., MOHAMMEDANISM (2nd Edition, New York 1953)

Goodman, Jeffrey WE ARE THE EARTHQUAKE GENERATION (Berkley Books, New York 1979)

Greenhouse, Herbert B., THE ASTRAL JOURNEY, (Avon Books, New York, 1976)

Guillaume, A. ISLAM (Penguin Books)

Guillaumont, A., H.-Ch.Puech, G. Quispel, W.Till and Yassah 'Abd Al Masih GOSPEL ACCORDING TO THOMAS. (Harper & Row, © E.J. Brill 1959)

Guthke, Karl S. THE LAST FRONTIER subtitled: *Imagining Other Words From the Copernican Revolution to Modern Science Fiction.* Originally published as DER MYTHOS DER NEUZEIT, 1983. English translation by Helen Atkins, (Cornell University Press, Ithaca and London 1990)

Hal, Lindsey. THE 1980's COUNTDOWN TO ARMAGEDDON (Bantam Books 1981)

Harvey, Andrew LIGHT UPON LIGHT, Inspirations from RUMI (North Atlantic Books, Berkeley, California 1996)

Hawking, Stephen W., A BRIEF HISTORY OF TIME. (Bantam Books

1988).
Hertzberg, Arthur (edited by) JUDAISM, (George Braziller, New York 1962)
Hexter, J.H., General Editor THE TRADITIONS OF THE WESTERN WORLD, (Rand McNally & Co. Chicago 1967)
Hunt, Lynn POLITICS, CULTURE, AND CLASS IN THE FRENCH REVOLUTION (University of California Press, Berkeley 1984)
Jayakar, Pupul KRISHNAMURTI, a biography (Harper & Row, San Francisco)
Jung, Carl, G. MAN AND HIS SYMBOLS, (Dell Publishing Co., Inc, New York, 1964)
Kapuscinski, Stanislaw BEYOND RELIGION, Volume I. (Inhousepress 1997, 2001; Smashwords Editions 2010).
Kapuscinski, Stanislaw BEYOND RELIGION, Volume II. (© Stanislaw Kapuscinski 1999, Inhousepress, 2000; Smashwords Editions 2010).
Kapuscinski, Stanislaw DICTIONARY OF BIBLICAL SYMBOLISM (Copyright © 2000 Stanislaw Kapuscinski, Inhousepress, First limited ed. 2001, now also available as eBook)
Kapuscinski, Stanislaw THE KEY TO IMMORTALITY—*A Commentary on the Gospel of Thomas* (Copyright © 1997 Stanislaw Kapuscinski, First limited edition, Inhousepress 2002; Smashwords Editions 2010)
King James Version of the HOLY BIBLE, (Thomas Nelson Inc., New Jersey)
Krishnamurti, Jiddu EXPLORATION INTO INSIGHT (Harper & Raw, San Francisco 1979)
LeCron, Leslie M. SELF HYPNOTISM (Signet Book, 1970).
LeCron, Leslie M. THE COMPLETE GUIDE TO HYPNOSIS (Harper & Row, 1971)
Lewis, Ewart. MEDIEVAL POLITICAL IDEAS, *Defensor Pacis*. (Alfred A. Knopf Inc., 1954)
McNall Burns, Edward WESTERN CIVILIZATIONS, 8th Edition, Volume 1. (W.W.Norton & Co. Inc., New York 1973)
Mindell, Earl VITAMIN BIBLE, [Warner Books, 1985]
McQuade, Walter and Aikman, Ann STRESS (Bantam Book 1975)
Mendum, J.P., VOLTAIRE' PHILOSOPHICAL DICTIONARY (Boston 1836)
Mindell, Earl VITAMIN BIBLE, [Warner Books, 1985]
Mitchell, Stephen A. & Black, Margaret J. FREUD AND BEYOND(Harper Collins publ. 1995)
------- Montreal GAZETTE, (Associated Press) January 23-25, 1999.
Murphy, Joseph THE AMAZING LAWS OF COSMIC MIND POWER (Parker Publ. Co., Inc. West Nyack, N.Y.. 1965)
Naisbitt, John & Aburdene, Patricia MEGATRENDS (William Morrow, New York 1983)
Naisbitt, John & Aburdene, Patricia MAGATRENDS 2000 (William Morrow,New York 1990)
Netherton, Morris, Ph.D. and Shiffrin, Nancy PAST LIVES THERAPY (Ace Books, New York 1979)
Nicholson, R.A. LITERARY HISTORY OF THE ARABS (Cambridge University Press)

Nietzsche, Friedrich Wilhelm THUS SPAKE ZARATHUSTRA (1844-1900)
O'Flaherty, Wendy Dniger HINDU MYTHS (Penguin Books, London 1975)
Pagels, Elaine, THE GNOSTIC GOSPELS (Vintage Books, New York 1981)
Pauling, Linus HOW TO LIVE LONGER AND FEEL BETTER (Avon Books, New York 1987)
Paulson, J. Sig / Dickerson, Ric REVELATION The Book of Unity. (Unity Books, Unity Village, Missouri 1976)
Pearce, Joseph Chilton EXPLORING THE CRACK IN THE COSMIC EGG (Washington Square Press, Pocket Books 1975)
Pearson, Carol S. THE HERO WITHIN (Harper Collins Publ. 1998).
Prabhupada, A.C. Bhaktivendanta Swami. SRIMAD-BHAGAVATAM (The Bhaktivendanta Book Trust. Los Angeles, California)
Raup, David M.: EXTINCTION: BAD GENES OR BAD LUCK? (Norton, New York 1991)
Reid, T.R., *Feeding the Planet*, NATIONAL GEOGRAPHIC Oct. 1998
Ropp, Robert de THE MASTER GAME (Delacorte, 1968).
Robinson, James M. General Editor THE NAG HAMMADI LIBRARY [In English] (Harper Collins, San Francisco 990)
Russell, Bertrand WISDOM OF THE WEST (Crescent Books, Inc., London 1959)
Russell, Peter THE TM TECHNIQUE (Arkana, Penguin Group 1998)
Scholer, D.M., NAG HAMMADI BIBLIOGRAPHY (Leiden 1971)
Schulman, Arnold, BABA (Simon & Shuster, Canada).
Seneca, Lucius Anneus (4.B.C.-65 B.C.) From his essay *On the happy Life*.
Shakespeare, William, The Unabridged. JULIUS CAESAR. (Courage books, Philadelphia, London 1989,1987)
Shakespeare, William, HAMLET (ibid.)
Socrates, DIALOGUES OF PLATO, (Random House, New York 1937).
Spencer, John and Anne: WORLD'S GREATEST UNSOLVED MYSTERIES, (Headline Book, London)
Theodosakis, Jason M.D., M.S., M.P.H.; Adderly, Brenda M.H.A.; Fox, Barry Ph.D. THE ARTHRITIS CURE (St. Martin's Paperbacks 1997)
Tipler, Frank J., THE PHYSICS OF IMMORTALITY, (Anchor Book, Doubleday, New York 1994)
Toffler, Alvin FUTURE SHOCK (Pan Books London 1975)
Waldrop. M. Mitchell COMPLEXITY, subtitled *The Emerging Science at the Edge of Order and Chaos.* (A Touchstone Book, Simon & Shuster, New York 1992)
Walter, W. Grey THE LIVING BRAIN (Penguin Books 1961)
Walton, Mary DEMING MANAGEMENT METHOD (Berkley Publishing Group 1988)
Watson, Lyall LIFETIDE (Coronet Books, Hodder and Stoughton 1979)
Watson, Lyall SUPERNATURE (Coronet Books, Hodder and Stoughton 1974)
Watson, Lyall LIGHTNING BIRD (Hodder and Stoughton Ltd., Great Britain).
Weil, Andrew M.D., SPONTANEOUS HEALING (Ballantine Books,

New York 1995)
  Weinberg, Steven THE FIRST THREE MINUTES (Basic Books, New York 1977)
  Williams, John Alden, Editor, ISLAM (George Braziller, New York 1962)
  Yeats-Brown, F. YOGA EXPLAINED (Victor Gollancz Ltd, 1937, London)
  Young, Robert, LL.D,. ANALYTICAL CONCORDANCE TO THE BIBLE (WM. B. Eerdmans Publ. Company 1980)

A Word about the Author

Stanislaw Kapuscinski, (aka **Stan I.S. Law**), architect, sculptor and prolific writer was educated in Poland and England. Since 1965 he has resided in Canada. His special interests cover a broad spectrum of arts, sciences and philosophy. His fiction and non-fiction attest to his particular passion for the scope and the development of human potential. He authored more than thirty books, twenty of them novels.

Under his real name he published seven non-fiction books sharing his vision of reality. He also composed two collections of poems in his original native tongue in which he satirizes his view of the world while paying homage to Bozena Happach's sculptures.

Finally, he and his wife publish two blogs online, which, to date of this printing have been already visited by hundreds of thousands of people. We both hope you'll enjoy them as much.

Acknowledgments

I would be remiss were I not to thank my many friends for their comments, advice, and proofreading, none more so than Madeleine Witthoeft who's editing raised this book to acceptable literary standards. As always my gratitude to my wife, Bozena Happach, who put up with being a grass widow for weeks on end, and then offered me her inspired insights.

Sincerely,
Stanisław Kapuściński

Smashwords wrote in their Annual Review:

If you write a book that touches your readers' soul, or inspires them with passion or knowledge, your readers will market your book for you.

I've done my part. The rest is up to you.
And if you enjoyed my efforts, please write a (brief) review.
Your thoughts are important to me.

DELUSIONS

Pragmatic Realism

Stanislaw Kapuscinski

INHOUSEPRESS, MONTREAL, CANADA
http://inhousepress.ca

www.ingramcontent.com/pod-product-compliance
Lightning Source LLC
Chambersburg PA
CBHW021038090426
42738CB00006B/137